Horror Films by Subgenre

A Viewer's Guide

Chris Vander Kaay *and*
Kathleen Fernandez-Vander Kaay

McFarland & Company, Inc., Publishers
Jefferson, North Carolina

Names: Vander Kaay, Chris author. |
Fernandez-Vander Kaay, Kathleen, 1979– author.
Title: Horror films by subgenre : a viewer's guide / Chris Vander Kaay
and Kathleen Fernandez-Vander Kaay.
Description: Jefferson, North Carolina ; McFarland & Company, Inc.,
Publishers, 2016. | Includes bibliographical references and index.
Identifiers: LCCN 2015049029 | ISBN 9780786498376 (softcover : acid free paper) ∞
Subjects: LCSH: Horror films—Catalogs. | Horror films—History and criticism.
Classification: LCC PN1995.9.H6 V36 2016 | DDC 791.43/6164—dc23
LC record available at http://lccn.loc.gov/2015049029

BRITISH LIBRARY CATALOGUING DATA ARE AVAILABLE

ISBN (print) 978-0-7864-9837-6
ISBN (ebook) 978-1-4766-2283-5

Front cover image of zombie © 2016 sumnersgraphicsinc/
iStock/Thinkstock

Printed in the United States of America

McFarland & Company, Inc., Publishers
Box 611, Jefferson, North Carolina 28640
www.mcfarlandpub.com

William and Darlene Fernandez
and all of the dedicated fans and filmmakers
who have made the horror film
genre worth exploring

Acknowledgments

We would like to thank the filmmakers who were kind enough to help make this book a reality: Dave Payne, Kevin Greutert, Rodrigo Gudiño, Daniel Stamm, Brad Sykes, Ryan Mantione, Charles Band, Simon Barrett, David Barker, Ethan Wiley, Jim Mickle, Larry Fessenden, Eric Red, Christian Stella, Ronit Vanderlinden, James Palmer, Evan English, Jeremy Kasten, Andrew van den Houten, Joe Egender, Eric England, Paul Campion, Shawn Angelski, Dylan Lewis, Scott Glosserman, and Kerry Prior.

We also want to acknowledge those people whose work inspired us to become writers: Chris Carter, Neil Gaiman, and J. Michael Straczynski.

And finally, to those people in our lives who inspire us every day to keep writing: Brian Turner, Gailmarie Pahmeier, and Alan Heathcock.

Table of Contents

Preface 1

Abduction Horror 3

Alien Horror 6

Animal Attack Horror 9

Anthology Horror 13

Apocalypse and Post-Apocalypse Horror 16

Asylum Horror 20

Back from the Dead—Revenant Horror 24

Basement Horror 27

Battle with the Devil Horror 30

Body-Snatching Horror 33

Buried Alive Horror 37

Campground Horror 40

Cannibal Horror 43

Carnival-Circus Horror 47

Children in Danger Horror 50

Church-Convent-Monastery Horror 53

Comedy-Horror 56

Crazy Family Horror 59

Creepy Kid Horror 62

Crime Horror 65

Cult Horror 67

Demon-Possession Horror 70

Doll-Puppet-Ventriloquist-Dummy Horror 74

Doppelganger–Evil Twin Horror 77

Dream Horror 80

Ecological Horror 83

Filmmaking Horror 86

Found Footage Horror 89

Ghost Horror 92

Giallo Horror 95

Holiday Horror 98

Humans Hunting Humans Horror 101

Infection Horror 105

Invisible Being Horror 108

Literary Horror 111

Modern Zombie Horror 113

Mummy Horror 117

Nazi Horror 120

Old People Horror 124

Out-of-Control Machines Horror 127

Pregnancy Horror 129

Prison Horror 132

Psychic–Mental Powers Horror 135

Redneck Horror 138

Repressed Sexuality Horror 141

Road-Travel Horror 144

School Horror 147

Serial Killer Horror 150

Shape-Shifter Horror 152

Siege Horror 155

Single Location Horror 158

Single Person Horror   162

Slasher Horror   165

Split Personality Horror   169

Spooky Old House Horror   171

Stalking Horror   174

Subway Horror   177

Surgical-Medical Horror   180

Swamp Horror   183

Terror in Suburbia Horror   186

Theatrical Performance Horror   189

Tool Horror   193

Underwater Horror   197

Urban Legend Horror   200

Vampire Horror   202

Voodoo Zombie Horror   206

War Horror   210

Werewolf Horror   212

Western Horror   216

Witchcraft Horror   219

(Zombie *see* Modern Zombie Horror;
    Voodoo Zombie Horror)

Further Resources   222

Index   223

Preface

When we view light with the naked eye, we experience all of the light combined into a single visual phenomenon. But what we see of light is not all that there is to see. When a solid beam of light passes through a prism, the light is dispersed into a full spectrum, a rainbow of colors from red to violet.

If the filmic genre of horror is the solid beam of light, then the various horror subgenres are the colors which make it up. This book breaks the horror genre down into subgenres—seventy-five of them—and analyzes the characteristics of each.

Horror is, on the yearly average, the genre with the most films produced and released (this includes on-demand and home release films). With rabid devotion, from creators as well as fans, that body of horror film grows exponentially every year. And though horror as a genre is extremely popular, some devotees voraciously consume certain kinds of films while avoiding others entirely. What does that say about the films and their audiences?

Certainly, any well-studied horror film buff can recognize that certain monsters, story elements, and themes can be seen as social and psychological commentary. But what about the making a movie within one sub-category as opposed to another? Is that choice already making some kind of commentary?

Each subgenre of horror taps into a unique part of human psychology and offers some dark commentary on our cultural circumstances. By examining the individual pieces, we begin to recognize patterns that both unite and divide us.

This book is intended primarily as a "diagnostic manual of horror," a guide for film aficionados to consider the many facets of fear. It is also intended as a primer for the vast and varied horror film world.

The seventy-five subgenres are featured alphabetically—the only way to categorize such disparate material, so as not to show favoritism. Each contains an introduction to the subgenre through a short observation of each one's philosophical underpinnings. Following that is a portion called "Elements of the Subgenre" where we note aspects of these films common enough to be considered standard or canonical elements. This is followed by "Recommendations from the Subgenre," where we discuss three or four films that give a fairly comprehensive overview of the subgenre and its subject matter and tropes. These films were not chosen because of their previous historical significance or their enduring popularity, but rather because of their appropriateness as a representative of the subgenre. They should not be considered the three or four best films of their subgenre, but the three or four most appropriate examples of their subgenre.

The number of recommendations and elements vary according to subgenre; each one has at least two elements and three recommendations. If there are more in an individual category, it is because the subgenre has a broader base to cover and it benefits the reader to note the extras.

Finally, each section is closed out with "Other Titles of Interest," where we list other movies that may touch on the subgenre material but were not covered in detail in the "Recommendations from the Subgenre" section.

Abduction Horror

In the history of horror film, the most popular films are often the ones with the least likelihood of real-world occurrence. Perhaps a sense of escapism offsets the audiences' reaction of visceral fear?

Not so with abduction horror. Though the individual circumstances of an abduction film might be slightly outlandish or stretch the boundaries of reality, the idea of someone being grabbed from their home, workplace, or a public street, and held or tortured without explanation is a concrete and disturbing reality. From drug-related kidnappings in South America to beheadings of foreign "infidels" in the Middle East, the world is used to the idea that, at any moment, one human being could simply capture and possess another.

Add to that the dual fear of abduction: Both the abductee *and* the person to whom the abductee is connected (family, friend, colleague, etc.) have to live with the fear and uncertainty. Of course, the immediacy of the abductee's situation is more frightening, but there is no doubt that a spouse or parent is every bit as terrified of never seeing their loved one again as the abducted person is of never being seen again.

Most of all, perhaps, is the sense of helplessness that an audience member feels regarding their inability to prevent an abduction. In films, the abductors are always prepared, armed, crazed, and more powerful. Any resistance from an abductee would almost certainly spell an immediate death, rather than the prolonged and anxiety-inducing capture that was clearly intended.

Luckily for the characters in the stories, abductions almost never work out the way the abductors intended. Murphy's Law (which states that "Anything that can go wrong, will") is in full and glorious force in the world of horror film, and even the meticulously laid plans of devious kidnappers will never end up the way they want. When people decide to operate in a world outside of the law, they can't expect the law to protect them from whatever comes about as a result. This subgenre can, and often does, overlap with the Crime Horror subgenre.

Elements of the Subgenre

Shifting Loyalties: In a story that pits two groups (or two individuals) against each other, the best drama happens when one begins to reconsider their allegiances. And it's not always the one you think. While it might be one of the kidnappers who has sympathy for a hostage, it might just as easily be one of the abductees who decides to make a deal with one of the kidnappers to take out the others and split the ransom money between them. You just never know who you can trust.

Powerless Law Enforcement: This will become a common trait in many subgenres of horror (terrible things can't happen if the police kept showing up to protect and serve, right?), but it is never more apparent than in the abduction subgenre. The police and other authorities are usually incompetent, absent, corrupt, or somehow involved in the abduction themselves.

A Show of Force: In order for an abduction to continue without concern of an escape or struggle, the abductors have to make it clear that they are serious and will do *anything* they have to do to succeed. The act might be violent, psychological, or sexual, but the abductors always have at least one disturbingly tense moment where they remind the hostage (and the audience) just how far they will go.

Recommendations from the Subgenre

The Last House on the Left (1972)

Directed by Wes Craven
Written by Craven (based loosely on the Ingmar Bergman film *The Virgin Spring*)
Starring: David Hess, Richard Towers, Martin Kove

Two girls on their way to a rock concert cross paths with a group of escaped criminals. After the brutal ordeal of their rape and capture, they are killed; later, through an unbelievable coincidence, the criminals stay in the house of one of the slain girls' parents. The parents learn of the murders and take bloody revenge. The film is an unrelenting and graphic expression of the frustration of America at the end of the 1960s. While the second half of the film reflects more of a revenge film sensibility than an abduction one, the first half is undeniably one of the most harrowing depictions of a kidnapping and murder depicted in cinema up to that point. The movie paints the police as bumbling and incompetent, even going so far as to have comical music when the cops appear on-screen, showing that the parents have no recourse but to take the law into their own hands.

An unforgettable entry in the abduction subgenre, it was the first film for college professor and iconic horror director Wes Craven. It was originally intended by producer Sean S. Cunningham as a way to cash in on the grindhouse movie boom; Craven instead made a dark and thoughtful rumination on humanity's propensity for violence and revenge. The performances, in particular David Hess (who also provided the unusually serene soundtrack), are gritty and realistic, and the film explores several themes that Craven would revisit throughout his career, including murderous revenge and booby-trapping houses. Craven and Cunningham would not work together again, but both went on after this film to create two of the most iconic horror villains of all time, Jason Voorhees and Freddy Krueger (who Craven has said got his last name from the villain in *The Last House on the Left*, Hess' Krug).

The Disappearance of Alice Creed (2009)

Written and Directed by J. Blakeson
Starring: Martin Compston, Eddie Marsan, Gemma Arterton

This taut, claustrophobic thriller revolves around two lovers who abduct a woman in order to ransom her. Secrets are slowly revealed during the abduction, including the fact that one of the kidnappers is also in a relationship with their abductee. In the tradition of the great British thrillers of the 1970s, *The Disappearance of Alice Creed* makes a big impact with limited resources. Duplicity, constant psychological tension, and clever story turns make it a worthwhile investment for a horror fan looking for an intelligent and moody character piece.

With a cast of only three people (Martin Compston, Eddie Marsan, and *Hansel & Gretel: Witch Hunters* star Gemma Arterton) and two major locations, the film lives and dies by the skill of its performers and the twisty, intricate plot. Much of the credit must go to writer-director J. Blakeson, who previously scripted the horror sequel *The Descent: Part Two*, for ratcheting up the tension and eliciting such effective and frightening performances. While not a horror film in the graphic sense, the intensity and implied violence of *Alice Creed* will keep even the most jaded horror fan's attention.

PVC-1 (2007)

Directed by Spiros Stathoulopoulos
Written by Dwight Istanbulian, Spiros Stathoulopoulos
Starring: Hugo Pereira, Daniel Páez, Merida Urquia

The story of *PVC-1* was based on a true story which the director heard about and became fascinated by. A Colombian family is besieged by a gang looking for money; the gang eventually straps a bomb inside a PVC pipe around the wife's neck. With no money to pay the ransom and have the bomb removed, the family races against time to get the mother to the National Guard bomb squad to have it defused before it detonates. The performances are honest, with no Hollywood artifice, and the jittery handheld cinematography adds to the tension of the dangerous real-time journey. *PVC-1* is by turns beautiful, frustrating, and revelatory; the horror industry could learn a valuable lesson from its excellent execution of an original and inexpensive story conceit.

PVC-1 is not only an amazing and refreshing exercise in "new wave" moviemaking (the entire film is shot in one uninterrupted take), it is also a disturbing and realistic film about very personal horrors. Writer-director Spiros Stathoulopoulos brings an artistic sensibility to the panicked proceedings, giving moments of relief with oddly serene scenes like the handcart trip on the train tracks with the disabled navigator.

Daylight (2010)

Directed by David Barker
Written by David Barker, Michael Godere, Ivan Martin, Alexandra Meierhans
Starring: Alexandra Meierhans, Ivan Martin, Michael Godere

What starts as a pleasant vacation for a Swiss husband and his pregnant wife becomes a nightmare of survival when the kind gesture of giving someone a ride turns into a carjacking and eventually a full-blown kidnapping. With lush cinematography, compelling performances from the kidnappers and the abductees, and a thoughtful and nuanced screenplay, *Daylight* succeeds in reinventing the abduction subgenre with the simple idea that audiences will care about complex and subtle characters. Lead actress Alexandra Meierhans does an excellent job of bringing to life the role of the fearful pregnant captor, a character that could easily have become a cliché of the genre.

Director David Barker cleverly plays back and forth with the audience's expectations of the kidnappers for the first half of the movie, challenging the viewer to intuit the motivations on their own. The pacing of the film is surprisingly subdued for the subject matter, and the

juxtaposition of the calm filmic style with the looming threat makes for a jarring experience, in an interesting and positive way. It's a bold work that comments on religion, existentialism, and the comparison of the American dream to its dark unfulfilled mirror image. Rarely has a suspense film been so quiet and looked so beautiful.

Other Titles of Interest

Kiss the Girls (1997), *Megan Is Missing* (2011), *Shuttle* (2008), *Funny Games* (1997 and 2007), *Summer's Moon* (2009), *Red Eye* (2005), *Kidnapped* (2010), *Captivity* (2007)

Irene (Alexander Meierhans) takes matters into her own hands to free herself from captors in 2010's *Daylight* (courtesy David Barker).

Alien Horror

Human beings have strived since the discovery of outer space to break free of our world and explore the far reaches of the cosmic expanse. We've traveled as far as we could travel on our own, and we have sent probes unimaginable distances to explore the edges of our solar system and gather some understanding of what may wait for us out there.

We're enamored with the idea of intelligent life somewhere other than this planet. The key word being *intelligent* life. Evidence of alien microbes might thrill scientists, but the rest of us want to find alien intelligence that has something to teach us—the holy grail of space exploration.

If we're honest with ourselves, the truth behind our obsession with finding other intelligent life is because we're not particularly interested in the intelligent life that surrounds us day to day. As a species that has grown in intelligence and sophistication, we've thrived on this planet, essentially making it our own. But our pettiness and squabbling is depressing. We can't get along with our fellow man, and so we seek some other consciousness or psychological connection in the universe.

The irony of that desire is that we must know how unlikely it is. Not only is it improbable that another race of intelligent creatures exists near enough to us that we would be able to travel to them and communicate, but the challenge of finding common ground would be an even greater obstacle. We find ourselves unable to meaningfully connect with others who have had the same experiences as beings on the same planet, and we imagine a meeting with beings having no connection to our language, culture, or biology would lead to a more profound interaction.

The hubris of believing we could effectively interact with a species from another planet is matched only by the desperation of humanity's need to find it. The desire of a lone human, emotionally alone in the world and desperately seeking something that makes him understand and feel, is the perfect analogy for the Earth in general: a single speck of life in a vast vacuum of indifference, spinning endlessly but never getting any closer to another source of life.

And when, in horror films, we finally do make contact with other forms of life, we're always optimistic about the connection. Then we inevitably learn that, to the alien, our planet is little more than a place to refuel ... or have a bite to eat.

Elements of the Subgenre

People as Objects: It seems that aliens aren't just stronger and more technologically advanced than humans, they also believe themselves to be so superior to us that they look at humanity as tools for various uses. We're incubators for new aliens, meat puppets to be controlled, food to be processed, or guinea pigs for various awful experiments, but we're certainly not their equals or even creatures worth protecting.

Of Unknown Origin: Though the home worlds and origins of many alien species have been explored in a variety of science fiction films, that element is almost always a source of mystery in the alien horror film. Not knowing where a creature came from and what it is capable of doing always makes for a more frightening experience, not to mention that it always leaves the door open to expand on the mythology when the film is popular enough to garner a sequel.

Recommendations from the Subgenre

Alien (1979)
Directed by Ridley Scott
Written by Dan O'Bannon, Ronald Shusett
Starring: Sigourney Weaver, Tom Skerritt, Harry Dean Stanton

In the distant future, the seven-member crew of the commercial spaceship *Nostromo* is wakened from their cryogenic sleep when the computer detects a distress signal of alien origin. Searching the craft from which the signal originated, they find a bay full of eggs, and one of the creatures from within the eggs attaches itself to one of the crew. After using the crewman as an incubator, a larger life form bursts from his body and escapes into the *Nostromo*, lurking the halls and killing off the rest of the crew.

Coming two years after the release of the original *Star Wars*, *Alien* was a masterpiece of sci-fi horror that reminded audiences that space could be scary as well as adventurous. Utilizing the vastness of the universe to create isolation, the film pits the crew against an unknown adversary with which they are unequipped to deal.

Director Ridley Scott had only one completed film to his credit, the period adventure *The Duellists*, when he embarked on this project. Teaming with producer Walter Hill (already known for his gritty crime pictures *The Driver* and *The Drowning Pool*) to create a lived-in world and using designs from *Necronomicon* artist H.R. Giger to create the iconic alien creature, Scott launched one of the most commercially successful science fiction franchises of all time. The series later served as an artistic proving ground for filmmakers David Fincher and James Cameron.

Slither (2006)

Directed and Written by James Gunn
Starring: Nathan Fillion, Michael Rooker, Elizabeth Banks

When a meteorite crashes in the woods near a small South Carolina town, an alien parasite crawls out and takes over the body of Grant, a local car dealer who is cheating on his wife. After Grant's body and his behavior go through some severe changes, his wife and the town police chief learn the truth of the quickly spreading infestation, and team up to stop the spread of the parasites before the entire world is taken over.

Equal parts gross-out effects and hilarious character observation, *Slither* is the modern comic answer to John Carpenter's seminal alien invasion film *The Thing*. Embracing the classic alien invasion elements of the small town, the noble but ill-prepared lawman, and the virus-like spread of the alien menace, the film cleverly puts many of the clichés on their head by surprising the viewer with an unconventional love story and some very icky visuals.

The film was directed by James Gunn before he became famous for *Guardians of the Galaxy* (in which Gunn re-used *Slither* cast members Gregg Henry, Michael Rooker, and Nathan Fillion). The effects work in large part because they are practical physical effects, and they hold up under scrutiny better than the CGI creations of the same era. The entire film plays as a darkly comic tale of infidelity and what kind of terrible things can be brought home from careless carousing. Gregg Henry's sincere histrionics help him stand out in a stellar supporting cast. Knowledgeable viewers might catch cameos from Troma founder Lloyd Kaufman and *The Devil's Rejects* director Rob Zombie.

Bad Taste (1987)

Directed by Peter Jackson
Written by Peter Jackson, Tony Hiles, Ken Hammon
Starring: Terry Potter, Peter O'Herne, Peter Jackson

All residents of the small town of Kaihoro, New Zealand, have disappeared without a trace, and it's up to four members of the Astro Investigation and Defence Service to solve the mystery. The investigators discover that the entire citizenry has been turned into alien fast food, and that the aliens have now disguised themselves as humans. The all-out intergalactic war that ensues involves chainsaws, rocket launchers, punchbowls full of vomit, and brains being held in place by a strategically secured hat. Though the outer trappings of the plot echo other alien invasion films and television shows (including the classic "To Serve Man" episode of *The Twilight Zone*), nothing can prepare the viewer for the intensely hilarious and disgusting *Bad Taste*. The threadbare plot is little more than an excuse to keep the wild set-pieces coming in fast succession, and the mostly amateur cast does an admirable job of attempting to play the ludicrous material as seriously as possible.

The first film from *Lord of the Rings* director Peter Jackson, *Bad Taste* was shot over a series of years with Jackson himself directing, co-writing, producing, co-editing, and starring (in more than one role). It was the first in his trilogy of gory horror comedies (the others were *Meet the Feebles* and *Dead Alive*) before making *Heavenly Creatures* and finding mainstream and critical success. Created with ingenuity on a tiny budget, the film was eventually completed with funding help from the New Zealand Film Commission.

Other Titles of Interest

Strange Invaders (1983), *Species* (1995), *Invaders from Mars* (1953 and 1986), *Signs* (2002), *Predator* (1987), *Dark Skies* (2013), *The Darkest Hour* (2011), *Lifeforce* (1985), *Grabbers* (2012), *Fire in the Sky* (1993)

Animal Attack Horror

If we were to catalog all the ways we are inferior to most of the animals with which we share the planet, it would be a long and disheartening list. We cannot run with the speed of cheetahs or lions; we cannot swim with the speed and dexterity of dolphins or sharks; we do not have the strength of the gorilla, the sting of the scorpion or the olfactory senses of the bear. Still, man is able to hold onto his position at the top of the food chain, comfortably removed from the threat of predation. But as horror films remind us, this circumstance can deteriorate quickly.

It is usually at society's highest point of decadence and insensitivity that something truly horrifying happens. Take, for example, the stock market crash that ended the Roaring Twenties and ushered in the Great Depression. In a society where we are consuming more meat than ever before—while knowing little about the animals we devour, their living conditions or modes of death—where creatures are kept in zoos and circuses for our entertainment, where beauty and cleaning products are tested on defenseless rabbits and simians, the inevitable turnabout can't be very far away.

Humanity didn't gain superiority by luck, though; our technology and resourcefulness have helped us reach the summit of the natural order. We have overpowered nature by adopting its innovations. Airplanes, motorcycle helmets and knives are just manufactured replicas of natural abilities and defenses we've witnessed in the animal kingdom. We've risen above nature by stealing from it and improving on it.

And that is how the shift will happen. Our trust lies in the technology, intelligence, and common interest of humanity; when technology fails, and intelligence has been stunted by a reliance on that technology, humanity panics. Panic breeds fear, and then common interest goes out the window. Then, while the remnants of humanity are fighting amongst themselves for the few resources at their disposal, perhaps some of nature's other creatures will realize that there is a vacuum in the position of power. And nature abhors a vacuum.

Elements of the Subgenre

Outrageous Dismissal of Something Important: Where would the animal attack film be if everyone used common sense and didn't do anything mean or stupid? Sure, there's a shark out in the water, but that's not a good enough reason for the mayor to close the beach on a holiday weekend, right? Who cares if that bear is minding its own business, we have a gun and we can shoot at it, right? What could possibly go wrong?

The One Who Gets It: Almost everyone in this genre is living their human-centric life and not caring about the creeping menace that is about to destroy them. One person, however, knows *exactly* what is going on. Maybe he's the wise old Indian man, or the crazy guy in the diner, or the persnickety biologist from some northern coastal city. If only someone would listen to them.

Recommendations from the Subgenre

The Birds (1963)
Directed by Alfred Hitchcock
Written by Evan Hunter (based on the novella by Daphne DuMaurier)
Starring: Tippi Hedren, Rod Taylor, Suzanne Pleshette

Lawyer Mitch meets Melanie, and their flirtatious practical jokes lead Melanie to travel to Mitch's home town of Bodega Bay to gift him with a pair of lovebirds. While in town, Melanie is witness to a series of seemingly unmotivated attacks on humans by birds of several varieties. After surviving a swarm at the local school and an explosion at the gas station, Melanie and Mitch learn that the bird attacks are spreading, and that their home is no longer a secure refuge.

Never one to shy from a challenge, director Alfred Hitchcock found some of his most insurmountable ones during the making of *The Birds*. Using author DuMaurier's novella as a loose inspiration, he and screenwriter Evan Hunter (better known as crime novelist Ed McBain) structured a deceptive script that evolved from playful romance to suspenseful thriller. The lack of resolution to the mysterious attacks leaves the audience with lingering fear at the fade-out.

After changing the landscape of modern horror with *Psycho* three years earlier, Hitchcock decided to change the technology of film with this release. He eschewed the traditional music score for a focus on an elaborate soundscape; he also pioneered a new photographic process with Walt Disney studios animator Ub Iwerks that allowed for greatly improved visual detail in the effects sequences. Though *The Birds* is remembered historically as one of the great thrillers of all time, it was nominated for only one Oscar, for visual effects—which it lost to *Cleopatra*.

Phase IV (1974)
Directed by Saul Bass
Written by Mayo Simon
Starring: Michael Murphy, Nigel Davenport, Lynne Frederick

After a largely unexplained cosmic event, colonies of ants all over the world have begun to change rapidly, developing a massive hive mind and destroying most of the natural predators in their ecosystems. A small team of scientists heads to the desert to observe their behavior, finding strange towers made by the ant population. One scientist wants to communicate with the ants, another wants to destroy them. The lead scientist attempts to destroy the towers and escalates the standoff into a war.

Beautiful photography and a complex and confounding story make *Phase IV* both rewarding and frustrating in equal measure. A product of its increasingly cynical era, the movie toys with some interesting philosophical questions while always skirting the inherent silliness of many disaster movies of the 1970s. Somehow accomplishing the unlikely task of making an army of ants seem frightening, the film also plays with the scientific underpinnings of the event in much the same way as Michael Crichton's *The Andromeda Strain*, and with similar intellectual (rather than emotional) effect.

Phase IV was directed by famed title sequence creator Saul Bass, whose openings dazzled audiences in films as wide-ranging as *Vertigo*, *West Side Story*, and *Goodfellas*. It was his only feature film as director. When *Phase IV* was a box office failure, Bass was relegated back to his position as title designer for the rest of his career. The stunning close-up photography of the ants was effective and eerie, and fares better in modern viewings than the practical effects of other films of the era. In the lead role of Dr. Lesko, Michael Murphy (seen in many great films of the era like *MASH* and *Manhattan*) effectively underplays to the story's strange events.

Bear (2010)

Directed by John Rebel
Written by Ethan Wiley, Roel Reiné
Starring: Brendan Michael Coughlin, Patrick Scott Lewis, Katie Lowes

Two brothers and their girlfriends are on a road trip when their vehicle breaks down in a remote stretch of wilderness. They are confronted by a curious bear, which they shoot and kill. The bear's mate finds and attacks them, imprisoning them in their vehicle and bringing buried familial conflicts to the surface.

Blue the Grizzly Bear imprisons four friends in their car in 2010's *Bear* (courtesy Ethan Wiley).

On its face, *Bear* seems like a run-of-the-mill animal attack movie and a perfect template for the subgenre; however, there are clever subversions within the concept, making the bear the sympathetic character and even showing a flashback of the bear's interaction with his dead mate. Unlike many "kids in the woods" movies, this film effectively makes them unwanted interlopers rather than simplistic victims to a simple menace.

There are subtle hints at a possible supernatural explanation during the monologue that discusses Native American folklore and through the uncharacteristically focused behavior of the bear. This pays off in a surprisingly touching finale that turns the villain of the piece into an intelligent and complicated character (made all the more impressive by the fact that he is an animal). A script by Roel Reiné and *House* writer Ethan Wiley does a lot of narrative work with little production value, and the result is a rare animal attack film that considers whether or not the animal may have had a point. A combination of well-orchestrated animal attack sequences and quietly intense existential conflict between the couples in the vehicle make this an interesting hybrid film.

Jaws (1975)

Directed by Steven Spielberg
Written by Carl Gottlieb (based on the novel by Peter Benchley)
Starring: Roy Scheider, Robert Shaw, Richard Dreyfuss

Sheriff Martin Brody is worried about the safety of the tourists on Amity Island after a shark attack causes mass panic. He struggles with the mayor, who refuses to shut down the beach because he fears a loss of revenue over the Fourth of July holiday. Brody decides to take matters into his own hands, working with marine biologist Matt and professional shark hunter Quint to find and kill the shark before it can kill more people.

The "Quint"-essential animal attack film of all time, *Jaws* not only created the template for the modern monster movie, but also invented the summer blockbuster film. The likable lead that no one believes, the stubborn bureaucrat, the obsessed Ahab figure, and the epic third act confrontation are all on stunning display in this masterpiece exercise in character-driven thrills.

Jaws was based on the novel by Peter Benchley (the producers optioned it before it was even published). It was Steven Spielberg's second theatrical project after the well-received drama *The Sugarland Express*. The notoriously troubled water shoot off the coast of Martha's Vineyard in Massachusetts led to creativity on Spielberg's part about concealing the appearance of the shark until late in the film, a decision that ended up giving the film much more tension. The iconic theme was composed by John Williams, who Spielberg worked with for the second time here and with whom he collaborated on over twenty other features.

Other Titles of Interest

Piranha (1978), *Burning Bright* (2010), *Black Sheep* (2006), *Willard* (1971 and 2003), *Eight-Legged Freaks* (2002), *Arachnophobia* (1990), *Snakes on a Plane* (2006), *The Ghost and the Darkness* (1996), *Night of the Lepus* (1972)

Anthology Horror

Though many horror fans love solid characterization, interesting plot twists, and a slow but steady pace, just as many have a special place in their hearts for the movies that get straight to the violence and craziness.

The desire to "get to the good parts" of a movie has been around a long time, even before the advent of technologies that allowed us to go straight to them, like VCRs, DVD players, and clips on YouTube. Keeping the viewer's attention has been getting harder and harder.

This goes a long way towards explaining the resurgence of the anthology horror film. It has been around in many genres for a long time; celebrated director D.W. Griffith made one of the most expensive films of the silent era with *Intolerance: Love's Struggle Throughout the Ages*, an anthology spanning the fall of Babylon and the crucifixion of Christ all the way up to the tragedy of a young couple's broken relationship. However, the format had gone out of vogue for most of the modern filmmaking era, occasionally resurfacing for a star-studded entry like *Dead of Night* or *Tales from the Crypt*. For the most part, though, anthology horror was relegated to television.

The combination of a shortening attention span, an explosion of venues for film and video consumption, and the ease of technology that allowed unproven filmmakers to create short-form work, all combined in a perfect storm of changes that brought the subgenre of anthology films back into the popular consciousness. Able to communicate over long distances due to emerging communication and editing technologies, filmmakers and friends could work on projects together without ever meeting or being in the same place. The expense and complication of creating an entire feature film was replaced with the ability to connect with others of like mind who were also working on smaller projects, and unite to bring them to audiences. And audiences were ready for them.

Elements of the Subgenre

The Linking Element: While some anthologies are simply four or five unconnected stories that simply exist together because they have an overriding theme or genre (horror, usually), the more popular tack is that of the wraparound story. The wraparound creates a bit of connective tissue between them, whether it be one person recounting all of the tales, or a character recurring in all of them, or all the stories taking place in a single spooky town.

The Standout Entry: It is impossible to produce a film made up of several smaller films without audiences immediately creating a scale of quality for them. And in all films, there will be a couple of decent entries and one that seems out of place or uninspired; but there will be one that everyone agrees is the best part of the film, the most clever use of the conceit, and certainly the one that makes the entire film worth watching.

Recommendations from the Subgenre

Black Sabbath (1963)

Directed by Mario Bava
Written by Mario Bava, Alberto Bevilacqua, Marcello Fondato
Starring: Boris Karloff, Mark Damon, Michèle Mercier

A trio of scary short stories, introduced by a spectral Boris Karloff. In the first, a woman returns to her house at night to find she is being stalked by an unseen threat that continually plagues her with unwanted phone calls. In the second, a man returns home to his family after killing a supernatural creature, and his family begins to suspect that he may not have returned unchanged. And in the third, a woman takes a piece of jewelry from the dead body of a woman being prepared for burial, only to learn that even death doesn't stop someone from reclaiming what is rightfully theirs. Three tales spanning time and locale, Mario Bava's *Black Sabbath* makes use of the director's experience shooting Technicolor epics to bring a fevered palette to horror; his previous horror offering, *Black Sunday*, was in monochrome. Shooting the film with the knowledge of its international audience, Bava effectively creates an atmosphere that can be enjoyed with nearly no dialogue at all.

The film was released stateside by American International Pictures, the company responsible for much of Roger Corman's early filmic output. The film underwent several changes prior to its American release, cutting some of the more overt violence and removing many of the references to casual sexuality. Though he appears in only one of the stories, Karloff also acts as the host, leading the audience from segment to segment. Bava was likely inspired to add this as a reference to Karloff's similar work on the television series *Thriller*.

V/H/S (2012)

Directed and Written by Matt Bettinelli-Olpin, David Bruckner, Tyler Gillet, Justin Martinez, Glenn McQuaid, Joe Swanberg, Chad Villella, Ti West, Adam Wingard, Radio Silence
Starring: Adam Wingard, Hannah Fierman

A masked burglar (Calvin Reeder) explores the mysterious tape room in the 2012 anthology film *V/H/S* (courtesy Simon Barrett).

A group of unlikely investigators is hired by an unknown person to burglarize a rundown house, something they decide to do while recording themselves. Once in the house, they discover a huge collection of old VHS tapes which contain horrifying footage. Soon something dark and possibly supernatural is happening inside the house.

Combining the anthology film structure with the grimy aesthetic of the found footage-fake documentary arena, *V/H/S* succeeds brilliantly in breathing new life into both. The segments range from darkly comedic (the manic pace and hilarious costumes of *10/31/98* balance out the action-oriented scares) to uncomfortably realistic (the quiet voyeurism of Ti West's *Second Honeymoon*). The wraparound story of the house is effective without wearing out its welcome.

V/H/S was created by several luminaries of the modern independent horror movement: West (*House of the Devil*), Simon Barrett (*You're Next*), Joe Swanberg (*24 Exposures*), and David Bruckner (*The Signal*). The project was a brainchild of Brad Miska, founder of the horror website Bloody Disgusting; it was followed by two successful sequels, *V/H/S/2* and *V/H/S: Viral*, which extended the mythology of the mysterious tapes and their hold over the populace and gave other horror industry luminaries a chance to experiment in the found footage arena.

Trick 'r Treat (2007)
Written and Directed by Michael Dougherty
Starring: Anna Paquin, Dylan Baker, Brian Cox

On Halloween night in a small Midwestern town, several dark stories are unfolding simultaneously. A young virgin decides not to go with her friends to a party, only to be stalked by a vampire; the school principal's candy has a little something extra inside for the neighborhood kids; the ghosts of children killed in a school bus crash return from the grave; and a miserable old recluse learns just how far one child will go to get a Halloween treat. Combining the anthology horror subgenre with the storytelling device of the "town with buried secrets," *Trick 'r Treat* is a fun revisiting of classic horror clichés that all end with a unique spin. Utilizing *Pulp Fiction*–style storytelling where seemingly disparate tales end up interweaving and interacting with each other in surprising ways, it is as clever as it is spooky.

Produced by *The Usual Suspects'* Bryan Singer, the film is directed by Singer collaborator Michael Dougherty and even uses an actor from their previous film project, Brian Cox from *X-Men 2*. The wraparound story of the masked boy was inspired by an animated short that Dougherty produced nearly a decade earlier called *Season's Greetings*. The film never received a full theatrical release, but it found a dedicated and rabid cult following upon its DVD release which led Dougherty to produce a similar Christmas-themed horror film called *Krampus* as well as beginning pre-production on a *Trick 'r Treat* sequel.

The Signal (2007)
Directed and Written by David Bruckner, Dan Bush, Jacob Gentry
Starring: AJ Bowen, Justin Welborn, Anessa Ramsey

Over the course of a single evening, a young married woman and the man with whom she is having an affair learn that some kind of strange transmission has made its way into the telephone, television, and radio signals of the city in which they live. As they attempt to find each other and get to safety, they have to deal with the citywide bouts of random violence that have plagued many of the people who have been exposed to it. A brilliant conceit for a standalone film is made even more interesting by the addition of the anthology format, splintering the straightforward narrative of the lovers into three pieces directed by three different directors. Each segment retains many of the same characters and circumstances, but they filter the concept of the world through a different sensibility (violent splatter film in one, dark comedy in another, love story in the final one). This linking element, along with the excellent lead performances (AJ Bowen deserves special note for his seamless shift from horror to comedy), makes *The Signal* a standout entry in the anthology film arena because it engages the viewers in each segment with equal intensity and the viewer requires each piece to solve the overall puzzle.

Director David Bruckner combined this anthology experience with the found footage style for a segment in the abovementioned *V/H/S*, while Jacob Gentry created the popular *My Super Psycho Sweet 16* film series. Actor Bowen has become something of a patron saint of great independent horror films, starring in *House of the Devil*, *You're Next*, and *The Sacrament*. Though *The Signal*'s budget was low, the quality is high, and the filmmakers even make a knowing reference to their filmic competition with an opening "slasher film" in-joke that shows the vast difference between standard low-budget fare and the smart material delivered here.

Other Titles of Interest

Kwaidan (1964), *Creepshow* (1982), *Twilight Zone: the Movie* (1983), *Three Extremes* (2004), *Trilogy of Terror* (1975), *Cat's Eye* (1985), *Fear(s) of the Dark* (2007), *Two Evil Eyes* (1990), *Tales from the Hood* (1995)

Apocalypse and Post-Apocalypse Horror

The modern American enjoys his or her amenities: electricity, air conditioning, deodorant, and plentiful food. The last few thousand years of our existence have been aimed at making things better for the next generation of humanity, creating ways to preserve and extend life, to ease and avoid pain, and in that we have been successful.

There has been a strange side effect of that ability to be safe on a daily basis and to live a long and healthy life. Humanity has found a way to use the built-in biological responses like fear, anger, and violence in ways that ancient man would never have expected. We combine the instinctive nature of our ancestors with the complex critical thinking skills that have come about with the advent of modern man, and an entirely new set of problems have emerged.

Many of the so-called advances of modern humanity are constructs that inherently create more complications. From education comes a hierarchy of intelligence; from money comes obscene wealth and crippling poverty. One could argue that, before the advent of higher thinking, the only thing that differentiated one man from another was his ability to hunt and his speed in fleeing from predators. Every day was a struggle to survive, but it was at least an honest struggle.

This is why today's man secretly craves the concept of the apocalypse. Though modern times do provide us with luxuries and niceties, they also provide us with the time to create anxiety and the things to create anxiety about. The apocalypse and (if you survive the initial apocalypse) the post-apocalyptic results are the great equalizer to marginalized people who are frustrated and held back by the framework of the society into which they were born.

When life is boiled down to mere survival, it is an even playing field. Two people trying to escape from a band of cannibalistic hunters won't be comparing the size of their houses or the prestige of their jobs; they'll simply be working to keep from becoming a meal. And with that desperation comes a clarity and simplicity missing from modern life, a compelling biological imperative that overrides social status and familial expectation. The cry of survival trumps all, and the post-apocalyptic landscape is the perfect representation of that secret desire.

Elements of the Subgenre

The Opening Exposition: Sometimes it's fancy, with accompanying visuals and a dramatic narrator, and other times, it's just a quick text crawl across the screen before the action begins. It's always there, though, the classic opening that spends thirty seconds explaining what went wrong with humanity to bring us to this current state of cannibalism or zombie outbreak or futuristic prison. And, often hilariously, the date on which humanity's fall took place has already passed during a modern viewing of the film.

Brand New (Old) Technology: With the end of normal civilization comes the ingenuity for humanity to continue surviving. One of the recurring elements of the post-apocalypse subgenre is the creation of new machines and tools from the parts of old obsolete ones, the earliest form of steampunk in the filmic world. Old moonshine distilleries turned into water purifiers, lawnmower blades turned into makeshift swords, cars and trucks cannibalized and reformed into desert survival machines—anything left behind that isn't useful in its old form becomes something new and likely dangerous.

Recommendations from the Subgenre

Mad Max (1979)

Directed by George Miller
Written by George Miller, James McCausland
Starring: Mel Gibson, Joanna Samuels, Steve Bisley

In the inhospitable landscape of post-apocalypse Australia, Officer Max Rockatansky is one of the last lines of defense against roving motorcycle gangs who terrorize and steal from anyone they find. After disrupting the gang and unsuccessfully attempting to bring members to trial, Max becomes the target of revenge. Gang members murder his wife and infant child, sending him into a rage-fueled quest for vengeance across the empty highways of the Outback.

Combining the worldwide fear of ecological ruin with the fuel shortages that had countries like Australia and the United States panicking, *Mad Max* was one of the first films to codify the growing fears of the future into the genre we now know as the post-apocalypse film. Rampant violence, ineffective government, and dwindling resources are part of the nightmarish everyday for the survivors in dystopian Australia, and the lengths they will go to for supplies and revenge create some of the most stunning car chases and stunt work ever committed to film.

The first feature film for director George Miller (who left his job as a medical doctor to pursue a film career) was the perfect calling card for his career as an idiosyncratic visionary. Produced on a tiny budget that belied its complicated action sequences, the film launched the career of then-unknown Australian actor Mel Gibson and held the Guinness World Record for most profitable film until the release of *The Blair Witch Project* twenty years later.

Escape from New York (1981)

Directed by John Carpenter
Written by John Carpenter, Nick Castle
Starring: Kurt Russell, Ernest Borgnine, Harry Dean Stanton

In the future year of 1997, New York City is a walled-off prison city containing the worst offenders of a troubled society. When the president's airplane is hijacked by terrorists, the president uses an escape pod, only to crash in the city. With a ticking clock on the president's life and a major peace treaty ready to fall apart, the police make a deal with a disgraced former Special Forces soldier-turned-criminal named Snake Plissken: go into New York City to find and save the president in less than twenty-four hours in exchange for a full pardon.

Post-Watergate cynicism, a jet black sense of humor, and a one-eyed anti-hero combine to make *Escape from New York* one of the great high-concept oddities of the early 1980s. Stunt casting of *Halloween* lead Donald Pleasence and musician Isaac Hayes help to deliver exactly the kind of fun you would want from an exploitation film like this.

After the huge hit of *Halloween* and the moody atmosphere of *The Fog*, director John Carpenter delivered a dark science fiction thriller that was equal parts dystopian vision and political satire. It was a re-teaming of Carpenter and Kurt Russell, who'd worked together on the TV movie *Elvis*. The success of this film launched a collaboration that spanned over fifteen years and included a sequel, *Escape from L.A.* The film has enjoyed long-standing cult popularity. A remake has been talked about for years.

The Battery (2012)

Directed and Written by Jeremy Gardner
Starring: Jeremy Gardner, Adam Cronheim, Alana O'Brien

In a post-apocalyptic New England ravaged by a zombie outbreak, two baseball players travel aimlessly together attempting to stay alive. One has acclimated well to the new rules of the world, the other is reserved and introspective, burying himself in music and memories of the world before the fall. Personality clashes and interactions with other groups of survivors change the dynamic for the two, who end up coming to an understanding just as they find themselves imprisoned with no reasonable means of escape.

The world of *The Battery* is familiar to post-apocalypse fans, but the characters are not. Rather than the crudely drawn clichés of survivors who have compromised themselves and become monsters, in this film's leads (compellingly played by Jeremy Gardner and Adam Cronheim) are real humans still adjusting to the recently destroyed way of living. The film is full of uncharacteristically quiet passages of introspection, and the change of pace for a post-apocalypse film is refreshing and emotional.

Ben (Jeremy Gardner) and Mickey (Adam Croheim) are on their lonely quest for survival in 2012's *The Battery* (courtesy Christian Stella).

The film was directed by writer-star Jeremy Gardner for the unbelievably low sum of $6,000, a sum that becomes more astounding when the stunning location photography is taken into account. The cast, who worked from a broad concept rather than a script, feels appropriate, intimate, and totally realistic for the world of the film, and the chemistry between the two leads is excellent (even when they're fighting).

Other Titles of Interest

Doomsday (2008), *The Road* (2009), *Blindness* (2008), *Hell* (2011), *The Quiet Earth* (1985), *The Divide* (2011), *Dead End Drive-In* (1986), *A Boy and His Dog* (1975), *The Book of Eli* (2010), *Soylent Green* (1973)

Asylum Horror

We humans like to hide our issues, whether behind a focused smile or a security gate in an exclusive neighborhood. We're not always successful. Emotional and psychological problems occasionally creep out into the light of day, making others uncomfortable and confused, wondering why this person can't just keep it together like the rest of us. The presence of people with obvious problems is a reminder of the fact that we, too, have secrets that could come spilling out at any moment.

Our reaction to that realization is a strange one: Rather than having sympathy for someone who is simply unable to continue doing what we ourselves are none too fond of doing, we find a place to hide them away, a place with "others of their kind." In essence, we take those undesirable parts of humanity and store them in a place that is the physical equivalent of the dark hole in which we bury the issues in our minds: the asylum.

In much the same way that we cannot hide forever the dark parts of our own psyche, we also cannot keep from eventually taking an unflinching look at the parts of humanity that we have hidden away. Sometimes it comes in the guise of reform, when the Department of Health closes down a care facility and the public is made aware of the appalling conditions that the residents have had to suffer. Sometimes, as in the case of horror films, it comes when someone who feels they don't belong inside an asylum is forced to remain there due to unforeseen circumstance.

It could be an electrical malfunction that lets the patients loose on the orderlies, or a lie told about an upstanding individual that leads to their incarceration; it could even be as simple as a wrong turn made down a dark road on a stormy night that puts innocent drivers in the clutches of the denizens of the asylum.

Whatever the cause, the moment humanity fears has arrived: the time that all the darkness which was hidden away has free rein. Trapped within the confines of a place created for undesirables, we know now that we're in a place where the social contract doesn't exist, there are no rules, and nothing is certain. So we are either crushed by the natives for being different, or we accept the truth and succumb to the ways of the locals. It's hard to say which is a worse fate.

Elements of the Subgenre

Who's Really Crazy?: A classic trope of the asylum film is the question of whether the people inside the walls of the asylum are really any more disturbed than the people running it. The uncaring orderlies, the nurses who dose without conscience, and the wild-eyed therapists who might just be pushing an unstable person to see what happens when he breaks down, are all aspects of the universal idea that the ones trying to make the patients better may be just as much of a problem themselves.

The Very Unreliable Narrator: The trope of the unreliable narrator is a fairly consistent device within the horror arena, as twists and surprise motivations often come to light in the closing frames of a movie. Nowhere is this more effective or more appropriate than in the asylum horror film, where we are always suspicious of a subjective reality that we will learn is imaginary or somehow the events are not what they seem. And this narrator may not be lying to us; it may just be that he doesn't know any better.

Recommendations from the Subgenre

Asylum Blackout (2011)
Directed by Alexandre Courtès
Written by S. Craig Zahler, Jérôme Fansten
Starring: Rupert Evans, Dave Legeno, Anna Skellern

Three friends struggling to keep their band together work days in the cafeteria of a psychiatric facility for the criminally insane to pay the bills. One day there is a power outage which locks the external doors but causes the cells to unlock, trapping everyone inside the building together. After first trying to help the guards escort the inmates back to their rooms, the friends eventually find themselves simply trying to barricade themselves in the kitchen and survive an all-out assault from the angry and disturbed inmates.

A fun throwback to the single-location, high-concept horror-thrillers of the late '70s and early '80s (the film itself takes place in 1989), *Asylum Blackout* is a clever exercise in violence and paranoia. The seemingly straightforward narrative drops hints that all may not be what it seems, allowing for a believable delivery of the inventive climax. The recurring theme of the loss of bodily dignity (from having parts removed to being tied down naked in front of others) plays on masculine fears to create a smart flipside to the films of Sam Peckinpah and John Woo.

Before making this his feature film debut, director Alexandre Courtès was part of a Grammy-winning music video–directing team called Alex and Martin (with Martin Fougerol). An excellent cast of British character actors (including *Batman Begins'* Richard Brake and *Hellboy's* Rupert Evans) help flesh out characters that could easily be lost in the chaos and action. Cinematographer Laurent Tangy evokes a surprisingly rich mood with a half-million dollar budget. Dave Legeno, MMA fighter and action film star, played a supporting role; his tragic early death cut short a promising career that included a recurring role as Fenrir in the *Harry Potter* movie series.

Alone in the Dark (1982)
Directed by Jack Sholder
Written by Jack Sholder, Robert Shaye, Michael Harrpster
Starring: Jack Palance, Donald Pleasence, Martin Landau

Dr. Dan Potter begins his new job at a psychiatric facility, working with several dangerous patients who decide among themselves that Potter has killed their previous doctor and is now after them. One night the power goes out, leaving the city in darkness. The deranged inmates use the opportunity to escape the facility and head toward Dr. Potter's house. Potter and his family blockade themselves inside the house, unable to communicate with the outside world, and battle the patients in order to survive the night.

A fascinating gem of the 1980s horror arena, *Alone in the Dark* balances genuine scares with some thoughtful rumination about the origins of insanity and a little bit of satire about the scant differences between the people inside the asylum and the ones running it. Familiar faces like Jack Palance (during a low in his career) and Donald Pleasence (enjoying success in the wake of the *Halloween* series) make an effective impact as the asylum heavies; their presence looms large over the young doctor played by Dwight Schultz, an actor who would find huge television success a year later with *The A-Team*.

Influenced by the writings of psychiatrist R.D. Laing, writer-director Jack Sholder created this concept as one of the first films to be produced in-house by distribution company New Line Cinema. Sholder went on to direct *A Nightmare on Elm Street 2: Freddy's Revenge*, the second installment in the horror series that made New Line hugely successful. Though the punk band in the script was made up, real-life group The Sick Fucks got the gig and kept their very recognizable band name in the film. Distinctive character actor Erland Van Lidth (playing child molester Ronald Elster in this film) was also a medal-winning wrestler, an opera singer, and a member of the Dutch royal family.

Session 9 (2001)

Directed by Brad Anderson
Written by Brad Anderson, Steven Gevedon
Starring: David Caruso, Peter Mullan, Josh Lucas

An asbestos removal company run by Scottish immigrant Gordon Fleming starts working on the massive job of cleaning up the Danvers State Hospital, a mental facility long closed and abandoned. There is in-fighting among the antagonistic crew members along with a quickly approaching deadline. The discovery of valuable items in the crematory distracts some of the crew from their work. Some lunchtime research into the facility's past, by listening to recordings of therapy sessions, reveals some dark truths about the facility itself and perhaps some of the people currently working there.

Session 9 is a psychological thriller which plays for every moment of its running time with the possibility that events could be supernatural or the work of deranged humanity, and that ambiguity makes for an effective viewing experience. The film is smart in its use of sound over images for particular revelations; the sequences of the crew member listening to the multiple-personality therapy sessions are creepily effective in their simplicity, and the ultimate reveal is played with audio over a single close-up shot of an actor's face.

Before director Brad Anderson scared audiences with suspense films like *The Machinist* and *Transsiberian*, he directed this low-budget psycho-thriller. It was one of the first films shot on high-definition digital video; the image accentuates the fantastically dilapidated Danvers State Hospital, a practical location in which they shot before it was partially torn down. An excellent cast of character actors, from Brendan Sexton III to the brilliantly tortured Peter Mullan, give the uncomfortable subject matter some much-needed emotional weight.

The Cabinet of Dr. Caligari (1920)

Directed by Robert Wiene
Written by Carl Mayer, Hans Janowitz
Starring: Werner Krauss, Conrad Veidt, Lil Dagover

In the mountain village of Holstenwall, a carnival entertains the locals while young Francis pursues Jane. Francis encounters the mysterious Dr. Caligari at the carnival, and Caligari awakens his mystical somnambulist Cesare to predict the death of Francis' friend. While investigating the murder, Francis finds that Jane is in danger from the somnambulist, and that Dr. Caligari's secret past is connected to a nearby psychiatric hospital. Journeying to the hospital to learn the truth, Francis finds out that everything he believed has been turned upside down.

This silent film is still watched by modern audiences. It's one of the earliest examples of both a true horror film and a German Expressionist masterpiece. The flat painted backgrounds and wild makeup designs add to the nightmarish quality of the film, which already boasts unusually shaped props and doorways which defy geometry and proper function.

Director Robert Wiene teamed with a pair of writers (both of whom would go on to write for another Expressionist master, Nosferatu's F.W. Murnau) whose vision for the project was nearly brought to screen by Fritz Lang. Actor Conrad Veidt, playing the somnambulist Cesare, later found great success in British and American films. He played the dastardly Nazi Major Strasser in Casablanca near the end of his career. The disturbing performances and designs in the film all become clear with the revelation in the asylum at the end, an ending often cited in film history as the origin of the cinematic twist ending.

The streetlights are lit to ward off the mysterious murderer who stalks the city of Holstenwall at night in the 1920 German expressionist classic The Cabinet of Dr. Caligari.

Other Titles of Interest

The Ward (2010), *Gothika* (2003), *Bedlam* (1946), *The Jacket* (2005), *Insanitarium* (2008), *Stonehearst Asylum* (2014), *Shutter Island* (2010), *The Ninth Configuration* (1980)

Back from the Dead—Revenant Horror

One of the reasons narrative fiction (literary or filmic) is so much more popular than documentary narrative is because fiction is allowed to draw conclusions and make connections that are outside of the scope of a story attempting to report the truth. A documentarian may believe that something is connected psychologically or spiritually or even circumstantially, but if he or she does not have the evidence to prove it, it cannot credibly be included. Fiction writers are not bound by the same code of ethics.

This appeals to humanity, because creating our own stories is one of the only ways that we can combat what we believe to be an indifferent and often arbitrary world. Terrible things happen at a moment's notice, people die unexpectedly, matters are left unresolved, and we as humans simply have to let it happen. There is no email address through which we can submit feedback to a higher power in order to alter events that have already taken place.

But there is the opportunity to contextualize it, to brainstorm around it and try to find meaning within it. The power of fiction is to make visible the invisible lines that connect random events and tragic circumstances, to give death a meaning and suffering a nobility. The power of fiction is to, at the very least, give humanity a sense that at some point, for someone, the events of all our lives have a profound meaning.

That human desire for cosmic balance, that hope for justice that extends beyond our own mortality, is the same trait that draws us to stories about revenants, those who have returned from the dead. Though the prospect is frightening to us, because we know that to return from the dead must involve some sort of otherworldly magic or dangerous technology that could threaten us, we are still subconsciously drawn to the idea.

We want someone to be able to come back, to wrong a right or finish something left undone. There is a sense of peace in the idea that a man or woman could return from the grave with a single goal in mind, driven by nothing more than a very human need to get something finished.

Sometimes, the wandering revenant could be here for years, attempting to remember or accomplish something difficult or unobtainable; other times, the revenant is here for mere hours, returned only to extinguish an offending life or save an innocent one. Then they'll turn and wander back into the ocean or grave from whence they came, satisfied that in some way, the business left unfinished by death was completed in spite of death.

Elements of the Subgenre

Rooting for Them to Die: Though there are some subgenres where you root for a character to die, it's never as strong as it is in the revenant horror film. The revenant, sometimes in the form of a neighborhood gentleman like the one played by Peter Cushing in *Tales from the Crypt*, is usually a kindly person who was abused before they were killed, and the supernatural revenge they seek is particularly satisfying to the audience because the people who tormented them were so truly terrible.

They're All Connected: Inevitably, if a person is returning from the grave to seek revenge on more than one person, those victims will have worked together to harass the deceased. In many revenant horror stories, we follow a character tangentially connected to the story (an investigator or concerned girlfriend) who wants to know what is happening and eventually realizes that the deaths are all connected to some terrible event which they never knew about and which reveals the disturbing truth.

Recommendations from the Subgenre

They Came Back (2004)

Directed by Robin Campillo
Written by Robin Campillo, Brigitte Tijou
Starring: Géraldine Pailhas, Jonathan Zaccaï, Frédéric Pierrot

The dead have suddenly started to return to life. And unlike in most monster movies, they're not here to kill or destroy; they simply wish to learn how to live again. In a small French town, the returned people are not accepted easily, and many are given menial tasks due to their childlike nature and inability to function the way they had previously. The returned do not accept their fate, though, sabotaging the infrastructure of the town and attempting to leave en masse, with many of their loved ones caught in the middle.

A haunting film that toys with elements of zombie storytelling without ever falling into the flesh-eating and post-apocalyptic clichés of the subgenre, *They Came Back* is a film as much about mood and theme as it is about its central protagonists. It effectively shows the global circumstances on a personal level, dealing with a single town's reaction. (This concept was later reworked to great results on HBO's *The Leftovers*.) Its portrayal of marginalized citizens stuck in dead-end jobs and treated as less than human reflects modern social hierarchies without coming across as too obvious.

Four years after French writer-director Robin Campillo brought this quiet rumination on death to the screen, he co-wrote the Oscar-nominated *The Class*. *They Came Back* never allows its outlandish premise to outweigh the human drama, and Campillo's focus on the mundane activities surrounding the return (medical examinations and census updates) helps to anchor the film in an effective near-reality. Its central premise was so strong and mysterious that Fabrice Gobert re-imagined the concept as a French television series with 2012's *The Returned*. The series proved so popular that the American network A&E produced an English-language remake.

Deathdream a.k.a. Dead of Night (1972)

Directed by Bob Clark
Written by Alan Ormsby
Starring: John Marley, Richard Backus, Lynn Carlin

In Vietnam, U.S. soldier Andy Brooks is killed in combat, and his family is informed. His mother will not accept the truth, and she is vindicated when Andy shows up at their front door, very much alive. His mother is thankful but his father suspects that something strange is happening, due to Andy's bizarre behavior and his habit of disappearing nightly. The truth is that Andy is a monster subsisting on blood. The police give chase, only to discover that Andy was slowly dying again and had begun to prepare for it.

Inspired by the classic nightmare wish scenario in the short story "The Monkey's Paw," *Deathdream* has a disturbing concept that uses its undead protagonist to reflect on the losses incurred by the still-raging Vietnam War. Though produced by Canadian filmmakers, the movie is a decidedly American tale, showing the devastation that war has on the family. John Marley and Lynn Carlin play the tortured parents, while Richard Backus lurks and leers as the not-quite-right Andy.

After the success of their first collaboration *Children Shouldn't Play with Dead Things*, director Bob Clark and writer Alan Ormsby reunited for this more serious outing. Their careers would diverge for several years, with Clark finding success with a series of iconic films (*Black Christmas*, *Porky's*, and *A Christmas Story*) and Ormsby working in action and horror (*The Substitute* and the *Cat People* remake). They reunited for a couple of projects in the late 1980s. Ormsby also handled the makeup effects in the film while working with young artist Tom Savini (this was only his second film). Savini went on to create some of the horror industry's greatest makeup works in *Dawn of the Dead* and *Friday the 13th*.

The Revenant (2009)

Written and Directed by Kerry Prior
Starring: David Anders, Chris Wylde, Louise Griffiths

Lieutenant Bart Gregory was killed under strange circumstances while serving in Iraq. His friend and girlfriend attend his funeral. Bart discovers that he is some kind of supernatural creature (settling on a revenant after deciding against vampire or zombie) who needs blood to survive and goes dormant during daylight hours. He and his friend become nighttime vigilante heroes, murdering and feeding on criminals, until the girlfriend finds out the truth and the authorities start a manhunt to catch them.

Lieutenant Bart Gregory (David Anders) finds he has returned from war, but isn't quite the same, in 2009's horror-comedy *The Revenant* (courtesy Kerry Prior).

The Revenant, a clever horror comedy, sets itself up (with its wartime theme) to be a film loaded with social commentary about American overreach, only to pull a reversal that ends up commenting on the bizarre nature of celebrity in a media-driven world. Great chemistry between David Anders and Chris Wylde as the friends turned avenging angels, along with meta-winks to other supernatural creatures (isn't it gargoyles who go dormant in daylight?), give the film a fun perspective and keep the proceedings from getting bogged down.

Director Kerry Prior began his career as a special effects artist in the late 1980s, working on the *Nightmare on Elm Street* series and forging a good relationship with director Don Coscarelli. *The Revenant* was his first major directorial work. Also serving as producer, writer, visual effects supervisor, and editor (under the pseudonym Walter Montague Urch, a reference to respected revenant authors from the past), Prior put his decades of knowledge to great use in creating a film that feels much larger and more complex than its modest budget should allow. Prior's film is not to be confused with the western survival film starring Leonardo DiCaprio, reeased in 2015.

Other Titles of Interest
Maniac Cop (1988), *The Ghoul* (1933), *The Tomb of Ligeia* (1964), *Blood Creek* (1964), *Cemetery Man* (1994)

Basement Horror

Physically and psychologically, the basement is a place we think of as beneath us. Nothing we truly value in our home belongs in a basement. Our surplus and cast-off belongings are sent there, perhaps as the last stop on the journey to the curb. All the unattractive and noisy mechanical elements of our homes—hot water heaters and air conditioning ducts and fuse boxes—are hidden away in the corners of the room under our feet.

The lighting is sparse and dismal. The heating and cooling vents that keep the rest of the house a consistent temperature are absent from the basement, and the result is a strange underground biosphere.

For those who live there, it is a comment on their perceived value to us. Forsaken members of the family, grown children who should have long since found their way in the world, exist quietly beneath us, the faint glow of their nighttime television watching the only reminder of their disturbing presence.

Though these objects (and people) seem displaced from our everyday life, they are still there. While that box of toys in the corner may no longer be useful to you, it hasn't reached the curb yet. There is still something there that prevents you from giving in and saying goodbye. The basement, with its valueless objects that we are still unable to let go, is the ground zero for the hoarder. We know the problem has gotten unmanageable when the material suited for the basement overflows into the rest of the house.

And so it sits, in the darkness, a confused catch-all for things unwanted. Like that small "room" in the back of the mind that holds onto things like guilt and embarrassment, the basement is the destination for unnecessary but emotionally resonant things which we don't want others to see but from which we can't fully separate. The basement is premature burial for things not yet dead. In their way, these things hold onto us as much as we hold onto them.

Elements of the Subgenre

The Naked Light Bulb: No one puts real effort into decorating the basement, because no one really cares what it looks like. No curtains on the windows, no carpet on the floor, and certainly no attractive coverings for the stark light bulbs on the ceiling. Likely they're hanging from a loose cord, and one bump will send them swinging wildly back and forth, throwing shadows in looping circles across the dirty brick walls.

The Other Room in the Basement: We don't know why it's there or what it's used for, but even within the basement, there is yet another door that leads to something even more unpleasant. The furnace closet, the tanning room, the tool storage—whatever is in there is the least needed and the most creepy.

Recommendations from the Subgenre

The Cellar (1989)
Directed by Kevin Tenney
Written by David Henry Keller, John Woodward, Darryl Wimberley
Starring: Patrick Kilpatrick, Chris Miller, Suzanne Savoy

In the 1800s, Native Americans anxious to prevent white men from taking their land, created an evil hybrid monster that would attack only them but could be kept at bay using talismans. In modern times, a family moves into a house located on the same land where the creature was created. The oldest son notices that something in the house is strange but his family doesn't believe him. The son decides to take matters into his own hands to gain proof of the monster's existence.

Tapping into a uniquely American paranoia (that the land grab our ancestors pulled could come back to bite us), *The Cellar* is a fun combination of supernatural threats and adolescent struggle that is reminiscent of Disney's darker live-action fairy tale fare like *The Watcher in the Woods* and *Something Wicked This Way Comes*. The classic Hitchcock concept of the single protagonist no one believes is made more effective in that it is a child of divorce, scared of the shapeless menace in the basement.

Director Kevin Tenney cut his teeth on low-budget horror exploitation fare like *Night of the Demons* before he was hired for this film. He was brought on to replace John Woodward, a first-time director who had written the screenplay and had already fallen several days behind the shooting schedule. Though there are many recognizable faces in the film (including character actor Patrick Kilpatrick and television mainstay Suzanne Savoy), the real surprise is Chris Miller as Willy Cashen. Miller went on to work for Dreamworks Animation, writing for the *Shrek* film series and receiving an Oscar nomination for Best Animated Feature for directing *Puss in Boots*.

The Evil Dead (1981)
Written and Directed by Sam Raimi
Starring: Bruce Campbell, Ellen Sandweiss, Betsy Baker

Five college students venture into the Tennessee hills to stay in a cabin in the middle of nowhere for spring break. They find some strange books and tapes in the basement and play a tape recording of incantations in another language. The incantations awaken an ancient evil in the forest which systematically begins to attack, kill, or possess members of the group.

An intense and energetic film which has left its distinct visual mark on the horror world, *The Evil Dead* is something of a hybrid oddity. A mix of visceral horror and winking humor, it synthesizes a new kind of monster, combining elements of zombies, cannibals, demon possession, and infection horror. The fruit cellar, with its hanging gourds and constantly dripping water, is eerily effective and sets up great scares later when possessed people start getting imprisoned there.

The first official release from director Sam Raimi (though he and his creative team, including actor Bruce Campbell, had made amateur films for years previous) is a *tour de force* masterpiece of low-budget ingenuity and inventive cinematic lunacy. Cameras were mounted to planks of wood and bicycles, smashed through windows, spun, and tilted awkwardly to create a sense of confusion and vertigo that effectively puts the viewer in the shoes of the characters. The plot of the film, focused on a "book of the dead" and its ability to wake ancient monsters, is heavily influenced by writer H.P. Lovecraft, even going so far as to name the book the Necronomicon after the fictional book that appeared in his writings.

Night of the Living Dead (1968)

Directed by George A. Romero
Written by George A. Romero, John A. Russo
Starring: Duane Jones, Judith O'Dea, Karl Hardman

For some unspecified reason, dead bodies began returning to life and cannibalistically attacking the living. A disparate group of survivors converge on a small country farmhouse.

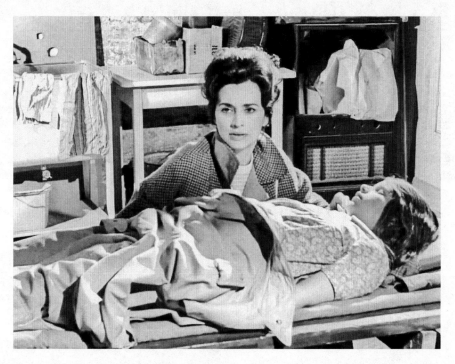

Helen Cooper (Marilyn Eastman) hides in the basement hoping her daughter (Kyra Schon) will recover from an attack in 1968's seminal *Night of the Living Dead*.

While watching the news on TV and talking among themselves to try and understand the scope of the phenomenon, the group begins to splinter when they can't decide on the best method for staying alive and avoiding the throngs of living dead. The bickering and disagreements come to an end when a horde of the living dead attack the farmhouse, slowly killing or dragging away the people inside.

One of the most important horror films in history, *Night of the Living Dead* was both a re-invigoration and reinvention. Stunning cinematography, a new spin on a classic monster, and some scathing political commentary combined to create one of the seminal films of all time, horror or otherwise.

Night of the Living Dead places most of its most important and iconic moments in the basement. The revelation of what a zombie bite does to its victim, along with the aftermath of that zombie's attack, take place in the basement, and the entire crux of the film hangs on the decision to flee the house or barricade themselves in the basement. The final tragic moments in the life of survivor Ben play out once he emerges from the basement.

Other Titles of Interest

Basement (2010), *Don't Look in the Basement* (1973), *The Basement* (2011), *The Silence of the Lambs* (1991)

Battle with the Devil Horror

In the long history of villainy there has always been one ultimate Big Bad, one malevolent character whose motivations are darkest, whose machinations are most complex, whose reach is widest and whose influence is the most insidious. He goes by many names: Lucifer, Satan, the Dark One, the Adversary, The Devil.

He is the King of the Fallen, the ruler of all the dark, shapeless beings that hide in the shadows from the light of God and the sight of humanity, the ruler of Hell. He is the embodiment of all we fear and dread.

Whether he exists or not is largely irrelevant to his ubiquitous presence in the genre of horror. In fact, it can be argued that his existence as a presence in the movies (rather than in the real world) says more than the idea of whether or not we believe in him in our everyday lives.

The true discussion of the concept of good and evil, the idea of whether or not there is a component of spirituality beyond the biological and psychological, is a question that most human beings don't wish to spend much time considering. The simplicity of a codified legal system, a structure created by moral boundaries and social expectation, allows for the freedom of humans to not really consider the full weight of their every action. A purchase made at one department store instead of another could mean the supporting of child labor or unsafe work environments for the people who manufactured that product; however, because the purchase of an object at a department store could never be seen as a legally binding crime or even generally a social miscue, we feel comfortable giving the action no more thought. Our rules have been laid out for us in black and white, and we have not broken them.

This is perhaps why the idea of the battle with the Devil is an appealing subgenre in horror. When characters battle the Devil in a film, they battle a person, a figure, a face (sometimes a recognizable one, as in the case of Gabriel Byrne in *End of Days* or George Burns in *Oh God, You Devil!*). And, in giving a personification to evil, we have relieved ourselves of the idea that the Devil might be everywhere. As long as Old Scratch is fighting with Daniel Webster for his soul or plotting the downfall of an up-and-coming young lawyer, then he might not be the stray thought you had about lying to your spouse about something important, or the fact that you kept quiet about the guy who slipped a pill into his date's drink at the bar.

Giving the Devil a form doesn't just make it easier for movie heroes to battle him on the big screen; it also makes it easier for us to absolve ourselves of the idea that the Devil might be just a little bit us.

Elements of the Subgenre

Hey, I Recognize Satan: He is the most heinous villain the history of humanity, so it should come as no surprise that every actor wants to portray him. Nearly no other figure in filmic history can claim to have been played by as varied a list as Harvey Keitel, Elizabeth Hurley, Tim Curry, Robert DeNiro, Al Pacino, Viggo Mortensen, Walter Huston, Donald Pleasence, Burgess Meredith, Jack Nicholson, and Peter Fonda.

A Contest for Your Soul: If the Devil is involved in your story, you can be sure that he has some kind of wager placed on the outcome. Sometimes it's a contest to prove to God that people are bad, sometimes it's a competition with other demons to gain possession of an already possessed soul, and sometimes it's against the humans themselves (who seem to think that they're clever enough to outwit the Prince of Darkness). These films often stand in as the cosmic screen on which the gamblers watch the humans try to escape the inevitable.

Recommendations from the Subgenre

The Devil's Advocate (1997)

Directed by Taylor Hackford
Written by Tony Gilroy, Jonathan Lemkin (based on the story by Andrew Neiderman)
Starring: Keanu Reeves, Al Pacino, Charlize Theron

Young Florida lawyer Kevin wins a controversial case which draws the attention of a prestigious New York City law firm run by John Milton. Heading to the city with his wife Mary Ann to join the firm, Kevin becomes enmeshed in troubling moral dilemmas. Mary Ann becomes so emotionally troubled by what she experiences with the people at the firm that she is driven mad and placed in a psychiatric care facility. As his personal life continues to fall apart and his professional life grows, Kevin discovers the true identity of the mysterious man who hired him.

An updating of *The Devil and Daniel Webster* by way of John Grisham, *The Devil's Advocate* uses the modern world of business, law, and finance to stand in for the age-old conceits of power, deceit, and greed. Over-the-top yet somehow appropriate performances accentuate the creeping menace of the film, nicely realized in CGI sequences of demonic creatures crawling just under the skin of seemingly normal humans. Al Pacino has a great time chewing the scenery as The Devil-John Milton (a reference to the author of the Devil's greatest story, *Paradise Lost*).

Director Taylor Hackford was known for his character-driven dramas *An Officer and a Gentleman* and *Dolores Claiborne* before venturing into supernatural territory in this film; he would return to character drama for the Oscar-winning *Ray*. This was his second collaboration with scripter Tony Gilroy; they would work together again on *Proof of Life* before Gilroy found success with *The Bourne Identity* and its sequels. It was released three years after Keanu Reeves' success in *Speed* but two years before Reeves' *The Matrix* changed action films forever; this film was a big-budget disappointment that exemplified Reeves' struggle to find vehicles for his talent.

Angel Heart (1987)
Directed and Written by Alan Parker (based on the novel by William Hjortsberg)
Starring: Robert De Niro, Mickey Rourke, Lisa Bonet

In 1955, New York City private investigator Harry Angel is hired by a wealthy and mysterious man to look into a missing persons case. His investigations lead him to New Orleans, where he discovers that the man he is seeking may have sold his soul to the Devil, and since then has been going through some hellish machinations to get himself out of the deal. Harry's investigation leads to dead bodies in every direction. After falling for the missing man's daughter, Harry begins to suspect that the man's past and his own are irrevocably intertwined.

A clever combination of the battle-with-the-Devil subgenre and the detective story, *Angel Heart* is most effective in the moments where it leans on its film noir roots. The film captures the seedy appeal of period New York City and New Orleans, and while the central mystery may not be difficult to figure out, the journey to the revelation is never boring.

Alan Parker was a successful commercial director before he transitioned to cinema with the critically and commercially successful films *Midnight Express* and *Fame*. He adapted the William Hjortsberg novel *Falling Angel* fairly faithfully, and the film was critically well-received. It underperformed theatrically, possibly due to the controversy involving a horror-laced sex scene between Rourke and Lisa Bonet (known to TV viewers as Bill Cosby's daughter Denise on *The Cosby Show*). Though the truth about the Devil's identity comes late in the film, director Parker does a great job of seeding clues to the revelation throughout.

Satan Hates You (2010)
Directed and Written by James Felix McKenney
Starring: Don Wood, Angus Scrimm, Christine Spencer

Representatives of both Heaven and Hell are very interested in the lives of Marc and Wendy. Marc is a maniac driven by homicidal impulses that root from his innate homophobia and fear of being identified as gay himself; Wendy is a free spirit, doing anything that feels good in the moment and facing the unfortunate consequences of her actions. Their lives begin to drift closer together while also spinning out of control. Perhaps only the words of televangelist Dr. Michael Gabriel can save them.

A truly bizarre and one-of-a-kind film, *Satan Hates You* is gleefully perverse and funny while simultaneously strangely sincere about the material it purports to mock. Nearly impossible to categorize (you get a disturbing medical procedure, a rave, and consistent evil commentary from two demons that are Hell's equivalent of Statler and Waldorf), the film exists in its own world and by its own logic.

Though it's silly on its surface, director James Felix McKenney's film comments on subjects like religious bigotry and homophobia while simultaneously skewering an obscure corner of the film universe: Christian apocalypse films of the 1970s. Working with the lowest of low budgets, McKenney (the idiosyncratic mind behind other crazed auteur works

Angus Scrimm as televangelist Dr. Michael Gabriel in 2010's *Satan Hates You* (courtesy Larry Fessenden).

like *Automatons* and *Hypothermia*) uses the familiar faces of genre veterans Angus Scrimm (*Phantasm*) and Michael Berryman (*The Hills Have Eyes*) to recapture the unintentional cheesiness and melodramatic importance of films like *A Thief in the Night* and *The Burning Hell*.

Other Titles of Interest

Devil (2010), *Constantine* (2005), *To the Devil a Daughter* (1976), *House of the Devil* (2009), *The Mephisto Waltz* (1971), *End of Days* (1999), *The Omen* (1976)

Body-Snatching Horror

The death of the body is supposed to be the physical form's last journey. Regardless of one's spiritual beliefs, all religions tend to agree with the central tenet that the human body is a physical one, meant for eventual decay, and that we will all end up back in the life cycle of the Earth, decomposed and returned to the soil, broken down to the key components that made us alive in the first place.

It is this belief in the finality of physical death that often makes people uncomfortable with the idea of dead bodies. They represent everyone's fate, that hunk of unmoving dead matter that currently resembles the person it inhabited, and will soon be little more than elements spread back out through the biosphere. Since early man's days, we have feared being around the dead, perhaps fearing that constant reminder of an end that waits patiently for us.

But there are those certain few who think otherwise. The human body, even when non-functional, is still a human body, after all. Enterprising doctors and scientists learned that, even though a dead human body couldn't react the way a living one did, it could still be useful for learning about anatomy and teaching skills of surgery.

Humanity always finds a way to profit from anything, including death. In a time when the science of medicine was young, and the world was still a place where every crime could not be solved with DNA evidence and forensic cleverness, the strange career of the body snatcher was as real as it is bizarre. His sole job was to find corpses of different sizes, genders, and maladies, and provide them to medical schools and science academies for study and practice.

The practice eventually became illegal for numerous reasons, up to and including the fact that many religions are opposed to disturbing the body after death. But this wasn't the only reason it was made illegal, of course; and the truth is a much more disturbing one.

If the human psyche can become comfortable enough around the remains of another human being that they can package and sell that body for money, then what is one more minor leap, from finding dead bodies in a cemetery to creating dead bodies of your own? Body snatching became a crime because the very nature of making money off human corpses encouraged far more serious crimes.

The illegality of an act never stops people from trying to profit from it. In 1978, the body of Charlie Chaplin was stolen from its resting place and his widow received a ransom demand of $600,000. The two "kidnappers," auto mechanics from Bulgaria, thought stealing the body would solve their financial problems. They were given time in prison, and Charlie Chaplin was re-buried in a concrete grave to prevent another theft. Unlike many subgenres in the horror film world, this one is based entirely in fact.

Elements of the Subgenre

Mixing Social Classes: This is a big part of the genre, because higher social classes that would need the bodies (scientists, doctors, medical schools) would never do such a job themselves, and are required by the dictates of decency to find someone desperate (and likely from a lower social class) to do the dirty work. This creates a rare situation where the lower classes are able to provide something that the upper classes need, and it gives them a modicum of power.

Escalation from Body Theft to Murder: In stories like this, there are never enough easily accessible bodies to fill the quota. At some point, an enterprising provider discovers that, if he is more active in the making of bodies, he can profit more from their sale. The stories almost inevitably blur the line (and then cross over it) between brokering in the aftermath of death and causing it outright.

Forensic Morality: The element of rationality from the doctors and scientists, that rigorous scientific testing can and will lead to cures for all diseases and maladies, is what allows such horrible behavior to continue. These stories usually have moments of lucidity or recognition regarding the complicity of the high-minded moralist in the resulting deaths.

Recommendations from the Subgenre

The Body Snatcher (1945)

Directed by Robert Wise
Written by Philip McDonald (based on the story by Robert Louis Stevenson)
Starring: Boris Karloff, Bela Lugosi, Henry Daniell

The Body Snatcher is a film about a driven surgeon whose desire to help a young paralyzed girl recover from her injuries causes him to enter into an unholy bargain with a coachman who provides bodies for his research. It is one of the first films to touch on the grisly subject matter in the conservative Hollywood of the day, and it creates many of the touchstones for the subgenre: a rich and educated doctor relying on a wily lower-class cabman to provide him with the cadavers; moving the story from creepy illegality to cold-blooded murder; and good people going well past the bounds of decency, and all because they believe the greater good can be served. The lush black and white cinematography is gorgeous and evocative, and belies the movie's meager budget.

It is a classic in the genre that should be even more well-known than it is, considering the involvement of several screen icons: director Robert Wise (who would later go on to direct *The Day the Earth Stood Still* and *The Haunting*), author Robert Louis Stevenson (upon whose short story the script is based), and one of the greatest horror producers of all time, Val Lewton (whose name became synonymous with low-budget, intelligent psychological horror films in the 1940s). Though Karloff and Lugosi share a scant few scenes, it is great to see them on-screen together, and their last shared moments are some of the highlights of the film. It's ostensibly a non-supernatural story of real-life medical horror, but there are hints at the end that perhaps a person's soul lives on after death, giving the premise of the film that much more impact.

Burke and Hare (2010)

Directed by John Landis
Written by Piers Ashworth, Nick Moorcroft
Starring: Simon Pegg, Andy Serkis, Tom Wilkinson

This horror-comedy is loosely based on the real-life case of William Burke and William Hare. Given that it is a comedy (in the credits it says "This is a true story. Except for the parts that are not"), it's safe to assume that the exploits of the two men who murdered sixteen people and sold their bodies to a medical college are somewhat altered for humorous effect. There's nothing funnier than desecrating someone's final resting place—or at least that's what this film would have you believe. Though the film does sport the same classic tropes of the subgenre, they are played to more comedic effect, particularly regarding the intelligence of the two leads.

The film is directed by the king of the horror-comedy, John Landis, who made audiences laugh and scream previously with *An American Werewolf in London* and *Twilight Zone: The Movie*, as well as creating the iconic Michael Jackson video *Thriller*. The two hapless killers, played by Simon Pegg and Andy Serkis as a fun comedy duo, are woefully out of their league, and the film plays like a classic comedy from Ealing (a studio known in the 1950s for their dark comedies starring Alec Guinness). An able supporting cast of recognizable British faces, from Tom Wilkinson and Tim Curry to Hammer Horror icon Christopher Lee, gives the film an air of respectability that is intentionally undercut by the black humor.

The Doctor and the Devils (1985)

Directed by Freddie Francis
Written by Ronald Harwood (based on an earlier screenplay by Dylan Thomas)
Starring: Timothy Dalton, Jonathan Pryce, Twiggy

Based on the same true-life case of grave robbing as *Burke and Hare*, and also bearing a distinctly British air (though one of costume—period drama rather than straight-faced black comedy), *The Doctor and the Devils* changes the names involved but keeps the same story of a driven doctor breaking the laws and mores of the Victorian era by purchasing cadavers from grave robbers. The film exudes an atmosphere of dread, and the imagery is stunning, but it's definitely more a drama than a horror film in its depiction of the disparity of wealthy and poor as the true evil of the story. Unrelentingly bleak but visually arresting, the film was a tough sell, and after its theatrical release it has been largely forgotten.

The film was produced by Mel Brooks, who is most well-known for his raunchy comedies, including *Blazing Saddles* and *History of the World, Part 1*. He did produce a few British period dramas of note; the first was *The Elephant Man*, an Oscar-nominated drama about the titular tragic historical figure. His follow-up was this film, directed by Freddie Francis, a cinematographer and director whose stellar career included work on *Dune*, *Cape Fear*, and the brilliant *The Innocents*. A pre–*Star Trek* Patrick Stewart and Stephen Rea (before he was known for his collaborations with director Neil Jordan) round out an excellent cast who have the task of bringing grim subject matter to life. Future James Bond Timothy Dalton excels as the titular doctor, and the film focuses as much on the toll of the proceedings on its characters as it does on the macabre details of the acts themselves. Many crew members came to this film from *The Elephant Man*, but this project came nowhere near *Elephant Man*'s box-office success.

I Sell the Dead (2008)

Written and Directed by Glenn McQuaid
Starring: Dominic Monaghan, Larry Fessenden, Ron Perlman

As grave robber Arthur Blake sits in prison, awaiting his death by hanging, he recounts the tale of his life of crime to a sympathetic priest. Thus begins *I Sell the Dead*, the humor-

ous tale of two corpse-stealers who learn that there's more than just dead bodies to be found buried in the ground. A horror-comedy that works because of its knowing references to previous films of the subgenre and the excellent comic timing

Arthur (Dominic Monaghan) and Willy (Larry Fessenden) find more than they expected inside a coffin in 2008's *I Sell the Dead* (courtesy Larry Fessenden).

of its leads, the film cleverly reinvents the body-snatching subgenre by cross-pollinating it with aliens and vampires. Clever plays on the conventions of the subgenre, such as when the grave robbers get rid of a troublesome doctor by giving him a vampire in a coffin instead of a corpse, help to elevate it above the typical clichés we've come to expect in films of this type.

The sense of humor veers wildly from slapstick comedy (Larry Fessenden's hilariously broad performance when carrying his own decapitated head) to quiet character observation (Ron Perlman and lead actor Dominic Monaghan are subtly effective in the wraparound confessional scenes). The film is a clever throwback to the classic horror anthology entries from British production company Amicus (a Hammer competitor known for films like *The Vault of Horror*, *Tales from the Crypt*, and *Asylum*). Director McQuaid shows off his horror knowledge with characters that are clear references to classic horror films (in particular, a fun nod to the masked daughter from *Eyes Without a Face*) and a cast of recognizable genre actors, including *Phantasm*'s resident Tall Man, Angus Scrimm.

Other Titles of Interest

Corridors of Blood (1958), *Frankenstein* (1931), *Re-Animator* (1985)

Buried Alive Horror

Death is inevitable. However, this is not something of which we like to be constantly reminded.

Much of what humanity spends its time doing, from watching television and reading books to visiting doctors and exercising, is designed to either distract us from the inevitability of death or to help delay it. In its way, the inevitability of death is more responsible for shaping the psychology of any individual human being (perhaps even the entire human race) than any of the actual events of life itself.

Many religions do focus on death, even going so far as to meditate frequently with death as the focus of their meditation. Buddhism, Judaism, and Islam all focus very strongly and specifically on the idea of death in various ways. It is believed that, by not turning a blind eye to the inevitable end that we all go through, we can replace the sense of morbid anxiety with a calmness and a sense of direction in life that is not driven by our buried fears.

The buried alive subgenre of horror fully embraces that focus. There are many viewers who are unable to watch horror movies that involve being buried alive, citing reasons as far-ranging as a sense of claustrophobia to restlessness regarding a movie with such a limiting locale. The deeper truth, however, is that a movie where a person is buried alive gives the audience no choice but to spend time thinking about death. Watching a character in the confines of a tiny box buried under the ground (the place where most bodies will end up after death) traps the audience in a box of their own making; they've put death into a container in their mind so that they don't have to think about it regularly, and now they find themselves locked inside it.

Being buried alive reminds us of the immediacy of death, and it forces us to stare mortality right in the eyes. We may deal differently with the discomfort, but we all have it. Because we know that, even if the hero of our movie has the luck of being found before the air runs out and he is saved from his earthen grave … it is only a matter of time before he will end up there again. Permanently.

Elements of the Subgenre

Very Tight Quarters: While being buried underground is terrifying no matter what your locale is, you don't tend to find a lot of horror movies where the people buried under the ground have wide-open spaces with plenty of leg room. Generally, the fear comes from the tiny area and no hope of escape; and the smaller the space, the more frightening the situation.

Panic Sets In: At some point during the ordeal of being buried, the human mind can't take it. Every film about being buried alive involves at least one moment where the interred but living victim screams, laughs, cries, and generally loses their mind, with all their histrionics lost to the world.

Recommendations from the Subgenre

The Vanishing (Spoorloos) (1988)

Written and Directed by George Sluizer (based on the novel *The Golden Egg* by Tim Krabbé)
Starring: Bernard-Pierre Donnadieu, Gene Bervoets, Johanna ter Steege

Rex and Saskia are a Dutch couple vacationing in France. They get separated at a gas station and this leads to Saskia's disappearance. For three years, Rex seeks the truth of his girlfriend's disappearance, becoming obsessed with finding out what happened and unable to move on in his life. When the man responsible for Saskia's disappearance approaches Rex and offers him a dangerous way to find out exactly what happened to her, Rex has to decide if his desire to know the truth is stronger than his will to survive.

Spoorloos is one of the greatest Hitchcock films that Hitchcock never made. A simple plot hinging on the most intimate and everyday fears, the kidnapping of a loved one, is turned into a tragic mystery of epic emotional proportions. The brilliance of including the entire story from the villain's perspective makes this film a unique accomplishment in creating a mystery that shows you the answer but still keeps you guessing.

Tapping into the nearly universal fear of being buried alive, director George Sluizer created a suspense film masterpiece from Tim Krabbé's novel *The Golden Egg*. The devastating ending is a smart turn that is completely expected and yet totally unwanted, making the final moments even more emotionally resonant. The two male leads play off each other well, but it is the performance of Johanna ter Steege (given only minutes to make an impact before disappearing forever) which connects with the viewer and pulls us through the journey. In 1993 Sluizer directed the American remake which had a happy ending. It was not well received by audiences or fans of the original film.

Buried Alive (1990)

Directed by Frank Darabont
Written by Mark Patrick Carducci, David A. Davies
Starring: Tim Matheson, Jennifer Jason Leigh, William Atherton

Joanna has been cheating on her husband Clint with a doctor named Cortland; Joanna and the doc want to get rid of Clint so they can sell his business and move to California together. Using a serum from a poisonous tropical fish that she got from Cortland, Joanna poisons Clint and he seemingly dies. After his burial, Clint awakens from what was actually just severe paralysis and slowed heart rate, and escapes his grave. Vowing revenge, he constructs an elaborate plan to make Cortland and Joanna turn on each other right before he punishes them forever.

Heavily influenced by the gothic romance horror of Edgar Allan Poe (in particular his story "The Premature Burial"), *Buried Alive* is a taut thriller whose made-for-cable origins belie its energy and inventiveness. A cast of recognizable faces from big films (Atherton from *Die Hard* and Matheson from *Animal House*) acquit themselves nicely in this modern noir.

Director Frank Darabont was a gun for hire—just a few years past his scripting work on *A Nightmare on Elm Street 3: Dream Warriors* and *The Blob*—when he directed this project. His skill behind the camera led to greater opportunities, and four years later he directed the Oscar-nominated *The Shawshank Redemption*. He returned to horror (and cable television) as the writer and developer of the popular zombie series *The Walking Dead*.

Nine years after *Buried Alive* was released, actor Tim Matheson returned to reprise his role and direct the sequel *Buried Alive II*.

Open Grave (2013)

Directed by Gonzalo López-Gallego
Written by Eddie Borey, Chris Borey
Starring: Sharlto Copley, Thomas Kretschmann, Erin Richards

A man awakens to find himself lying in a large earthen pit full of dead bodies, with no memory of who he is or how he arrived there. Pulling himself out with the assistance of a

Amnesiac John (Sharlto Copley) wakes to find himself in a pit filled with corpses in the 2013 thriller *Open Grave* (courtesy Dylan Lewis).

woman, he flees to a nearby house and discovers that there are other people hiding there. They also have no memory. As they begin to look into the mystery, they learn that they all previously knew each other, that the amnesia was chemically induced, and that there is a virulent plague that is slowly destroying humanity.

Open Grave plays effectively by keeping feet in two different camps: the buried alive film and the amnesiac film. The main characters are truly put through the wringer in this twisty thriller that toys with supernatural and science fiction theories for the complicated situation before revealing a surprisingly plausible medical explanation.

After the low-budget success of *King of the Mountain* and a foray into found footage filmmaking with *Apollo 18*, director Gonzalo López-Gallego brought this internationally minded thriller to the screen. The script from sibling writing team Eddie and Chris Borey creates solid material for great character actors Thomas Kretschmann and lead Sharlto Copley, who burst onto the scene four years earlier in the similarly grimy sci-fi–tinged action film *District 9*.

Other Titles of Interest

Kill Bill (2003 and 2004), *Premature Burial* (1962), *Blood Simple* (1984), *House of Usher* (1960)

Campground Horror

The clichéd explanation for humanity's fear of the wilderness usually involves fears of getting lost, being attacked by animals, and dying in the midst of the elements. And while those things can happen, the strangest part of the idea of going camping and staying in the woods has relatively little to do with such simple fears.

The biggest and most confusing aspect of the idea of camping is the inherent falseness of the entire endeavor. Even the description of it, "getting back to nature," insinuates that we have ever been there before. We as a species are far enough removed from being a creature of nature that anything we might know about wilderness survival was far more likely learned from watching the Discovery Channel than from any internal instinct or primal call to action. All of our "returns" to nature are handled under strict guidelines and supervision, with camping plots worked out so we have enough space to feel free, but not so much that we can't see our fellow campers in their RVs, eating store-bought hot dogs over a tiny fire.

The dynamic for children is even worse, given that they rarely have any choice in the matter. One mistake made during the school year, or whispered conversation about parents' marital problems, and a child may find him or herself separated from family and society for an entire summer, forced to sleep in bunk beds with strangers and trust their lives to people barely older than them; their "guardians" are obsessed with having sex and getting drunk. There may be a crazed man in a mask stalking through the woods and attempting to murder an entire camp one person at a time; but on the other hand, there are lecherous counselors and bullying to contend with, and no escape at the end of the day like there is during the school year.

The insult and indignity of being attacked or killed in the woods is matched by the futility of being there in the first place. Some campers might be out to prove to themselves they can survive or thrive, but most everyone else is there out of some sad circumstance that was beyond their control: a trip forced on them by family or an outing thought to be fun for a young couple in love. The ultimate irony of the campground horror subgenre is that most of the people who die at the hands of the slasher or the monster were people who never wanted to be there.

Elements of the Subgenre

Terrible Camp Leadership: The people who run the camps in these movies should be arrested for child endangerment (and based on their non-existent screening policy, they may have been already). If they're not off in the woods somewhere getting high or having sex, then they're driving into town for supplies and leaving thirty kids unsupervised in the woods. That is probably not the environment the parents expected.

The American Northeast: There are summer camps everywhere, but something about the American Northeast seems to draw the filmmakers, because *Friday the 13th*, *The Burning*, *Sleepaway Camp*, and many others all set their camps in the New England area. Maybe it's the beautiful beaches and wilderness, maybe it's the mild summers, and maybe it's that the serial killers in New York are less frightening than the ones in Texas.

Why Was This Place Shut Down Again?: In many of the campground horror films, the camp in question is re-opening for some reason, and the reason never seems to be good. It's not just that the funding fell through or paperwork got lost; the reasons vary from children drowning to counselors being murdered to the poor caretaker being severely burned and disfigured. The question of why the new owner wouldn't have wanted to just make a new camp instead of buying an old one with a terrible history (and possibly a "death curse") is never addressed.

Recommendations from the Subgenre

Friday the 13th (1980)
Directed by Sean S. Cunningham
Written by Victor Miller, Sean S. Cunningham
Starring: Betsy Palmer, Adrienne King, Kevin Bacon

In 1958, two camp counselors are murdered in a cabin at Camp Crystal Lake, which leads to its closing. Twenty-one years later, new owner Steve hires a group of teenagers to help him clean up the camp in preparation for its re-opening. As the cleaning and repairing commence, along with the drug use and sexual activities, a killer arrives at the camp and starts bumping off the counselors and the owner.

Two years after the runaway success of *Halloween*, writer-director Sean S. Cunningham cemented the popularity of the new slasher subgenre with *Friday the 13th*, a $500,000 film that earned over one hundred times its budget in its theatrical release. Taking the structure of the mysterious killer and grafting it onto the world of the campground was a successful gambit for the creative team, who made a surprisingly competent horror film with notable nature cinematography and one of the great horror scores of all time by composer Harry Manfredini.

Cunningham, already somewhat notorious for producing Wes Craven's *Last House on the Left*, returned to horror with this film. Working with writer Victor Miller, who had already collaborated with him on two low-budget family films, they fashioned a series of set-piece murders and a twist ending that became the template for slasher films for the next decade. The film spawned the longest-running theatrical horror film franchise in history, with ten sequels, a remake, and a tangentially related television series.

Camp Blood (2000)

Directed and Written by Brad Sykes
Starring: Jennifer Ritchkoff, Michael Taylor, Tim Young

In the woods of Camp Blackwood, two tourists fall victim to a serial killer wearing a clown mask. Later, young Tricia, her friends and a guide venture into Camp Blackwood for themselves. After the first night camping, they all wake to find the burned corpse of their guide on the fire, and they panic. Not knowing how to escape the woods, they are slowly hunted down and killed by the murderous clown until only Tricia is left.

A love letter to the classic campground horror films of the 1980s, *Camp Blood* took its name from the original *Friday the 13th* film (it was the nickname for the camp; the title of the original script was *A Long Night at Camp Blood*). The homage hits all the same notes as its progenitors, from the eccentric locals to the surprising reveal of the murderer to the sequels (*Camp Blood* has three).

After an early career establishing himself behind the camera in numerous technical posi-

Survivor Tricia (Jennifer Ritchkoff) finds herself captured by a slasher known only as The Clown in Brad Sykes' *Camp Blood* film series (courtesy Brad Sykes).

tions, filmmaker Brad Sykes directed his first film *Camp Blood*. He shot it back to back with its sequel in 2000; Sykes revisited the franchise again in 2005 for *Within the Woods*, the title of which references the original short film version of Sam Raimi's *Evil Dead* (another film about teens in the woods). If that weren't enough reference to Raimi's film, the credits of *Camp Blood* reveal that the killer clown was played by Shemp Moseley; in the *Evil Dead* films, people who worked as stand-ins for actors were often referred to as Fake Shemps in reference to Three Stooges member Shemp Howard, a childhood favorite of Raimi's.

Sleepaway Camp (1983)
Written and Directed by Robert Hiltzik
Starring: Felissa Rose, Jonathan Tiersten, Christopher Collet

Young Angela, at the beach with her father and brother, witnesses their deaths in a motorboat accident. Years later, as a young teenager, she lives with her aunt and cousin, and is getting ready to leave for summer camp. While dealing with the bullying and isolation at the camp, Angela also learns that someone has been killing off all of the people who have hurt or made fun of her. Could the killer be her kind, protective cousin?

A confusing, bizarre, and sometimes unintentionally hilarious piece of mid–1980s horror weirdness, *Sleepaway Camp* has gone down in history as the film with one of the most notorious endings of all time. One of the few campground movies to focus specifically on the campers rather than the counselors, the film was daring in its time for its graphic disposal of several pre-teen characters in creative and disturbing ways.

Robert Hiltzik, a lawyer, wrote, produced, and directed the film, and has the distinction of having worked only on films in the *Sleepaway Camp* franchise. Though the second and third installments of the series were from other creators (who distanced themselves from the gender commentary of the original), Hiltzik returned to the franchise twenty-five years later for *Return to Sleepaway Camp*. The enduring cult popularity of the original film found its way into pop culture, being referenced in various degrees on the animated series *Robot Chicken*, several heavy metal albums (including from Camp Kill Yourself, the band fronted by Deron Miller, husband of *Sleepaway Camp* actress Felissa Rose), and the summer camp comedy *Wet Hot American Summer*.

Other Titles of Interest

The Burning (1981), *Grizzly* (1976), *Campfire Tales* (1997), *Timber Falls* (2007), *Cabin Fever* (2002), *Wolf Creek* (2005)

Cannibal Horror

The act of cannibalism is a taboo in nearly every society on Earth. It is such a taboo, in fact, that there has basically never been an opposing argument to its illegality, nor has there really been any kind of theoretical intellectual consideration for its presence as a possible lifestyle alternative.

Let's look at the act in detail. Cannibalism is (for the purposes of discussion in a horror film book) the devouring of human flesh by another human. It is common knowledge that cannibalistic predation happens in nature all the time with other species; sometimes it's an act of desperation in times of great need, and sometimes it is simply something that one animal of a species does to another because it wants to eat. So in a biological sense, the idea of cannibalism is not uncommon or surprising to us.

Nor is the concept of eating meat. If that were the sticking point with people, it might be understandable; the idea of ending another living creature's life, cutting it to pieces, and putting it inside yourself so you can continue living instead of it, is a strange one. We have become used to it because it is an act of sustenance. However, this is not the element of cannibalism that bothers us, because this element is something we do multiple times every day.

So if cannibalism is not an unusual circumstance in nature, and it's pragmatically no different than the eating of meat from other creatures, then what is it that makes it such a taboo to us? Certainly, in horror films, if someone is a cannibal, it is unlikely that he waits around for a person to die of natural causes before eating him, so there is an obvious fear of being murdered and turned into food. But we fear cannibals more than we fear regular murderers, even though our demise is the same in both. Why?

If we're honest with ourselves, it's because we believe there is something else besides just meat in a human body. Whatever it is, the spirit or soul, the unique element that makes us who we are as opposed to just another version of someone else, that element was housed inside our body. This biological vehicle carried an individual within it, and we recognize and respect it. Whether we think further about the spiritual aspect of it, or simply acknowledge that someone else's body should remain their property, even after their death, all of us buy into it.

Well, almost all of us...

Elements of the Subgenre

The Slow Revelation: In cannibal movies, it's rare that the film cops to the fact that people are being eaten for a good bit of the film. Though the audience knows it's coming (and likely, the advertising has already given it away), the film takes its time to establish the location and the characters (or, more appropriately, the menu) before the disturbing moment that the victims realize the jerky they bought isn't exactly what they thought.

Eating Like Animals: Because of the savagery and barbarism of the act itself, it should come as no surprise that the people who are eating other people do so with a total lack of manners or regard. There is no silverware to be found, no polite conversation or napkins tucked into shirt collars. By embracing an animalistic psychology on feeding, the people have reduced themselves to animals in behavior as well.

Recommendations from the Subgenre

We Are What We Are (2013)
Directed by Jim Mickle
Written by Nick Damici, Jim Mickle (based on the original screenplay by Jorge Michel Grau)
Starring: Julia Garner, Ambyr Childers, Bill Sage

When the matriarch of a backwoods family dies, the family is left to try and recover. A rainy season floods the area, and the local doctor comes upon human remains which have floated downstream. Connecting the discovery of the human remains to his autopsy findings (which revealed the matriarch's postmortem Parkinson's diagnosis), the doctor begins to suspect that the family was eating human beings, and that they might be in some way connected to the disappearance of his daughter years earlier.

Based on the Mexican film *Somos Lo Que Hay* from filmmaker Jorge Michel Grau, *We Are What We Are* takes the disturbing premise of the original and relocates it to the mountains of eastern America to good effect. The film is an exercise in uncomfortable silence and creeping dread, perfectly embodied by the slowly rising level of rainwater in the ravines throughout the town. It takes its time in revealing the truth of the family's reasoning for their behavior, and by the time the viewer sees the origin of their beliefs, the explanation is as horrifying as it is expected.

For director Jim Mickle and scriptwriter Nick Damici, this was their third film together (after *Mulberry Street* and *Stakeland*). They populated it with recognizable faces like Bill Sage and Kelly McGillis (miles away from the glamour of *Top Gun*). The real standout performance here is from Michael Parks, a great character actor whose career lagged in the 1980s and 1990s, until a series of horror films brought his subtle skills back into the public eye: *From Dusk Till Dawn* and *Grindhouse* led to *Red State* and this film. The religious commentary in the movie is unsubtle but extremely effective, touching on subject matter that Mickle and Damici previously explored in the vampire film *Stakeland*.

The Parker family dinner for Frank (Bill Sage), Rory (Jack Gore), Iris (Ambyr Childers), and Rose (Julia Garner) in the 2013 horror remake *We Are What We Are* (courtesy Jim Mickle).

Ravenous (1999)

Directed by Antonia Bird
Written by Ted Griffin
Starring: Guy Pearce, Robert Carlyle, Jeffrey Jones

After his cowardice accidentally leads to a victory in the Mexican-American War, Lieutenant Boyd is sent to command a tiny fort in Nevada. Leaving the fort to find a traveling party lost in the winter weather, Boyd and his men discover that all the members of the party were killed and eaten by one man who now attacks and kills everyone but Boyd. Healing from the attack and surviving by feeding on the body of one of his men, he eventually returns to the fort only to find that he has been replaced ... by the man who tried to kill him.

A clever combination of the cannibal film and the more supernatural concept of the Wendigo, *Ravenous* is a hybrid western-horror-comedy-action that defies simple categorization. Much of the film is noteworthy, from its unconventional take on the cowardice of heroes and the likability of villains to the fantastically strange score by Michael Nyman and Blur frontman Damon Albarn.

Antonia Bird was an experienced director of British film and television work when she was called on to replace original director Milcho Manchevski after three difficult weeks of shooting. The script by *Ocean's 11* writer Ted Griffin has his trademark dark humor throughout; the game cast, including Robert Carlyle, Neal McDonough, and Jeremy Davies, makes great use of it. *Ravenous* was the last theatrical release from the very talented Bird before her tragic death from cancer in 2013.

Delicatessen (1990)

Directed by Jean-Pierre Jeunet, Marc Caro
Written by Marc Caro, Jean-Paul Jeunet, Gilles Adrien
Starring: Dominique Pinon, Jean-Claude Dreyfus, Marie-Laure Dougnac

In a rundown apartment building in post-apocalyptic France, wanderer Louison arrives looking for a job. He is hired as a maintenance man and is paid well by the owner, who also runs the butcher shop downstairs. As Louison becomes close to the butcher's daughter and many of the tenants, he begins to suspect that the plentiful meat in the shop window might be coming from someplace less than reputable. Fearing he knows too much, the butcher schedules for Louison to be next on the menu.

An endlessly inventive and visually stunning work, *Delicatessen* is the distinctly French answer to the post-apocalypse. At times spooky but never menacing (unusual, considering its subject matter), the film creates a nebulous future world that could just as easily be part of an imagined past or a wild alternate reality. The lead character's former career as a circus clown juxtaposed against the dour modern world strikes the perfect balance between humor and pathos, and reminds the viewer of Charlie Chaplin's lovable Tramp.

Before venturing off on his own to direct the big-budget *Alien: Resurrection* and the Oscar-nominated *Amelie* and *A Very Long Engagement*, director Jean-Pierre Jeunet worked with partner Marc Caro on two films, the first of which was *Delicatessen*. Released in the U.S. with the poster stating "Presented by Terry Gilliam," the film is clearly influenced by Gilliam's body of work, in particular the homage to *Brazil*'s rebel plumber in the shape of *Delicatessen*'s vegetarian rebels, the Troglodistes. This was the first collaboration between Jeunet and actor Dominique Pinon, who would go on to work together six more times.

Other Titles of Interest

Doctor X (1932), *Cannibal Ferox* (1981), *Welcome to the Jungle* (2007), *Anthropophagus* (1980), *Wrong Turn* (2003), *Parents* (1989), *Sweeney Todd: The Demon Barber of Fleet Street* (2007), *Eating Raoul* (1982), *Frontier(s)* (2007)

Carnival-Circus Horror

"Nobody trusts a carnie, not even other carnies." While that statement may not be fully accurate, it is a well-known cliché. And the reason it's persisted so long is because people who work for carnivals seem to have done little to nothing to dissuade the public at large from feeling that way.

There is relatively little that would make townsfolk feel better about the rickety, rust-covered rides scattered across the field where the carnival or circus sets up, or the sickeningly delicious foods available at the concession stands that seem like such a fun idea when you start them and feel like an epic culinary mistake halfway through. Perhaps this deficit could be overcome if there weren't so many other unsavory aspects of carnival and circus life.

When they appear, it seems sometimes as if there is no warning. One moment, there is nothing but an empty field where cows used to graze before the local farm closed down. Then one day, with seemingly no preparation or advance notice, fifteen flat-bed trucks are parked in the field, flattening the grass and assembling the brightly colored coasters, tents, games, and booths that will be open in a few short hours.

And they're gone just as quickly. Three days of frivolity and fun, loud music and excited screams, haunted houses and dancing animals, clowns and ringmasters and soaring swing rides. And the next day ... silence and an empty field. We're instinctively mistrusting of people who show up in our lives, have a great time for a very short time, and then disappear. Usually, it's followed by revelations of missing money, pregnancy, or the discovery of an unpleasant disease.

Add to this the point behind the carnival or circus itself: to get as much money from a town as one can before picking up and leaving to go do the same thing somewhere else. The impermanence of the job feels like it would breed a certain type of individual, a drifter with no ties to home or family, a person whose moral code might reflect the attitude he has when he's taunting passersby to play his carnival game: whatever it takes to get them to come over.

Like the five-day-old caramel apples that can be purchased there, these places seem sweet at first, covered in an enticing candy shell. Only after we bite through it do we discover the rot that lies at its center.

Elements of the Subgenre

A Look Inside the Tent: A staple of the circus-carnival film, the tent is the place where people congregate to watch animal acts and feats of impressive skill and dexterity. But in horror film, it is also the place where children might peek at an inopportune time and witness something disturbing (a murder or the secret plotting of the freak show denizens) that no one will believe.

Hidden Behind a Painted Smile: The eerie and completely false smiles painted onto the faces of the clowns are off-putting for numerous reasons, not the least of which is that it becomes difficult to tell what the person is really thinking or feeling. But the disguised face, hidden under makeup to prevent easy identification, gives rise to uneasiness about how, if they were to attack and disappear, you would ever be able to know who they truly were.

Recommendations from the Subgenre

Carnival of Souls (1962)

Directed by Herk Harvey
Written by John Clifford
Starring: Candace Hilligoss, Frances Feist, Sidney Berger

In the car with her girlfriends, Mary finds herself the only survivor of an accident caused by a drag race which sent the vehicle careening off a bridge and into the river below. Her memory murky, Mary leaves town to piece her life back together. She gets a job as a church organist and finds herself drawn to an eerie closed-down carnival nearby where she catches a glimpse of an ethereal man who begins following her everywhere she goes. No one sees or hears him but Mary, and he gets closer with every sighting.

A quiet, moody film that slowly works its way into the audience's mind through suggestion rather than outright action or violence, *Carnival of Souls* is a sterling example of the shift in horror during the 1960s. The grainy black and white photography, combined with the unusual lighting scheme and the haunting organ score by Gene Moore, gives the film an air of otherworldly surrealism. Lead actress Candace Hilligoss' subdued performance is eerily appropriate.

Shooting on a shoestring budget outside the studio system, director Herk Harvey put his skills as an industrial film producer to good use in creating this cult classic for less than $40,000. Aside from coming up with the story concept, producing, and directing, Harvey also appears as the pale-faced ghoul who keeps showing up to haunt Mary. Like the similarly low-budget *Night of the Living Dead*, the film passed immediately into the public domain due to a copyright mistake. And as a result, there are numerous releases of the film from different distributors, all of which add to its constant presence in the video market and its enduring cult popularity.

Something Wicked This Way Comes (1983)

Directed by Jack Clayton
Written by Ray Bradbury (based on his own story)
Starring: Jason Robards, Jonathan Pryce, Diane Ladd

In the small Illinois town of Greentown, young Will Holloway and his friend become fascinated when a sinister-looking carnival seemingly springs up in seconds on the edge of town. The carnival master, Mr. Dark, has his sights set on acquiring souls from the town by using his Carousel, Mirror Maze, and the help of his collection of strange companions. Only Will and his mild-mannered librarian father can save the town from the clutches of Mr. Dark's Pandemonium Carnival.

Equal parts "coming of age" story and epic battle of good versus evil, *Something Wicked This Way Comes* is the rare film that balances those two disparate sensibilities well. The cast is excellent across the board. Jonathan Pryce, a relative newcomer in 1983, would find a successful career in fantasy for years to come, from *The Adventures of Baron Munchausen* to the *Pirates of the Caribbean* franchise.

Working for Disney to produce a mature dark fantasy film in the vein of *Watcher in the Woods* and *Return to Oz*, director Jack Clayton brought his years of technical expertise to the film as well as a reputation for success in similar subject matter with his work on *The Innocents*.

The original draft of the script was written by author Bradbury himself, though subsequent drafts would distance the writer from the project and the material from its original source. A delicate balancing act of horror and pathos, the film did not connect with audiences at the time, earning less than half of its production budget back. In recent years, audiences have rediscovered the film, and Disney has announced plans for a remake.

The Devil's Carnival (2012)

Directed by Darren Lynn Bousman
Written by Terrance Zdunich
Starring: Sean Patrick Flanery, Briana Evigan, Jessica Lowndes

Three people are simultaneously losing their lives for different reasons: John commits suicide over grief after losing his son; Ms. Merrywood is killed by police in a shootout; and Tamara is murdered by her boyfriend. They then wake up in the twisted carnival that is Hell. They meet the denizens of the carnival, learn of their fate through the telling of Aesop's fables, and eventually come face to face with Lucifer himself.

Combining fantastically bizarre set design, an epic tale of Heaven versus Hell, and a plot in which damned characters sing about their fates, *The Devil's Carnival* is nothing if not bold. Trained singer-performers Paul Sorvino and Emilie Autumn share screen time (and songs) with horror icons Bill Moseley and Briana Evigan, and somehow the warped logic of it all ends up working.

Director Darren Lynn Bousman was coming off a successful run of *Saw* films when he teamed with writer-composer Terrance Zdunich for *Repo! The Genetic Opera*. With a surprise cult horror-musical hit on their hands, they re-teamed for this film. It was originally conceived as the first in a possible trilogy; Bousman and Zdunich have already collaborated on the second installment in 2014, with a road tour and album release expected similar to the original's.

Killer Klowns from Outer Space (1988)

Directed by Stephen Chiodo
Written by Charles Chiodo, Stephen Chiodo
Starring: Grant Cramer, Suzanne Snyder, John Vernon

Young teen lovers Mike and Debbie see what they believe to be a comet falling to earth in Crescent Cove, California. They find a strange circus tent, and upon entering, they discover that a local farmer has been captured and cocooned inside of cotton candy. Chased and attacked by monstrous-looking alien clowns, they try to warn the sheriff and the rest of the town. No one believes them until the carnivorous clowns have kidnapped many of the towns-folk to take home as meals.

Borrowing the classic "teens in trouble" template from *The Blob* and reworking it into a colorful nightmare of circus violence, *Killer Klowns from Outer Space* is a wild hybrid film in a category of its own. Though never too serious, the film explores the sci-fi extrapolations of alien clowns in surprising depth. A hilarious appearance from character actor John Vernon as the dubious sheriff is the icing on the very tongue-in-cheek cake.

Stephen Chiodo was an animator and special effects designer with his two brothers at Chiodo Bros. Productions when he decided to direct this film as his first feature. With previous experience on movies like *Pee-wee's Big Adventure* and the *Critters* series, the Chiodo brothers were the perfect candidates for this high-concept black comedy. The film has garnered an impressive cult following. Offshoots include a series of action figures, Halloween masks, a re-released soundtrack, and decades of homage and imitation from numerous sources—not the least of which is the hip-hop group Insane Clown Posse.

Other Titles of Interest

Freaks (1932), *Vampire Circus* (1972), *The Funhouse* (1981), *The Last Circus* (2010), *Santa Sangre* (1989), *Freaked* (1993), *Dark Ride* (2006), *Circus of Horrors* (1960)

Children in Danger Horror

There is a biological imperative at play any time a child is in danger. Our parental instincts are awakened at the mere idea of child endangerment, even for those who have not yet been (or never will be) parents. What seems like a protective and selfless act is in fact rooted in the very strongest of selfish motivations; keeping some part of ourselves alive and continuing past our own existence.

The built-in, knee-jerk reaction that humanity has to the cries of a child in pain or fear is a psychological pressure point to which most people will bend, and the careful use of such pressure points within a horror film makes the likelihood greater that an audience will be moved to feel anxiety and fear.

The ultimate irony, of course, is that our instinctive protection of children stands in juxtaposition to the truth that children are better survivors than adults are. Certainly, there are the formative years right after birth, when awareness of the world is nearly nonexistent and the ability to feed and clothe oneself has yet to be gained. But there is a certain point after which children are far better equipped to survive miserable, dangerous, or psychologically troubling circumstances.

If we have, as children, had no major troubles or struggles, then we are weaker as adults due to the simple fact that we haven't had to conquer or recover from anything. Spoiled children find their adult years confrontational and often unsuccessful, because the rest of the world isn't ready to hand them everything they want the moment that they ask. Children who have been through hardships and deprivation are prepared for a somewhat unfeeling existence where unpleasant things happen to people who don't deserve them. The children of struggle grow up to survive; the children of easy living collapse under the pressure.

And this is the irony that we create, in life and in art. We fear for the safety of our children, and in doing so, we make them less likely to be able to survive an unsafe situation. In a world where sharp corners have no padding, germs and dirt aren't always whisked away by Mom's bottle of antibacterial gel, and every challenge doesn't automatically get you an "A" for effort, the coddling we give to our children might be hobbling them in the future.

Perhaps horror films have something to teach us about that. Seeing children in danger taps into the strongest of protective emotions, and maybe we need to feel that in order to deal with it. To put it in its place and remember that, while we never want our children to hurt, we may sometimes want them to learn. And though no bad experience is fun to have, it can be invaluable in creating a better survivor.

Elements of the Subgenre

The Kids Have to Save Themselves: This element is an extension of the existential crisis at the center of any horror film, the fact that no one is going to help you. It is given greater weight here, however, because the central figures seem so helpless and weak. But ingenuity and no small amount of sneakiness usually helps them win the day.

The Unbelievable Threat: It is likely that whatever threat is bearing down on the children is going to be impossible to believe. It's hard enough for children, generally known for their vivid imaginations and tendency to exaggerate, to convince adults that anything they're saying is the truth; but when it's a vampire next door or a monster in a pit in the yard or an alien that looks like the neighbor, there's no reason to even try.

Recommendations from the Subgenre

M (1931)

Directed by Fritz Lang
Written by Thea von Harbou, Fritz Lang
Starring: Peter Lorre, Otto Wernicke, Ellen Widman

A small community in Berlin lives in fear due the predatory acts of a child serial killer. After another child disappears, the police begin to crack down on the activities of criminals. Desperate to stop the police from further prying into their shady businesses, the criminal bosses meet and decide to start their own manhunt for the killer. With the police and members of the underworld both closing in on him, the solitary child killer has now become the victim himself.

A haunting thriller that pits villains against one another while the victims, families, and the law are shoved aside, *M* is a masterpiece of social commentary. It was also a technological advancement in film. Its use of sound in the film, particularly killer Peter Lorre's whistling refrain, is impressive in an era where sound was so new. The noir lighting and shadowplay give *M* a nightmarish, otherworldly sense that intensifies as the child killer comes closer and closer to capture.

Fritz Lang had already found great success directing *Dr. Mabuse* and *Metropolis* when he teamed with wife and co-writer Thea van Harbou to make this film, which he considered his greatest work. The lead performance was both a blessing and curse to Peter Lorre, who was recognized widely for his work but was then typecast as a villain for most of his career. Hollywood remade the film in 1951 with Joseph Losey directing.

Pan's Labyrinth (2006)

Written and Directed by Guillermo del Toro
Starring: Ivana Baquero, Sergi López, Doug Jones

When her pregnant mother remarries the violent Captain Vidal, young Ofelia moves with her into Vidal's stronghold. While exploring the property, Ofelia discovers a labyrinth which leads her to a faun who believes that she is the spirit of a deceased princess from another world. Given three tasks that will bring her immortality if successfully completed, Ofelia attempts to accomplish them while also suffering through the struggles of her real life as her mother's pregnancy faces serious troubles and Spanish rebels threaten to storm the stronghold.

Combining the coming-of-age elements of his previous film *The Devil's Backbone* with the fantastical creatures and locales from *Hellboy*, director Guillermo del Toro created *Pan's Labyrinth*, a dark *Alice in Wonderland* story set in post–Civil War Spain. Mixing del Toro's frequent acting collaborators Federico Luppi and the spectacular Doug Jones with Spanish and Mexican actors known well in their home countries, the film built a global audience with a universal story.

Shifting back and forth between personal indie stories (*Cronos*) and big-budget studio films (*Blade II*), del Toro finally found the right balance with this film. In many ways a spiritual sequel to *The Devil's Backbone*, the story owes a debt to Catholic iconography and belief. The design of the Pale Man is equal parts Arthur Rackham art and symbolic stigmata. The film, well received by critics and audiences, went on to win three Academy Awards.

City of Lost Children (1995)

Directed by Jean-Pierre Jeunet, Marc Caro
Written by Marc Caro, Jean-Pierre Jeunet, Gilles Adrien, Guillaume Laurant
Starring: Ron Perlman, Daniel Emilfork, Dominique Pinon

In a fantastical French seaside town, someone has been kidnapping young children. Former sailor One is enraged when his hungry young adopted brother is taken. He joins ranks with a child thief named Miette, and their journey brings them to an ocean rig populated by a maniacal elderly scientist, a talkative brain in a glass cabinet, and six clones with narcolepsy who have been kidnapping the children in order to steal their dreams.

Effectively blending a fairy tale sensibility with hints of steampunk and circus gothic, *The City of Lost Children* is a delightfully ambitious children's story that succeeds with inventiveness and black humor. Ron Perlman, an American actor known best for *Hellboy* and *Sons of Anarchy*, acquits himself well in the central role (which he performed phonetically, as he speaks no French), as does Dominique Pinon in *seven* roles. The set design and cinematography are stunning. The film captures the audience right from the opening moments of the child's Christmas-themed nightmare.

This film was the last on which Jean-Pierre Jeunet and Marc Caro worked together before embarking on their solo careers. The score by frequent David Lynch collaborator Angelo Badalamenti is at turns haunting and whimsical. The retired circus freaks and performers who populate this unusual city by the sea are a fun prototype for the family of junkyard misfits that Jeunet introduces us to in *Micmacs*. The entire film bursts with an infectiously fun absurdity.

Other Titles of Interest

Insidious (2010), *Poltergeist* (1982 and 2015), *The Devil's Backbone* (2001), *Fragile* (2005), *The People Under the Stairs* (1991), *Mama* (2013), *Hurt* (2009)

Church-Covent-Monastery Horror

The idea of sanctuary is one that is largely lost on modern humanity. When we think of the word, we have little consideration for its origin, seeing it mostly now as a name for places that protect plants and animals, or perhaps a political term for refugees or defectors from one country to another (often used interchangeably with "asylum"). The word, however, has its origins within the sacred halls of the church.

From the fourth century to the seventeenth century in England, a fugitive or criminal was able to escape at least the immediate dangers of capture and arrest by entering a church and requesting sanctuary. At the time, the country's church was so strong that, if the minister allowed the fugitive to stay, that fugitive was immune to arrest for as long as he remained within the walls of that religious establishment. For a time, that was the main definition of sanctuary: the protection extended to individuals within the protected walls of the church.

Eventually the power of the church began to wane, and so did the power of the word which described the church's ability to protect. The word became commonplace, often used to reference parts of the church itself such as the meeting area (alternately known as the synagogue or the chapel) and even the altar itself. Broadly, sanctuary became used as a term of spiritual significance, with the walls of the church now symbolic defenses against the darkness which runs rampant through the rest of the world. To be within a church was to have spiritual sanctuary.

It is with all of those various meanings at play that the subgenre of the horror film within the church, convent, or monastery becomes its most effective and ironic. The standard perception of a sanctuary in modern times, seen as an oasis of safety where someone can escape to have peace and tranquility, is just as much at risk of destruction as the religious perception of it within the confines of a horror film. The place often thought of as one of safety, the confines of the church, is the place where we remove the armor that protects us from the world and allow our vulnerabilities to show.

It is for this reason that the presence of horror is so powerful. We are unprepared for it, here in the holy of holies, the place in which we seek enlightenment and truth. The darkness of the world and its evils should have no place here, and so we are caught off-guard. The danger is not just physical but psychological; if we are not safe in a church, where can we possibly be safe? It is this juxtaposition that makes the subgenre unique and powerful.

Elements of the Subgenre

Power Corrupts: Often in church horror, it isn't just a single person or monster to contend with; there is a bureaucracy. The churches in these films hold sway and power over people, and often they grow so powerful that they start to become corrupt themselves, caring only about their continued acquisition of control. You're not just battling a single creature, you're battling a conspiratorial ideology.

The Questionable Minister: An effective way of sustaining tension until late into the third act of the film, the phenomenon of the Questionable Minister is based on the concept of a religious figure who might just as easily be good or evil. Their odd behavior and seemingly shifting allegiances will keep the characters and the audience guessing until the truth is finally revealed in the end.

Recommendations from the Subgenre

Viy (1967)

Directed by Konstantin Ershov, Georgi Kropachyov
Written by Konstantin Ershov, Georgi Kropachyov, Aleksandr Ptushko (based on the short story by Nikolai Gogol)
Starring: Leonid Kuravlyov, Natalya Varley, Aleksey Glazyrin

A neophyte priest is given the unenviable task of standing guard and praying over the body of a woman believed to be a witch. Standing inside a circle of chalk, he is not to venture outside of its protection for three days. The spirit of the woman returns along with several demons to coax him out using whatever means they can.

A wild and unexpected film to come out of its place and time in history, *Viy* is generally considered to be the first horror film made in Soviet-era Russia. Based on the short story by writer Nikolai Gogol, *Viy* was able to skirt some of the issues of Russian censorship by claiming to be based on folk myths, though history suggests that perhaps Gogol made up much of the mythology himself. A film comprised of several vignettes, all of which are carried primarily on the back of Leonid Kuravlyov as young seminary student Khoma, the movie's sensibilities vacillate between dark horror and broad comedy.

Neither Georgi Kropachyov nor Konstantin Ershov had directed a film before *Viy*, both having worked in the Russian film industry as actors and production designers. The effects, which do not hold up well on modern viewing, were ambitious for their day. The film's restless intensity and cinematography style are echoed in Sam Raimi's *Evil Dead* films. A remake, also filmed in Russia, was begun in 2006; after shooting nearly half the movie, the production was shut down to convert the film to 3-D, an expensive and time-consuming process. It was finally released to Russian theaters in 2014.

Prince of Darkness (1987)

Written and Directed by John Carpenter
Starring: Donald Pleasence, Jameson Parker, Victor Wong

A Catholic priest discovers a hidden church building that houses a long-held secret. He recruits a university professor and his quantum physics class to help him understand what they have found in the basement of the building: a vat of pulsating green liquid that seems to be alive and broadcasting complex data. As the group studies the vat, they become surrounded by seemingly zombified homeless people who imprison them inside, and the liquid begins to escape its container and possess the students.

A chamber piece horror film that explores the strange convergence of religion and cutting-edge science, *Prince of Darkness* is a tense thriller that also rewards the more thoughtful viewer. Bringing back cast members of previous films (Pleasence from *Halloween*, Wong and Dennis Dun from *Big Trouble in Little China*) to work with unknowns for this low-budget project, director John Carpenter assembled a diverse cast that is a welcome change from the primarily white faces in typical horror. The re-imagining of biblical creation through a scientific lens makes for fun theorizing, but Carpenter wisely knows when to put the science aside and create some effective scares.

After the big-budget disappointment of *Big Trouble in Little China*, Carpenter went back to his roots to write and direct this small film with big ideas. He wrote the script under the pseudonym Martin Quatermass, a reference to the British horror–sci-fi *Quatermass* films which influenced this film's concept; those films were written by Nigel Kneale, with whom Carpenter had worked on *Halloween III: Season of the Witch*. As one of the zombie homeless people, musician Alice Cooper used one of his famous stage props to impale an escaping scientist.

The Hunchback of Notre Dame (1923)
Directed by Wallace Worsley
Written by Perley Poore Sheehan, Edward T. Lowe Jr. (based on the novel by Victor Hugo)
Starring: Lon Chaney, Patsy Ruth Miller, Norman Kerry

Deformed Quasimodo works as a bellringer in the Notre Dame Cathedral. One day while being publicly punished, he is saved by Esmeralda, and his feelings for her grow. Esmeralda's true love, Phoebus, is stabbed and nearly killed by one of her other jealous suitors, and she is framed for it and sentenced to death. Quasimodo rescues her and takes her to the cathe-

Claude Frollo (Nigel De Brulier) attempts to stop Quasimodo (Lon Chaney) from leaving the safety of the cathedral in 1923's *The Hunchback of Notre Dame*.

dral for sanctuary, holding off the people who wish to take her away and eventually sacrificing himself to save her life.

Hugely successful and influential on generations of horror films, *The Hunchback of Notre Dame* was also the film that turned Lon Chaney from a makeup-covered bit player into a genuine Hollywood superstar. Taking the broad outlines of the Hugo novel, with changes to appease censors of the day, the film began Universal's tradition of the sympathetic monster that would continue into *Frankenstein* a decade later.

Though it was studio director Wallace Worsley who helmed the film, it was a labor of love for lead actor Chaney, who willed the project into existence and did his own makeup. It was Universal's most successful silent film, making in excess of $3 million. When the film went into the public domain in 1951, nearly all of the original 35mm prints were destroyed. Copies of the film that still exist are taken from the lower-quality 16mm prints; some footage is gone forever.

Other Titles of Interest

The Church (1989), *The Convent* (2000), *The Devils* (1971), *Alucarda* (1977)

Comedy-Horror

Horror and comedy don't seem like they should work together. Unlike genre hybrids like romantic comedy and science fiction–action, horror and comedy would seem on their face to be opposed to each other, at cross purposes ideologically. One seems to want you to enjoy yourself, and the other seems to want you to endure something, to survive an unpleasant experience and come out on the other side a changed person. So why is it that the subgenre of the horror comedy is so prevalent and often so successful?

The truth is fairly simple, and it springs from the connections that horror and comedy have as regards the audience's similar reactions to both. There are essentially two places from which humor is born: surprise (when something is funny because it is not expected) and awkwardness (when something is funny because of how uncomfortable it is). Surprisingly, the same two elements make up what scares people in film: Surprise translates to shock, those moments that startle you because they come from out of nowhere; and awkwardness, which becomes dread in a horror context. Though their goals might be different, comedy and horror are working with the same two principles.

This is further strengthened when we look at the subtle elements of each that already exist within the other before the two genres even begin to combine. Human beings automatically tend to respond to situations that alarm them or make them nervous by laughing, even when it may be inappropriate. It is a biological response that is often uncontrollable, and anyone who has ever seen a horror movie in a packed theater knows what it's like to have a particularly effective scare sequence undercut by the giggles of a fellow audience member. The intrusion of horror into comedy can be seen subtly, too, known to any unsuspecting victim of an insult comic who finds him or herself the target of cruelty and derision from the performer. The longer you stare at the family photo that is filmic genres, the more you notice that these two distant cousins look very much alike.

If there is a spectrum of emotion in the world of film, it seems at first that horror and comedy would be on opposite ends of it; but a closer examination reveals that perhaps the spectrum is in fact a loop that continuously circles back upon itself, and that the two genres which at first seemed to be the furthest apart are in fact the ones which connect the entire spectrum together.

Elements of the Subgenre

Too Much Blood: Sometimes, something that is scary in one capacity is humorous in another, and it is often just a matter of degrees. Just the right amount of blood can be a terrifying sight on screen, but by quadrupling that same amount of blood, those absurd gallons of red spilling across the screen suddenly becomes a little silly.

Juxtaposition: The most effective weapon of the horror comedy is juxtaposition. The makers of a smart comedy horror film knows that it can get great laughs from putting certain incongruous things next to each other on screen, from suave vampires and bumbling rednecks to silent masked killers and talkative hostages.

Recommendations from the Subgenre

Abbott and Costello Meet Frankenstein (1948)

Directed by Charles Barton
Written by Robert Lees, Frederic Rinaldo, John Grant
Starring: Bud Abbott, Lou Costello, Lon Chaney, Jr.

Baggage clerks Chick and Wilbur are hired to deliver wax figures of iconic monsters to a nearby wax museum. Little do they know that the wax figures are in fact the real bodies of Count Dracula and the Frankenstein Monster. After getting in trouble for losing the figures, Chick and Wilbur become even more tangled in the complicated caper when it is revealed that Dracula wishes to make the Frankenstein Monster more easily controlled by implanting Wilbur's simpleton brain to replace its current one.

After successfully combining several of their horror characters in previous crossover films, Universal took a big gamble by letting Abbott and Costello Meet Frankenstein. The addition of comedic characters helped to add to the stakes of the film (the audience feared more for the likable comic leads), and it was a box office success. The real treat of the film is in seeing the return of Bela Lugosi, Lon Chaney, Jr., and Glenn Strange in the roles that had made them famous. In Lugosi's case, this was the only time he ever reprised on-screen the role of Dracula.

Charles Barton was primarily known for his many collaborations with Abbott and Costello when he stepped in to make this horror hybrid, and his deft balancing of the two genres made the film a success and had him returning for *Abbott and Costello Meet the Killer, Boris Karloff*. The cameo by Vincent Price as the Invisible Man at the end of the film was intended as nothing more than a final joke, but when the film was a financial success, the

Invisible Man became the focus of the second of four comedy-horror follow-ups. Abbott and Costello then met Dr. Jekyll and Mr. Hyde and the Mummy.

Shaun of the Dead (2004)

Directed by Edgar Wright
Written by Simon Pegg, Edgar Wright
Starring: Simon Pegg, Nick Frost, Kate Ashfield

After being dumped by his girlfriend for having no ambitions, aimless Shaun goes out for a night of drinking with his slacker friend Ed. As they recover, they realize that a zombie apocalypse has gripped London. Suddenly filled with a renewed motivation for survival, Shaun and Ed risk traveling the streets of London to save Shaun's mother and girlfriend, only to end up stuck in a closed bar and going nowhere again.

A British cult comedy which took the U.S. by storm because of its knowing references to both slacker culture and the beloved films of George A. Romero, *Shaun of the Dead* is a triumph of comic timing, sincerity, and brilliant technical innovation. Filled to the brim with visual allusions to great zombie movies, from Shaun's sleepy opening zombie walk to his employment at Foree Electric (a reference to *Dawn of the Dead* star Ken Foree), the movie is as reverent to the history of zombies as it is self-effacing about the aimless British youths who make up its cast. The chemistry between lead actors Pegg and Frost is impressive, and led to several more filmic team-ups.

Director Edgar Wright had already worked with Pegg and Frost on the British sitcom *Spaced* (even directing a zombie-themed episode) when they decided to team up and create this zombie romantic comedy. Sharp-eyed British television fans will see cameos from some of their favorite stars, from *The Office*'s Martin Freeman to *Little Britain*'s Matt Lucas. The members of the band Coldplay pop up as zombies. Some of the film was shot in Ealing Studios, an appropriate location for the film given Ealing's reputation for producing the darkly comedic thrillers *The Ladykillers* and *Kind Hearts and Coronets*.

Rubber (2010)

Written and Directed by Quentin Dupieux
Starring: Stephen Spinella, Jack Plotnick, Wings Hauser

As a group of people watch through binoculars from seats located in the middle of the desert, a rubber car tire suddenly gains sentience. After learning to stand upright and roll, it focuses on crushing and destroying other things by rolling over them. When simply rolling isn't enough to destroy them, the tire discovers that it also has some psychokinetic abilities, and uses them to explode a series of objects: a glass bottle, a rabbit, a crow, and eventually a maid at a motel. The audience in the desert is slowly poisoned by an accountant as the tire goes on a murder spree fueled by its rage after witnessing a tire fire.

A horror film that is making fun of horror films, an arthouse film that comments on itself while insinuating that it has bad intentions towards its viewers, *Rubber* is a film that is better to experience than to explain. Though played with a straight face, the film is a series of puzzle box meta-jokes, from the murderous tire to the hilariously incongruous presence of early '80s tough-guy actor Wings Hauser. Much of the pleasure of the film will derive from the audience's appreciation for (and tolerance of) deadpan absurdity.

Before directing *Rubber*, Quentin Dupieux was already famous as an electronic musician called Mr. Oizo. After an American festival run for the film that varied in reception from highly positive to confounded to furious, the movie was released on-demand. Dupieux has since made three other movies: *Wrong, Wrong Cops* (starring *Twin Peaks'* Grace Zabriskie and musician Marilyn Manson), and *Reality*.

Other Titles of Interest

Evil Dead 2: Dead by Dawn (1987), *Gremlins* (1984), *An American Werewolf in London* (1981), *Night of the Creeps* (1986), *The Fearless Vampire Killers* (1967), *The Frighteners* (1996), *Fright Night* (1985), *Tremors* (1990)

Crazy Family Horror

All families are dysfunctional to some degree. The idea that there is a perfectly well-adjusted family out there in the world somewhere, getting along well with every member and enjoying all the holiday meals they attend, doesn't seem realistic to us. The secret desire to feel like no one else gets along with their family, the same as us, is one of the elements that unites most anyone on the planet who has any level of consistent contact with their extended family.

But there is solidarity in that understanding, and not just with people in other families who also feel like their relationship with their loved ones is weird. Each member of the family is united in their awareness of the dysfunction; we may not get along, but we are all doing it together.

Whether we are able to admit it or not, we are also secretly pleased to have our family as the object of blame or ridicule. No one likes the idea of having to admit to a fault or a quirk that might make others take notice or feel uncomfortable. Where would we be without the ability to blame Mother for not having us try more foods when we were young (which is why you now can't eat certain vegetables), or Father for not hugging us enough (which is why you have intimacy issues)? We wouldn't admit to appreciating the excuse, but we certainly make use of it whenever it is convenient.

The push and pull of family, the desire to be part of it and the need to have an identity separate from it, always makes for compelling drama, and compelling drama can become riveting horror with the right execution. As the people who know your secrets, the ones who helped to define who you were during your formative years, they are unique in the world. You will introduce yourself to everyone else you will ever know, but your family knew you before you knew yourself enough to even make an introduction. You may leave them physically, but they will always be a part of you psychologically and genetically.

Solidarity and dysfunction, secrets and influence, psychology and genetics … family is the place where science and belief have equal sway, where a bad habit can become a lifestyle and a childhood mistake can live forever in the quiet pauses during Thanksgiving dinner. It's no surprise that a fertile psychological playground like that would find its way into the horror film.

Elements of the Subgenre

The White Sheep: In a normal film, the outcast of the family is the black sheep, so it makes sense that the outcast in a crazy family horror film would be a decent person. They are often the traitors who have sympathy for the captors or victims, and they end up betraying the family in order to help the victims escape, often at the cost of their own lives.

The Family House: A staple of the subgenre is the family house, the place that would seem idyllic from the outside but secretly harbors some of the most frightening atrocities you could possibly imagine. The house itself is often the most symbolic element of the stories, representing the friendly public persona that humanity puts on their darkness so that a simple glance would never tell the whole story.

Recommendations from the Subgenre

The Texas Chain Saw Massacre (1974)
Directed by Tobe Hooper
Written by Tobe Hooper, Kim Henkel
Starring: Marilyn Burns, Gunnar Hansen, Edwin Neal

Two siblings and their three friends make a cross-country drive to Texas to check on their grandfather's grave after hearing reports of grave robbing. While traveling, they decide to visit the family property as well. After a run-in with a crazed hitchhiker, they find the childhood home and decide to spend some time looking around. Two of the friends head to a nearby pond, only to stumble onto someone else's home, and their venture inside leads to an encounter with a crazy masked murderer. The kids are picked off one by one until only sister Sally is alive, captured by the masked killer and his family, and seated at the dinner table for a truly disturbing dinner.

One of the most notorious and influential horror films of all time, *The Texas Chain Saw Massacre* is a film whose exploitation title hides its heavy psychological resonance and artistic merit. With a minuscule budget and a cast of unknown or non-professional actors, a group of friends in Texas created what is consistently credited as one of the ten scariest films of all time.

Tobe Hooper was a college filmmaker and documentarian when he teamed with writer Kim Henkel to create the script for this film. Enduring a hellish shoot that included rotting food during long nighttime takes, costumes which were heavy and hot, and perhaps even some mind-altering substances ingested by cast and crew, the project was the epitome of independent shoestring filmmaking. The film was an enormous hit, spawning six more films in the franchise. Director Hooper returned for the second film, original writer Henkel came back for the fourth, and cinematographer Daniel Pearl returned to shoot the 2003 remake.

The Baby (1973)
Directed by Ted Post
Written by Abe Polsky
Starring: Anjanette Comer, Ruth Roman, Marianna Hill

Ann, a social worker still traumatized from an accident that severely injured her husband, is assigned to a new case with the Wadsworth family. Upon meeting them, she discovers that the clan includes a mentally impaired twenty-year-old man who is being treated like an infant by his mother. The boy has no name and is abused by the family. Ann wants to get him out of the house and to a safe place where he can develop emotionally, but the Wadsworths aren't going to give up Baby so easily.

As bizarre and blackly hilarious as it is frightening, *The Baby* is a quintessential example of the subgenre which was inspired by entries like *Spider Baby* and the television series *The Addams Family*. Couched as a film about a kindly woman saving a man-child from a monstrous family, it takes a clever last-act turn for a surprising reveal that gives the viewer reason to rethink what they've just seen.

Ted Post, a versatile director who had worked in science fiction (*Beneath the Planet of the Apes*) and westerns (*Hang 'Em High*) and was best known for his run on the series *Peyton Place*, directed this dark horror-comedy. The script was written by television scribe Abe Polsky, who also served as producer. The film was part of horror's commentary on the growing feminist movement in America, seen in other films of the era like *Season of the Witch* and *Rosemary's Baby*.

Pink Flamingos (1972)

Written and Directed by John Waters
Starring: Divine, Mink Stole, Edith Massey

After transvestite Babs Johnson is voted Filthiest Person Alive by a local Maryland tabloid, rivals Connie and Raymond Marble plot to unseat her. With their underground business of kidnapping young women and forcibly impregnating them to sell their children to lesbian couples, they believe they should be the rightful holders of the title. After a battle of propaganda that involves mailing human feces to each other and murdering police officers, Babs and her family win the day with a live trial and execution that takes place in front of the cameras of the local media.

A film whose unique appeal seems to exist outside the ability to easily describe (a relief to any writer attempting to summarize its horrific events), *Pink Flamingos* was the movie that, along with some of Andy Warhol's cinematic output, began the phenomenon of "trash cinema." Dark humor, graphic sexuality, absurdism, animal abuse, and cannibalism are elements of the ramshackle plot that builds to the most notoriously gross ending in film history.

Baltimore film icon John Waters had produced several shorts and a couple of no-budget features before embarking on *Pink Flamingos*, which brought him dubious recognition in the filmmaking world. Gaining a huge cult following due to its midnight movie screenings (along with films like *El Topo* and *Night of the Living Dead*), it led to a series of successful pairings of Waters and lead actor-actress Divine that culminated in the musical comedy *Hairspray*. The film was banned by Australia, Canada, and Norway upon its initial release, as well as being edited heavily for content in other countries as well.

Other Titles of Interest

The Old Dark House (1932 or 1963), *House of 1,000 Corpses* (2003), *The Hills Have Eyes* (1977 and 2006), *American Gothic* (1988)

Creepy Kid Horror

If we remove the biological necessity of reproducing in order to keep the human race alive and look at the actual process and result of child-bearing, most people would admit to its strangeness. The idea that tiny parts of two different humans can combine (within the body of one of those humans) and begin to expand into a miniature version of a person using half of the genetic information of those two humans seems like an outlandish science fiction concept. That the person would then grow to the size of a watermelon and then decide to force its way out into the world in the most inconvenient way possible is not just weird but somewhat horrifying. Finally it will arrive in the world completely helpless and its needs and wants will become the responsibility of the very people whose genetic makeup it borrowed in order to form itself.

Free of the moral and psychological implications of what a child represents, the factual circumstance of its existence can in some way be seen as an example of humanity caring for a parasite that pragmatically gives it nothing in return. Eighteen years of providing food and protection are repaid only in an emotional and biological sense: the pride we have in their accomplishments, and the inborn desire to see our genes continue on after our deaths. We heap enormous amounts of expectation onto that relationship as a result. Children are hope for the future.

That is why it feels like such a betrayal when children go wrong. Hearing about a neighborhood murder is devastating, but there is an added level of confusion and revulsion when we learn that it happened at the hands of a child. We can somehow accept that an adult human, ravaged by the miserable realities of the world, can lose perspective and hope and lash out in desperation; the idea that a child could do the same makes no sense to us. In our collective human psyche, children represent innocence, and nothing is more tragic than the recognition that innocence has been corrupted. Our pride in their accomplishments vanishes, because no painting on the refrigerator or story told at bedtime can wipe away the memory of that level of darkness. If children are our hope for the future, then the occurrence of sudden and unexplained violence from those children gives us pause on an existential level: Is this what our future will be?

Elements of the Subgenre

That's Not an Innocent Smile: Sure, the kid may look sweet, with batting eyes or shrugging shoulders, but the kind smile you see when you're looking turns dark and creepy just moments after you turn away. Whatever is on that child's mind during that smile, you don't want any part of it.

Who Drew This?: A crayon drawing found in the trash can or reported by a teacher often gives a disturbing insight into the twisted mind of the child, with bright red slashes representing the blood gushing from the stick figure family killed by the tiny smiling child with the gray knife scribbled into his hand.

Recommendations from the Subgenre

The Bad Seed (1956)

Directed by Mervyn LeRoy
Written by John Lee Mahin (based on the novel by William March and the play by Maxwell Anderson)
Starring: Nancy Kelly, Patty McCormack, Henry Jones

When a classmate of her daughter Rhoda's dies under mysterious circumstances, mother Christine is first concerned that Rhoda might be scarred by the trauma. But revelations about disagreements between Rhoda and the classmate along with the discovery of one of the dead student's items in Rhoda's room, give Christine reason for pause. While attempting to learn what her daughter had to do with the crime, Christine discovers that they are both related to a notorious serial killer, and that genetics might have driven her daughter to homicidal impulses.

The film generally credited with igniting the popularity of the creepy kid subgenre, *The Bad Seed* is a fun viewing experience that is the template for all the films which have come since. The eerily cheerful, soft-voiced performance of Patty McCormack immediately makes an impact, and the brilliance of the film is in allowing viewers to have a sense of her true nature before any revelations are made.

Mervyn LeRoy had just completed the Oscar-winning war comedy *Mister Roberts* when he signed on to make this big-screen version of the successful stage play. Censors of the day insisted that the moviemakers change the ending so that the mother survived and the child died; the original, darker ending can be found in the 1985 television remake. The film was nominated for four Oscars, and was one of Warner Bros.' biggest hits of 1956. The closing credits sequence, in which evil child Rhoda is finally "punished," comes from a curtain call moment created during the run of the stage play.

The Children (2008)

Directed by Tom Shankland
Written by Paul Andrew Williams, Tom Shankland
Starring: Eva Birthistle, Stephen Campbell Moore, Jeremy Sheffield

Casey is the teenage daughter of a British couple who are spending New Year's at a country estate with the rest of the extended family. Several of the children seem to be coming down with some sort of illness that induces vomiting. Late in the night, the cat goes missing, and the behavior of the children turns from simply sick to outright violent. As the violence escalates and Casey begins to suspect that the illness is causing it, she tries to escape with her aunt, only to find that it is happening elsewhere too.

Cleverly combining the outbreak film with the creepy kid subgenre, *The Children* is a slow burn horror film that takes its time to make the outlandish premise fully believable. Leaning more on suspense than graphic violence, the film toys with its audience in the same playful way a child might (but with bloodier results). The child actors are both frightening and sympathetic, particularly Hannah Tointon as Casey, and the final reveal in the closing moments is a well-earned tragedy.

Tom Shankland had already directed several short films and a horror feature called *The Killing Gene* when he wrote and co-directed this project. His skill behind the camera won him several television jobs, from *The Fades* to *Ripper Street*, and he was the sole director of all eight episodes of the award-winning first season of the series *The Missing*. Lead actress Hannah Tointon found success in international television, appearing on BBC's *The Hour* and Showtime's *Penny Dreadful*. Cinematographer Nanu Segal's stunning visuals were featured in several other British horror films of the time, including *Donkey Punch* and *Shrooms*.

Children of the Corn (1984)
Directed by Fritz Kiersch
Written by George Goldsmith (based on the story by Stephen King)
Starring: Peter Horton, Linda Hamilton, Courtney Gains

Burt and Vicky are a couple traveling cross-country to Seattle when they stop in Gatlin, Nebraska, after accidentally hitting and killing a child with their car. While searching for his family, they find that all of the adults of the town are gone; the children have formed some kind of strange cult and killed all the parents. Vicky and Burt try to survive the violence as there is a power struggle in the cult. The creature that they worship shows up to demand a sacrifice.

A frightening American updating of the 1976 Spanish film *Who Can Kill a Child?* (with some added supernatural elements), *Children of the Corn* combines the creepy kid subgenre with the road travel subgenre for a generally positive result. Peter Horton and Linda Hamilton are a believable onscreen couple, but it is young actor Courtney Gains whose go-for-broke performance left the strongest impression. He made an equally strong impression five years later in the horror-comedy *The 'Burbs*.

Director Fritz Kiersch chose the iconic short story by Stephen King as his first feature film. He would end up using writer George Goldsmith's draft of the script rather than King's own. A filmic version of the story closer to King's script (and to the original story) reached television screens in 2009. With a budget of less than $1 million, the 1984 original earned over $14 million at the box office, and it spawned one of the longest running horror film franchises with eight sequels. (Only the first three were theatrical releases, with the others going straight to DVD.)

Other Titles of Interest

Village of the Damned (1960 and 1995), *Alice Sweet Alice* (1976), *Audrey Rose* (1977), *The Brood* (1979), *Pet Sematary* (1989), *Mikey* (1992), *The Good Son* (1993), *Wicked Little Things* (2006)

Crime Horror

To establish the effectiveness of the subgenre of crime horror, the first things to establish are the parameters of what a crime horror film is. After all, nearly everything that happens in a horror film can be considered a crime in one way or another. Stalking, murder, and cannibalism are types of crimes, but they are not the crimes to which this subgenre refers.

The subgenre is in many ways similar to the western horror or comedy horror, in that it takes from two genres and creates a hybrid. It is the juxtaposition of these two genres, and the dynamic created in their combination, that makes this unique. Unlike the other genres, however, the two dueling storylines often feel separate, and it is their jarring and unexpected meeting that gives the crime horror subgenre its specific sensibility.

Often the film begins with the crime or the criminals, and the film does a great deal of work convincing you that this is what the main focus of the story is going to be. A kidnapping, a robbery, a jailbreak, these are set-piece action and suspense beats that are right at home in any story of anti-heroes and their lives. The turn usually comes about when the criminals have begun their criminal escapade or are on their way to escaping the law, and it is frequently at the halfway point of the film. It is here that the horror element rears its head.

This subgenre of horror is different from any other horror film in which the supernatural doesn't pop up until partway through the movie because the mere presence of criminals makes it an entirely different kind of story. Criminals in the midst of an illegal pursuit are unable to call the police or seek assistance from anyone; because they have broken the law, the law is no longer there to protect them. Add to that the fact that criminals are often unsavory, immoral figures; this does away with the expected dynamic of heroes versus monsters. We may root for the criminals to survive and escape the danger, but we may just as easily hope that whatever hellish creature is pursuing them gets its chance to deliver divine retribution for the wrongful acts they have perpetrated. The simple answers are gone, and it is now a struggle between varying degrees of villainy. Virtue and karma are no longer part of the equation in the world of the crime horror; power, deceit, and pure blind luck are the only commodities that matter.

Elements of the Subgenre

The Easiest Job You Ever Worked: Isn't that always the promise in a film with a crime as the centerpiece? "One more job, and then I'm out." In crime dramas as well as horror films, the promise is always that the job will be easy, no one will get hurt, and in two weeks you'll be laughing about this on some island in the South Pacific. It usually ends bad in a crime drama, but in a horror film, it's so much worse.

They're All Bad, But He's Not As Bad: A crime drama off-shoot of the "hooker with a heart of gold" cliché is the "gentleman criminal." He may rob banks or steal famous paintings, but he's so polite and handsome, and he won't hurt people if he doesn't have to. So, if you have to choose between the monster, the psychotic and obsessed police officer, or the gentleman criminal, there's really no question where your loyalties end up.

Recommendations from the Subgenre

From Dusk Till Dawn (1996)

Directed by Robert Rodriguez
Written by Quentin Tarantino, Robert Kurtzman
Starring: George Clooney, Harvey Keitel, Juliette Lewis

Bank robber brothers Seth and Gordon Gecko have just finished a job in Texas and are looking to get over the border. Taking ex-minister Jacob and his family hostage in their RV, they escape into Mexico and wait at a seedy bar to meet with their contact. Suddenly, the dancers and staff of the bar lock the door and reveal themselves to be vampires, and they start feeding on all the truckers and bikers within. Seth, Jacob, and a handful of other survivors make a stand, but after one of them is bitten and turns, it becomes a grueling struggle to stay alive until morning.

Creating a film that is quite literally one-half crime story and one-half horror film (it makes its transition at almost the 45-minute mark), *From Dusk Till Dawn* is a fun and surprising action-horror that takes the best of its multiple inspirations. With great turns from reliable actors Harvey Keitel and Juliette Lewis, this was the film that proved *ER* heartthrob George Clooney was also a matinee star.

Writer Quentin Tarantino was hired by special effects icon Robert Kurtzman to turn his vampire idea into a script, and after Tarantino's huge success with *Pulp Fiction*, he turned to filmmaker friend Robert Rodriguez to direct it. The film has many cameos from '70s exploitation stars like Fred Williamson and John Saxon, continuing Tarantino's interest in resurrecting actors as he previously did in *Pulp Fiction* (John Travolta) and would do again in *Jackie Brown* (Pam Grier and Robert Forster). A throwaway Texas Ranger character was played by Michael Parks; he became an icon who popped up later in *Kill Bill* and both Rodriguez's and Tarantino's entries in the *Grindhouse* film.

Whisper (2007)

Directed by Stewart Hendler
Written by Christopher Borrelli
Starring: Josh Holloway, Sarah Wayne Callies, Michael Rooker

Ex-convict Max is trying to make a respectable living with his fiancée Roxanne, but money troubles have forced him back into a life of crime. The job he takes with his old partner involves the kidnapping and ransom of an eight-year-old boy named David. After the kidnapping, they hide out in a small house in the middle of nowhere to await the ransom money. David seems to have an ability to get people to do violent things, and he begins making the criminals turn on each other.

Using a similar conceit to the crime thriller *Suicide Kings*, *Whisper* adds a demonic angle and a series of shifting loyalties to make for a smart and worthwhile viewing. Television stars Josh Holloway (*Lost*) and Sarah Wayne Callies (*Prison Break*) play the sympathetic criminal leads in over their heads, while *Psych* star Dulé Hill gets a chance to play against his comedic television type.

This film began Stewart Hendler's career as a feature film director. He went on to create the popular *Halo 4: Forward Unto Dawn* webseries, and remade the classic horror film *Sorority Row*. Cinematographer Dean Cundey brought the stunning visuals of his previous work on *Halloween* and *Jurassic Park* to this beautifully shot film. Future stars of *The Walking Dead* Callies and Michael Rooker worked together for the first time here, and *Glee* star Corey Monteith gives an early film performance.

Kill List (2011)

Directed by Ben Wheatley
Written by Amy Jump, Ben Wheatley
Starring: Neil Maskell, MyAnna Buring, Michael Smiley

Disturbed ex-soldier Ray works as a hitman now, though he has struggled with the job and his family is running out of money. He takes a new job that involves three people who need to be killed. As he finds and eliminates his targets, he begins to suspect that the job is not as straightforward as he first thought. When he decides to abandon the task, the client threatens to murder him and his entire family if the job isn't completed.

A fascinating hybrid movie that owes its aesthetic to the gritty British crime movies of the 1970s and its plot to *The Wicker Man*, *Kill List* is a triumph of independent British cinema. Touching on war trauma, snuff films, and the home life of the career criminal, the movie has a lot to say about violence and its effects on the people around those who inflict it. The live wire performances from Neil Maskell and Michael Smiley keep every frame of this film taut with anticipation.

Ben Wheatley was receiving positive acclaim for his previous crime film *Down Terrace* when he decided to incorporate that crime sensibility with a horror edge for this film. The script was co-written by Amy Jump; the two have collaborated on three other projects since. Steve Oram and Alice Lowe, actors who played small roles here, went on to star in Wheatley's *Sightseers*, based on characters they created themselves. Wheatley's success in the British film arena and his idiosyncratic style (seen best in *A Field in England*) led to work on BBC's *Doctor Who*.

Other Titles of Interest

Botched (2007), *Seven* (1995), *From Hell* (2001), *Anamorph* (2007), *I Saw the Devil* (2010)

Cult Horror

There are numerous elements in the cult horror genre that tap into deep psychological fears. The idea of a foreign belief system that has swayed so many people, the systematic isolation and secrecy, the seemingly good-natured facade that covers a much darker agenda—these are all things that immediately give us pause collectively, because they stand counter to what we feel as a society that enjoys the benefits of free speech and individual pursuit.

There is another fear, equal in its intensity but opposed in its origins, that also makes the idea of a cult frightening to us. And that is, simply, that we are on the outside of something, looking in. The concept of a cult immediately brings up fears and questions that are similar to the issues that most teenagers deal with in high school: the question of popularity and fitting in. The cliques that we remember from school, the groups who had their chosen form of speech and dress, have in their make-up that same dogged determination to be different from everyone else by all doing the same thing differently. Black clothes and mascara for some, tank tops and tattoos for others, and still others dress in the coolest clothes and follow the latest trends. For students who aren't lucky enough to have the proper perspective about the questionable value of going along with the crowd, much of high school feels like an attempt to form yourself into something that others will hopefully appreciate but at the very least tolerate.

The loss of identity associated with cults is the same loss of identity that comes with attempting to be accepted into a popular group of kids; we don't like the idea that someone would judge us for something as shallow and superficial as that, but it would be worse if they judged us and found us lacking. We may not like the rules, but we usually abide by them, if we want to survive the high school experience psychologically intact. It is this psychological phenomenon, the idea of hating something that you also want to be embraced by, that makes the concept of cults so uncomfortably effective.

Humanity has a natural curiosity, a natural desire to be accepted, and a fear of being passed over or left out. We do stupid things that cost us time and money and pride because we think they might help us connect to people whose values we don't even necessarily share; we buy cars and houses to impress neighbors and family members; we seek tenuous connections to celebrities through pictures and autographs; we develop relationships with people we don't like in the hopes of attaining things they have. We are fearful of the idea of cults because, in some ways, we know we're just as susceptible to the sway of the crowd as anyone else. We might one day turn around to realize that the group with the ridiculous outfits and outdated beliefs who only listen to and interact with other members of the group, is the group you worked so hard to join, and you can't remember why.

Elements of the Subgenre

The Middle of Nowhere: Though the idea of isolation is a common element in horror films, there is an interesting psychology for its necessity in the cult horror film. The strange communal living facilities that house cults in the middle of forests or on an island are isolated not because the cult members need to be able to kill and sacrifice with impunity (we won't find that out until act three); their reasoning is that the outside world won't understand or appreciate what they're trying to do, and so they have sequestered themselves for their own safety. Don't you believe it.

They Seemed So Nice: The shift comes so quickly into religious fervor and violence that we sometimes forget that they were somehow able to hold it together and seem normal and peaceful long enough to welcome some unsuspecting characters in. The first half-hour of the experience is often pleasant, calm, and beautiful, which makes the eventual revelation that much more disturbing.

Recommendations from the Subgenre

The Wicker Man (1973)

Directed by Robin Hardy
Written by Anthony Shaffer (based on the story by David Pinner)
Starring: Edward Woodward, Christopher Lee, Britt Ekland

Devoutly religious Police Sergeant Howie travels to the isolated island of Summerisle to investigate the disappearance of a young woman. He is disturbed by activities on the island which hearken back to the pagan traditions of the pre–Christian culture. Upon discovering that the islanders make a human sacrifice every year in exchange for a good harvest, he knows that he must find the girl before the ceremony begins.

An insidious film that sneaks up on its audience as cleverly as it does its lead character, *The Wicker Man* is a fascinating look at the battle of old versus modern belief systems. Woodward is perfect as the devout policeman, and his likability makes the notorious ending all the more tragic. The only clue to the deceit is the presence of Hammer horror star Christopher Lee, whose intimidating appearance always spells trouble.

Director Robin Hardy teamed with novelist and playwright Anthony Shaffer (at the urging of Christopher Lee) to create this unexpected film. Before its release, there were many cuts to the film, and additional ones were made upon its distribution to the U.S.; the footage was lost in subsequent years, and it wasn't until 2001 that the majority of it was reassembled into a "director's cut." A 1989 sequel treatment by writer Shaffer was never filmed. In 2006 director Neil Labute helmed the critically panned Nicolas Cage remake. Robin Hardy returned to the concept in 2011, creating the pseudo-sequel *The Wicker Tree*. He has since been working on securing funding for *The Wrath of the Gods*, which would be the final film in a trilogy.

Race with the Devil (1975)

Directed by Jack Starrett
Written by Lee Frost, Wes Bishop
Starring: Peter Fonda, Warren Oates, Loretta Swit

Two motorcycle shop owners and their wives are on an RV vacation in central Texas. In a desolate area, they accidentally witness a satanic ritual sacrifice and barely escape with their lives. After finding indifference when trying to report the crime, the foursome decides to leave the area for their safety, only to find out that the cultists are not just a tiny group in one isolated town.

A clever combination of the cult horror film and the road picture very popular in the era, *Race with the Devil* borrows the framework of *Easy Rider* and builds it up with elements of *The Wicker Man*. The surprising addition of the big chase scene in the third act takes the film into areas generally unexplored in the claustrophobic confines of cult horror, to fun effect.

Lead actors Peter Fonda and Warren Oates (frequent collaborators and unquestionable icons of the late 1960s and early 1970s) are excellent in what could be stereotypical roles, and *M*A*S*H* series star Loretta Swit makes one of her few theatrical appearances. The script by Lee Frost and Wes Bishop came after they collaborated on several other exploitation titles like *Chain Gang Women* and *The Thing with Two Heads*. *Race with the Devil*, along with *Easy Rider* and *The Texas Chain Saw Massacre*, painted an unflattering picture of what young America thought of the Deep South at the time. A similar movie was made by horror icon Wes Craven two years later: *The Hills Have Eyes*.

Holy Ghost People (2013)

Directed by Mitchell Altieri
Written by Kevin Artigue, Joe Egender, Mitchell Altieri, Phil Flores
Starring: Emma Greenwell, Joe Egender, Brendan McCarthy

Charlotte wants to solve the mystery of her sister Liz's disappearance. She recruits an alcoholic ex–Marine, Wayne, to look into it, and the investigation takes her to the Appalachian Mountains. She encounters a religious group called the Church of One Accord, led by the charismatic Brother Billy. They handle poisonous snakes and seem to have some answers to the secrets surrounding the whereabouts of Liz.

Charismatic preacher Brother Billy (Joe Egender) shows the frightening extent of his faith in the 2013 film *Holy Ghost People* (courtesy Joe Egender).

Capturing the mood and mystery of a real way of life in certain parts of rural America, *Holy Ghost People* strikes a delicate balance between humanizing and vilifying its story's central figures. Joe Egender as Brother Billy gives a star-making performance. The use of real snakes in many of the church sequences brings a heightened level of tension to the proceedings.

Mitchell Altieri had already worked as a team with Phil Flores (under the name The Butcher Brothers), directing *The Violent Kind*, *The Hamiltons* and its sequel *The Thompsons*, and the remake of *April Fool's Day*. Altieri went solo to direct this film. Along with producer Kevin Artigue, Altieri co-scripted the film with Egender and former directing partner Flores. The public domain documentary *Holy Ghost People* (1967) is where the film got its name as well as much of its subject matter. Lead performers Emma Greenwell and Brendan McCarthy had previously dabbled in horror on the HBO series *True Blood*.

Other Titles of Interest

Sound of My Voice (2011), *Savage Messiah* (2002), *Martha Marcy May Marlene* (2011), *Helter Skelter* (1976), *The Sacrament* (2013)

Demon-Possession Horror

Demon possession horror is a well-visited subgenre because there is so much about demon possession that is still mysterious and confusing. Stories and myths speak of demons as living creatures with higher thinking and intelligence, but no corporeal shape; they simply borrow the bodies of humans to do whatever they want whenever they can. This is an effective fear to accentuate within the demon possession arena, because loss of control is one of the most anxiety-inducing fears in human existence. We don't just fear that some other person might be possessed by a demon and that we will have to battle it; we also wonder what it could be that allowed a demon to take over that person, and what would stop it from taking us over as well.

On top of the fear of losing control, we also fear that we are woefully unequipped to deal with the problem once it presents itself. One of the most terrifying things about an exorcism in film is that there is never any guarantee that it is going to work. If it did, no one would think it was suspenseful when a person seemed to be driven by demonic forces; other characters would simply call their local medium-priest-voodoo practitioner and have the demon quickly and conveniently removed. The problem is, it never works out like that.

And why should it? Demons, traditionally seen in Judeo-Christian belief as fallen angels cast out of Heaven because of their unwillingness to obey, thrive on chaos. But, when we decide to wage battle with them, we do so by enacting rituals. Rituals are nothing more than religious rules and actions that we believe will chase away the demons and keep them at bay. Why, if these creatures were cast out of Heaven for not obeying the most powerful being in existence, do we expect that they're going to listen to us when we tell them what to do? Our desire for process and ritual, our instinct towards order and justice, stands in total opposition to everything that a demon represents.

The biggest fear of all is that a demon will have sway over someone we care about. Since demons have no shape, we can only battle them by battling the shape that they have taken over; it is no coincidence that they like to find the vulnerable and seemingly innocent. The more painful it would be to fight against a particular individual, the more likely that is the person they would want to possess. Like a terrorist who attacks and then hides in a building full of children, they are taunting us to use force against them when we know that it will only harm innocent bystanders. Demons don't die and aren't wounded; they are only cast out to wait patiently for their next vessel. The possessed are the ones who suffer all the real damage.

Elements of the Subgenre

Casting Them Out: The promise of a demon-possession horror film is that, if you wait long enough, there is going to be an exorcism, and it's going to be *the* set-piece. From *The Exorcist* to *The Devil Inside*, the audience expects that the deal is generally going to be the same: You can scare us, you can surprise or fool us, but by the end of the film, that demon had better get tossed out (either from a house, a person's body, or perhaps the window that overlooks a really long stairway).

They Sure Do Love the Ladies: Though there certainly are prominent films in which men become possessed by demons (*Deliver Us From Evil* is a recent example), the overwhelming percentage of people in these films being possessed by the male demons are women. There might be some kind of misogynistic gender commentary on the insidiousness of both demonic and feminine evils ... or it might just be that filmmakers think it's more frightening when a woman has a scary monster voice coming out of her.

Recommendations from the Subgenre

Demons (1985)

Directed by Lamberto Bava
Written by Dardano Sacchetti, Dario Argento, Lamberto Bava, Franco Ferrini
Starring: Urbano Barberini, Natasha Hovey, Fabiola Toledo

After being accosted in the subway by a man passing out free tickets to a movie screening, Cheryl and her friends decide to attend the show. The movie involves the possession of a person through the wearing of a strange ceremonial mask. One of the patrons puts on a prop mask in the lobby and finds that it possesses her. She goes on a bloody rampage, biting and possessing others. Unaffected audience members try to escape only to find that all the exits have been sealed.

One of the earliest examples of meta-horror, in which the events of a horror film have an effect on inhabitants of the so-called real world (this was similarly explored in the 1987 film *Anguish*), *Demons* is equally a tense chamber piece horror film that excels in moments of special effects–driven violence. A true exploitation film in every sense (the motorcycle sword sequence alone wins it that title), the film has fun playing up the juxtaposition of the fancy film premiere and the ancient evil stalking the theater.

Lamberto Bava, son of Italian horror master Mario Bava, had already worked on many films as assistant director and directed horror entries *Macabre* and *A Blade in the Dark* when he made this film. Two of his script collaborators, Franco Ferrini and Dario Argento, were responsible for some of the most famous Italian horror films ever made, including *Deep Red* and *Opera*. The meta nature of the story became more complicated in *Demons 2* (directed and written by the same team), in which the tenants of a high-rise building become possessed by watching the first film on television. The *Demons* series continued for seven more entries (one again directed by Bava), but none connected to the original narrative, and the titles were primarily used as a marketing strategy.

The Last Exorcism (2010)

Directed by Daniel Stamm
Written by Huck Botko, Andrew Gurland
Starring: Patrick Fabian, Ashley Bell, Caleb Landry Jones

Disillusioned faith healer Cotton Marcus has decided to invite a film crew to watch him perform his last "exorcism," a process he believes to be a sham and wishes to have documented as such. The girl suffering from demon possession is not as simple a case as Cotton first thought, and he decides to stay a while and try to help her. Cotton and the film crew learn that the family has hidden secrets, that the demon inside the young girl may be real, and that the folks who live nearby may not be as warm and forthcoming as he had previously believed.

Taut, surprising, and cleverly executed, *The Last Exorcism* breathes life into a tired formula by combining demon possession horror with the fake documentary style and a focus on fundamentalist rather than Catholic exorcism. A brilliant lead performance from the underappreciated Patrick Fabian strikes exactly the right balance of cynicism and genuine compassion, and Ashley Bell's tortured performance brings sympathy along with the scares.

Heavily influenced by the real-life documentary *Marjoe* (about a one-time child preacher who allows a documentary crew to film his "performances"), the movie is a nearly flawless execution of the found footage style, thanks in large part to the direction of Daniel Stamm (who two years earlier made the chilling suicide fake doc *A Necessary Death*). It's a surprisingly subdued and thoughtful film from producer Eli Roth, whose other films include *Cabin Fever* and *Hostel*. The shock ending divided audiences and left little room for a sequel—which made it strange when a sequel did indeed show up in 2013.

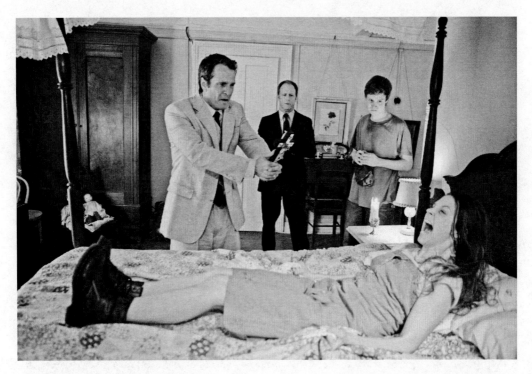

Minister Cotton Weary (Patrick Fabian) attempts to exorcise young Nell Sweetzer (Ashley Bell), while her brother (Caleb Landry Jones) and father (Louis Herthum) watch helplessly, in 2010's *The Last Exorcism* (courtesy Lionsgate Publicity).

Drag Me to Hell (2009)

Directed by Sam Raimi
Written by Sam Raimi, Ivan Raimi
Starring: Alison Lohman, Justin Long, Dileep Rao

In an attempt to impress her boss at the bank, loan officer Christine rejects the pleas of an elderly gypsy woman regarding her mortgage. The tough decision wins her favor at work, but the woman later accosts her in the parking garage and places a curse on her. Christine begins to panic that the curse is real when she sees the specter of a demonic entity following and taunting her. She seeks the help of a fortune teller and an exorcist, and learns that the only way for her to get rid of the demonic force which wants to pull her into Hell is to pass the curse onto someone else.

As hilarious and unexpected as it is shocking, *Drag Me to Hell* was a comedy-action-horror hybrid that somehow found a fairly sizable audience despite its mysterious and overly dramatic advertising campaign. A game cast of actors plays the pitch black comedy with straight faces. Special credit should be given to Alison Lohman and Lorna Raver for their commitment to character (and willingness to beat the crap out of each other).

Between the big-budget studio projects *Spider-Man 3* and *Oz the Great and Powerful*, visionary director Sam Raimi made this low-budget passion project. Scripted by Sam and his brother Ivan (who also scripted the similar *Army of Darkness*), the film is a return to the *Evil Dead* universe in all but cast and title. The script was written a decade before it was finally made, as Raimi's attention was drawn away from the project by the *Spider-Man* series.

Other Titles of Interest

The Rite (2011), *The Amityville Horror* (1979 and 2005), *Paranormal Activity* (2007), *Jennifer's Body* (2009), *The Exorcist* (1973), *Burnt Offerings* (1976), *Fallen* (1998)

Doll–Puppet–Ventriloquist-Dummy Horror

They look like us, somewhat. Though there is a crude simplicity to their design, as if the objects were designed for children by other children. Superficially, their shape is our shape.

Our soul is not their soul, though. There is no life within, no humanity filling up that human form. Some dolls, puppets, and ventriloquist dummies talk, but they do so through a power beyond them. From the ventriloquist's arm to the puppeteer's unmoving lips to the mechanical voice box activated by a pulled string, these human-like objects do their best to mimic us because it is in their design to do so.

The juxtaposition between their innocuous appearance and the spiritual emptiness is what gives us pause around them. Their frozen smiles and empty eyes, forever unchanging and always watching, disturb us because we know that when we look into a set of eyes, the eyes should look back. To stare into the face of a doll is to stare into the unaltered face of something that never lived, or is already dead. It doesn't move, but it looks like it should.

And yet … nothing terrifies us more than the idea that it might move. In the seconds before the light is switched off in a child's bedroom, the child sees the puppet or doll laid on top of the toy box, blank face turned away from them. Then, darkness fills the room, and the child can't help but wonder: Where is the puppet looking now? I can't see him, but can he see me?

It is a surprising irony that we are unnerved by dolls because they seem human but not human enough, when it is absolutely certain that being more human would make them all the more unnerving to us. We think they're so creepy when they sit, motionless; but they're dolls, and it's unnatural for them to do anything else. So, of course, in horror films, they all do something else.

It might be an annoying voice that only we hear, or a sudden appearance in the hallway; it might be more active and destructive than that, escalating to a full assault with kitchen knives. Or, even more frightening than that, it might be smart enough to be playing with you. A slight movement that perhaps was in your head, or a blink from seemingly frozen eyes, and you're suddenly back in that childhood bedroom yourself, wondering whether or not he can see you while you sleep.

He can.

Elements of the Subgenre

Is That Where He Was Before?: The slow burn element of this subgenre comes from toying with the character on-screen and, by association, the audience, by making them question if it really moved. Is the doll possessed? Is someone playing tricks on them? Were the puppet's hands folded a minute ago? These moments are the calm before the storm.

If You're Not Strong, You Have to Be Creative: Even if we buy into the idea that dolls have somehow come to life, we still know that they're small and weak, and can't move around very quickly. So if they're going to be convincing killers, they have to come up with some clever ways of dispensing with their victims. Dropping chandeliers on them, choking them from the back seat, and suffocating them while they sleep are just some of the tactics that living dolls use to keep up with the stronger and more athletic slashers.

Recommendations from the Subgenre

Child's Play (1988)

Directed by Tom Holland
Written by Don Mancini, John Lafia, Tom Holland
Starring: Brad Dourif, Catherine Hicks, Chris Sarandon

When serial killer-voodoo practitioner Charles Lee Ray is injured and trapped in a toy store by police, he uses a voodoo incantation to put his soul into the body of a nearby doll. The doll is later purchased by a struggling single mother for her son, who loves the doll, calls it Chucky and begins communicating with it. As a police officer begins to suspect that someone is cleaning up some messes that Ray left behind, the single mother realizes that her son isn't making up the tales of interactions that he is having with the toy.

Child's Play, a surprisingly effective hybrid of shocks and comedy, finds its humor not in the absurdity of the premise, but in the juxtaposition of the innocent appearance of the character and his heinous acts. Combining the classic slasher tropes with the more mainstream mystery elements of a police procedural, it boasts some great practical Chicago locations and a knowing script that keeps the audience surprised even when they think they're ahead of the curve.

Director Tom Holland had already found success in horror-comedy with *Fright Night* (1985) before launching this last major slasher franchise of the 1980s. Excellent (and complicated) practical effects from designer Kevin Yagher brought Chucky to life as brilliantly as Brad Dourif's vocal performance did. The successful film spawned five sequels, all written by the original scripter, Don Mancini.

Dead Silence (2007)

Directed by James Wan
Written by Leigh Whannell, James Wan
Starring: Ryan Kwanten, Amber Valletta, Donnie Wahlberg

When Jamie and his wife receive a ventriloquist's dummy in the mail, they are reminded of an old poem about someone named Mary Shaw who loved dolls. Later, Jamie discovers his wife dead in the apartment and the dummy near her body, and learns that it was owned by the mysterious Mary Shaw who was from his hometown. He goes back to his home town to find out about the doll's connection to his wife's death, and learns that his family is connected to the history of the murderous woman.

A combination of the ventriloquist dummy story and the evil old woman story, *Dead Silence* is a fun film that combines old-fashioned spooks with modern gore and style. While much is made of the twist ending (a twist that was not particularly surprising), the film itself stands as a fairly strong entry in the genre with great use of silence as a narrative device that hearkens back to the gimmick in Vincent Price's *The Tingler*.

The second venture into horror for director James Wan and writer Leigh Whannell after working on the first three realistically violent *Saw* films, *Dead Silence* brought back many of the same crew members (and star Donnie Wahlberg) for this very supernatural outing. This was the first film in which director Wan worked with cinematographer John R. Leonetti, with whom he later teamed on the successful horror series *Insidious*. Leonetti had previously worked in the creepy doll genre as cinematographer on *Child's Play 3*, and later directed the doll-centric spin-off of *The Conjuring*, *Annabelle*.

Puppetmaster (1989)

Directed by David Schmoeller
Written by Charles Band, Kenneth J. Hall, David Schmoeller
Starring: Paul Le Mat, William Hickey, Irene Miracle

Just before World War II, puppeteer Andre Toulon tapped into the secret of creating living puppets. He constructed and hid several of them before killing himself just as Nazis discovered his whereabouts. Decades later, a group of psychics are contacted by the owner of the inn where Toulon died, and they are told that this may be the final resting place of Toulon. As they arrive at the inn and start to investigate, they find themselves the victims of the murderous impulses of Toulon's nightmarish creations.

An intentionally cheesy film that combines killer puppets, Nazis, and a group of investigative psychics all residing in a hotel in California, *Puppetmaster* succeeds grandly in its attempt to be an entertaining B-movie. The presence of Oscar-nominated William Hickey

Murderous puppet Blade stalks the halls of a Bodega Bay hotel in 1989's *Puppet Master* (courtesy Ry Mantione).

as Toulon is as welcome as it is brief. The real stars of the film are Pinhead, Blade, and Leech Woman, the pint-sized villains who wreak havoc on the band of psychics.

Though it was directed and co-written by David Schmoeller (who had already directed *Tourist Trap* and *Crawlspace*), *Puppetmaster* is known primarily as a creation of producer–co-writer Charles Band. Founder of Full Moon Pictures, the production company that pioneered direct-to-video filmmaking in the 1980s, Band made *Puppetmaster* one of their most successful series, garnering nine sequels over twenty-three years. The only unofficial entry in the series is *Puppet Master vs. Demonic Toys* (2004), a crossover film which aired on Syfy and which Charles Band had no involvement in creating.

Other Titles of Interest

Dead of Night (1945), *Dolls* (1987), *Pinocchio's Revenge* (1996), *May* (2002), *Devil Doll* (1964), *Magic* (1978), *Blood Dolls* (1999), *Annabelle* (2014)

Doppelganger–Evil Twin Horror

Though the idea of another human being walking through the world with your face and doing whatever he or she pleases is a terrifying thought, there is also some element of secret wish fulfillment within it as well, and that is why the doppelganger horror subgenre is such a frequently visited arena.

We obviously don't hope for the existence of a dark and twisted version of ourselves wandering around, doing terrible things in our name; but we are aware of the fact that most people tend to have a dark side within them. That dark side can sometimes be fairly tame, thinking only of hurting people who have wronged us or wronged our loved ones, and never beyond the capacity that we wish them to understand their errors. But that dark side can also manifest internally in much less socially acceptable ways, fantasizing about the death of people who we don't like or the easy things we could do to get away with criminal acts. We all know that it's there, and we all deal with it.

What if you could externalize it? If you could remove every dark thought and impulse and put it out into the world as another human being, then the caveat would be that it isn't you any more. It looks like you and sounds like you, but it is evil, free and apart from yourself. And as such, perhaps there is some way that you could fight it.

The idea is appealing to us for a number of reasons, the first of which is that we would no longer have to claim the darkness as part of ourselves. It is distinctly someone other than us, and so we have the psychological rationale that we are no longer the creator of those thoughts and desires. And secondly, the idea of a person's darkness being externalized and made physical means that he or she could defeat it. And if that were a possibility, then that would make him or her the hero, rather than the villain.

We all think that we would like to become better people, but most of the effort involved is complicated and involves a lot of introspection and recognition of uncomfortable truths.

The much easier avenue of having your worst aspects come to life so you can kill them and save yourself and everyone else is far more preferable.

Elements of the Subgenre

Seeing the Other You: There is frequently a point in doppelganger horror where the beleaguered decent person finally finds the person pretending to be them, and they have to deal with the fact that true evil is walking around in the world with their face on. Sometimes they meet face to face, sometimes they see it on a video recording, and sometimes they watch another person interacting with others at a distance, but this is the moment when the terrifying possibility becomes the undeniable reality.

Overlapping Lives: Once a person discovers they have a doppelganger, they often begin to insinuate themselves into the other person's life, interacting with others as that person, until eventually they are indistinguishable from each other, and then one of them decides they want to replace the other.

Recommendations from the Subgenre

Obsession (1976)
Directed by Brian De Palma
Written by Paul Schrader, Brian De Palma
Starring: Cliff Robertson, Geneviève Bujold, John Lithgow

After real estate magnate Michael Courtland botches the ransom delivery for his wife and daughter, they are killed in a car accident along with their kidnappers. Michael remains obsessed with his dead wife, building a shrine of the church where they originally met to honor her memory. When he goes back to the original church fifteen years later, he meets a young woman who looks exactly like his deceased wife. After falling in love with and marrying her, Michael finds the nightmare starting all over again when his new wife is kidnapped and ransomed just like before.

Inspired in large part by Alfred Hitchcock's seminal *Vertigo*, *Obsession* is a masterful lookalike thriller whose title is a perfectly appropriate description of the lead character's frame of mind. Beautifully shot by Oscar-winning cinematographer Vilmos Zsigmond, the film is driven forward by Bernard Herrmann's passionate score. Lead actor Cliff Robertson never allows his character's obsession to take away the audience's empathy for him.

Brian De Palma had a good year in 1976, teaming with Stephen King for *Carrie* and with *Taxi Driver* writer Paul Schrader for this film. Schrader's original draft was much longer and more complicated, and he was unhappy with the truncated story that De Palma delivered. De Palma revisited the doppelganger theme throughout his career in *Femme Fatale* and *Raising Cain* (the latter starring *Obsession*'s John Lithgow). Over a decade after playing a doppelganger herself, actress Geneviève Bujold played a woman in love with her own set of doppelgangers in David Cronenberg's *Dead Ringers*.

Inland Empire (2006)
Written and Directed by David Lynch
Starring: Laura Dern, Jeremy Irons, Justin Theroux

Nikki Grace, a struggling actress, auditions for a role in a film called *On High in Blue Tomorrows* in hopes of re-igniting her flagging career. Her neighbor predicts that she will get the part, along with some other ominous musings. She does indeed get the part, and begins an affair with the lead actor as they are filming. As she loses the ability to distinguish her own life from the life of her character, events from the story and her own past begin to mingle until she is no longer certain of who she is.

Another haunting, elliptical story from the king of the surreal, *Inland Empire* is both a perfect example of a David Lynch film and an exciting experiment in mystery filmmaking. It uses the classic Lynch elements of the multiple narratives, the lead woman in undefined but troubling circumstances, and the possibility of a second person who looks just like the first (also seen in *Mulholland Drive* and *Lost Highway*). The film also explores the psychology of Hollywood and its love affair with itself.

Using actors he'd worked with previously, like Laura Dern, Justin Theroux, Harry Dean Stanton, and Grace Zabriskie, Lynch fashioned this film in an unconventional way: Rather than handing out a completed screenplay, he gave actors new pages every day before they shot. The film was Lynch's first project using digital video rather than film, and he liked the experience so much that he has decided not to use film for any future projects. Though he has worked on short films and the re-launch of the television series *Twin Peaks*, 2006's *Inland Empire* was the only feature film Lynch directed for nearly a decade.

Basket Case (1982)

Written and Directed by Frank Henenlotter
Starring: Kevin van Hentenryck, Terri Susan Smith, Beverly Bonner

Duane Bradley comes to New York City with two things: a locked basket in his hands, and revenge on his mind. He checks into a cheap hotel and unlocks the basket to reveal Belial, his conjoined twin brother who was surgically separated from him at a young age. Belial and Duane are unhappy about the separation, and have traveled to the city to seek revenge on the doctors responsible for separating them. When Duane begins to have feelings for a sweet nurse named Susan, the interloper could be the thing that destroys the brothers' special connection.

A film with simplistic but memorable effects and a psychologically fascinating pair of lead characters, *Basket Case* became one of the most unlikely cult hits of the 1980s. The combination of seedy New York City locations and the grainy image of the 16mm film stock give the film its distinctive look and feel. Lead actor Van Hentenryck's performance is appropriately quirky.

Frank Henenlotter had made several short cult films before embarking on this first feature, which he scripted and edited himself. Though the budget was minuscule (barely $30,000), the Belial effects were ambitious, particularly the stop-motion attack sequence near the end of the film. The advertising campaign was a smart ploy, with commercials made up simply of various filmic characters asking Duane "What's in the box?" It spawned two sequels, both of which were written and directed by Henenlotter and starred Van Hentenryck.

Other Titles of Interest

The Man Who Haunted Himself (1970), *Black Swan* (2010), *The Broken* (2008), *The Other* (1972)

Dream Horror

There is an inevitability to sleep that makes it frightening in a way most real-world fears never reach. Sharks can be scary, but you can always stay out of the water, and you're never required to go camping or participate in a séance with your friends. But sleep? Everyone succumbs.

People sometimes try to escape sleep, like Nancy did in the most well-known of all dream horror films, *A Nightmare on Elm Street*; but it eventually catches up with you, either from the sheer bodily exhaustion that forces you into hibernation, or by the trickery of those around you, medical professionals and caring parents who just want to help you.

More frightening than that is the alternative to dreaming: death. When Wes Craven first started exploring the idea of a dream killer, he based it on a true story about a man who feared falling asleep and being killed; and when he fell asleep, he did indeed die. But the truth of the matter already was, he was dead either way, because lack of sleep can cause hallucinations, severe health conditions, and eventually death. When your dreams are a threat to you, there is no solution or escape.

But possibly the most disturbing aspect of dreams as a realm for horror is the fact that, often in horror films about dreams, it is not an invading force that enters your dreams and wishes you harm (as in child killer Freddy Krueger), but simply a betrayal by your mind itself.

Dreams are a phenomenon within humanity and many higher-level animals that we don't entirely understand. We know that we do it, and that we need to do it in order to remain sane and alive, but beyond that, much of it still remains shrouded in mystery. It is one of our only biological functions for which science has yet to pinpoint a fully understood reason for its existence.

Whether they are color or black and white, whether you remember them or not, or whether you have any level of control within them, dreams are still an unsolvable question to humanity, as close as the back of our hands and as confusing and alien as the ocean floor. This psychological mystery gives it an air of menace and threat, a fog-shrouded place in our own heads that waits patiently for sixteen hours a day, until the sun sets and the body is at rest, when it can begin to drag the mind and soul through the most horrifying places imaginable.

Elements of the Subgenre

Messing with Timelines: In films about dreams, the landscape of the mind and its many other strange abilities are often addressed, resulting in things like prophetic dreams that foretell of later events, repeated or similar scenes or images, and dreams helping people travel into the past or future, or access hidden memories. This results in many movies of this subgenre also toying with the idea of linear storytelling.

Someone Not Knowing They're Asleep: A classic trope of the genre is a sequence that starts normally, gets dangerous or weird, and is then revealed to be only a dream. This happens in most films of the subgenre, and often the audience is as unaware of the dream sequence as the characters themselves.

Surrealistic and Expressionistic Imagery: Because the realm of the mind is limitless in its boundaries, filmmakers often embrace artistic movements that push the boundaries of realism in order to visually reflect the unreal nature of the dream state. This manifests in multiple ways, from virtuoso visual sequences of color and set design, to simple image manipulations like lengthening shadows or putting door frames slightly off-kilter.

Recommendations from the Subgenre

Phantasm (1979)

Written and Directed by Don Coscarelli
Starring: A. Michael Baldwin, Reggie Bannister, Angus Scrimm

Though *A Nightmare on Elm Street* is the best-known horror film dealing with dreams, director Don Coscarelli's surreal film *Phantasm* made it to theaters first, a full five years before Wes Craven took audiences into the nightmare world of Freddy Krueger. Chronicling the story of two brothers who become embroiled in an intergalactic invasion of Earth by way of a local cemetery, the film is not only about dreams; it is a film that operates on dream logic, folding over itself in a non-linear fashion and negating its own story even as it continues headlong towards an absurd but visually stunning climax. With villains like the Tall Man, a nightmarish vision of a funeral director with long hair who bleeds yellow blood; the deadly flying silver spheres (practically created by painting softballs and throwing them from behind the camera); and the tiny robed minions from another dimension who bear more than a passing resemblance to the Jawas in *Star Wars*, *Phantasm* has the distinction of being one of the only horror films whose icons were more memorable than they were understandable. Much of the explanation for the mythology came in subsequent installments of the series.

Revealing only in its final act that the film is both a horror and a science fiction film, Coscarelli audaciously toys with audience expectations and pulls the rug out from under viewers on more than one occasion. The revelation of the true identity of the lady in lavender is one of the more wild moments. It was Coscarelli's first horror movie after two mild successes in the family-friendly arena, and the film took his career in a whole new direction. While viewers may not understand everything that happens, memories of the imagery and the mood will remain long after the viewing is over.

In Dreams (1999)

Directed by Neil Jordan
Written by Bruce Robinson, Neil Jordan (based on the story by Bari Wood)
Starring: Annette Bening, Robert Downey, Jr., Aidan Quinn

Claire Cooper is traumatized by the death of her daughter. She discovers that her nightmares are actually visions seen through the eyes of the killer; he is preparing to kill again, and Claire can do nothing about it, because she is locked in an asylum and no one believes her. This psychological horror film effectively couples unnerving dream sequences with Claire's sense of helplessness, putting the audience into the shoes (and mindset) of the imprisoned but still driven heroine.

Director Neil Jordan, known previously in the horror world for his direction of *Interview with the Vampire*, creates a recurring visual reference (an entire town submerged in a reservoir) that is haunting and beautiful, and much of the takeaway of this film is in its excellent cinematography and set design. An excellent cast led by Annette Bening brings humanity to what could easily be a technically clever but empty film, with Stephen Rea and Paul Guilfoyle particular standouts in small but important roles as the psychiatrist and detective. The only sour note in an otherwise excellent film is the performance of Robert Downey Jr. as the killer. Several years away from his career resurgence with *Iron Man*, Downey was temporarily released from jail to finish shooting this film.

Paperhouse (1988)

Directed by Bernard Rose
Written by Matthew Jacobs (based on the novel by Catherine Storr)
Starring: Charlotte Burke, Glenne Headly, Gemma Jones

Based on the novel *Marianne Dreams*, *Paperhouse* tells the tale of an ill 11-year-old named Anna whose drawings begin to take on a life of their own in her dreams. The dreams begin to spell danger for her and the young disabled boy she meets within a magical house she drew that comes to life when she sleeps. The concept of simple children's ideas becoming the source of nightmarish reality is well orchestrated, and this film seems to have had an influence on director Joe Dante's similarly themed *The Hole*. *Paperhouse* was unfortunately lost in the aftermarket due to an underwhelming theatrical performance. It's a dark, complex film that touches on horror elements while also embracing the trappings of a children's fantasy.

The expressionistic take on the house in her dreams is impressive, as is the direction by British filmmaker Bernard Rose. This was his first major film; two years later he would helm the first entry in the slasher franchise *Candyman*. The imagery, particularly of the blinded ogre which appears in the dream after Anna makes a poorly drawn picture of her father and then scribbles his face out, is simple and terrifying. With excellent performances from young actors Charlotte Burke (who never made another film) and Elliott Spiers (who played the wheelchair-bound boy in the film and who made only one other movie before a tragic death in 1994), this film will appeal to discerning audiences of any age.

Donnie Darko (2001)

Written and Directed by Richard Kelly
Starring: Jake Gyllenhaal, Maggie Gyllenhaal, Jena Malone

To call *Donnie Darko* simply a film about dreams would be to call *Citizen Kane* an exposé of the newspaper industry. Written by director Richard Kelly, it depicts a month in the life of troubled teen Donnie Darko, who is having visions of a rabbit from the future who warns him about the coming end of the world. Kelly's audacious first feature film incorporates such disparate elements as insanity, prophetic dreams, time travel, and possible super powers. It's a unique and distinctive work that clearly marks the beginning of an idiosyncratic career for the director. The whole film has a nightmarish quality, from the incongruous slow-motion scenes to Donnie's uncomfortable confessional moments in the psychiatrist's office, and it comes as no surprise in the end when it seems probable that nothing we ever saw was actually real.

Kelly went on to make the much-maligned *Southland Tales* and the confusing but fascinating *The Box*. *Donnie Darko* built an enormous cult following (and an unfortunate sequel, *S. Darko*, that the director has clarified that he had no interest in or involvement with) and also started the careers of brother and sister actors Jake and Maggie Gyllenhaal, who play siblings in the film. Carefully chosen music, an eye for period detail, and a great supporting cast that includes Patrick Swayze and Mary McDonnell all combine to make a thoughtful, bizarre, challenging, and humorous film that defies strict categorization and even definitive explanation. A later director's cut and commentary helped to explain some things, but others still remain a mystery. Those looking for simple answers, look elsewhere.

Other Titles of Interest

Vampyr (1932), *Jacob's Ladder* (1990), *Flatliners* (1990), *Bad Dreams* (1988), *Dreamscape* (1984)

Ecological Horror

In 1978, *I Spit on Your Grave*, a disturbing exploitation film about rape and bloody revenge, was released to much controversy. It was an amateur project, with exactly the kind of stilted performances, uninspired direction, and rampant nudity and violence one would expect from a grindhouse film of the time.

The story (what little there was) follows an aspiring writer who moves to a small town to work, only to be raped and left for dead by a group of men. After crawling back to her house bleeding and in pain, she slowly recovers from her injuries and then makes her presence known in the town. She eventually revisits every one of the men who attacked her and kills them.

While this film is by no means an artistic achievement, it does prove something that should be fairly obvious in terms of audience reaction: Given that an audience could endure watching someone brutalized in the way that the lead character was in *I Spit on Your Grave*, they will be one hundred percent behind the recovery and overly violent retribution that will be revisited on the perpetrators.

In the best and worst way, the ecological horror subgenre has the same end goal in mind. In an ecological horror story, the filmmaker makes a pact with the audience to recognize who the villain is, and the villain is us. If an ecological film is a rape-revenge film, we are the rapists, and the Earth is the victim we have savaged over and over again.

Though no intelligent human would root for the demise of his or her own race, we can at least understand the tendency of nature to rise up against us: to mutate pollen so it will make us suicidal as in *The Happening*, or to use our own pollution against us as in *The Toxic Avenger*.

We don't like it, but we understand it. The Earth has been abused ritually and callously by us for years without ever fighting back. We've done nothing to help her recover from the wounds we've inflicted, and we go back to our everyday lives as if we've done nothing wrong. It seems only fair that, one of these days, she's going to look to even the score.

Elements of the Subgenre

It's Not Nice to Fool with Mother Nature: In every outdoor excursion, there's always at least one guy who thinks he's too cool to be a decent human being and caretaker for the Earth.

He leaves his campfires burning, he throws his trash in the woods, and he recklessly tramples exotic and endangered habitats just for a laugh. And when you mess with Mother Nature like that, you'd better be ready for some serious vengeance.

A Messenger Is Spared: If nature is rising up against humanity and establishing its new rules of order, then nature must leave someone alive to bring that message to the rest of humanity. Often in ecological horror, one of the interlopers will see the error of their ways and, because of that, they will survive to return and warn humans about their hubris, serving as disciples of nature spreading the message to change humanity's destructive ways.

Recommendations from the Subgenre

Long Weekend (1978)
Directed by Colin Eggleston
Written by Everett De Roche
Starring: John Hargreaves, Briony Behets

Peter and Marcia are a couple on vacation for a weekend camping trip. As they bicker and their relationship becomes strained, they are also being dismissive with their behavior towards the environment around them; they litter the unspoiled wilderness, destroy insects with spray cans, kill a dugong, and start a fire in the brush. Nature lashes back at them, defending itself against the thoughtlessness with methods violent and subtle. An ecological horror film that cleverly disguises itself for the first act as a relationship drama, *Long Weekend* was an Australian answer to the eco-disaster films of the U.S. like *Day of the Animals*. Strong and naturalistic performances from lead actors John Hargreaves and Briony Behets are aided by patient direction and animal attacks that feel organic and frightening rather than exploitative and silly.

After success directing many hours of television and a soft-core comedy called *Fantasm Comes Again*, director Colin Eggleston brought this film to the screen. The script was written by Everett De Roche, an American who wrote for Australian television before becoming known for his Outback thrillers *Patrick*, *Road Games*, and *Razorback*. At the time of the original's filming, Eggleston and Behets were married. Australian director Jamie Blanks, known in the States for *Urban Legend* and *Valentine*, returned to his native country to remake the film in 2008, his version starring native actress Claudia Karvan and *Person of Interest*'s Jim Caviezel.

The Last Winter (2006)
Directed by Larry Fessenden
Written by Larry Fessenden, Robert Leaver
Starring: Ron Perlman, James Le Gros, Connie Britton

When the naked body of a research team member is found in the snow in the Arctic National Wildlife Refuge, environmentalist James and drill base commander Ed try to figure out what happened to him. They initially suspect it to be poisonous gas leakage from rapid climate change but many people at the research facility sense that nature itself is killing to protect its well-being. The spectral "ghosts" in the oil for which they're drilling start to attack everyone at the camp, until only a handful are left. Combining elements of eco-thriller, arctic isolation *a la The Thing*, and cinematography reminiscent of Kurosawa's *Dersu Uzala*, *The*

Last Winter is a thoughtful horror film with an important message. The central mystery of what killed the team member is nothing more than an excuse to gather people of opposing viewpoints on a stark and threatening landscape to watch them struggle. Great performances from Ron Perlman and a pre–*Friday Night Lights* Connie Britton cement the film in a strong reality, with writer-director Larry Fessenden creating a smart fusion of natural and supernatural fears.

Oil drilling supervisor Ed Pollack (Ron Perlman) finds trouble in the Arctic National Wildlife Refuge in 2006's eco-horror *The Last Winter* (courtesy Larry Fessenden).

The most expensive and complex of Fessenden's films, it continues to showcase his interest in environmental issues (an interest begun in *No Telling* and continued past this film to his most recent work, *Beneath*). In a quick flashback cameo, Fessenden's son Jack plays the young version of James Le Gros' character; Jack has appeared in many of his father's films, and has gone on to direct many of his own projects as well.

The Ruins (2008)

Directed by Carter Smith
Written by Scott B. Smith (based on his own story)
Starring: Jena Malone, Laura Ramsey, Shawn Ashmore

A group of American tourists and a German man searching for his brother find more than they expected when they come upon a Mayan ruin in the jungles of Mexico. They become trapped on the ruins when villagers refuse to let them leave. Overnight, two of the injured members of the group discover that some of the vine vegetation has begun to work its way into their wounds. With no escape from the ruins possible due to the murderous villagers, the group has to figure out how to contend with the intelligent plant life which is slowly devouring them. A smart film whose unlikely premise is delivered believably through subtle effects and smart direction, *The Ruins* is a fun roller coaster ride which unfortunately only found its audience upon its DVD release. Though it stars many younger actors like Jena Malone (*Donnie Darko*) and Shawn Ashmore (*X-Men*), this film is not a typical teen horror entry; it relies on great performances and suspense rather than gimmicks and gore

After directing a short film featured in the popular anthology series *Boys Life*, director Carter Smith made this his debut feature. Teaming with writer Scott B. Smith, whose previous work on *A Simple Plan* was Oscar-nominated, they made the film with Ben Stiller's production company Red Hour. A different, darker ending was shot, adhering more closely to the ending of the book, but the studio preferred the happier one. The other version can be seen on the unrated cut.

Other Titles of Interest

The Happening (2008), *The Bay* (2012), *Prophecy* (1979), *The Thaw* (2009)

Filmmaking Horror

"Pain is temporary, film is forever." This famous saying appeared on-screen in the 1987 film *Three O' Clock High* and has also been attributed to celebrities as varied as Michael J. Fox, Peter Jackson, and John Milius. Interestingly, the quote is often associated with filmmakers who are trying to convince actors to do things for a movie that could be extremely dangerous. Funnily enough, it works.

There is something magical about the presence of a movie camera; it changes people's willingness and attitude. And it's not just the people involved in the film. When a movie camera appears in a public place, the people in that place are suddenly far more permissive to the activities of the people behind the camera, and far more interested in the activities of the people in front of it. In all likelihood, it is because there is some level of truth in that adage: Film *is* forever. Notwithstanding the thousands of movies from the silent era that were lost to age and disintegration, the sense is that if something is captured on film, it is there for posterity. Societies and political parties may come and go, standards and mores may change, but the images committed to film will be there as a moving monument of a specific piece of history. We sense that, and we cater to it.

But why do we trust the people behind the camera? If anyone can operate a camera, does the mere fact that a camera is being used mean that there is some inherent level of credibility to the person using it? Of course not; but the kinds of people who use the camera in the filmmaking horror subgenre, to manipulate and torture and record suffering, know how to play on the instinctive draw of a captured image. For as long as there have been images of any kind, there have been images of violence captured. Just as most of humanity is drawn to the immortality of being captured on film, there has always been a smaller group of people equally drawn to manipulating that instinct in others, whether to objectify them sexually, to manipulate them emotionally, or to capture the image of their abuse physically.

The irony of the adage is that, by making an image of something that was emotionally or physically damaging, they have in fact made that pain permanent. The expression should more accurately be "Pain is temporary, but film makes it last forever."

Elements of the Subgenre

It's All Part of the Story: One of the most popular misleads in the Filmmaking Horror subgenre is the scene where important people are killed and it makes a gigantic and seemingly unfixable change in the story. Then the camera pans out to reveal that the whole thing was just part of a movie within the movie, complete with a winking cameo and a tech guy holding a smoke machine.

References Galore!: Because filmmakers who make Filmmaking Horror films assume that their audience is aware of the meta-narrative, they love to include numerous references to other films, thereby tipping their hats to educated film fans who will catch all of the clues and visual cues.

Recommendations from the Subgenre

Peeping Tom (1960)

Directed by Michael Powell
Written by Leo Marks
Starring: Carl Boehm, Moira Shearer, Anna Massey

After a childhood of constant observation and psychological experiments from his researcher father, Mark Lewis has found that he has his own peculiar obsession with filming things. He works with a film crew, as well as taking pin-up pictures on the side. The murder of one of the stars of his most recent movie gets the police interested in him as a suspect, while his relationship with a new tenant in his house threatens to reveal the true nature of his obsession with recording: capturing the fear as his victims realize that they are going to die.

A shocking film for its time that still has an impact now, *Peeping Tom* is a visual stunner that has influenced many great filmmakers including Martin Scorsese and Jim McBride. The focus on filmmaking and the real-life effects of those films on emotionally troubled characters rings even more true in today's media-driven society. This film was a precursor to the camera-bearing killers of the recent fake documentary-found footage horror movement.

Director Michael Powell was known for lavish collaborations with co-director Emeric Pressburger, such as *The Red Shoes* and *Black Narcissus*, when he embarked on this very personal and controversial film. The movie was so poorly received by contemporary critics that it essentially destroyed any chance of Powell continuing to work as a director in the U.K., a country notorious for its sexual repression (a theme that was clear here). Though written by Leo Marks, the project is clearly Powell's; he even appears on-screen, playing the killer's father in flashbacks.

Mulholland Drive (2001)

Written and Directed by David Lynch
Starring: Laura Harring, Naomi Watts, Justin Theroux

A car accident brings amnesiac Rita into the life of acting hopeful Betty, and the two of them begin to look into Rita's past life and why she would have a huge sum of money and a mysterious blue key in her purse. At the same time, Betty scores an audition for a new film for a filmmaker with a troubled home life. When Rita finds a blue box that matches her key, she unlocks the box, and massive and mysterious changes plague her life.

A puzzle box of a movie with a puzzle box as a plot point, *Mulholland Drive* is exactly the kind of visually stunning and narratively confusing work one would expect from David Lynch. With characters that border on absurdity and plot threads that vanish at the mid-point, the film is as frustrating as it is compelling. At a certain point the viewer realizes that the mystery is likely not to be solved but the journey is worthwhile.

While not a horror film in the strictest sense, its palpable weirdness and unnerving nature will haunt viewers long after it is over. Lynch initially created the film as a pilot for ABC-TV, and when it was nixed, he reworked the concept and made a feature film with (somewhat) more closure. Breakout performances from Naomi Watts and Justin Theroux add a level of emotion that is often absent from Lynch's surreal work. Humorous showbiz cameos from Billy Ray Cyrus and *Twin Peaks* alums Angelo Badalamenti and Michael J. Anderson add to the dark take on the seedy side of Hollywood.

A Cat in the Brain (1990)

Directed by Lucio Fulci
Written by Lucio Fulci, Giovanni Simonelli, Antonio Tentori
Starring: Lucio Fulci, David L. Thompson

Italian horror director Lucio Fulci (a real-life figure playing himself in the film) has been questioning his sanity due to a series of murders taking place in Rome and visions of sequences from his own horror movies. He contacts a local psychiatrist who agrees to see him and help him deal with the intrusion of his cinematic life on his real one. The psychiatrist turns out to be disturbed, and he goes on a murder spree that is carefully executed in order to make Fulci (and the police) believe that Fulci is the real killer.

A brilliant bit of self-referential horror filmmaking, *A Cat in the Brain* (also known as *Nightmare Concert*) is a clever coda to Fulci's successful film career. Using himself as the focus of a story about the psychological damage that horror imagery can cause, Fulci plays with many of the genre clichés (from hypnotism to the "wrongfully accused man" concept) in this horror version of Fellini's classic film about filmmaking, 8½.

Fulci, a mainstay in the Italian horror movement of the late 1960s through the 1980s, cleverly found a way to utilize footage from his previous films by framing them as flashbacks and fantasy sequences. The wraparound story involving the psychiatrist (shot at the world famous Cinecitta Studios) pushes the threadbare narrative forward, but the film is primarily a love letter to the many fans of Fulci's often graphic genre work.

Behind the Mask: The Rise of Leslie Vernon (2006)

Directed by Scott Glosserman
Written by Scott Glosserman, David J. Stieve
Starring: Nathan Baesel, Robert Englund, Scott Wilson

Taylor Gentry and her camera crew are making a documentary about Leslie Vernon, a hopeful slasher killer who is preparing for his debut in hopes of achieving the same level of recognition of his heroes Freddy and Jason. As Taylor becomes hesitant about the crew's participation in what will be a wholesale slaughter, she decides to try and help the teens escape Leslie's attacks, only to discover that their behavior was factored into Leslie's plans all along. A smart satire on the tropes and clichés of the horror genre that embraces them while subverting them at the same time, *Behind the Mask: The Rise of Leslie Vernon* is an accomplished treatise on horror filmmaking while still remaining frightening and humorous. A disarming lead performance from Nathan Baesel makes Leslie an interesting figure, a likable slasher. The shift from fake documentary to traditional slasher film for the last act is a surprising and effective move, placing the audience into the shoes of the victims.

Leslie Vernon (Nathan Baesel) emerges from the fog in his full costume, ready to embark on the first official slaughter of his slasher career, in the horror-comedy *Behind the Mask: The Rise of Leslie Vernon* (courtesy Scott Glosserman).

After shooting a single short documentary film, Scott Glosserman made this fake documentary his first feature. The script was co-written by agent David J. Stieve, hitting all the classic tropes. Familiar horror faces fill the supporting roles: Robert Englund and Scott Wilson deliver brilliant character turns, and *Poltergeist*'s Zelda Rubinstein makes one of her last film appearances. Numerous references to other horror characters, from *Hellraiser*'s Pinhead to *Halloween*'s Dr. Loomis, are peppered throughout for diehard horror fans.

Other Titles of Interest

Urban Legend: Final Cut (2000), *Halloween: Resurrection* (2002), *Wes Craven's New Nightmare* (1994), *Spliced* (2002), *Popcorn* (1991)

Found Footage Horror

The fake documentary film, frequently referred to as Found Footage when discussed in terms of horror films, is one of the youngest of the subgenres of horror because the fake documentary is the most recently invented genre in the history of film. While many of the other genres, such as westerns and gangster films, date to the late 1800s and early 1900s, and other genres like comedy and drama predate even the creation of film itself, the birth of the fake documentary can be traced back to somewhere around the late 1960s or early 1970s.

It is a young genre because it is driven by the technology that creates it. The documentary film has existed for a very long time, but it was only with the creation of more easily affordable and mobile camera equipment that the idea of pretending to be a documentary became an achievable goal in a film. And since its creation, the world of horror film has changed greatly.

In many ways, the camera has done away with the need for survivors in a story. In previous decades, one of the many victims of a serial killer or monster or other horror conceit needed to survive to the end and escape, so that someone could live on to tell the story of the event, to build it into a mythic horror tale. Now, with the advent of the ever-present and constantly recording camera, there is no need for a person to spread the legend; the camera does all that work, and the people involved in the story can now become what the killer always wanted them to be: victims and nothing more.

The found footage horror film has also been integral in disabusing humanity of the notion that a camera somehow translates to safety or security. Since the creation of the video camera, society has been attempting to use it as a deterrent to violence and crime, thinking that people would not commit heinous acts if they were being recorded because they did not want people to know that they did them. The found footage film has helped to cement what we have suspected all along: that people who are willing to do terrible things to other people are likely not stopped by the presence of a camera. In that way, it has neutered any possible safety or security that the camera once offered. Now the camera is the final witness to the violence, and can do absolutely nothing to stop it.

Elements of the Subgenre

Just a Group of Friends Heading to…: Though there are several ways to set up a found footage horror film, there is no doubt that most of them involve a small group of friends or family members innocently on their way to [insert your mundane event here] when a supernatural event reared its head, and they happened to be recording while it all happened.

The Unfinished Film: Almost as ubiquitous as the "group of friends" aspect of the story is the element of the making of some kind of film, often a documentary. The production of the film-within-a-film was started before anyone realized the full extent of the danger, and the documentary is left incomplete; of course, a whole other film came about as a result of their tragedy.

Recommendations from the Subgenre

Cannibal Holocaust (1980)

Directed by Ruggero Deodato
Written by Gianfranco Clerici
Starring: Robert Kerman, Carl Gabriel Yorke, Francesca Ciardi

An American film crew disappeared in the rainforests of the Amazon while attempting to shoot a documentary about its cannibal tribes. Anthropologist Harold Monroe decides to venture back into the woods to find out what happened to them. He makes a deal with local villagers for reels of film left behind by the film crew. Watching the footage, Harold is horrified to see that the film crew was responsible for the rape of a woman from a cannibal tribe, and that the cannibal tribe hunted them down and took revenge. Though only the last portion of the film qualifies as true found footage, *Cannibal Holocaust* is the most well-known and perhaps notorious example of a fake documentary in the history of horror film. Juxtaposing very convincing gore effects with actual footage of animal slaughter, it builds a sense of *cinéma vérité* realism of the most uncomfortable kind.

Ruggero Deodato was a successful Italian director who had already made several films (including a cannibal film called *Jungle Holocaust*) when he embarked on the making of this controversial project. The film was eventually seized and the moviemakers were charged with obscenity; the director was accused of creating a snuff film. Deodato actually hindered himself in that regard, having asked his lead actors to sign an agreement not to appear in other work for a year after the film, and their absence seemed proof to the public that they had really died during the making of the movie. He was eventually cleared of all charges. *Cannibal Holocaust*'s violence towards animals and the graphic imagery and sexual assaults continue to keep it on a list of banned films in many countries.

A Necessary Death (2008)

Directed and Written by Daniel Stamm
Starring: G.J. Echternkamp, Matthew Tilly

Film student Gilbert decides that, for his first foray into filmmaking, he wants to make something that will get everyone's attention. He looks for a subject who is willing to let him film their last days of life before they commit suicide. When he finds a man dying of a brain tumor, it seems like he is the perfect choice. While shooting the film, Gilbert starts to realize that his desire to capture the film that he set out to make may be having a serious effect on the decisions that his subject is making in real life.

This is a fake documentary so convincing that even screening audiences aware of its fictional nature walked out near the intense ending, *A Necessary Death* is a remarkable accomplishment in capturing fear without resorting to graphic imagery. Gilbert and the dying Matthew have excellent chemistry, and their evolution throughout the shoot is handled with skill and subtlety.

German filmmaker Daniel Stamm wrote and directed short films before making *A Necessary Death* his feature debut. Doing a lot of his own camerawork and writing the script, he brilliantly captures the quiet discomfort and shifting emotions of his subject matter. The film won the Audience Award at the American Film Institute Festival. Stamm's skills in creating an effective false reality helped to win him the job of directing 2010's *The Last Exorcism*. G.J. Echternkamp, who plays Gilbert, also served as the film's producer, and has worked extensively in traditional documentary filmmaking as well.

The Blair Witch Project (1999)

Written and Directed by Eduardo Sánchez, Daniel Myrick
Starring: Heather Donahue, Joshua Leonard, Michael C. Williams

What better way to introduce a film than with the opening text of the film itself: "In October of 1994, three student filmmakers disappeared in the woods near Burkittsville, Maryland, while shooting a documentary. A year later their footage was found." The simplicity of that statement perfectly matches the unsophisticated style and the blunt effectiveness of *The Blair Witch Project*, the fake documentary horror film that changed the course of horror filmmaking. Supposedly unearthed footage of the week-long ordeal of Michael, Joshua, and Heather (actors who played versions of themselves and kept their own names), the film is an example of threadbare production value and conceptual brilliance combining to make a *vérité* horror film unlike anything audiences had experienced. The performances are raw and honest, the footage is stark and beautiful, and the film's answers about the central mystery are effectively ambiguous.

Created as a concept years earlier by directors Sánchez and Myrick, the film hit theaters in 1999 at a time when media were finally reaching the Internet and fandom was becoming mainstream. The success of the film was due in large part to the surefire advertising gimmick (was it real or not?) and its bragging rights about the production cost (likely less than $500,000). The film was the progenitor of the very successful found footage horror movement. There was a not-very-successful sequel, *Book of Shadows: Blair Witch 2*, which the original filmmakers were not involved in making.

Other Titles of Interest

As Above So Below (2014), *June 9* (2008), *Home Movie* (2008), *Atrocious* (2010), *388 Arletta Avenue* (2011), *Troll Hunter* (2010), *Cloverfield* (2008)

Ghost Horror

There's something sad about the idea of ghosts. Human ghosts, that is, rather than spirit entities or other non-corporeal intelligences that haunt us in the physical world. Part of the sadness comes from the realization of one possible afterlife that differs little from our current life.

Cursed to spend eternity wandering around the same house or grounds, unable to touch or interact with anything, barely aware of their own existence outside of the anger and confusion that accompany the meeting of new, living tenants, ghosts inhabit a tragic and forlorn afterlife. Those being plagued by the ghost may have no idea how to rid themselves of it, but in all likelihood the ghost doesn't have any answers, either.

Some ghosts are lucky enough to come in contact with seekers who wish to help them move on to another plane of existence by resolving some unfinished business or allowing some truth to come to light that will finally allow the poor soul to rest in peace; far more frequently, though, it seems as if the answers that the human tenants seek tend to be self-serving plans to simply chase the ghost away. The experience of a ghost is one of an unwanted amnesiac playing out practiced routines in an attempt to give itself meaning, and that is the root of the sadness.

Layered more deeply within that sadness is a commentary on the psychology of humanity as a whole. That we would believe in the idea of something greater than simple biology, a soul or life that can transcend the body and continue on forever, is understandable; that we can think of nothing more interesting for that life to do than to wander around its old home in the same clothes, caught in a sad rhythm of its former life, is depressing because of what it says about the human imagination.

We hope to live on after the moment that our body stops functioning, and that is an almost unfathomable feat of desire that borders on a miracle. That we have a total lack of interest in doing anything other than what are already doing here and now is the revelation that makes it truly tragic.

Elements of the Subgenre

She Doesn't Know She's a Ghost: It is rare that the ghosts in these films ever know that they are ghosts. They never seem to have an awareness of their own deaths. Part of the task of the person afflicted by the haunting is often just convincing them that their life is in fact over and that they have no place in the living world any more, sometimes by burying their remains or solving the mystery of their passing.

Reflections and Flickering Lights: There are certain things all ghosts seem to be drawn to doing. Peeking over the shoulders of people in reflections and then disappearing when they turn to look for them is one of their favorites. The same is true of flickering lights; they love to show up when the lights are dimming, although it's also possible that their arrival is what causes the lights to flicker in the first place.

Recommendations from the Subgenre

Seventh Moon (2008)
Directed by Eduardo Sánchez
Written by Eduardo Sánchez, Jamie Nash
Starring: Amy Smart, Tim Chiou, Dennis Chan

Yul and Melissa, young American honeymooners, arrive in a remote Chinese village during the Hungry Ghosts festival. Here they learn of the legend that in the seventh month, the gates of Hell are opened and the souls of the dead can walk amongst the living. The honeymooners are later caught outside at night after their driver abandons them. They learn that the ghosts hunt the living during their time back in this world, and the two have to try and survive until sunrise.

A visceral, action-driven ghost story, *Seventh Moon* is as exciting as it is original in its use of ghosts as a frightening physical presence. Beautiful Chinese location photography brings a well-needed sense of place to the story, and lead actors Tim Chiou and Amy Smart are likable while still portraying believably ignorant Americans.

Half of the directing team that brought the world *The Blair Witch Project* in 1999, Eduardo Sánchez was already well versed in scaring the viewing public when he made this film. Re-teaming with screenwriter Jamie Nash, with whom he created the tense sci-fi horror film *Altered*, Sanchez created vicious villains in the Hungry Ghosts, an effectively exaggerated version of real Chinese myth. Released through Sam Raimi's Ghosthouse distribution company, the film was unfortunately lost on audiences, but gained a following over the years. Sánchez and Nash worked together again on *Lovely Molly*, *VHS 2*, and *Exists*.

The Eye (2002)

Directed by Danny Pang, Oxide Pang Chun
Written by Danny Pang, Oxide Pang Chun, Yuet-Jan Hui
Starring: Angelica Lee, Lawrence Chou, Jinda Duangtoy

Mun, a blind violinist, gets an eye cornea transplant that gives her back her sight. Mun soon becomes disturbed by haunting visions and images, and decides to find information about the eye donor. She learns that the woman whose eyes she received was a psychic who could see otherworldly images and predict coming disasters, and Mun has now inherited that ability.

Filled to the brim with spooky visuals and clever plot machinations, *The Eye* is a smart horror-thriller that works as much with its emotional content as it does with its scares. It's a supernatural continuation of *Wait Until Dark*, with the blind woman now the recipient of even more terror with the regaining of her sight. Lead actress Angelica Lee finds the right mix of innocence and resolve.

The Pang Brothers (Danny Pang and Oxide Pang Chun) had worked on several features as editors and writers, and had co-directed the action film *Bangkok Dangerous*, when they signed on to make *The Eye*. The film was an international production, using Malaysian and Chinese actors and Thai crew along with the Hong Kong directors. An international success, it was theatrically released in the U.S. The film was remade several times, including an American version with Jessica Alba. The Pang Brothers also made two sequels.

100 Feet (2008)

Directed and Written by Eric Red
Starring: Famke Janssen, Bobby Cannavale, Ed Westwick

Narrowly escaping prison time for killing her abusive police officer husband in self-defense, Marnie Watson is imprisoned in her own New York apartment by an ankle bracelet that won't allow her to stray more than 100 feet. While attempting to adjust to her new life as a single woman under house arrest, she finds romantic interest from a local delivery boy and finds evidence in the house that her husband was a dirty cop. Her new life is shattered by the discovery that her husband's vengeful ghost has taken up residence in the house, torturing her in death as he did in life, with the full knowledge that she has no means of escape. The very definition of a chamber piece, *100 Feet* takes place for 90 of its 96 minutes inside Marnie's nearly empty home. The film effectively taps into the claustrophobia and isolation of the locale.

100 Feet is a visceral thriller that gives a physicality to the supernatural elements. Director Eric Red was well suited for this material after his script work on the vampire tale *Near Dark*. Solid central performances from *Boardwalk Empire*'s Bobby Cannavale and particularly *X-Men* star Famke Janssen elevate an already smart script. Borrowing elements from the film noir genre to build a slow burn mystery reveal about the husband's past, the film does a great job of marrying supernatural dread with real-world suspense.

Other Titles of Interest

The Uninvited (1944 or 2009), *13 Ghosts* (1960), *Dark Water* (2002 and 2005), *Ju-On: The Grudge* (2002), *Pulse* (2001 and 2006), *Stir of Echoes* (1999), *The Fog* (1980 and 2005)

Marnie Watson (Famke Janssen) is a prisoner in her home in the 2008 supernatural thriller *100 Feet* (courtesy Eric Red).

Giallo Horror

Most mainstream film fans are not familiar with Giallo. Perhaps they've heard of the film *Giallo* (though probably only because of the appearance of Academy Award winner Adrien Brody), or they might have stumbled across an article in a film magazine that discussed the influence of Dario Argento and Mario Bava on an entire movement of film in Italy in the 1970s.

Giallo (an Italian word meaning yellow) originated in Italy, and its inspirations were surprisingly widespread. Giallo is the carrier of the torch for certain film traditions, while being the birthplace of others. The onscreen violence and sexuality would lead one to believe that the grindhouse films from America were their primary influence. The irony, of course, is that much of the makeup of the Giallo films came from higher-end and far more artistic sensibilities. In the 1970s, the master of suspense, Alfred Hitchcock, only made two films before his death (*Frenzy* in 1972 and *Family Plot* in 1976). Though his output had slowed from the heyday of his career, his influence was still apparent in films of the day, and it is from there that Giallo took many of its key elements.

Beautiful cinematography, murder mysteries, visually arresting set-pieces and cutting-edge fashions were all aspects of Hitchcock's most well-known works, and Giallo found a life for them all after the director's career slowed down (in tandem with another young American filmmaker, Brian De Palma, who was clearly as influenced by Hitchcock's work as the Italians were). Though there was a tradition of the serial killer film in the 1990s, no one has taken the mantle of the artful suspense-thriller in the same way that Giallo did.

The many elements that Giallo borrowed from Hitchcock show the influence of his work on the Italian film scene in the 1970s, but the elements that the Italians themselves added to the mix brought about the creation of another subgenre. The shockingly graphic death scenes and the frank sexuality—new elements for American audiences seeing these Giallo films for the first time—helped to gain certain filmmakers notoriety, but also led to a less artistic and more money-driven subgenre of film we now call the slasher film.

Combining the first-person perspective of the mystery killer (begun in the Giallo films and seen later in the slashers *Halloween*, *Black Christmas*, and *Friday the 13th*) with the emphasis on death and sexuality, but with less of a focus on the cinematography or fashion (and reducing the virtuoso set-pieces to increasingly graphic gore scenes), the American equivalent of the Giallo did what the American version of any filmic movement does: make more money.

Though Hitchcock's work will always be better remembered, and the slasher films were always more profitable, the Giallo films will have a place in history as the evolutionary middle step between Norman Bates and Michael Myers.

Elements of the Subgenre

The Mysterious Black-Gloved Killer: One of the most common elements of the Giallo is the mystery of the killer's identity. Filmmakers found a way to continue showing the murders without revealing the identity: put black gloves on the hands of the killer so there'd be no clues about gender and skin color identification. That way, they get the best of both worlds: the graphic depictions of victims' deaths, and a slowly building mystery that is never betrayed by costumes or personal appearance.

The Intrepid Investigator: All Giallo films involve a central mystery, and a mystery has to be solved. The Giallo films were smart in that they generally had the investigator as an everyman (or woman) caught up in the murders, rather than the standard police officer. This differentiated the genre from the previous Italian police crime thrillers, called Poliziotteschi.

Recommendations from the Subgenre

Bird with the Crystal Plumage (1970)
Written and Directed by Dario Argento
Starring: Tony Musante, Suzy Kendall, Enrico Maria Salerno

Sam, an American writer staying in Rome with his girlfriend, struggles with writer's block. After he witnesses the attempted murder of a woman in an art gallery, his passport is seized by the police, who know he is an important witness and need to keep him in the country. Sam decides to investigate the attack, which is believed to be connected to a series of other murders in town. As he gets closer to the answer, he finds that the killer is aware of his investigation, and could be targeting his girlfriend as the next victim.

A beautifully shot and daring entry into the relatively new subgenre of Giallo film, *Bird with the Crystal Plumage* helped to codify most of the well-known elements seen in later entries.

Incorporating a last-act twist reveal into the murder investigation, the film breathed new life into the tired crime drama and put the Italian thriller film on the map internationally. The participation of an American (often, an artist) in overseas intrigue became one of the most revisited of the classic Giallo tropes, started here with Tony Musante's stymied writer.

Dario Argento was already a successful film critic and screenwriter (having co-written the script for Sergio Leone's *Once Upon a Time in the West*) when he took this on as his first directing job. Writing the script himself, Argento wisely surrounded himself with industry greats: The music was composed by Ennio Morricone, and the cinematographer was Bertolucci and Coppola collaborator Vittorio Storaro. The film won the Edgar Allan Poe Award for Best Motion Picture, and was critically well-received in Italy and the U.S. Argento went on to create the classic film *Suspiria* and to help George A. Romero produce the zombie sequel *Dawn of the Dead*.

Giallo (2009)

Directed by Dario Argento
Written by Jim Agnew, Dario Argento, Sean Keller
Starring: Adrien Brody, Emmanuelle Seigner, Elsa Pataky

In Turin, Italy, a killer known only as Yellow has been abducting women by inviting them into his taxi, drugging them, and then mutilating their bodies. Detective Avolfi is working to help French stewardess Linda find her sister Celine, recently abducted by Yellow. They discover that Yellow is not just his name, but his description, and they follow an unorthodox investigative method to try and save Linda's sister.

Nearly forty years after he codified the subgenre with his directorial debut, director Dario Argento returned to it with *Giallo*. A film that is as much a knowing nod to the great Giallo films of the past decades as it is an original work, *Giallo* is able to be more direct about its killer's motives than censors would have allowed in the 1970s. In typical fashion for the subgenre, an Italian director is in charge of an international cast that speaks primarily English.

Dario Argento had just completed *Mother of Tears*, the last film in his Three Mothers trilogy, when he started work on this film. Co-writer Sean Keller would go on to write the Nicolas Cage thriller *Rage*. Argento cast Oscar-winning actor Adrien Brody in dual roles as the police inspector and the mysterious killer. Brody was directed to an Oscar in *The Pianist* by Roman Polanski, and in this film, he acts opposite Polanski's wife Emmanuelle Seigner. Two years after her work in *Giallo*, Elsa Pataky joined the cast of the *Fast Five*, becoming a continuing cast member of the highly successful *Fast and the Furious* franchise for two more installments.

Berberian Sound Studio (2012)

Written and Directed by Peter Strickland
Starring: Toby Jones, Cosimo Fusco, Antonio Mancino

Gilderoy, a mild-mannered sound engineer, has come to Italy to work on a film by a respected Italian director. He is surprised to find that the film is a graphically brutal horror-thriller called *The Equestrian Vortex*, but he decides to keep his promise to complete it. The relentless repetition of the images he has to watch begin to get under his skin, leading to a series of strange hallucinations that have him questioning how he even got to the studio in the first place.

A tricky narrative that shifts between various realities as Gilderoy begins to lose track of where he came from and who he is, *Berberian Sound Studio* is a sure-handed thriller that uses skillful manipulation of sound to create a thick and foreboding atmosphere. Toby Jones, known best for his work in the *Hunger Games* film franchise and as the voice of Dobby in the *Harry Potter* films, is a marvelous revelation here, evolving from fastidious and nervous English speaker to cruel taskmaster speaking in fluent Italian. The period detail of the costumes and the Italian sound studio in the 1970s is evocative.

Peter Strickland completed the feature drama *Katalin Varga* before embarking on this film; however, he'd had a practice run on the project, having made a short film version of it in 2005. Cinematographer Nicholas Knowland previously worked on a series of live concerts and music videos, along with the visually stunning Quay Brothers films *Institute Benjamina* and *The Piano Tuner of Earthquakes*. The film won several British Independent Film Awards. Strickland followed up a well-received Giallo film with a psycho-sexual thriller of a similar vein, *The Duke of Burgundy*.

Other Titles of Interest

Deep Red (1975), *A Lizard in a Woman's Skin* (1971), *Don't Torture a Duckling* (1972), *Twitch of the Death Nerve* (1971), *Black Belly of the Tarantula* (1971), *Blood and Black Lace* (1964)

Holiday Horror

No one wants their holidays ruined. Holidays are supposed to be the times that we rest, reflect, and spend time with loved ones. We put up with the minor annoyances of the world on holidays, like our favorite stores being closed and our least favorite family members showing up for a meal and gifts, because everything else about a holiday is great. It's nice to have time off from work (or school), and there's a sense of happiness that tends to unite people.

Why do horror movies always have to ruin the things we love the best?

Horror movies have no interest in what we want or what we like; they are only interested in what we can survive. And though the idea of being stalked and killed by a madman on any day of the year is an unpleasant one, somehow horror movies seem to know that it's that much more of an offense to do it on a holiday. Our days of celebration are sacred, and not just in the religious sense; our governments have made decrees about them and made allowances for anyone who works for our country to take those days for themselves.

These days are our safe inlets from the hustle and bustle of everyday life, the tiny tide pools of joy and calm that remind us why any of the craziness of normal society is worth enduring. And it is for this exact reason that the horror movie loves to attack the holiday.

The expression "adding insult to injury" is an excellent encapsulation of the motivation behind the horror movie obsession with holidays (aside from the obvious desire to brand a killer with a theme and costume that can be revisited many times within a lucrative film franchise). The holiday is a place for happiness and for family, for introspection and a positive outlook on life. The horror movie loves nothing more than irony (except perhaps a good death scene), and there is very little more ironic than the fear and isolation of a horror movie taking place right in the middle of the festivities. The injury may be that you're going to die, but the insult is that all of those presents are going to forever go unopened.

For some reason, we respond to it—perhaps with amusement, perhaps with discomfort, but there is something in it that moves us. The scares and surprises of any day can be effective in a horror film, but there's a little extra something to the bright red of a victim's blood juxtaposed against the merry green of a Christmas sweater.

Elements of the Subgenre

Themed Kills!: Why would you go through all the trouble of coming up with a holiday theme for your film if you weren't going to milk that gimmick for all it was worth, from the set design and costuming to the ridiculous ways that the victims are taken out? From Christmas tree cookie cutters to Halloween masks to a New Year's Eve countdown, anything can be deadly in the hands of the right maniac.

A Bad History with the Day: In the holiday horror genre, the holiday being shown in the film is never the first tragic version of the holiday. The murders being witnessed are inevitably connected to some old tragedies from previous holidays that created a psychological trauma in the killer, and that trauma is being played out on a later holiday that triggers their fury.

Recommendations from the Subgenre

Black Christmas (1974)
Directed by Bob Clark
Written by Roy Moore
Starring: Olivia Hussey, Keir Dullea, Margot Kidder

At the beginning of a college's Christmas break, a group of sorority sisters find themselves plagued by an obscene caller. A man has made his way into their sorority house and has begun targeting the girls, killing them one at a time. As the body count rises and the corpses disappear, it is ultimately pregnant Jess who must face off against the killer all by herself.

When *Black Christmas* was released in 1974, it set a new standard for horror films, in many ways creating the template for the slasher horror film which *Halloween* popularized a few years later. The excellent juxtaposition of cheery holiday parties and decorations against the dark violence hiding in the attic makes for a gripping film that holds up better than its 2006 remake.

Bob Clark, who would later become famous for another memorable holiday film (*A Christmas Story*), used the first-person camera technique to hide the identity of his killer and smartly updated the classic "The call is coming from inside the house" urban legend which was used to similar effect in *When a Stranger Calls*. The film boasts an impressive cast of actors who were all known for iconic performances: Olivia Hussey in *Romeo & Juliet*, Keir Dullea in *2001: A Space Odyssey*, and Margot Kidder in *Superman*. The intentionally ambiguous ending allowed for a sequel that somehow never happened, though rumors persist that the original *Halloween* was secretly intended as a follow-up.

My Bloody Valentine (2009)

Directed by Patrick Lussier
Written by Todd Farmer, Zane Smith, John Beaird, Stephen Miller
Starring: Jensen Ackles, Jaime King, Tom Atkins

On Valentine's Day 1997, six miners are trapped after a cave-in. Six days of searching by a rescue team finds five of them dead and one comatose. A year later, the comatose miner wakes and goes on a rampage, killing several kids partying in the abandoned mine. A decade after that tragedy, the mine owner has just passed away, and the aged survivors of the rampage find that someone else has started killing all over again.

A remake that retains the overall concept of the original, but reworks it for modern audiences, the 2009 *My Bloody Valentine* is an unabashed B-movie that revels in its exploitation roots. Television stars Jensen Ackles (*Supernatural*) and Kerr Smith (*Dawson's Creek*) work well alongside genre veterans Tom Atkins (*The Fog*) and Kevin Tighe (*Rose Red*), and the film's pacing helps to keep audiences focused on what's coming, rather than the questionable plot elements that have just passed.

Patrick Lussier was a longtime collaborator with horror icon Wes Craven, editing many of his films, before getting his chance to direct a theatrical release with the Craven-produced *Dracula 2000*. After two *Dracula* sequels and the direct-to-video *White Noise 2*, Lussier directed this film, a major 3-D release. The darkly humorous script was co-written by Todd Farmer, who previously brought humor to another well-known franchise with *Jason X*. Farmer worked with Lussier again on *Drive Angry*, and he also pops up in a small role in this film as Frank, the sleazy trucker.

Jensen Ackles as Tom Hanniger in the 2009 remake of *My Bloody Valentine* (courtesy Lionsgate Publicity).

Happy Birthday to Me (1981)

Directed by J. Lee Thompson
Written by John C.W. Saxton, Peter Jobin, Timothy Bond
Starring: Melissa Sue Anderson, Glenn Ford, Lawrence Dane

Ginny is a sweet girl, excelling in high school and a member of the "Top Ten," the school's smartest and most successful students. No one would know that she had recently survived a terrible accident that claimed the life of her mother. As Ginny becomes one of the few survivors of a killer who is taking out members of the Top Ten, she works to regain some of her lost memories from before the accident in the hopes of remembering some secret that might save her life.

Embracing the elaborate death scenes and multiple twist revelations of the still-new slasher subgenre, as well as their tendency to focus on special occasions as their backdrop, *Happy Birthday to Me* is an effective continuation of those themes. Lead actress Melissa Sue Anderson, just off her successful television run on *Little House on the Prairie*, does well in the role of the memory-challenged Virginia, and her scenes with classic marquee star Glenn Ford give the film its best moments.

The slasher film was gaining notoriety, as was evidenced by the fact that respected director J. Lee Thompson (who made the original *Cape Fear* and two entries in the *Planet of the Apes* series) signed on to make this movie. The script was rewritten several times, including during the shooting, and many of the film's clues seem to point to the original ending, with Virginia killing while possessed by the spirit of her dead mother. Producers John Dunning and Andre Link were so aware of the popularity of the holiday gimmick while shooting this film that when it wrapped, they almost immediately began production on *My Bloody Valentine*.

Other Titles of Interest

April Fool's Day (1986 and 2008), *Easter Bunny Kill Kill* (2006), *Memorial Day* (1999), *Silent Night Deadly Night* (1984), *Mother's Day* (1980 and 2010), *New Year's Evil* (1980)

Humans Hunting Humans Horror

Many of the advancements humanity has made have their roots in the desire to be the first to reach the top of a quickly narrowing pyramid of superiority. But with dominance comes a level of complacency. The dark beating heart of the hunter still resides in us, not satisfied to follow the unnecessary parts of ancient man's psyche into the rubbish bin of evolution. Their very instincts were for survival and dominance, and they are not easily quelled. The boredom and listlessness of modern life, the lack of challenge to simply stay alive, pushes people to pursue socially acceptable pastimes such as game hunting, martial arts, and paintball battles.

But the true goal of what they're striving for in those activities, the thrill of possible injury or death, the true and total domination of another creature, are hampered by things like safety gear, rules and regulations, and weaponry that takes the challenge of survival away.

The only true challenge to the cunning of a human is the cunning of another human. Often in horror stories, the struggle exists between two individuals. That is further sharpened in the humans hunting humans subgenre, because roles are assigned by the hunter, not by nature. The hunter, often a wealthy person or a domineering social structure, makes the decision and the boundaries for the competition, often with seemingly insurmountable odds.

This dynamic, of the wealthy hunters who have achieved, acquired, or consumed everything legal and reasonable to that point, and needing to venture into the realm of human hunting to quench a darker need, creates a class dynamic of haves versus have-nots, a story as old as the class system itself.

And therein lies the true desire of the hunter: not to be back in his savage state, spending his days trying to survive by killing when he has to, but to be strong enough and cunning enough that he stands even outside his own species. That he, as a human, has achieved something more than the rest of his species; that he has combined the savagery of ancient man and the technology, cunning, and intelligence of modern man to create something more than man itself.

The genre has been alive and well since the adaptation of the story *The Most Dangerous Game* (mentioned below), and has popped up in places as varied and unusual as the futuristic Ray Liotta film *No Escape* and the John Leguizamo comedy *The Pest*.

Elements of the Subgenre

Wealthy and Powerful Hunters: It is almost dictated by the confines of the genre that a wealthy and powerful figure (or organization) would be the ones doing the hunting (or at the very least, doing the facilitating of the people hunting each other). Whether it be governments, multinational entertainment companies, or billionaire playboys looking for dangerous adventure, the ones orchestrating the hunt will have deep pockets and vast resources, which makes the challenge all the more difficult for the individuals being hunted.

Ingenuity in a Pinch: The hunted always seem to find some way to utilize cleverness, previous intelligence about unrelated material, and unconventional weapons and methods, to gain an advantage. A man who likes to go outdoor camping suddenly finds his survival skills in great demand; a college graduate remembers from a science class that the liquid from a certain plant is an effective neurotoxin; and the list goes on, as the hunted becomes determined to use their one unbreakable weapon, intelligence, to help even the odds.

Changing the Game: The event the audience witnesses this time around isn't just business as usual; someone wants to create an uprising, fight the power, alter the rules, or take down the whole system. Part of the appeal of the subgenre is for audiences to connect with the underdog, and for them to have a chance of not only surviving themselves, but of making it possible for others to survive as well.

Recommendations from the Subgenre

The Most Dangerous Game (1932)
Directed by Irving Pichel, Ernest B. Schoedsack
Written by James Ashmore Creelman (based on the story by Richard Connell)
Starring: Joel McCrea, Fay Wray, Leslie Banks

Based on the 1924 short story by Richard Connell, *The Most Dangerous Game* tells the story of shipwreck survivors who find themselves on a private island. The owner, Count Zaroff, makes clear his plans to use the survivors as prey, to be released on the island so he can hunt them down. Beautiful black and white cinematography and stunning locations balance out a surprisingly dark story for its time, one that pushed the boundaries of pre–Hays Code Hollywood by having Zaroff find his fate sealed when (spoiler alert) he is devoured by his own ravenous hunting dogs. As this film is the progenitor of all the other films in the subgenre, its impact is diminished slightly by what has come since (including a 1945 remake of the film by the same studio, *A Game of Death*), and by the limitations of the time; however, the film still holds up as a classic of the subgenre and a great example of filmmaking of the period.

An impressive level of talent was involved in bringing the tale to life on the big screen. It was written by James Ashmore Creelman and directed by Ernest B. Schoedsack, filmmakers who already had an impressive résumé when they embarked on this project (and who also united to create one of the most well-known films of all time, *King Kong*). The cast boasted scream queen Fay Wray, with *Sullivan's Travels* star Joel McCrea in the heroic lead and Hitchcock regular Leslie Banks as the villainous hunter Zaroff. This film gained notoriety years later when lines were used as parts of the Zodiac Killer's messages sent to newspapers (chronicled in the 2007 David Fincher film *Zodiac*).

Shipwreck survivor Bob (Joel McCrea) confronts Count Zaroff (Leslie Banks), the villainous owner of the island on which he has landed, in 1932's *The Most Dangerous Game*.

Battle Royale (2000)

Directed by Kinji Fukasaku
Written by Kenta Fukasaku (based on the story by Koushun Takami)
Starring: Tatsuya Fujiwara, Aki Maeda, Takeshi Kitano

In a near-future world, the population is kept in check by having classes of Japanese children sent to a battlefield to kill each other until there is only one child left. *Battle Royale* pulls no punches with its subject matter. Weapons are handed out (some of the humor of the film comes in the disparity between their weapons), rules and boundaries are given, and neck collars with explosives are attached to all the children. Then the three-day melee begins, and if they don't whittle themselves down in three days, they all die.

Brutal, frightening, bizarrely humorous, and unflinching in its portrayals, the movie is a dystopian vision from respected career writer-director Kinji Fukasaku (known by American audiences primarily for the *Battle Royale* films and the arthouse entry *Rampo*). Cult director-actor Takeshi Kitano (*Sonatine, Johnny Mnemonic*) appears at the beginning of the film as an instructor, and the shocking culmination of his talk sets the tone for the entire film. The movie was highly influential on Quentin Tarantino, who cast *Battle Royale* actress Chiaki Kuriyama as a deadly assassin in his action-revenge film *Kill Bill*. *Battle Royale* has often been credited with being the inspiration for *The Hunger Games*. Director Fukasaku died during the making of the sequel and his son Kenta stepped in to finish the filming.

Deathsport (1978)

Directed by Allan Arkush, Nicholas Niciphor
Written by Nicholas Niciphor, Donald E. Stewart
Starring: David Carradine, Claudia Jennings, Richard Lynch

Deathsport explores a futuristic world where prison inmates have to fight for their freedom in a dangerous bloodsport game on "destructo-cycles." One of the players, David Carradine, decides to escape the games with the help of a female guide, but the other players won't make it easy for them. Navigating mine fields, Death Machines, other riders, and mutant cannibals, they make their way across an apocalyptic landscape to save the guide's missing child.

The film's origins are almost as interesting as the film itself. Producer Roger Corman, king of the B-films, had a model of learning about advance buzz for an upcoming hit movie release, and then making a quick and cheap knock-off to cash in on the popularity much in the same way that the modern production company The Asylum works, with films like *Transmorphers* and *Paranormal Entity*. This was his method in creating *Death Race 2000*, a futuristic racing movie modeled on the big-budget studio release *Rollerball*. Interestingly, *Death Race 2000* did good business and Corman decided to rip himself off by creating *Deathsport*. Genre mainstays David Carradine (who was also in *Death Race*) and Richard Lynch were joined by Playmate and actress Claudia Jennings in one of her last performances before a tragically young death. The film never attained the cult status of its predecessor, due in large part to its hectic plot and pacing (director Allan Arkush was brought in to replace the original director, a first timer who never directed another film). *Deathsport* has largely been forgotten outside of exploitation cinema arenas.

Series 7: The Contenders (2001)

Written and Directed by Daniel Minahan
Starring: Brooke Smith, Mark Woodbury, Michael Kaycheck

Series 7: the Contenders is framed as a marathon of episodes of a very popular reality television series in the near future where regular people are given the chance to win money by killing off their competitors. It is both satirical and touching in its portrayal of America's obsession with violence and media, and the lives that are ruined in the wake of that pursuit. Combining commentary about media consumption with an Orwellian outlook on our collective controlled future, the film balances the dark absurdity of the games themselves with compelling human stories from the contestants (including the heartbreaking reunion of former lovers who are now pitted against one another in the game). Cleverly reinventing the subgenre by showing hunting as no longer a taboo and hidden practice, but now a popular and beloved game show that audiences flock to in record numbers, the movie has some important commentary regarding the state of entertainment in the new millennium. However, the filmmaker effectively keeps the commentary from intruding on what is an excellent and surprising low-budget action-drama.

Director Minahan went on to a successful television career, directing great HBO series like *Game of Thrones*, *True Blood*, and *Deadwood*. The film is a clever conceit, and an incredibly strong central performance from Brooke Smith as the pregnant returning champion anchors the emotion of the premise. The film came out in 2001 after the premieres of *The Real World* and *Survivor*, but before the glut of reality programming took over the majority of cable and network television, and its prescience regarding the depths to which a series will go in order to get viewership is spot-on.

Other Titles of Interest

The Running Man (1987), *Hard Target* (1993), *The Woman Hunt* (1972), *Bloodlust* (1961), *I Come in Peace* (1990)

Infection Horror

All of us are afraid to die, that is certain. But if we were forced to choose how we died, it is a safe bet to say that no one would pick dying from an infectious disease. There are some things worse than death, and that is one of them.

Becoming infected by a debilitating and ravaging disease isn't just another way to die; it's the slowest and most miserable way that humanity knows of to naturally die (meaning, without the aid of another human doing horrible, torturous things to you). With a disease, it isn't enough that you're dying; it's also the indignity of having your body betray you, as you are conscious enough to see it happening. Normal functions go awry, and no matter what you say or do, it's going to keep heading inexorably towards death.

To add insult to the injury, this indignity becomes coupled with enforced isolation. Any virulent disease horrible enough to exist in a horror film is most likely 100 percent contagious and 100 percent fatal. Which means that, if you contract it, the best you can hope for is to be left alone for the rest of your unpleasant life; but the greater likelihood is that you'll be starved or beaten, and then have your body disposed of in some way involving fire. It really doesn't get more horrible than that.

We don't spend much time in our lives angry at diseases, wondering what they have against us. We believe them to be doing simply what is in their nature, continuing to spread their microscopic offspring into further parts of a single body, and out to other bodies. It seems to be action without malice, a creature only doing what it knows.

The disease, however, has more in common with the slasher killer than one would expect, at least in the world of horror films. The same group of young teenagers may go to an old cabin or an abandoned hospital to hang out and drink beer, and none of them are expecting to be dead before the weekend is over. Whether by machete to the face or through the liquidation of internal organs, the slasher and the disease have the same goal in mind: killing off the group, one by one. The victims are unaware and helpless, and until one of them figures out how to fight back (with a weapon or a last-second visit to an emergency room), there is no escape.

Diseases may not have personalities or higher thinking, they may not plot your demise with pleasure; but they do want you dead, because that is what they do. And while what they do may not be personal, it is absolutely intentional.

Elements of the Subgenre

Someone Has It, But They're Not Telling: No one wants an infected person in their group, because it raises the likelihood of infection spread; but no one wants to be the person who is kicked *out* of the group for being infected. The terror of being left alone while dying of a degenerative disease is often a strong enough fear that people will keep the knowledge of their own infection hidden, even though they are always found out and they have usually infected someone else because of it.

Ravaging the Human Body: It wouldn't be an infection horror movie if the audience wasn't required to watch in disturbing detail as a human being's body shuts down on-screen: vomiting, weight loss, burst blood vessels, hacking cough, loss of hair (and hair growth in strange places), and insanity.

Recommendations from the Subgenre

The Crazies (1973)
Directed by George A. Romero
Written by Paul McCollough, George A. Romero
Starring: Lane Carroll, Harold Wayne Jones, Will MacMillan

The residents of tiny Evans City, Pennsylvania, are worried about their safety after a series of violent events have plagued the town. The events were precipitated by a chemical spill from a military plane crash which contaminated the water and has the locals acting crazed. While trying to escape the infected people and avoid the military quarantine of the town, they discover that planes with nuclear weapons will destroy everything if the infection gets out of hand.

Riding high off the governmental paranoia witnessed during Watergate, *The Crazies* combined that foreboding sense of mistrust with continuing fears of biological warfare to make a powerful story of survival. A smart script paints the everyman leads as societal back-bones (nurses, firemen, ex-soldiers), juxtaposing them against compassionless troops and helpless scientists. The revelation of the town's final fate is all the more frightening because it is unfortunately a plausible outcome.

George A. Romero had already become world-famous for his work on *Night of the Living Dead*, and had revisited the horror arena once with *Season of the Witch*, before making this film that hearkens back to many of *Living Dead*'s worldwide catastrophe themes. Working from an original script by Paul McCollough, which dealt primarily with the outbreak and survival, Romero expanded the element of the military presence. Bill Hinzman, remembered well as the cemetery zombie in Romero's first film, returned here as one of the crazies and also served as director of photography. The film's title was changed from the original (and not very scary) *Code Name: Trixie*.

Carriers (2009)

Written and Directed by David Pastor, Alex Pastor
Starring: Lou Taylor Pucci, Chris Pine, Piper Perabo

In the near future, a deadly virus spreads across the world and wipes out the majority of the population. Two brothers and their girlfriends decide to make the dangerous journey to a motel on an isolated beach so they can hole up and wait for the disease to run its course with the rest of the world. On the journey, they struggle with near exposure to the disease, attacks from other survivors, and tough decisions about leaving loved ones behind.

Equal parts infection horror, road film, and relationship drama, *Carriers* is a surprisingly affecting story of familial bonds tested by the ravages of disease. Pucci and Pine have an excellent and believable rapport as brothers, but Christopher Meloni and Kiernan Shipka as the father and infected daughter inject the film with its strongest emotional impact. The story is clearly influenced by the work of Stephen King, in particular the short story "Night Surf," an outbreak tale which exists in the same world as his book *The Stand*.

Having previously worked in Spanish television and short films, the sibling directing team of Alex and David Pastor made this their first feature film. Though it was shot in 2006, it wasn't released until 2009, to capitalize on the new fame of lead actor Pine in the *Star Trek* re-launch. Four years later, the brothers worked on another thoughtful and unique outbreak film, the award-winning *The Last Days*. Actress Kiernan Shipka later found television success as Don Draper's oldest child on *MadMen*.

REC (2007)

Directed by Jaume Balagueró, Paco Plaza
Written by Jaume Balagueró, Luiso Berdejo, Paco Plaza
Starring: Manuela Velasco, Ferran Terraza, Jorge-Yamam Serrano

Television reporter Angela Vidal and her cameraman Pablo are doing a straightforward documentary about the night crew of a local Barcelona fire station. The station receives a call about an elderly woman trapped inside her apartment, and the film crew follows them to the complex. They discover that the old woman is very sick, along with other tenants, and everyone inside is immediately quarantined, including Angela and Pablo. As the danger of the infection turns violent, Angela attempts to find a way out of the building. A relentless thriller made disturbingly realistic because of its dogged determination to conform exactly to the rules and style of actual news camera footage, *REC* is a Spanish-language horror film that became an international phenomenon. A smart script takes advantage of a low budget to set nearly the entire film inside a single apartment building, allowing an epic outbreak to take place on a small scale. Though hidden behind the camera for most of the film, Pablo Rosso as the cameraman is a great companion to Manuela Velasco's determined reporter.

Jaume Balagueró and Paco Plaza had previously worked in horror (Plaza directed *Romasanta: The Werewolf Hunt* and Balagueró made *The Nameless*) when they teamed up to make the documentary *OT: la película*; using that experience helped them to create the reality of this film. The film was remade for American audiences as *Quarantine* (changing the explanation of the disease from spiritual to medical in origin), which was successful and spawned a direct-to-DVD sequel. However, the original series had such loyal fandom that it has since garnered three additional entries in the series, two of which bring back Manuela Velasco and one of which is a darkly comic prequel.

Other Titles of Interest

Warning Sign (1985), *Rabid* (1977), *Salvage* (2009), *The Stuff* (1985), *Infection* (2005), *Shivers* (1975)

Invisible Being Horror

The fear of an invisible antagonist certainly makes sense on its surface. From a strictly pragmatic point of view, someone who can move through the world unseen by others is a formidable foe for a host of reasons: An attack could come at any moment, there is no place guaranteed to be safe, and it is nearly impossible to form a plan of defense because you never know whether or not the invisible intruder is standing nearby and listening.

Beyond the difficulties of dealing with an invisible entity, there are also the psychological factors to take into consideration. These resonate strongly and make the invisible being subgenre a prolific one.

There is a level of violation inherent in the idea of an invisible person (or creature) invading your space. That violation can take the form of small and frightening moments (such as noises in the silence or the fog of breath on a pane of glass) as well as violent encounters (varying from being knocked unconscious to being sexually assaulted to being outright murdered). With an invisible foe, there is never a time when you are allowed to feel safe, except for the false safety a victim feels before they're aware of the fact that an invisible foe exists. The power of the invisible creature is that, by the very nature of its abilities, the victim can never be sure if it is in the room with them. In a way, that means it always is.

Perhaps the greatest victim of the invisible foe is that of privacy. In a world that has slowly and quietly been losing its privacy since the invention of technologies which capture reality for posterity (from still images to moving pictures), the invisible villain can also be seen as simply a voyeur, taking away the only moments that we ever truly have to ourselves. Like hidden cameras recording your most private moments, the invisible creature doesn't actually have to attack you in order to violate you. The mere awareness on the part of the invisible voyeur's victim, the knowledge that their most private thoughts and actions have been played out in front of an unknown audience, is enough to cause the kind of emotional damage and fear to which any real-life victim can relate.

Elements of the Subgenre

Secret Nudity: In most of these stories, it is only the person's body which has become invisible, and not their clothing. So it stands to reason that, if a person is running around on the screen and you can't see them, then they must be naked. It was particularly an insinuation of old Hays Code films, when actual nudity was not permitted on screen.

The Dent in the Chair: When a character is invisible, the audience is as clueless about their presence and location as the characters in the story. But a smart filmmaker finds ways to hint to the viewer about their presence with close-ups on things like depressions in chairs or handprints on tables.

Recommendations from the Subgenre

The Invisible Man (1933)

Directed by James Whale
Written by R.C. Sherriff (based on the novel by H.G. Wells)
Starring: Claude Rains, Gloria Stuart, William Harrigan

A mysterious man, his head bandaged, arrives in a Sussex inn to rent a room in which he wishes to be left entirely alone. The man is Dr. Jack Griffin, and he is hiding a secret: He discovered a formula to turn things invisible, and used it on himself. Struggling with his sanity due to the physical changes and because of the volatility of the ingredients in his formula, Griffin begins murdering and terrorizing the police, his loved ones, and total strangers in a bid to dominate the world. A new science-tinged horror entry in the Universal canon to stand alongside *Frankenstein*, *The Invisible Man* is an exciting film with visual effects that were ahead of their time and still dazzle today. In his first major performance on film, Claude Rains is a force to be reckoned with, playing a formidable villain while acting through face-obscuring bandages or performing as nothing more than a bodiless voice.

James Whale had already brought the seminal *Frankenstein* (1931) to the screen when he returned to horror film for the third time; his second horror film, 1932's *The Old Dark House*, is a classic of the genre in which he worked with *Invisible Man* star Gloria Stuart for the first time. Whale collected collaborators as he worked, and he brought comic actress Una O'Connor from this film along with him to *Bride of Frankenstein* (1935). The special effects, including covering the background and the actor in black velvet to simulate invisibility, were brilliant in their practical simplicity. Rains suffered from claustrophobia, and several of his shots were completed by a double.

Hollow Man (2000)

Directed by Paul Verhoeven
Written by Gary Scott Thompson, Andrew W. Marlowe
Starring: Elisabeth Shue, Kevin Bacon, Josh Brolin

Scientist Sebastian Caine has made a breakthrough that could change the world: the ability to turn living creatures invisible. He volunteers for the human trials himself, but it is later revealed that reverting back to visibility is not yet possible. While awaiting his fate in quarantine (and learning that his ex-girlfriend Linda is now dating one of his fellow doctors), Sebastian begins to lose his grip on reality. He escapes, raping his neighbor and killing the head of the research program, after which he decides to get revenge on Linda. A reinvention of *The Invisible Man* for the modern age, *Hollow Man* utilized nearly seventy years of advancing film technology to vividly capture the classic "science gone wrong" story. Starring Kevin Bacon, who (unlike Claude Rains) had to show up every day of shooting naked and painted green, the film treats the vanished scientist as even more dangerous and frightening than the original, raping and murdering with impunity.

Paul Verhoeven was a respected Dutch filmmaker who had already made the fantastical *RoboCop* and *Starship Troopers* before tackling this big-budget spectacle. Verhoeven worked with Alec Gillis and Tom Woodruff to create effects as stunning as the giant bugs they made for *Starship Troopers*; the effects were nominated for an Oscar. It was the last American film for Verhoeven before returning to his home country to make *Black Book*. Screenwriter Andrew Marlowe went on to create the popular television detective series *Castle*. A thinly connected direct-to-DVD sequel was released six years after the original.

Memoirs of an Invisible Man (1992)

Directed by John Carpenter
Written by Robert Collector, Dana Olsen, William Goldman (based on the story by H.F. Saint)
Starring: Chevy Chase, Daryl Hannah, Sam Neill

Stock analyst Nick Halloway tries to sleep off a hangover in the bathroom of a laboratory where a shareholder's meeting is taking place. The building's computer malfunctions and causes a meltdown. The building is evacuated, except for the sleeping Nick, and he wakes up to find that he has been rendered invisible. When a CIA agent discovers that a living human survived the explosion, he decides to try and capture and recruit him to be a spy-assassin.

An unusual hybrid of science fiction suspense, special effects razzle-dazzle, and physical comedy, *Memoirs of an Invisible Man* is a strange but fascinating experiment. With several great supporting actors like Sam Neill, Michael McKean, and Stephen Tobolowsky, it's a shame none of them were given the lead role that Chevy Chase sleepwalks through. The visual effects are stunning throughout, with particular standouts being the aftermath of the meltdown that causes his exposure and the images of food traveling through his invisible body.

John Carpenter returned to the studio system with this film after working on the indie projects *Prince of Darkness* and *They Live*. Original screenwriter William Goldman and original director Ivan Reitman both left the project, reportedly due to disagreements with star Chase. In one of only a handful of scores not composed by Carpenter himself, Shirley Walker acquits herself nicely; they worked together again on *Escape from L.A.* and she created the iconic music for *Final Destination*. Carpenter also dropped his usual *John Carpenter's* above the title, knowing that a studio film would never allow him total creative freedom. His instincts were correct, as the watered-down studio version was poorly received by audiences and critics.

Other Titles of Interest

Invisible Avenger (1958), *Invisible Invaders* (1959), *The League of Extraordinary Gentlemen* (2003), *The Amazing Transparent Man* (1960)

Literary Horror

It is almost certainly not a coincidence that horror stories are, on the whole, narrative fiction stories. While there are true-life stories that are harrowing and violent and would seem to fit the description of horror, most of those films are not truly horror films. There is something that keeps us from calling them horror, as if the word "horror" is reserved for something so unreal that to call a true story a horror story would trivialize the true story and betray the definition of horror.

President Franklin D. Roosevelt, in his first inaugural speech, spoke the famous line "The only thing we have to fear is fear itself." The simplicity of those words betrays the complexity of the theory behind it. In any circumstance where a human being feels fear, he does so because the fear has been focused on an object (for example, a disease or a stock market crash); however, in almost every case of human fear, the feeling of fear comes before or after the actual circumstance that the person finds frightening. When we're in the midst of something that scares us (a car crash or a fistfight), we have relatively little time to be aware of anything beyond the immediate biological response to danger: It is "fight or flight." It is only before an event, as we imagine what *could* happen, or after an event, when we remember what *did* happen, that we are fearful.

That is because fear is a product of reflection, and it is why horror exists almost primarily as a creation of story. We do not think of the events of our lives as fodder for horror, no matter how bad they get; it is only a story, manipulated in various ways to do certain things to the psychology of a person, that creates horror. Horror is not something that exists in nature, but a thing we have created ourselves.

That is why the idea of literary horror crops up so often. The birthplace of horror is the story, created by the storyteller and committed to words, pages, or celluloid. Given that the written word is the most ubiquitous form of mass communication in the history of mankind, it certainly makes sense that many horror stories would have reverence for their origins. And in a genre where the better scare is almost always when you don't see the monster, it helps to have a figure at the typewriter, building a better monster in your mind than the filmmaker could ever put on screen.

Elements of the Subgenre

The Story They Can't Crack: Writers are constantly writing, but in the literary horror subgenre, it is the story they *can't* write that is often the focus. Some story is plaguing them, something they can't quite get right or that is too personal to tell or perhaps even a story that begins to take on a life of its own.

Just Like My Most Recent Novel: Writers will often get wrapped up in supernatural mysteries or murder investigations because something about the events described are eerily similar to a passage written in one of their own stories. The investigation begins in order to clear their names regarding possible involvement in a murder or any accusation of plagiarism.

Recommendations from the Subgenre

Misery (1990)

Directed by Rob Reiner
Written by William Goldman (based on the story by Stephen King)
Starring: James Caan, Kathy Bates, Richard Farnsworth

Romance novelist Paul Sheldon, on his way home from a snowy cabin retreat where he has written a very personal book about his life, has a car accident. He awakens to find that he is severely injured but has been rescued by Annie, a simple woman in a country house and a huge fan of his work. As he heals, Paul discovers that Annie is more than a fan; she is obsessed with him and his work, and will use violent means to get him to stay with her and continue writing stories about her favorite character of his, Misery Chastain. A fantastic battle of wills plays out within the cozy confines of a remote cabin in *Misery*, a chamber piece full of psychological terror and punctuated violence. Though she'd been acting for over fifteen years, Kathy Bates' performance earned her an Oscar and launched her to stardom, while James Caan got to play against his standard tough guy persona.

Rob Reiner had already made successful comedies (*When Harry Met Sally*), dramas (*Stand by Me*), and fantasies (*The Princess Bride*) when he made this his first horror film. It's the only Stephen King work ever to win an Oscar. Many members of the creative team returned to his material again in their careers: Bates played the lead in *Dolores Claiborne*, and writer William Goldman scripted *Hearts in Atlantis* and *Dreamcatcher*. The claustrophobic cinematography is thanks to Barry Sonnenfeld, longtime Coen Brothers collaborator and visually inventive director of *Get Shorty* and *Men in Black*.

Naked Lunch (1991)

Written and Directed by David Cronenberg (based on the story by William S. Burroughs)
Starring: Peter Weller, Judy Davis, Ian Holm

Writer William Lee's drug abuse is so bad that he hallucinates his typewriter coming to life as a large insect that gives him secret missions. After accidentally shooting his wife in the head during an attempt to reproduce William Tell's famous apple routine, he flees the law and hides out in a place called Interzone. Unsure of what is real and what is not, William finds himself wrapped up with another woman named Joan who is the spitting image of his deceased wife. When he tries to make his escape from Interzone, the entire nightmarish story begins to fold back in on itself. A translation of the title novel, a meta-narrative about the writing of it, and a hyper-stylized retelling of some of the events in the author's actual life, *Naked Lunch* is a nearly indescribable film based on a seemingly unfilmable story. Peter Weller and Judy Davis are excellent in their complex and confusing lead roles (Davis has two), but the "bugs" in the story are nearly as compelling, their effects and personalities remarkably realistic in a strange and captivating way.

David Cronenberg was no stranger to warped clinical psychology and insect creepiness, having directed *The Fly* and *Dead Ringers* before working on this film. He scripted the movie from Burroughs' book, and re-teamed with *Dead Ringers* cinematographer Peter Suschitzky to create the surreal world of Interzone. (Cronenberg and Suschitzky have worked together eleven times.) Beat poetry buffs will note that several of the characters in the story are stand-ins for many of Burroughs' writing contemporaries like Allen Ginsberg and Jack Kerouac.

In the Mouth of Madness (1994)
Directed by John Carpenter
Written by Michael De Luca
Starring: Sam Neill, Julie Carmen, Jurgen Prochnow

Insurance investigator John Trent is hired by a book publisher to look into the disappearance of Sutter Cane, an immensely popular horror novelist. Finding clues in the covers of Cane's previous books, he creates a map that takes him to a small New England town right out of Cane's books. Trent tries to leave to report his findings, but is unable to find his way out. He eventually finds Cane, who tries to convince Trent that he is in fact just a character from one of Cane's books.

Framing the whole story as a flashback tale told by an asylum-bound John, *In the Mouth of Madness* plays as a fevered remembrance of events not long past (or that may never have happened). With Sam Neill in the role of the skeptical detective, the film is a horror noir that enjoys twisting back over its own path and re-interpreting events from multiple perspectives, leaving the audience as confused as the investigator.

John Carpenter took a break from the action and effects of *They Live* and *Memoirs of an Invisible Man* to return to the thoughtful moodiness of *Prince of Darkness* for this film. With a script by well-known New Line producer Michael De Luca, Carpenter uses the proceedings to comment on horror art, the public's perception of it, and popular figures such as Stephen King (though many of its creatures are closer to H.P. Lovecraft's work). Before Carpenter signed on to direct it, both Tony Randel (*Hellbound: Hellraiser 2*) and Mary Lambert (*Pet Sematary*) were attached to the script, which had been around since the late 1980s.

Other Titles of Interest

Sinister (2012), *The Shining* (1980), *The Dark Half* (1993), *In a Lonely Place* (1950), *The Ghost Writer* (2010), *The Man from Elysian Fields* (2001)

Modern Zombie Horror

The modern incarnation of the zombie was created in equal parts by George A. Romero's *Night of the Living Dead* and the deluge of living dead inspirations and ripoffs that came about in the wake of that seminal film's popularity. This is one of the rare instances of a movie monster being entirely reinvented, and having that reinvention last longer than the initial incarnation did.

The reason is likely because of what zombies represent: *everything*. Zombies are the great malleable monster of our time, a creature so devoid of personality that we can paint any meaning we like on them, political or religious, environmental or psychological, and march them across the screen to carry our message. The absence of an agenda forces the audience (and the film's creators) to look within themselves and find the truth.

They began, in Romero's time, as a stepping stone monster that took us from the manufactured and relatively safe evil of the Universal-era monsters and ushered us into the uncomfortable and darkly realistic human killers that sprang up in the independent grindhouse horror films of the 1970s. Zombies were once human, and then became monsters, and it was our acceptance of them that led to our eventual recognition that a person could be a monster *before* they turned into a zombie.

And ever since then, they have stood as slowly moving monuments to whatever all-too-human fear we have faced after that: the rampant spread of disease (the AIDS epidemic explosion of the 1980s led to an upsurge of imported Italian zombie films), terrorism (the frighteningly empty streets of an abandoned London in *28 Days Later*), military overreach and chemical warfare (the chemical spill and cover-up of *Return of the Living Dead*) and financial collapse (the hilarious consumer greed on display in the original *Dawn of the Dead*).

Along with the reinvention of the zombie, Romero also brought other elements that have become synonymous with films about hordes of the undead: small groups of human beings attempting to survive the outbreak, only to fail because of their inability to deal with each other; set piece locations that speak ironically to the theme of the movie; and dark, nihilistic endings that stand in contrast to the hopeful endings of generations before. The only "happily ever after"s in these worlds are the satisfied groans of a well-fed zombie.

Elements of the Subgenre

It Spreads by Bite: Though there have been many changes in the history of the zombie, from moving slow to moving fast and from moaning to talking, one element of the zombie mythos remains the same: being a zombie is some kind of disease, and it spreads by bite. It might be a virus, or an alien presence, or even a demonic influence, but they all travel the same way.

The Government Is Over: Almost as common as the zombie threat itself is the total collapse of the government. Nothing resembling a cohesive modern political structure ever survives the initial outbreak, and societies become violent, driven now by individual need and conquest rather than the desire to work together and build something better.

Recommendations from the Subgenre

Fido (2006)

Directed by Andrew Currie
Written by Robert Chomiak, Andrew Currie, Dennis Heaton
Starring: Billy Connolly, Dylan Baker, Carrie-Anne Moss

In an alternate version of 1950s America, zombies rise from the grave only to be defeated, subdued, and turned into a servant class. Small-town couple Helen and Bill buy a pet zombie

Obedient zombie pet Fido (Billy Connolly) helps with yard work in the 2006 horror-comedy *Fido* (courtesy Lionsgate Publicity).

named Fido for their son Timmy. When Fido breaks loose of his electronic control collar and kills a neighbor, the villainous Zomcom security force takes Fido away in order to keep the community safe. But Timmy is unwilling to give up on his pet that easily, and he mounts a rescue mission to get Fido back. A satire of American family values, slavery, runaway animal films, and the atomic age, *Fido* is a fun exercise in taking a horror premise to its furthest comedic possibility. Playing the roles to deadpan perfection, Dylan Baker and Henry Czerny are hilariously sincere, and Billy Connolly does a great deal with a wordless lead performance. Impressive set and costume design vividly bring the *faux* '50s world to life.

Andrew Currie had already directed the Canadian dramatic thriller *Mile Zero* and two made-for-television films when he began working on this movie. Playwright and *O Brother, Where Art Thou?* star Tim Blake Nelson has a small but fun role. The film is clearly influenced as much by the melodramas of filmmaker Douglas Sirk as it is by shows like *Lassie* and *Rin Tin Tin*. Co-writer Dennis Heaton also created the short-lived Lifetime horror series *Blood Ties*.

Pontypool (2008)

Directed by Bruce McDonald
Written by Tony Burgess (based on his own story)
Starring: Stephen McHattie, Lisa Houle, Georgina Reilly

Former radio host Grant Mazzy has been reduced to hosting a local NPR–style radio show in the tiny town of Pontypool, Ontario, Canada. While butting heads with his producer and staff, Grant suddenly finds himself as the sole voice reporting an epidemic of violent attacks. The violence makes its way to the radio station, where Grant and his crew try to survive what turns out to be some sort of strange viral infection turning people into mindless killers.

Depicting the real-time dissolution of society due to an outbreak, *Pontypool* smartly captures the events through the eyes of a small and dedicated team of local news radio producers and rarely leaves the tiny station where they work. Stephen McHattie, a great Canadian character actor seen in dozens of films (including *The Fountain* and *A History of Violence*), does his best work here as the lynchpin of the film, playing the likably dour radio host. The film's use of sound and repetition is what makes the frightening premise work, introducing brief glimpses of violence only at key moments.

Bruce McDonald was the idiosyncratic director known for his musical fake documentary *Hard Core Logo* when he embarked on this ambitious book adaptation. McDonald worked from a script by Tony Burgess (translating his own material); they reunited for another film, *Cashtown Corners*, and there has long been talk of a sequel to *Pontypool*. The key revelation about the disease, having to do with the breakdown in communication through spoken language, is a distinctly Canadian concept, given their dual official languages.

Dawn of the Dead (1978)

Written and Directed by George A. Romero
Starring: Ken Foree, David Emge, Gaylen Ross

Two SWAT team members join two television employees in a helicopter to escape the zombie outbreak in the Philadelphia area. Fleeing for the suburbs, the group lands on top of a mostly empty shopping mall. After securing the building and clearing out the zombies within, the four create a makeshift existence for themselves free of the panic and carnage outside.

When a motorcycle gang lays siege to the building and breaks the secure barriers, the safe haven is destroyed and the four of them must fight for their survival once again.

Generally credited as the most popular and influential zombie film of all time (even surpassing its progenitor, *Night of the Living Dead*), *Dawn of the Dead* is a masterpiece of practical effects, social commentary, and independent filmmaking. The film is the first lead role for Ken Foree, who would pop up in numerous horror genre films like *Leatherface: Texas Chainsaw Massacre 3* and the *Halloween* remake. His somber and thoughtful performance is a spiritual continuation of Duane Jones' work from the original film.

George A. Romero was a decade past his premiere in *Night of the Living Dead* when he returned to the world that made him famous in this film. Once again serving as writer, director, and editor, Romero wisely decided to continue the story of the world itself rather than attempting to bring back any characters from the first film (most of whom had died). The scenes in the giant mall, the central location for most of the film's action, were shot in the real-life Monroeville Mall near Pittsburgh, Pennsylvania, which is still in operation today. Special effects legend Tom Savini not only did the superb effects in the film, he plays a featured role as a member of the marauding motorcycle gang.

Other Titles of Interest

28 Days Later (2002), *Zombieland* (2009), *Dead Alive* (1992), *Day of the Dead* (1985 and 2008), *World War Z* (2013), *Resident Evil* (2003), *The Beyond* (1981), *Warm Bodies* (2013)

Mummy Horror

The mummy film is a strange phenomenon within the world of the horror film. Rather than creating a frightening monster or building an allegorical villain based on the fears and desires of humanity, the mummy film simply takes an existing practice and brings it back into play thousands of years after its supposed end. Mummies are real things, unlike werewolves and vampires; they can be seen up close in museums, and we know the names of the people within the wrappings and quite a bit about their lives from the objects found buried with them. As far as a horror villain goes, the mummy is one of the least mysterious, the least threatening, and the most poorly dressed.

So why does the mummy have a place in the horror pantheon? The simple answer is juxtaposition. A mummy film almost never takes place in the era in which the mummy was buried (unless, of course, you have a flashback to establish the circumstances which brought about the mummy); they are almost always stories about people from later generations who have to deal with the mummy and its dark practices. It is the uneasy balance of the modern sensibility struggling against the unorthodox beliefs and arcane rituals that gives a mummy story its psychological weight. We pride ourselves on being a society of forward-thinkers, innovators, and creators; that a society so devoted to looking forward could be defeated by a creature so primitive and barbaric is a shock to our rational senses.

It is more than just the hubris and tragedy of being defeated by ancient beings that taps into the human psyche; there is a deeper thought process at work. The victims of a mummy in a horror film are not just victims of the hand of the mummy itself, but of the magic it wields and the followers it commands. This revelation gives us pause, because the ramifications push back against the rationality of our age. The man or woman inside those rags dedicated his or her life to pursuing the beliefs and rituals which would eventually bring him or her back to life; and within the world of the movie, it actually happened. That means that the archaic beliefs were correct, and if it is happening around us, there is no other recourse than for us to believe it as well.

The recent age of man, driven by logic and science, is comfortable with the mummy as an artifact of a superstitious age long past. The simple act of bringing that mummy back to life puts everything that we know and rely on in our society in question; because if those followers are right, then we're all wrong, and it may be too late to change sides.

Elements of the Subgenre

Curse of the Tomb: Mummies are one of the few monsters in horror that never just show up and terrify people. They're dead and buried deep in the ground, and in order for a person to be terrorized by a mummy, they have to excavate a long-forgotten tomb and disturb their slumber by reciting incantations or disrupting their eternal rest. Only people who do these things find themselves the victims of the curse of the tomb.

Reincarnated Love: The mummy still has his ancient beliefs, so when he awakens and sees a woman somewhere that reminds him even a little bit of a previous love interest, his assumption is always that she must be the reincarnated soul of his beloved. Now he can move on from searching for his lost love to kidnapping the reincarnation of his lost love.

Recommendations from the Subgenre

The Mummy (1932)

Directed by Karl Freund
Written by John L. Balderston (based on the story by Nina Wilcox Putnam and Richard Schayer)
Starring: Boris Karloff, Zita Johann, David Manners

While on an archaeological dig in Egypt in 1921, a group of explorers finds the tomb of Imhotep, a powerful Egyptian priest. When one of the archaeologists reads a scroll aloud, the mummified body of Imhotep comes back to life, escaping the tomb and, now using the name Ardath Bey, heading to modern-day Cairo. He insinuates himself into society, arranging for archaeologists to exhume the body of his long-lost love. When he meets the lovely Helen, he sees that she bears a striking resemblance to the woman from his past. He pursues her, thinking that Helen must be his love reincarnated.

A stunning piece of visual artistry whose goal is to instill awe rather than fear, *The Mummy* is perhaps the most artistic of the original Universal horror monster films. Boris Karloff forgoes the moaning and stomping of *Frankenstein*'s Monster to play the lovelorn and erudite Imhotep, appearing as the bandage-covered mummy for mere seconds of screen time early in the film. Much of the second act is comprised of an extended flashback showing Imhotep's past, and the set design and period detail are meticulous.

Karl Freund had already created stunning images as cinematographer on *All Quiet on the Western Front*, *Murders in the Rue Morgue*, and *Dracula* when he was hired to direct this film. With a script from John L. Balderston, Universal's go-to writer after the success of his work on *Dracula* and *Frankenstein*, Freund also brought back *Dracula* actors Edward Van Sloan and David Manners. This was the first of the Universal horror monsters not based on a novel; much of the mythos for *The Mummy* came from the real-life opening of Tutankhamun's tomb in 1922. A re-launch of the series, starting with *The Mummy's Hand* in 1940, led to more Universal mummy movies, this time with a mummy named Kharis. Hammer Films remade them in the 1950s and 1960s, and Universal created a new version of the series again in 1999.

The Extraordinary Adventures of Adèle Blanc-Sec (2010)
Written and Directed by Luc Besson (based on the stories by Jacques Tardi)
Starring: Louise Bourgoin, Gilles Lellouche, Jacky Nercessian

In 1912, journalist Adèle Blanc-Sec searches the world to find the mummified body of Patmosis, the personal physician of Ramses II. After obtaining the body, she seeks the help of eccentric Professor Espérandieu to reanimate Patmosis so the deceased physician can use his powerful abilities to save her comatose sister. She finds trouble when she learns that he has been arrested and will face the death penalty for bringing a flying dinosaur to life to wreak havoc in Paris. Adèle must find a way to capture the dinosaur and rescue Espérandieu if she is ever to reanimate the physician and bring her sister back. A remarkable adventure-fantasy, *The Extraordinary Adventures of Adèle Blanc-Sec* is a big-screen adaptation of the Jacques Tardi comic that was an early pioneer of the steampunk aesthetic. Similar in shooting style and visuals to the earlier *Sky Captain and the World of Tomorrow*, the film used live action footage and primarily computer generated locations to create its fantastical *faux*-past.

Director Luc Besson was an adventurous director determined to work in every genre by the time he made this fantasy film, already having produced the action-oriented *Leon the Professional*, the animated *Arthur and the Invisibles*, and the biopic *The Messenger: The Story of Joan of Arc*. Besson partnered with his cinematographer Thierry Arbogast for the ninth time (they have worked as a team on thirteen films). Professor Ménard is played by the intense French actor Philippe Nahon, remembered for his frightening presence in *Irreversible*, *High Tension*, and *I Stand Alone*. Though the film was approved by Jacques Tardi and intended as the first of a trilogy, no news about a sequel has surfaced since its release.

Bubba Ho-Tep (2002)
Written and Directed by Don Coscarelli (based on the story by Joe R. Lansdale)
Starring: Bruce Campbell, Ossie Davis, Ella Joyce

Elvis Presley didn't die in 1977; years earlier, Presley had switched places with an impersonator who then passed away, while Presley himself lived a quiet and happy life out of the spotlight. In his later years, a broken hip and coma leave him in a retirement home dreaming of the old days, with the staff assuming he's just another confused resident. When he learns that other elderly residents are having their souls sucked out by an ancient mummy, he teams up with an old black man who thinks he's John F. Kennedy to stop the mummy and save the home. Hilariously unbelievable and unpredictable, *Bubba Ho-Tep* is also a surprising and somewhat touching rumination on the struggles of getting older. In the role he was born to play, Bruce Campbell taps into the comedy of the *Evil Dead* series and laces it with morose subtlety to create the performance of his career.

Don Coscarelli was and will always be best known for his work on the *Phantasm* series, and much of that energy and style went into the making of this movie. He also brought some actors from the franchise with him, including Reggie Bannister, Heidi Marnhout, and Bob Ivy. The credits mention the return of Elvis in *Bubba Nosferatu: Curse of the She-Vampires*; this was originally intended only as a closing credits joke, but Coscarelli eventually wrote a sequel script which cast actor Paul Giamatti as Colonel Sanders. That film was nearly made in 2008 before its funding fell through.

Other Titles of Interest

Blood from the Mummy's Tomb (1971), *The Monster Squad* (1987), *Dawn of the Mummy* (1981), *Bram Stoker's Legend of the Mummy* (1998), *Tale of the Mummy* (1998)

Nazi Horror

Sometimes it's nice to have a bad guy that everyone can hate. In horror, you often want people to root for one person or group and against another, and it becomes troublesome to create three-dimensional villains with real-life motivations and reasons for the awful things they do. When faced with a situation like that, one of the tried and true solutions is to bring in the Nazis.

It's a rarity, in a world populated with rationalization, reinvention, temporary insanity, and deconstruction, that everyone across the world and across time (with the exception of a handful of addle-minded or attention-seeking weirdos) would agree that a single group of human beings had banded together to simply do something so unspeakably horrible that humanity as a species can agree they should never have existed. Nazis are that unspeakable universal horror; in some strange way, the hatred of what they did and what they stood for is a defining and uniting part of the human spirit since the Second World War, a signpost that has signaled what everyone can understand as too far and too evil. That kind of singular recognition and agreement, in a world of splintered beliefs and an almost total lack of reasonable and civil discourse, is almost unheard of.

And though it is a true evil upon which we as humans agree, there is also some level of satisfaction and relief at that recognition. Humanity, fearing its own faults and shortcomings (because we always know we have them), has always sought out a scapegoat to blame for whatever our problems are, whether it is truly their fault or not. The idea that there is a single group in man's history that fulfills every measure of the hyperbole normally leveled at other scapegoats is the ideal for us: They are the other, they are the evil, and I'm not them, so I am not evil.

But it can't ever be that simple. Every person who signed up to be a Nazi was a regular human being (except possibly for the deranged and diseased minds who created and implemented what became their agenda); at some point in their existence, they were either fooled into thinking they were doing something right (in the case of people who never saw the concentration camps or Nazi experiments), or they made a conscious decision at some point that what they were doing was a trespass, and that they were going to make that trespass willingly. Either situation is one that humans find themselves in (in lesser degrees) every day of their lives, being taken advantage of by smarter or more manipulative people to do things they shouldn't, or consciously stepping over the line of what any decent member of society could do in good conscience. It is because these people were human to begin with that we want to distance ourselves from them; because if they could do what they did, then what other human beings could as well? Do we see them every day? Do we know them? Are they us?

The Nazi subgenre has been alive and well since the early days of the Nazi empire, popping up in films as varied as *Casablanca* and various Three Stooges shorts. With the advent of the exploitation film of the 1960s and 1970s, Nazis came to the forefront again, embraced as villains in film when society felt sufficiently distant from the real-life events that made them so evil. Films like *The Frozen Dead* and *Ilsa: She Wolf of the SS* became commonplace, reaching a fever pitch when Nazis were the villains in laughably schlocky fare like *Iron Sky*.

Elements of the Subgenre

Secret Experiments: Because of the disturbing truth behind the Nazi experiments documented in the aftermath of World War II and brought to light during the Nuremberg War Crime Trials, it has become a common occurrence that the villainous Nazis in any horror movie are probably still conducting their experiments and attempting to mess with either human genetic make-up or possibly dark occult rituals.

Hiding in Plain Sight: Most Nazi horror stories don't take place during the actual period of Nazi occupation. Therefore, it's hard to just have Nazis walking around in public in a movie. The case is often that the Nazis have escaped arrest and are living in another country, disguised as an immigrant but still up to their old ways, as in the cases of *The Boys from Brazil* and *Apt Pupil*.

British Actors: Perhaps as a result of genuine German actors not wanting to play-act the atrocities of their fellow countrymen, most Nazi films end up casting respected British actors as the villains. From Ian McKellen to Ralph Fiennes to Peter Cushing, it's often the British actors who get the plum Nazi villain roles, perhaps because their accent is more pleasant.

Recommendations from the Subgenre

Dead Snow (2009)

Directed by Tommy Wirkola
Written by Tommy Wirkola, Stig Frode Henriksen
Starring: Vegar Hoel, Stig Frode Henriksen, Charlotte Frogner

During Easter vacation, seven students head to a mountain cabin to drink and party. While there, they learn of the legend of the nearby townsfolk who chased Nazi oppressors into the mountains, leaving them to freeze to death. The group also comes upon a cache of stolen goods which the Nazis had taken from the townsfolk. After helping themselves to the goods, they become victims of an onslaught by the reanimated and very angry Nazi zombies. "Zombie Nazi soldiers stalking Easter skiers to get their stolen gold back" is all someone has to say in order to get horror fans interested in *Dead Snow*, a hilarious send-up of the Nazi horror subgenre. Combining comedy, horror, and Indiana Jones-Allan Quatermain–type adventure, the film manages to stick the landing due to the commitment of the actors and the non-stop action.

After directing the similarly humorous (and violent) Norwegian *Kill Bill* parody *Kill Buljo*, Tommy Wirkola made this his second feature film. He co-wrote the script with Stig Frode Henriksen, who also stars in the film as the tragically over-killed Roy. The film's skillful mix of humor and action won Wirkola the directing gig on the fantasy-action film *Hansel and Gretel: Witch Hunters*; after its release, he re-teamed with Henriksen to make both *Kill Buljo 2* and *Dead Snow 2: Red vs. Dead*.

Shock Waves (1977)
Directed by Ken Wiederhorn
Written by John Kent Harrison, Ken Wiederhorn
Starring: Peter Cushing, John Carradine, Brooke Adams

Tourists on a pleasure cruise are endangered when the boat gets lost in a strange mist and is then damaged by a decrepit old ship in the water nearby. They evacuate their boat and arrive on a nearby island that has a run-down hotel run by an old man. Stranded on the island, they also learn that the old man is an ex–Nazi commander who created zombie soldiers capable of traveling underwater, and that their bodies reside in the wrecked ship. Disappearing tourists confirm their worst fears: The soldiers are hunting them down.

A horror film that barely skirts schlock by taking itself as seriously as a premise like this can be taken, *Shock Waves* is a surprisingly high-quality entry in the Nazi horror subgenre. The artfully rendered images of the film, including the slow reveal of soldiers rising from the water, take on a hallucinatory feel, hearkening back to Lucio Fulci's original *Zombi*. Brooke Adams' sincere performance helps to sell the proceedings, and the images of the goggled soldiers slowly stalking the vacationers are haunting.

Ken Wiederhorn won a Student Academy Award for his short film *Manhattan Melody* when he came on to direct this film as his feature filmmaking debut. He co-wrote the script with TV-movie screenwriter John Kent Harrison, and his cinematographer was *Manhattan Melody* co-creator Reuben Trane. Wiederhorn went on to direct the sequels to two very famous films, *Meatballs 2* and *Return of the Living Dead 2*. The horror pedigree of *Shock Waves* is impressive, with starring roles from John Carradine (who played Dracula in Universal's horror mash-ups *House of Frankenstein* and *House of Dracula*) and Peter Cushing (the lead in the majority of Hammer's seminal horror entries of the 1960s and 1970s).

The Devil's Rock (2011)
Directed by Paul Campion
Written by Paul Finch, Paul Campion, Brett Ihaka
Starring: Craig Hall, Matthew Sunderland, Karlos Drinkwater

Two New Zealand soldiers sent on a sabotage mission to the Channel Islands during World War II find a woman screaming in a tunnel deep underneath the island. They also discover a black magic book within the tunnels. The woman looks exactly like the deceased wife of one of the soldiers. They are captured by a Nazi colonel; he used the book to conjure a demon which has now taken the shape of the deceased woman, and who is intended to be used as a weapon for the Nazi army. Based in part on the historically true occupation of the Channel Islands by Germany, *The Devil's Rock* is a great war-horror film that combines Nazi menace, demonic books *a la Evil Dead* and H.P. Lovecraft, and unnerving claustrophobia and paranoia. In a strong central performance, Australian TV star Craig Hall emotes well while struggling with physical and psychological torment.

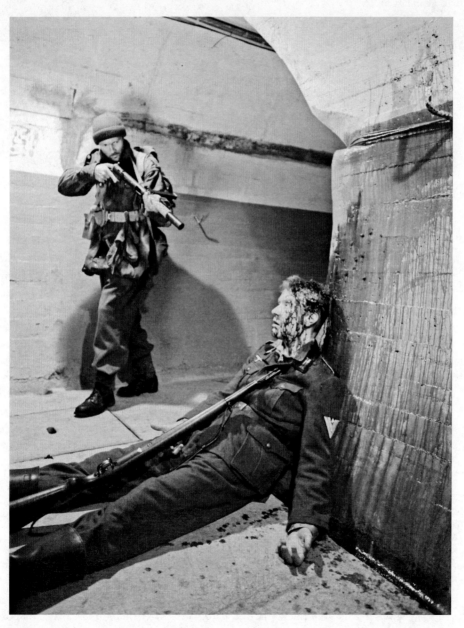

Captain Ben Grogan (Craig Hall) finds a dead soldier (Jonathan King) and much worse inside a German fortification in 2011's *The Devil's Rock* (courtesy Paul Campion).

After a long and impressive run of work doing visual effects on major films like *The Lord of the Rings* trilogy, *X-Men: The Last Stand*, and *Clash of the Titans*, Paul Campion made his feature directorial debut with this film. He also co-scripted with television writers Paul Finch and Brett Ihaka. Campion called upon many of his Weta Workshop co-workers to help him accomplish the impressive makeup of the film: Richard Taylor, Davina Lamont, and Sean Foot all worked at Weta, and they won a New Zealand Film and TV Award for their work here. Some of the scenes were done on location at Wrights Hill Fortress, an actual restored World War II bunker.

Other Titles of Interest

Invisible Agent (1942), *Outpost* (2007), *The Frozen Dead* (1966), *Oasis of the Zombies* (1982), *Frankenstein's Army* (2013), *Zombie Lake* (1981), *Ilsa, She-Wolf of the SS* (1975), *The Keep* (1983)

Old People Horror

The subgenre of horror that deals with the elderly seems to be built on the concept of dichotomy. If we fear an elderly character in a story, it must be because they are possessed of something, working against their natural state. We couldn't fear physical danger from them, as their advanced years have made them slower, less strong, and nowhere near as threatening. So we look at the elderly as villains in a horror movie in the same ironic way that we might with an innocent-looking figure like Chucky the doll in *Child's Play*.

But a secondary and more careful examination of their lives might show a slightly more complex breakdown of psychology for elderly villains. In many cases, being nearer the end of their lives than the rest of us, they become the very definition of a loose cannon. They're dangerous because they have nothing left to lose except a few short years that would likely be filled with medical issues and the loss of body and mind function. One never knows what they might do: steer the car into oncoming traffic, or crush some pills into the mashed potatoes. And in the aftermath of a circumstance that terrible, the inclination is to forgive the elderly person, who in our estimation must have been experiencing troubles related to nothing more than "getting on in years."

The idea that older people want to be young again is no great secret. Perhaps they harbor anger and maybe homicidal impulses towards the younger people who have marginalized them, taken away their rights, and placed them in care facilities far from the awareness of the rest of the world.

The term "bucket list" came about as a way to describe a list of things that a person wishes to do before they die. Most of the things on the list are life achievements, like re-visiting a place they always loved, or meeting a certain person that has always been a hero to them. We know, however, that inside, elderly people have the same desires, fears, and weird dark thoughts that the rest of us have. And in the world of the horror film, when an illness takes hold or an octogenarian recognizes the signs of dementia, we had all better hope that the things they want to cross off their bucket list are innocuous and socially acceptable.

Elements of the Subgenre

Crazy or Infirm: Some of the central fears humans have about getting old are also the focus of the plots of many "old people" horror films. Old age causes people to lose the use of their mental or physical abilities, and these movies often focus either on the dark tragedy of watching it happen, or the horror that results from the lengths they will go to prevent it.

The Long Buried Secret: The plots of these films often hinge on something that was hidden long ago, something that the general public would not know because it was covered up or forgotten about. Only the people old enough to have been around personally at the time know what truly happened.

Recommendations from the Subgenre

Hush…Hush, Sweet Charlotte (1964)
Directed by Robert Aldrich
Written by Henry Farrell, Lukas Heller
Starring: Bette Davis, Olivia de Havilland, Joseph Cotten

Decades after Southern belle Charlotte's married lover was brutally murdered by having his head and hands chopped off, aging recluse Charlotte still lives in the run-down plantation home with no one but her housekeeper. Cousin Miriam comes to help her transition out of the home, which is to be demolished to make room for a highway, and Charlotte's mental state deteriorates quickly. All is not as it seems in the house, though, and after the mysterious death of the housekeeper, clues begin to point towards a nefarious plan to drive Charlotte insane. *Hush…Hush, Sweet Charlotte* is a pitch black Southern gothic thriller with an impeccable cast of Hollywood veterans late in their careers. The film plays with character motivations and effectively shifts audience sympathies numerous times before the darkly humorous climax reveals the truth.

Director Robert Aldrich fashioned this film as a follow-up to his previous "aging beauties" thriller *What Ever Happened to Baby Jane?*, and it was equally as successful. It was nominated for seven Oscars (the most for a horror film until *The Silence of the Lambs*); the great cast included a reunion for Joseph Cotten and Agnes Moorehead, who had worked together early in their career with Orson Welles as Mercury Theatre players and co-stars in *Citizen Kane*. This was the last film appearance of Mary Astor, best remembered as the femme fatale in the film noir *The Maltese Falcon*. It was also one of the *first* performances for beloved character actor Bruce Dern.

The Taking of Deborah Logan (2014)
Directed by Adam Robitel
Written by Adam Robitel, Gavin Heffernan
Starring: Jill Larson, Anne Ramsey, Michelle Ang

Mia, the director of a documentary, brings a camera crew to the home of Sarah Logan. Her aged mother Deborah has started to show signs of Alzheimer's disease. Hoping that the funding from the documentary will help her to keep the house, Sarah agrees to let the crew chronicle Deborah's disease. As the crew begins to capture unusual and eccentric behavior, they wonder whether it is as a result of her disease, or some sort of dark influence whose origins reach back to a town tragedy from decades earlier.

A skillfully executed fake documentary that delivers more than the average because of its thoughtful story and great central performance, *The Taking of Deborah Logan* is a story that would be tragic and frightening even without its supernatural underpinnings. Soap opera veteran Jill Larson is heartbreaking in the lead role of Deborah, and Anne Ramsey does superb and subtle supporting work as the long-suffering daughter. This is one of the few fake documentary films that has a conclusion in which characters survive and there is an explanation for the documentary framework, and both are welcome touches.

Adam Robitel was not new to horror when he made this film, having worked variously as editor, actor, and producer on the anthology film *Chillerama* and the remakes *2001 Maniacs* and *2001 Maniacs: Field of Screams*. The film was produced by Bryan Singer, a director with whom Robitel had worked on *X-Men* (as an actor) and *Superman Returns* (as a behind-the-scenes videographer).

Exorcist III: Legion (1990)

Written and Directed by William Peter Blatty (based on the story by Blatty)
Starring: George C. Scott, Brad Dourif, Jason Miller

Fifteen years after the exorcism of Regan MacNeil, police lieutenant Kinderman finds himself once again becoming immersed in a series of violent crimes with ritualistic elements. He discovers that the deaths are connected to a long-dead serial killer, and that a patient in a psychiatric facility who seems to know something about the killings bears an uncanny resemblance to Father Karras, the priest who died performing the exorcism years earlier. Linking the serial killer to the exorcised demon, Kinderman battles the dead and the dying in an attempt to solve the case and keep his family safe. Ignoring the second sequel and connecting directly to the events of the original, *Exorcist III* manages to pull off the impressive feat of being a terrifying film on its own merits. The supernatural elements are seen through the lens of a police procedural this time, and the concept of elderly people with senile dementia being used as puppets for the soul of a killer is brilliant and haunting.

Though he was originally not interested in creating a sequel to his successful adaptation of the original, William Peter Blatty returned to the franchise after the commercial and critical failure of *Exorcist II: The Heretic*. Based on the novel *Legion* and focused on an ancillary character from the first book, the film places the great George C. Scott in the role of Kinderman in place of Lee J. Cobb, who passed away in 1976. The book and the original version of the film contain no exorcism at all, but the studio insisted on it, and Nicol Williamson's Father Morning was added in reshoots.

Other Titles of Interest

Rabid Grannies (1988), *Mercy* (2014), *Grandmother's House* (1988), *Homebodies* (1974), *Mom* (1991), *The Skeleton Key* (2005), *The Visit* (2015)

Out-of-Control Machines Horror

Humans are a clever and industrious species, especially when it comes to inventing methods by which we have to do less work. Our ingenuity is never better, or more positively noted, than when an emerging technology somehow has the potential to save the human race a little time or a lot of effort. We love finding something else that will do our jobs for us.

Sometimes, those things are machines or technologies; just as often, they are less fortunate people who have no choice but to do what we don't want to do. Cleaning houses, mowing lawns, picking fruit, assembling electronics—these are tasks that have been neatly divided between amazing new machines and the financially insecure working class. And because of that, we no longer have to do them ourselves.

We like it that way, and we are comfortable. The idea of having to go back to doing things the old-fashioned way is terrifying to us; just ask a teenager sitting in his room when the electricity and wireless Internet are down for longer than an hour. Though the tasks were recently ours to do in the historical scheme of things, we live in fear of the day that we have to go back to them.

And why should we have to go back? We invented machines to do these jobs for us, so why should we ever have to do them ourselves? The hubris with which we have decided that machines have been designed for a single purpose (the purpose which is most convenient to us) will someday be matched by the sense of loss and confusion we have when those machines suddenly decide to start doing what they want instead of what we want. We may have told the computer that it was supposed to remember and protect our information, but what the computer decides to do on its own is another story.

The true secret of the out-of-control machine subgenre is that it is not really about the machines at all. Yes, the trucks and computers and factories and satellites do represent some level of fear that humanity has about our creations becoming smarter and stronger than us and taking over the world. But the thing we're far more frightened of is what those machines represent: They stand in for the aforementioned working class, the people who do the jobs we don't want and never seem to get ahead because of it. The thing we really fear is their uprising, their recognition of the fact that we have made them machines for our ease. Someday, the working class people who are the backbone of any economy will see that they have been taken advantage of; and when that day comes, most of us will be praying for something as tame and unthreatening as the inconvenience of doing our own work again. Because the alternative is too frightening to consider.

Elements of the Subgenre

No Personality Here: Sometimes, machines in films do take on personalities, like the lovable robots of *Star Wars* or the cute appliances in *The Brave Little Toaster*. In the horror arena, machines get no personality. They may be alive, but their desires are bloodthirsty and single-minded. They are faceless monstrosities that must be defeated by us rather than understood or reasoned with.

Getting Medieval: Since it is always the modern technology that tends to go crazy and start killing people (it's never a windmill or a hand-cranked water pump), the only sure way to beat the attacker is to use human ingenuity and good old-fashioned technology: smash them with blunt objects, blow them up with dynamite, or maybe even splash some holy water around and perform an exorcism.

Recommendations from the Subgenre

The Car (1977)
Directed by Elliot Silverstein
Written by Dennis Shryack, Michael Butler, Lane Slate
Starring: James Brolin, Kathleen Lloyd, John Marley

In the quiet town of Santa Ynez, Utah, a series of violent hit and runs has the local community scared. Witnesses to the killings are stalked and killed by an unmarked black car. After the death of the sheriff, Chief Deputy Wade Parent gets on the trail of what is, according to witnesses, a driverless vehicle.

The relentless hunt of a slick metallic monster against the dusty backdrop of a small American town, *The Car* gathers tropes from many of the most popular horror subgenres (from road horror to stalking to out-of-control machines) and hybridizes them for a fun, if somewhat silly, result. Great supporting performances from veterans like John Marley and R.G. Armstrong give the film a believable sense of community; Marley and co-star Kathleen Lloyd reunited a year later for the horror sequel *It Lives Again*.

Though primarily a western director, having worked on *Cat Ballou* and *A Man Called Horse*, director Elliot Silverstein had directed one horror film, *Nightmare Honeymoon*, before making this film; he would later direct multiple episodes of the HBO horror series *Tales from the Crypt*. The script is by Dennis Shryack and Michael Butler, who would later revisit supernatural-tinged horror with *Pale Rider*. Silverstein followed the filmmaking template created by Steven Spielberg three years earlier with *Jaws* (which was itself an animal-based take on his own earlier out-of-control machine movie, *Duel*). Television star James Brolin had just finished his eight-year run on *Marcus Welby, M.D.* when he starred in this film. He returned to the genre very successfully two years later with *The Amityville Horror*. Child actress sisters (and future *Real Housewives of Beverly Hills* stars) Kim and Kyle Richards play Brolin's daughters.

The Mangler (1995)
Directed by Tobe Hooper
Written by Tobe Hooper, Stephen David Brooks, Harry Alan Towers (based on the story by Stephen King)
Starring: Robert Englund, Ted Levine, Daniel Matmor

Gartley's Blue Ribbon Laundry is dealing with some problems. After owner Bill Gartley's niece hurts herself on the laundry folding machine, spilling blood inside it, the machine seems to have a mind of its own and causes the death of an elderly worker. When a police officer investigates, he is soon convinced by his brother that the machine may have become possessed by a demon and is in need of an exorcism before it kills again. Squeezing mechanical horror from one of the most unusual and seemingly unthreatening killers in the history of horror film, *The Mangler* is a respectable attempt to take a ludicrous concept seriously. The presence of two iconic horror villains (Robert Englund was Freddy Krueger, and Ted Levine played Buffalo Bill in *The Silence of the Lambs*) working in a film based on a Stephen King short story holds promise, and in structure the story has potential. The biggest problem facing the movie is the visual style, overdoing the unnecessary moodiness and creep factor in order to compensate for a mostly immobile villain.

Director Tobe Hooper was nearly a decade out from *Texas Chainsaw Massacre 2*, his last successful film, when he came aboard this movie. Co-writing the script with previous collaborators Stephen David Brooks and Harry Alan Towers, he faced the daunting task of taking a wild premise that only had to last a handful of pages in a short story and turn it into a feature film. The film did poorly in theaters, but found an audience on DVD, which led to *The Mangler 2* and *The Mangler Reborn*, both direct-to-DVD releases.

Virus (1999)

Directed by John Bruno
Written by Chuck Pfarrer, Dennis Feldman (based on the comic book by Chuck Pfarrer)
Starring: Jamie Lee Curtis, William Baldwin, Donald Sutherland

An American salvage crew, caught in a typhoon, evacuate onto a seemingly abandoned Russian research ship in the eye of the storm. Exploring the ship, they find a single crew member alive and crazed, claiming that some kind of creature has taken over the ship. When they find a way to restore power to the vessel, they discover that an electronic life force has been constructing bodies for itself from parts of the ship and parts of Russian crew members. A clever reinterpretation of the haunted house framework that uses elements of *Frankenstein* with technology paranoia, *Virus* is a modern update of a classic horror concept. An eclectic cast of character actors brings an international sensibility to the story (a nice change of pace for a big-budget American film release), and the eye for maritime and technological detail is impressive.

Directed by visual effects master John Bruno, who worked with James Cameron to create the fantastic visuals of *Titanic* and *Avatar*, the film was based on the successful Dark Horse comic by writer Chuck Pfarrer. The plot was influenced heavily by director Bruno's experiences during Cameron's dives to the *Titanic* (including the introduction of the Mir space station into the story). The film was produced by *The Terminator* and *The Walking Dead* producer Gale Ann Hurd. Though it was not a success in its initial release, it has found a devoted following since.

Other Titles of Interest

Christine (1983), *Maximum Overdrive* (1986), *The Lift* (1983), *Deadly Friend* (1986), *Runaway* (1984), *Colossus: The Forbin Project* (1970)

Pregnancy Horror

Giving birth is the weapon humanity has against the constant attempt by nature to destroy us, the yin to death's yang. It is the way that people gain a measure of immortality in the physical world, a way to make sure that half of the genetic information that makes up who we are continues on after we're long gone. It's also an amazing way to bring together humanity, literally combining two separate human beings at a genetic level, knitting them together more closely than any relationship ever could. And the instinct that humans find in marginalizing or sacrificing themselves for the betterment of their child is one of the only instincts in humanity that is naturally a selfless one. There are many beautiful things about the idea of having children.

And there are many terrifying things. Childbirth has long been a source of many deaths for mothers, and even in our modern society, there is still a minor risk of a mother losing her life bringing a child into the world. And pregnancy itself is a source of much fear, for both parents. In a world that makes terminating a pregnancy difficult to impossible to do in a safe way, young people can suddenly find themselves discovering that their lives are no longer just their own, and that a decision made in the heat of passion can change an entire future lifetime.

But at its base, pregnancy is often scary to people because it is about unusual biology. Pregnancy is a "natural" thing, that is for certain, but it is not the default state. The human body goes through changes that are often inconvenient and confusing, and sometimes frightening and painful. Sickness, complications, cravings, even emotional instability, often root from the act of propagating the species. Not to mention that, at the end of the day, there is a tiny group of cells growing at an exponential rate inside of a person's body until it has gestated long enough, and then it will be making its way out in the most intimate way possible.

But we risk it all, because the biological imperative to continue the species is strong. There is an innate knowledge of our own death inside us from the moment we become self-aware, and perhaps it is the recognition that birth is the closest natural thing to living forever which pushes us into a procreation process that can be uncomfortable and dangerous. Because as director Alfonso Cuaron's brilliant film *Children of Men* reminds us, the only thing more frightening than being responsible for bringing a life into the world, is knowing that you can't.

The subgenre dates back to the 1960s, when taboo subject matter was finally allowed in mainstream films; before that, the anxiety of motherhood manifested as evil children movies in the *Bad Seed* vein.

Elements of the Subgenre

Terminate or Carry to Term: It is inevitable in a film about pregnancy horror that the subject of abortion will come up. Sure, it's controversial, but if you were pregnant with Satan's baby, wouldn't you consider the safe, legal, and rare option of exercising your rights?

Nature vs. Nurture: The age-old question of who is to blame for evil children often comes into play this early in the child's existence, as mothers fret that the child may already be evil, and that none of their unconditional maternal love will make any difference. More often than not in the pregnancy horror film, nature wins out.

Uncaring Medical Professionals: The only thing worse than prying neighbors or an uninvolved husband is the detached and clinical treatment that mothers receive from their medical caregivers. Women may have been giving birth since the dawn of humanity, but it doesn't mean that first-time mothers don't still have questions and fears, and the total lack of emotional investment from the doctors isolates them even more.

Recommendations from the Subgenre

Rosemary's Baby (1968)
Written and Directed by Roman Polanski (based on the novel by Ira Levin)
Starring: Mia Farrow, John Cassavetes, Ruth Gordon

Newlyweds Rosemary and Guy have just moved into a beautiful New York City apartment building. Guy is focused on his acting career, and Rosemary wants to start a family. After they meet the elderly Castavets, neighbors from down the hall, their fortunes seem to turn around. Guy finds great success in his career, and Rosemary learns she is pregnant. The happiness changes to paranoia as Rosemary begins to get sicker and sicker, struggling with uncaring doctors and distance from her husband, and starts to suspect that the child inside her may not be the product of hers and Guy's love, but something much darker. The pregnancy horror film by which all others are measured (and usually found lacking), *Rosemary's Baby* is the perfect matching of concept and creators. Mia Farrow is well cast as the innocent Rosemary. In the roles of seemingly supportive friends and family, John Cassavetes and Ruth Gordon excel. Beautiful cinematography accentuates the great set design for the apartment, in which most of the action of the film takes place.

Rosemary's Baby was only the fifth film for Polish director Roman Polanski, but his eye for detail and camera placement gave it a frightening authenticity. Writing the script himself from the novel by Ira Levin, the movie was actually produced by B-movie pioneer William Castle. Ruth Gordon won an Oscar for her portrayal of Minnie; it was her fifth nomination, two of them being for her scripting work with Garson Kanin for the Hepburn-Tracy comedies *Adam's Rib* and *Pat and Mike*. In one of his first film appearances, Charles Grodin appears as Dr. Hill; four years later, he would get his big break in *The Heartbreak Kid*.

Inside (2007)
Written and Directed by Alexandre Bustillo, Julien Maury
Starring: Alysson Paradis, Béatrice Dalle, Nathalie Roussel

Early on in her pregnancy, Sarah is in a car accident that takes the life of her husband. Still dealing with the aftermath of the event months later, Sarah is accosted and eventually assaulted by a mysterious woman who tries to get into her home. A brutal struggle for survival which leaves Sarah's mother and employer dead reveals the truth of the mysterious woman's obsession: She wants to take Sarah's baby at any cost.

A film so blunt and visceral that a second viewing may never be necessary, *Inside* is an audacious debut for a talented filmmaking duo. A small cast and only one major location do nothing to diminish the terrifying impact of the film, which combines moments of silent and nearly unbearable suspense (the scissors on the pregnant belly) with graphically realistic moments of prolonged violence (the hand pinned to the wall). The lead performance from Paradis as the brutalized but resourceful Sarah is affecting.

Julien Maury and Alexandre Bustillo are the creative minds behind this film, one of the premier entries in the ultraviolent French new wave of horror which also includes *High Tension* and *Martyrs*. The film plays with the clichés of the stalker film, embracing the pregnancy storyline and emphasizing a strictly female power struggle that ends up being all the more brutal because of it. The directing duo reteamed with actress Béatrice Dalle (who played the deranged and obsessive stalker here) for their follow-up, the supernaturally tinged *Livid*.

It's Alive (1974)

Written and Directed by Larry Cohen
Starring: John Ryan, Sharon Farrell, James Dixon

A young couple in Los Angeles are expecting their second child. Husband Frank is sitting patiently in the waiting room when screams are heard: The baby, monstrous and strong, murders everyone in the birthing room except for its mother and flees out into the night. As a manhunt for their child sweeps the city, PR consultant Frank loses his job because of the bad publicity. Soon he begins to suspect that the child might just be heading home to visit its family. The perfect thematic continuation of the fears raised in *Rosemary's Baby*, *It's Alive* extends past the pregnancy and embraces the fears of parenthood directly. Equal parts monster horror, domestic drama, and police thriller, the film is delightfully difficult to categorize and clever in its use of modern fears like pollution, medication, and abortion to fuel its heightened reality.

The movie was the first major hit for maverick writer-director Larry Cohen, who would go on to make the equally wild horror films *God Told Me To*, *Q*, and *The Stuff*. The film was part of the movement toward more socially conscious films in the 1970s, with a classic opening titles sequence and a score by Bernard Herrmann (one of his last before his death in 1975) adding to the time capsule quality of the movie when viewed in a modern context. The monstrous baby was the work of creature designer Rick Baker, six years before his Oscar win for makeup with *An American Werewolf in London*.

Other Titles of Interest

Grace (2009), *Devil's Due* (2014), *Xtro* (1982), *The Fly* (1986), *Demon Seed* (1977)

Prison Horror

Part of the challenge of any truly effective horror film is to take a seemingly normal place or circumstance and turn this mundane reality into a nightmarish experience that will breed the best kind of terror. It is a difficult balance to keep, because in order to make a story feel realistic, the elements of dread must make their way slowly into the world of the story; and a horror film which is slow in its descent into the fears and scares is a film that risks losing its audience.

It is for this reason that the prison is such a perfect location for a horror film, from a storytelling perspective. No one ever wants to be in prison; it's a miserable place that anyone in the world would avoid. It is extremely helpful to a storyteller trying to fashion a horror film if they can begin the first frame of their film in a place that everyone is scared to go.

The truth of our fear of prisons, however, goes deeper than the initial fear of the place. Many people temporarily go to prisons for reasons varying from conjugal visits to church outreach programs, so it's not the idea of the prison itself. It is the fear of remaining there. Humanity fears being confined, a fear that also taps into claustrophobia and being buried alive. We need no greater fear than to know that we will walk in the doors of a secure facility, and never be allowed back out.

If the skilled horror filmmaker adds to that already existing fear the idea that something else in the prison is to be feared, then the anxiety doubles. Something waits for us within those walls, something that could kill us (or worse); whatever it is, we will have to confront it and defeat it, or we will be killed. One thing is certain, however: We know there is no escape.

This would be a bad enough realization on its own, that your survival depends solely on your own resourcefulness. Add to that the realization that you are trapped in a building with the worst of society. In the same way that no one wants to go to a mental facility because it is the place we have chosen to send people we deem undesirable, we recognize that prison is the place for the violent, the perverted, the people that can't be trusted to stay within the boundaries of decency. They may now be your only hope.

Elements of the Subgenre

Don't Trust the Warden: The man who is in charge of the well-being of the entire prison population is never to be trusted, no matter what kind of film a prison story takes place in. In a prison horror film, however, it's usually much worse. Forcing prisoners to participate in secret experiments, making them work for no money, starving and beating them—corruption comes from the top down, and the top is where the warden lives.

The Bad Kind of Action: Rape is a cliché in any kind of prison film, and is probably more prevalent in prison movies than it is in actual prison. Of course, in a prison horror film, it's bound to be either more frequent or more violent than any other kind of film, and is likely to be handled in a less-than-artistic manner.

Recommendations from the Subgenre

Maléfique (2002)
Directed by Eric Valette
Written by Alexandre Charlot, Franck Magnier, François Cognard
Starring: Gérald Laroche, Philippe Laudenbach, Clovis Cornillac

Financial criminal Carrere is sent to prison, where he shares his cell with three other people. While serving their time, they find a journal hidden behind the bricks of the cell wall. The journal features occult imagery and incantations. As they begin dabbling with the material, one of them is killed by it and the others find their dark desires being granted in unusual and horrifying ways. As applicable for nomination in the single location horror film subgenre as the prison horror subgenre, *Maléfique* is a chamber piece film that is more disturbing, wild, and adventurous than you would ever imagine a film taking place inside a single prison cell possibly could be. The lead performances are riveting and powerful across the board, with Dimitri Rataud a standout as the child-eating Pâquerette. The languid pacing of the film early on accentuates the disturbing events and breakneck pace of the final act.

Eric Valette had only directed a few short films when he partnered with the writing team of Alexandre Charlot and Franck Magnier to make this movie. Valette's ability to wring scares from a meager budget won him an American directing job a few years later, remaking *One Missed Call* for English-speaking audiences. The practical effects, likely a necessity due to the small budget, work well in the setting and add to the grimy feel of the movie. Though the film was decidedly low-budget, it was well received and won several awards, including placing third in the Fantasia Film Festival for Best International Film.

Prison (1987)

Directed by Renny Harlin
Written by Irwin Yablans, C. Courtney Joyner
Starring: Viggo Mortensen, Chelsea Field, Tom "Tiny" Lister

Charlie Forsythe was put to death in the Creedmore Prison electric chair in 1964 for a crime he didn't commit. Forsythe's soul decided not to rest easy, waiting patiently inside the closed-down prison for thirty years until its re-opening. Forsythe begins killing his way through prisoners on his journey to find the man responsible for his death sentence. With the body count climbing, the prisoners have to find a way to get Forsythe to his intended victim before he kills them all. Filmed at the actual Old State Prison in Rawlins, Wyoming, *Prison* is a low-budget, gritty supernatural take on the subgenre of the prison film. The film has a cast of young actors on the verge of breaking into greater recognition: Tom Lister would be featured in big action films like *Universal Soldier* and *Posse*, Chelsea Field would make her name in respected horror indies like *Dust Devil* and *The Dark Half*, and Viggo Mortensen would gain worldwide fame as Aragorn in the *Lord of the Rings* trilogy.

Renny Harlin was a Finnish filmmaker with only one film, an action-thriller called *Born American*, to his name when he signed on to make *Prison* from a screenplay from Full Moon Pictures alumnus C. Courtney Joyner. Not too many prints were made and it was not strongly distributed by its producer, *Halloween*'s Irwin Yablans. The project did help to get Harlin a meeting with Bob Shaye at New Line Cinema, and the result was his directing gig on *A Nightmare on Elm Street 4: The Dream Master*. Composer Richard Band was also borrowed from the Full Moon stable to handle the scoring for the film.

Ghosts...of the Civil Dead (1988)

Directed by John Hillcoat
Written by Nick Cave, Gene Conkie, Evan English, John Hillcoat, Hugo Race (based on the book by
    Jack Henry Abbott)
Starring: David Field, Nick Cave

After a violent outbreak within a privately run maximum security prison, investigators must uncover the cause of the problem. It seems that the entirety of the prison's population, both the guards and the prisoners, have been intentionally antagonized, irritated, and manipulated into bringing about the violence in an attempt to feed into a political reality that will allow the prison owners to construct even more expensive and secure facilities. Shockingly based on true events that were chronicled in the book *In the Belly of the Beast*, *Ghosts...of the Civil Dead* is a frightening near-reality that reflects humanity's fears and hatred in the microcosm of the Australian penal system. Casting a critical eye on the business of incarceration, the film pulls no punches in showing the deprivation and brutality of the system, and points out society's complicity in allowing it to happen.

John Hillcoat was a rising talent in the music documentary world, having directed a film for the band INXS, when he made this movie; his career would take him into music videos for Manic Street Preachers and Depeche Mode before he returned to film for *The Road* and *Lawless*. Hillcoat co-scripted the film with producer Evan English and musician Nick Cave, who also has a role in the film; the two worked together again when Hillcoat directed Cave's screenplay for *The Proposition*. The film is difficult to find, as it has never had an American DVD release, but it is well worth the search.

Other Titles of Interest

Vincent Gil is Ruben, one of the enraged prisoners enduring brutality in a maximum security prison in *Ghosts...of the Civil Dead* (courtesy Evan English).

Beyond Re-Animator (2003), *Alive* (2002), *Haunted Prison* (2006), *Zombie Death House* (1987)

Psychic–Mental Powers Horror

The subgenre of the mental powers horror film is a two-edged sword: It is in many ways a wish fulfillment for the individual who is gifted with the powers, while simultaneously being the stuff of nightmares for those who have crossed that gifted individual.

The stories often begin the same way, with a weak-willed or ineffective person suffering abuse at the hands of uncaring peers. This can be in the halls of a high school, the break room of a workplace, or the basement of a foster parent's house. The treatment is harsh and unwarranted, and the audience immediately sympathizes with the victim. Then, at a pivotal point in the story, the character gains the ability to defend or protect him or herself, and the story shifts as the previously victimized character becomes the victimizer. Though the retribution may be bloody and deadly, we have watched the suffering for too long, and we are emotionally invested; revenge may not be right, but it is satisfying.

This is where the brilliance of the mental powers revenge story lies. Though most people sympathize with the mentally enhanced victim because they imagine themselves to be like him or her (an outcast or loner who just wants to be accepted and loved), the truth is that more often than not, we probably have more in common with the abuser than with the abused. An honest appraisal of our daily interactions with other people will often reveal cruel and unnecessary jokes at others' expense, animosity harbored against individuals because of what they have or what they represent, and no small amount of petty gossip.

We are all, in fact, both victim and abuser in various situations. When we watch a film that shows a physically diminutive person gaining the upper hand against aggressors (in the most satisfying way possible, because mental powers require no physical exertion, training, or discipline), we cheer because we connect with their plight and we approve of their over-the-top solutions. But the reason that these films are horror films, rather than feel-good fantasies, is because we secretly know that if this were to happen in the real world, we could all just as easily be on the receiving end of that vengeance.

Elements of the Subgenre

Frightened by Their Own Power: Before the shocking and somewhat relieving part of the film where the person with mental powers lets loose and fully embraces their own massive abilities, they tend to have some hesitation about what they are. They are held back, prevented from realizing their full potential, because they fear what they can do.

There Will Be Blood: Whether it's coming from the nose or eyes of the gifted psychic when they strain too hard to use their abilities, or the bodies of their victims, or from a bucket suspended above the stage that drops all over an innocent girl at the prom, there is the definite promise of blood.

Recommendations from the Subgenre

Carrie (1976)

Directed by Brian De Palma
Written by Lawrence D. Cohen (based on the story by Stephen King)
Starring: Sissy Spacek, Piper Laurie, John Travolta

Adolescent Carrie White is unpopular at school, the constant target of bullies. Her sexual maturity is treated as hostile by her devoutly religious mother. Carrie begins to realize that, with the coming of her physical changes, she has also developed some unusual psychokinetic abilities which scare her at first. Becoming comfortable with herself due to her new abilities and an unlikely date to the prom, all of her confidence and sanity are suddenly shattered by a cruel prank at the dance which causes her to lose control of her growing powers.

The greatest of the supernatural revenge stories, *Carrie* brought the world the first film from the mind of Stephen King and launched an already promising director to a decade of commercial and critical success. In diametrically opposed lead performances, Sissy Spacek is as sympathetic in her innocence and naiveté as Piper Laurie is loathsome in her demented religious fervor. Young unknowns P.J. Soles, Nancy Allen, and John Travolta were all on the verge of breaking out in huge films over the next few years. The prom tragedy and its aftermath go down in history as one of cinema's earliest mass bloodbaths; the death of innocent students was shocking in its day, and takes on a new resonance with more recent school tragedies.

Brian De Palma had already been heralded a young Hitchcock when he directed this film. Working from the story by King, writer Lawrence D. Cohen crafted the largely faithful screenplay; he would work on King's material again for television with *It* and *The Tommyknockers*. Both female leads were nominated for Oscars, a rare feat for a horror film.

Eyes of Laura Mars (1978)

Directed by Irvin Kershner
Written by John Carpenter, David Zelag Goodman
Starring: Faye Dunaway, Tommy Lee Jones, Brad Dourif

Fashion photographer Laura Mars is known for her beautiful but violence-tinged imagery. While struggling with the public perception of her work as degrading to women, Laura finds herself seeing first-person visions of people she knows being murdered. She goes to the police, who show her police photos of crime scenes that look almost identical to images she arranged for her photo shoots. As she tries to clear herself of any connection to the murders, she finds herself the new target of the killer through whose eyes she is seeing. An American example of Italy's Giallo genre, *Eyes of Laura Mars* is an impeccably directed thriller with great lead performances and a solid if predictable final reveal. Three years out from his star-making turn in *One Flew Over the Cuckoo's Nest*, Brad Dourif is excellent as the chauffeur, and Tommy Lee Jones breathes life into the tired cliché of the cop–love interest. But it is Faye Dunaway, shifting from glamorous photographer to tortured victim plagued by visions, who carries the film with her sympathetic portrayal.

Journeyman director Irvin Kershner was known for his solid crime and drama work like *The Hoodlum Priest* when he signed on to make this film. Teaming with writer David Zelag Goodman to adapt an original screenplay from *Halloween's* John Carpenter, Kershner made a box-office hit; he would direct another hit two years later with *The Empire Strikes Back*. Barbara Streisand was originally courted for the role of Laura Mars, and ended up recording a ballad for the film's soundtrack.

Phenomena (1985)

Directed by Dario Argento
Written by Dario Argento, Franco Ferrini
Starring: Jennifer Connelly, Daria Nicolodi, Donald Pleasence

Young Jennifer arrives at a Swiss boarding school, and after sleepwalking the first night, she sees a murder taking place. Fleeing into the nearby forest, she meets an entomologist who notices her uncanny ability to communicate with insects. She uses her skills to get the insects to help her figure out the identity of the killer through forensic means. Other students and faculty begin to think that Jennifer is possibly demonic and might be responsible for the killings herself. To clear her name and keep from being placed in an asylum, she must catch the real killer. Combining the supernatural elements of Argento films like *Suspiria* with the murder mystery of his earlier Giallo films like *Deep Red*, *Phenomena* is a fun and fantastical Italian horror film that buys fully into its own wild premise. Young Jennifer Connelly appears here in only her third film role, though she would be a recognizable name a year later starring opposite David Bowie in *Labyrinth*. The plot, mixing entomology science, serial killings, and somnambulism, is a mixed bag of fascinating concepts perhaps not fully explored, but nonetheless enjoyable.

Director Argento was fully a horror filmmaking phenomenon himself when he partnered with screenwriter Franco Ferrini for the first time on this film. Longtime Argento collaborative actress (and sometimes co-writer) Daria Nicolodi appears as Jennifer's chaperone. The movie was released in the U.S. as *Creepers*. The score was created by Goblin, the rock band who became synonymous with intense supernatural thrillers in the late '70s and early '80s.

Other Titles of Interest

Scanners (1981), *The X-Files: I Want to Believe* (2008), *Minority Report* (2002), *The Dead Zone* (1983), *The Fury* (1978), *Patrick* (1978 and 2013), *The Psychic* (1977)

Redneck Horror

In 1972, British director John Boorman created the granddaddy of all redneck horror films, *Deliverance*. Though its subject matter was distinctly American, it was perfectly appropriate that a man from a country almost two thousand years old would remind us that we, at the time barely on the cusp of our two hundredth birthday, were not quite as civilized as we would like to think.

That realization, that no amount of modern technology, picket fences, or polite conversation would protect us from the unchecked aggression of depraved humanity, tapped into a fear potent enough to revisit several times over the last four decades.

In the best and most effective films of the subgenre, civilized man recognizes his complicity in the situation. The crazed rednecks may emasculate, dehumanize, and ultimately kill many of the big-city interlopers, but they see it as retribution for crimes against them: giant companies are buying up their land or flooding their valley, blowing the tops off mountains or polluting their endless blue sky. Their vengeance is extreme, but not aimless; they're monsters, but they're human ones.

Civilized man is also complicit because he has grown complacent in his comfort, safely cocooned in the protection of society. Once he wanders into the woods, every moment is a challenge of survival: He must hunt his own food and create his own weapons, and one drink of the wrong water could lead to a debilitating illness.

In the end, even a civilized human knows what he must do to survive in a hostile landscape: He must become the monster in order to defeat the monster. Thousands of years of human evolution, society, and civilization are stripped away in hours, and in surviving by embracing humanity's base mentality, the "civilized" men have to live the rest of their lives knowing that the true darkness of the enemy's heart is inside them as well...

The genre has been alive and well since the release of *Deliverance*, with entries as varied as 1981's *Just Before Dawn* and the 1980 Troma classic *Mother's Day*; there are those who would even argue that the second *Friday the 13th* film, with Jason Voorhees as a potato sack–disguised redneck killer in the woods, falls into that category. And rednecks aren't just limited to America, certainly; Australian director Jamie Blanks entered the genre with 2007's *Storm Warning*, and even France got in on the action in 2004 with *The Ordeal*.

Elements of the Subgenre

A Simple Misunderstanding Gone Wrong: In civilized society, a simple misunderstanding such as fender bender or beverage spill can be straightened out by polite conversation and restitution. In the world of the redneck horror film, retribution must be served, even for an unintended accident. It starts as a minor issue, and by the end, bodies are piled high and blood vengeance has been sworn.

If We Could Only Get to...: The one thing that will make the displaced city dwellers safe from harm is always just frustratingly out of reach or unattainable. It might be a ham radio at the cabin, or the nearby town run by a different sheriff, or a tank of gas to get their vehicle rolling again, but it's always just slightly further away than the truck full of angry locals.

We Don't Need Your Fancy Machines: The redneck contingent doesn't need the compasses or hiking gear or satellite phones that the city folk bring with them when they venture into the wilderness (they seem to do without toothbrushes or silverware, too). The redneck horror villain prides himself on his ability to survive with nearly nothing, and finds no end of amusement in making untrained city people try to do the same by taking all of their advanced technologies and watching them flounder in the wild.

Recommendations from the Subgenre

Southern Comfort (1981)
Directed by Walter Hill
Written by Michael Kane, Walter Hill, David Giler
Starring: Keith Carradine, Powers Boothe, Fred Ward

Over a weekend of training maneuvers, it is clear that a group of Louisiana National Guardsmen are not versed in survival skills. After getting lost in the swamp, the squad decides that the only way to continue their mission is to borrow boats from a local bayou resident. A misunderstanding with blank rounds causes a death, the violence on both sides escalates, and the squad members find themselves trapped in the swamp and stalked by Cajun hunters angry about the death of their friends. Landing somewhere between *Deliverance* and director Walter Hill's previous *The Warriors*, *Southern Comfort* is a war story about warriors who are forced to fight people they believed to be their own countrymen. A solid cast of tough guy character actors, including Fred Ward, Powers Boothe, and Peter Coyote, is put through the wringer on practical locations in a swamp during a cold winter, and the struggle shows in the performances.

Hill was already a writer and producer, known for films like *The Driver* and *Alien*, when he and producing partner David Giler fashioned the script for this film. The film struggled to find an audience in its initial release, but gained a following in later years and is now thought of as one of Hill's strongest films. As the Cajun heavies, Brion James and Sonny Landham made strong impressions; a year later, James was featured in the sci-fi classic *Blade Runner* while Landham's career (which began in pornography) would eventually lead him to run for Republican office in Kentucky.

Madison County (2011)
Directed and Written by Eric England
Starring: Colley Bailey, Matt Mercer, Ace Marrero

A group of college students make a trek out to the wilderness-bound Madison County to meet the author of a book about notorious serial killer Damien Ewell. They search for the author and are unsuccessful in finding him, but they do find a lot of hostility from locals who don't like the group's goal of creating a class assignment out of their local tragedy. As they try to get out of town, the group finds that there is someone out in the woods who is angry enough to start killing them one by one. A film that owes a debt to the Southern rage films of the 1970s such as *Deliverance* and *Race with the Devil*, *Madison County* is a fun revisiting of the classic story of the big-city interlopers at the mercy of secretive locals. As the serial killer Damien Ewell, stuntman-actor Nick Principe (who played another masked killer, Chrome-

Crazed killer Damien Ewell (Nick Principe) stalks the woods looking for the terrified Brooke (Joanna Sotomura) in 2011's *Madison County* (courtesy Eric England).

Skull, in the *Laid to Rest* films) makes an eerie impression, even though much of his performance is behind a face-obscuring pig mask.

After making a few short films, Eric England took on the multiple roles of director, producer, writer, and casting director for this film. England worked with cinematographer David Starks to achieve the grainy style of the film, which hearkens back to the stark imagery of the original *Texas Chain Saw Massacre*. After successfully exploring the redneck horror genre with a limited budget here, England went on to make an interesting entry in the sexual body horror arena, *Contracted*.

Tucker and Dale vs. Evil (2010)

Directed by Eli Craig
Written by Eli Craig, Morgan Jurgenson
Starring: Tyler Labine, Alan Tudyk, Katrina Bowden

Tucker and Dale, simple-minded country boys, have purchased a run-down cabin in the middle of nowhere and are excited about their renovation vacation. A group of city kids are camping nearby. After a confusing interaction that ends with Dale saving one of them from drowning, the city kids seem to think that Tucker and Dale are crazed hillbilly killers. The city kids decide they have to try and kill the two of them before they are killed themselves. A series of bizarre accidents, in which the city kids keep dying, make it look to the surviving kids like Tucker and Dale keep murdering them. A brilliant comedic re-evaluation of the redneck horror subgenre that subverts expectations in a similar way to *Cabin in the Woods*, *Tucker and Dale vs. Evil* is a very smart film about very stupid people. Great chemistry between Tyler Labine and Alan Tudyk, as the nice but vacuous hillbilly friends, anchors a deceptively clever plot that flips all the conventions of the genre, from the "chainsaw dance" to the "wood-chipper disposal," and turns the supposed villains into confused pseudo-heroes.

Eli Craig had experience as an actor, writer, and director in a series of short films before making this his first feature. With writing partner Morgan Jurgenson he fashioned a film that found a surprisingly large audience, and the film did well in the horror-industry awards circuit with wins at Fangoria and Fright Meter. Labine and Tudyk announced during a festival appearance that there would indeed be a sequel to the film.

Other Titles of Interest

Eden Lake (2008), *Staunton Hill* (2008), *The Hills Run Red* (2009), *The Devil's Rejects* (2005), *Backwoods* (2008), *The Locals* (2003), *Breakdown* (1997)

Repressed Sexuality Horror

It's not hard to understand why films about repressed or damaged sexuality (especially as regards female sexuality) are so common within the American horror arena. With horror movies acting as a lens for the discussions, frustrations, and problems that are taking place within a society at a given time and place, one can clearly see how the mixed messages of American media can create problems with a person's level of comfort regarding their gender identity.

As a society, Americans have little to no tolerance when it comes to sexual predators preying on children, as is evidenced by the many laws we have created and the harsh punishments we inflict on those who cross the very clear set boundaries. In this respect, we have drawn a line of decency and propriety which we expect everyone to respect and obey. Our media conform to this idea, showing the people who break these taboos as deviants and psychologically disturbed loners. The stance is unequivocal.

And then there is everything else we see in media in America. The proliferation of social sexuality (used for everything from easily attained pornography to innuendo-laden commercials for fast-food restaurants like Carl's Jr.) has given rise to an inborn sense of sexual identification and sexual confusion in children and pre-teens (primarily girls) before they have even progressed biologically to the point that sexuality should even be an element of discussion or consideration.

A young woman may notice that the strong laws protecting her from being coerced into pornography when she is a child seem to dissipate quickly when she is of legal age, and she might find it confusing that the same father who threatens to beat up any boy who gets inappropriate with his daughter would also stare creepily at cheerleaders during a football game. The dissonance between what is being told and what is being shown creates a breakdown in the path to a healthy understanding of personal sexuality.

The confusing imbalance of America's desire to protect our children from unwanted sexuality while simultaneously bombarding them with it in movies, magazines, television shows, and billboards can easily translate into a series of psychological hang-ups in the mind of a particularly sensitive child. In real life, the results can be as varied as eating disorders, fear of intimacy, casual sexuality, and self-hatred; in horror films, the damage inflicted on a still-developing young mind can manifest in much more troubling ways.

Elements of the Subgenre

The Secret Slut: Films in this subgenre often seem to undercut themselves thematically by creating a character who has some kind of external fear or paranoia about intimacy that is in many ways contradicted by what we see them thinking about or fantasizing. In their heads, they have the freedom to go out and have rampant sex with multiple people, while remaining unable to even endure the touch of another human being in real life.

It's a Woman's Problem: In these films, men never seem to have any issues with repressed sexuality. It is only women who suffer from this crippling disorder, and in the same way that the women are simply the victims, the men are nothing more than the aggressors.

Recommendations from the Subgenre

Repulsion (1965)

Directed by Roman Polanski
Written by Roman Polanski, Gerard Brach, David Stone
Starring: Catherine Deneuve, Ian Hendry, John Fraser

Carol, a severely anxious woman living with her sister Helen, is left alone in their London apartment when Helen goes on vacation. Carol's anxiety intensifies due to the isolation, and the sexual discomfort she feels around men in her life begins to manifest in strange ways. She starts to have bizarre hallucinations about her apartment slowly crumbling, and believes that a man is constantly attempting to break in and rape her. Encounters with a suitor and her landlord turn the hallucinations into violent reality as she defends herself from unwanted attention. A chamber piece of unrelenting psychological tension, *Repulsion* is a tricky film whose perspective rarely deviates from that of the main character and keeps the audience firmly enmeshed in her slowly devolving mental state. A *tour-de-force* lead performance from French actress Catherine Deneuve is miles away from the sweet innocent that she played in 1964's *Umbrellas of Cherbourg*, and Deneuve delivers spectacularly. Oppressive set design and inventive camerawork help to add to the mounting claustrophobia of the apartment.

Though Roman Polanski had worked in the Polish film industry for several years, he had only directed one feature, *Knife in the Water*, before making this film. He co-wrote the script with Gerard Brach, with whom he would work again on *Cul-de-Sac* and *The Fearless Vampire Killers*. Cinematographer Gilbert Taylor had previous experience with beautiful black and white photography, having shot *Dr. Strangelove*, and he later worked on *The Omen* and the original *Star Wars*.

Excision (2012)

Written and Directed by Richard Bates, Jr.
Starring: AnnaLynne McCord, Roger Bart, Ariel Winter

Pauline is an unusual girl. She is obsessed with working in the medical profession, and has extremely disturbing daydreams that involve vibrantly bloody sexuality. She is unpopular at school, and is seeking someone with whom she can lose her virginity, while at home she is dealing with the fact that her younger sister is slowly dying of cystic fibrosis. After a frustrating rejection and a humiliating prank, the already unstable Pauline tries to gain some level of control in her life by embracing her interest in surgery and attempting to save her sister's life. A delicate balance of adolescent angst and suburban ennui, Excision takes elements known well in the drama arena and covers them with blood and quirkiness, to interesting effect. The film lives or dies on the performance of Pauline, and 90210 star AnnaLynne McCord is fearless in her portrayal of the mousy and disturbed girl and her over-the-top fantasy counterpart. Fun supporting roles are played by a series of recognizable faces, from Tracy Lords to John Waters to Marlee Matlin, raising the profile of this unusual and singular horror film.

Four years before Excision became a feature film, director Richard Bates Jr., had already produced it as a short film. Falling into the subgenre with more recent entries like Lucky McKee's May, the film received mixed reviews, but most made note of its visual flair. Bates' distinct mix of horror and commentary was on full display in his sophomore effort Suburban Gothic, which brought back Excision players including John Waters and lead actor Matthew Gray Gubler.

Disturbed loner Pauline (AnnaLynne McCord) is exotic and empowered in her dark and outlandish fantasies in the 2012 horror film Excision (courtesy Dylan Lewis).

Teeth (2007)

Written and Directed by Mitchell Lichtenstein
Starring: Jess Weixler, John Hensley, Josh Pais

Abstinence activist Dawn O'Keefe meets Tobey and, after spending a little time together, a casual outing becomes heated: Tobey tries to have sex with her when she doesn't want to. A graphic castration takes place mid-coitus, and Dawn discovers that she has a set of sharp teeth inside her vagina. Dawn is frightened of her body and its capabilities and of being arrested for the unintentional murder of Tobey.

Using the wildest urban legend imaginable to construct a fascinating fable of female empowerment, *Teeth* is as daring as it is unexpected. Jess Weixler, a writer-actress known for several independent films and a run on *The Good Wife*, plays the central role with a delicate balance of fear, confusion, and secret appreciation. The film does a great job of casting actors who can play the sleazy men in her life, of which John Hensley and Josh Pais are standouts.

Mitchell Lichtenstein was a working actor in films like *Streamers* and Ang Lee's *The Wedding Banquet* before making his feature directorial debut here. His script juggles dark humor, issues of female sexuality, and commentary on gender politics in a conservative climate, and its shifting tone and cleverness were influential on the later female-driven horror-comedy *Jennifer's Body*. Since his horror film debut, Lichtenstein made *Happy Tears*, an indie comedy-drama, and is returning to horror with the ghost story *Angelica*.

Other Titles of Interest

In the Realm of the Senses (1976), *Blue Velvet* (1986), *The Piano Teacher* (2001), *Dressed to Kill* (1980)

Road-Travel Horror

One of the linchpins of the horror genre is the fear of the unknown, of the strange place or person. Much of what scares us can come from the everyday and mundane, but in a horror film, there is something to be said for the wrong turn down a dark road or the questionable motives of a new neighbor.

That is why road travel is so effective as a horror film element. The simple act of having someone travel creates a character whose very existence is constantly out of place. They are the eternal stranger, and that can be used effectively to dual purposes. In the case of the Mysterious Stranger, he could be the strangler everyone in the town heard about on the news; or in the case of the Upstanding Vacationer, he could be out to enjoy a week off from work with a camping trip, only to discover unpleasant secrets in the cabins off the interstate.

The concept of traveling makes all places strange and ominous, stretches of empty road and deserted rest stops as the ever-widening circles of Hell. Whether the trouble follows you down that road (as in the case of John Ryder in the classic 1980s thriller *The Hitcher*) or simply strands you in the middle of it (like the inbred family's trap in *The Hills Have Eyes*), the journey down a road in isolated country has the effect of shrinking your hope of escape down to a slab of asphalt 25 feet wide and thousands of miles long.

The road travel element of horror also feeds into other well-known elements in the genre, from the seemingly pleasant family-owned businesses (a motel run by a man and his mother, or a small Texas gas station that sells smoked meat) to the strange psychological trap of the never-ending car trip (seen in films such as *Dead End* and *In Fear*) to the unforeseen accidents that trap people in life-threatening wrecks (like Adrien Brody in *Wrecked* and Stephen Rea in *Stuck*). No matter the preparation, the distance, or the passengers, no road trip in a horror movie ever ends the way it was intended.

Elements of the Subgenre

Trouble with the Car?: One of the great classic tropes of horror films across the board, the "car trouble" trope is most effectively used in the road-travel horror film. It might be frightening if your car doesn't start at night in your own driveway, but it is far more terrifying when you can hear the engine turn over but never start while you're watching the headlights slowly fade to black against the wall of pine trees on either side of you.

Fast-Draining Batteries: Perhaps it's a geographic thing, but right at the moment that a person or group of people get just far away enough from the safety of a city or rest area, the GPS or cell phone or flashlight never seems to be able to work properly, blinking on and off or just running out of power entirely.

Recommendations from the Subgenre

Duel (1971)
Directed by Steven Spielberg
Written by Richard Matheson (based on his story)
Starring: Dennis Weaver

David Mann is a traveling salesman on a long road trip through the California desert. After encountering a filthy truck on the road that continues to pull in front of him and slow down, the antagonism between them escalates from irritation to attempted vehicular homicide. David is terrified of the crazed truck driver, and can find no one who believes his story or is willing to help him. The mild-mannered salesman must find the strength and courage within himself to face down the aggressor alone, or end up a casualty littering the side of the desert highway. The high-water mark of the subgenre, Universal's *Duel* is one of the great made-for-TV movies; it was so well-received in the U.S. that Universal decided to release it theatrically overseas. A raw performance by Dennis Weaver holds the entire film together, and he appears in nearly every moment on screen. Though never seen, the antagonistic trucker is a brilliant and terrifying villain.

Steven Spielberg had directed several short films and episodes of TV's *Columbo* and *Night Gallery* when he came on to direct this film. Written by Richard Matheson, who adapted his own short story for the screen, the movie taps into the savage heart of humanity in its most simplistic forms: violence and survival. It was highly influential on the subgenre for decades to come; the makers of films like *Breakdown* and *Road Games* owe it a debt of gratitude.

Joy Ride (2001)

Directed by John Dahl
Written by Clay Tarver, J.J. Abrams
Starring: Steve Zahn, Paul Walker, Leelee Sobieski

When a young man's offer to drive a female friend across the country to go home from college for summer break is interrupted by his troublemaking brother, they make the most of the trip by buying a CB radio and interacting with truckers. They pull a prank on one of the truckers, pretending to be a woman interested in meeting up, and they convince him to come to a hotel room that is actually occupied by another surly man. When their prank escalates into murder, the three of them try to leave the area, only to find out that the trucker who killed the hotel room man is on their trail and knows what they did. A fun throwback to the road movies of the 1970s, *Joy Ride* owes a great deal to Spielberg's *Duel* for influence and mood. A likable trio of lead actors allows the audience to enjoy the bad behavior until it gets out of control in the second act. Paul Walker has never been better than he is when playing off Steve Zahn as antagonistic brothers. Though never appearing on-screen, *Silence of the Lambs* actor Ted Levine makes a frightening impact as the voice of trucker Rusty Nail.

J.J. Abrams was still primarily known as the creator of the television series *Felicity* and *Alias* when he teamed with Clay Tarver to write this film. John Dahl, already a hot commodity in high-concept thrillers like *The Last Seduction* and *Rounders*, was the perfect choice to direct. The moviemakers ended up filming five alternate endings, including one which deviated from the story for a full 29 minutes, all of which are available on the DVD release; ironically, the only version in which the villainous Rusty Nail survives is the official release, and it is that cut which was sequelized twice, as *Joy Ride 2: Dead Ahead* and *Joy Ride 3: Road Kill*. In both sequels, only Rusty Nail returns.

Wind Chill (2007)

Directed by Gregory Jacobs
Written by Joseph Gangemi, Steven Katz
Starring: Emily Blunt, Ashton Holmes, Martin Donovan

Two students splitting gas money to drive home from college for Christmas break are stranded in the midst of a snowbank on the side of an empty stretch of road after being forced off the road by a passing vehicle. After a few strange sightings of unresponsive people walking by the vehicle, they think help has arrived in the form of a highway patrolman. But after he assaults them and then vanishes, they find some evidence that the patrolman and the people they saw earlier died decades ago, and they've somehow become caught in a re-enactment of their deaths. Combining the road horror film with the classic "history repeats itself" ghost story, *Wind Chill* adds some great cinematography and an interesting final revelation to make this a welcome addition to the category. Though the cast is small, with only three lead characters, there are several familiar faces, including *The Devil Wears Prada*'s Emily Blunt and frequent Hal Hartley collaborator Martin Donovan.

Gregory Jacobs had already written and directed the well-received indie thriller *Criminal* when he brought this project to the screen. He had worked with director Steven Soderbergh as assistant director on nine films; Soderbergh backed this film financially through his and George Clooney's production company, Section Eight. Jacobs reunited with Soderbergh and *Wind Chill* writer Steven Katz on the Cinemax series *The Knick*.

Other Titles of Interest

Death Proof (2007), *Road Games* (1981), *Dead End* (2003), *Hush* (2008), *Drive Angry* (2011), *Jeepers Creepers* (2001), *Road Kill* (2010), *Hit and Run* (2009)

School Horror

School is a terrible place to be, on the best of terms. Regimented times for everything (from when you can eat to what time you're allowed to go back to your home), tiny metal boxes in which you have to house all of your belongings (and which can be searched without permission by an alarming number of other people), tiny rooms packed to the brim with other noisy, annoying kids, confusing lessons and arbitrary testing, and the indignity of having to ask permission (and be given documentation) in order to go to the restroom. That any of us survive it is truly amazing.

All of those unpleasant aspects of school might just be bearable, if they weren't coupled with the perfect storm that is adolescent angst. In the midst of the physical changes that human bodies go through during puberty (which cause their own problems at very inconvenient times in public), emotional changes rear their ugly head as well. Suddenly, everything is bigger, scarier, more upsetting, and downright tragic than it ever was before. Every decision is life or death, every interaction could change your social status, and every fashion decision could be a nightmare waiting to happen.

School isn't a nurturing environment that is meant to accompany a maturing young person into adulthood with understanding and knowledge; it is a war zone, meant to be survived. The rigid structure of hourly shifts in location and subject matter leave the average student woefully unprepared for a later professional life wherein personal responsibility and critical thinking skills are necessary. It is frightening and competitive, and it prepares you for almost nothing in later life.

But we keep doing it. Like a strange hazing ritual that old recruits force new recruits through because they don't want someone else to escape the indignity of having to survive it themselves, we do nothing to correct the weirdness, the cruelty, the violence, the strictness. We lament a generation of children who are not as intelligent or free-thinking as the one before, but we never bother to do the hard work of isolating the problem and changing it. The descent continues.

The work of education has little to do with the experience of attending school, and the horror genre does an excellent job of separating them. The real lessons to be learned in school, horror films tell us, are the ones about knowing which teachers might be aliens, which secrets are locked away in detention hall, and which students might be ready to reach in their coats for a weapon at any moment.

Elements of the Subgenre

Supernatural Analogies for the High School Experience: Though most notably seen on the movie and TV series *Buffy the Vampire Slayer*, the idea of using supernatural elements to express the struggle and angst of the school experience is something many films touch on. From vampires and werewolves as stand-ins for sexual frustration and bullying to selective murder as a representation of class popularity, the heightened emotions of school translate perfectly to the world of the horror film.

Dying to Be Popular: The way that students divide themselves into groups in school creates a hierarchy of popularity, and that division can lead to confrontation. The rivalries created in the halls of the school parallel gangs and armies constantly plotting to take each other out in the battlefield of the school hallway.

Recommendations from the Subgenre

Prom Night (1980)

Directed by Paul Lynch
Written by William Gray, Robert Guza, Jr.
Starring: Leslie Nielsen, Jamie Lee Curtis, Casey Stevens

On the six-year anniversary of her sister's death, Kim is preparing to attend her prom. Unbeknownst to Kim, her sister is dead due to an accident caused by four of her school friends. While preparing for the dance, many of the friends receive threatening phone calls, and the bodies of the prom victims begin to pile up as the friends separate to have sex, smoke pot, and enjoy their evenings.

Moviemakers raided the typical adolescent life for any events of significance to turn into slasher bloodbaths in the wake of the success of *Halloween*; *Prom Night* focuses on the high school rite of passage. The film borrows many elements of the new but already codified slasher playbook, including a past tragedy shown in the opening moments, victims picked off one by one, and even the appearance of Jamie Lee Curtis (who would also appear in *Terror Train* later this same year).

The release and success of *Prom Night*, along with *Friday the 13th* two months earlier, heralded the staying power of the slasher film and proved that new horror films didn't need famous faces or large budgets to find an audience. After a couple of low-budget action films, director Paul Lynch assembled this Canadian production. Its unexpected success brought other Canadian filmmakers into the game, with *My Bloody Valentine* coming the next year. *Prom Night* was a success that was followed by three largely unrelated supernatural sequels and a PG-13 thriller remake in 2008.

The Faculty (1998)

Directed by Robert Rodriguez
Written by Kevin Williamson, David Wechter, Bruce Kimmel
Starring: Elijah Wood, Josh Hartnett, Clea DuVall

An unlikely group of students—a nerdy photographer, a cheerleader, a pothead, a football player, and an outcast—stumble onto a conspiracy that seems to connect to all of the teachers and staff of their local high school. It seems that many of the instructors have been taken over by some kind of extraterrestrial hive mind presence, and are slowly recruiting the students of the school in order to spread their influence through the town. The students team up to find the origin and weaknesses of the alien menace and stop them before they quietly conquer the entire world. A clear homage to *Invasion of the Body Snatchers* by way of *The Breakfast Club*, *The Faculty* is a fun and knowing science fiction–action film with clever dialogue and a surprisingly talented cast of young actors. Utilizing a similar whodunit angle as the recent release *Scream* (in this case, "Who is the alien?" rather than "Who is the killer?"), the film does a great job of incorporating drug use, social cliques, and "adults just don't get it" attitude into an age-old invasion concept.

Two of Miramax's young shining stars, *Desperado* director Robert Rodriguez and *Scream* writer Kevin Williamson, teamed to bring this action-comedy hybrid to screen. A mild success upon release, the film built a cult following due to its self-awareness and allusions to other great alien films. Aside from *Invasion of the Body Snatchers*, there are clear references to *The Thing* and *The Stepford Wives*. Williamson was originally going to direct the film, but opted instead to direct his other script *Teaching Mrs. Tingle*.

Buffy the Vampire Slayer (1992)

Directed by Fran Rubel Kuzui
Written by Joss Whedon
Starring: Kristy Swanson, Donald Sutherland, Rutger Hauer

When Buffy Summers begins her senior year in high school, she expects the normal shopping and boyfriend events that anyone else would. She instead finds out that she is a chosen warrior known as the Slayer, a female vampire killer whose job is to protect humanity from the forces of darkness. After a successful run of vampire killings, Buffy becomes the target of Lothos, a vampire king known for having killed many past Slayers. An attack on the senior dance pushes Buffy into the unlikely position of protecting the entire school from a vampire onslaught. The film that spawned a television empire, *Buffy the Vampire Slayer* was a moderately successful comedy that was at its best when it balanced the fears of vampires with the fears of adolescence. Excellent characterizations from Paul Reubens and Rutger Hauer are largely lost amidst the straight-faced performances in the film, which give the entire movie a schizophrenic sensibility.

Screenwriter Joss Whedon had already worked on television as a story editor for series like *Roseanne* when his *Buffy* script was optioned for the big screen. Generally unhappy with the final product (and in particular, the performance of Donald Sutherland, who strayed from the script and improvised much of his dialogue), Whedon pitched the concept as a television series which was eventually picked up and which made only passing reference to events from the movie. Whedon's television series (he produced and wrote episodes) captured the dark, *Heathers*-esque comedy style that Whedon sought, and would eventually lead to the spin-off series *Angel* and a long run of sequel comics.

Other Titles of Interest

The Expelled (2010), *The Substitute* (1996), *Hell Night* (1981), *Dorm* (2006), *The Final* (2010), *Dance of the Dead* (2008)

Serial Killer Horror

Serial killers in film are both the progenitors of the slasher (because slashers *are* serial killers; they just do it with more flair and an eye for costuming) and also the safe haven to which horror and thriller films retreated in the wake of the slasher cycle.

The 1980s belonged to the slasher killer, with his stylish weapon of choice and his endless array of addle-minded teens ready to be killed in graphic and elaborate ways. The backlash to these slashers, however, was wide-reaching. The films became increasingly derivative while simultaneously getting more and more violent, until even the fans of the movies grew tired of the obvious template from which almost no film deviated. The ultra-violence was too much for religious organizations and parents groups, but still not enough for fans.

It was the 1990s, a decade known for its political correctness as well as its skill in merging commercial sensibilities with audience taste, that brought about the solution to the problem of slashers: the serial killer, the somewhat forgotten absentee father of the slasher who had waned in popularity in the 1980s because of his boring clothes and ability to fit into society.

What producers of serial killer films quickly figured out was that, much like a slasher, you could have a truly heinous villain as the centerpiece of your film; but unlike slashers, the villain needed a nemesis that the audience could ostensibly root for, exonerating the producers from any accusation of glorifying violence because they allowed the audience to cheer for the hero. Gone were the anti-heroes of the 1980s who joyfully murdered until the closing credits, replaced by the tortured human serial killers who secretly fed their dark desires while an upstanding member of law enforcement pushed himself (and perhaps his family) too far in an attempt to stop the killings.

By creating a believable human hero, one with a history and a family and flaws and feelings, filmmakers discovered that they could make the serial killer so much more vile and graphically violent by comparison. The horror fans who sought out the over-the-top violence of slasher films could be sated with the acts of these serial killers, while the mainstream film-going audiences could recoil in horror at their acts and hope desperately that the FBI agent or police detective or county sheriff would figure it out in time.

Though not as fantastic as the slasher, the serial killer, in all his clinically disturbed detail, is actually responsible for the increased level of realistic violence present in modern films. Masquerading as stories about heroes conquering the darkness, serial killer films actually made the landscape of horror film that much more dark.

Elements of the Subgenre

A Psychological Exploration: Unlike the masked killers of the slasher subgenre who seemingly kill with little or no purpose, the serial killer horror movie attempts to explain, diagnose, and perhaps even come to understand the thought processes and motivations of the central murderer.

Live to Kill Another Day: The very human killers in these films are often captured and studied, rather than killed like their murderous counterparts in other subgenres. Part of the reason is because it leads to the classic trope of the imprisoned killer interrogation, but mostly it is so that the killer may escape again in the event that the movie is popular enough to warrant a sequel.

Recommendations from the Subgenre

Psycho (1960)

Directed by Alfred Hitchcock
Written by Joseph Stefano (based on the novel by Robert Bloch)
Starring: Anthony Perkins, Janet Leigh, Vera Miles

First-time thief Marion Crane takes money from the bank where she works and flees town so she can be with her married boyfriend. While waiting it out in a rundown motel well off the main highway, she is killed by someone dressed in an old woman's clothes. Innocent-looking proprietor Norman Bates covers it up, believing his frail mother to be the killer. He disposes of Marion's car and body, along with the money, and believes he has succeeded. But a nosy detective and Marion's sister come looking for her, and his secrets don't remain buried for long. In all likelihood the most famous horror film in the history of American movies, *Psycho* is a masterpiece of suspense by the master of suspense himself, Alfred Hitchcock. Strong and sympathetic performances from Janet Leigh and Anthony Perkins help lull the viewer into false expectations that are shattered by the film's now well-known second act twist.

Already the most popular and successful film director in Hollywood, Hitchcock's daring experiment with *Psycho* was simple: make a mainstream film that no studio wanted because of its violence and prurient subject matter. He achieved it, though he had to make it low-budget, in black and white with his television crew. The film (and its original source novel by Robert Bloch) was inspired by the murders committed by Ed Gein; his story would later inspire other stories like *The Texas Chain Saw Massacre* and *The Silence of the Lambs*. *Psycho* was one of the earliest true horror films to be nominated for multiple Academy Awards, though it won none of them.

Henry: Portrait of a Serial Killer (1986)

Directed by John McNaughton
Written by Richard Fire, John McNaughton
Starring: Michael Rooker, Tom Towles, Tracy Arnold

Murderer and ex-convict Henry shares an apartment with his prison friend Otis and Otis' recently separated sister Becky. Henry reveals himself to be a cold-blooded serial killer to Otis, who decides to participate with Henry in a series of random killings, some of which they record. Henry develops a tentative relationship with Becky, and when Otis rapes and attempts to kill Becky, Henry murders him. The two of them are linked by the murder, and head off together for a new start, until tragedy occurs. A dark, brooding, relentless piece of *vérité* filmmaking, *Henry: Portrait of a Serial Killer* is an unflinching look at the most frightening parts of humanity. A virtuoso performance from genre favorite Michael Rooker (making his film debut here) is boosted by the presence of Tom Towles, a Chicago actor whose skill in playing unlikable figures is nearly unrivaled (see his performance in 1990's *Night of the Living Dead*).

Before finding wide audiences with thrillers like *Mad Dog and Glory* and *Wild Things*, director John McNaughton started his career with this disturbingly realistic low-budget film. Based broadly on the real-life killers Henry Lee Lucas and Ottis Toole, the film was completed in 1986 but not released until 1990 due to marketing concerns and issues with the ratings board. A surprise cult following arose around the film, and a barely related sequel, *Henry: Portrait of a Serial Killer 2: Mask of Sanity*, was produced in 1996 without the involvement of director McNaughton or star Rooker.

Man Bites Dog (1992)

Directed by Rémy Belvaux, André Bonzel, Benoît Poelvoorde
Written by Rémy Belvaux, André Bonzel, Benoît Poelvoorde, Vincent Tavier
Starring: Benoît Poelvoorde, Jenny Drye, Rémy Belvaux

Benoît is a dangerous serial killer who also happens to be a bit of a buffoon and an amateur philosopher. A documentary camera crew trails him as he does his work, killing old people and children and dumping their bodies over bridges in the dead of night. As they continue filming his exploits, they slowly become wrapped up in his activities, eventually coming to participate in some of the heinous acts themselves. Eventually, someone begins targeting Benoît in revenge for his murders, and the film crew learns that they have become targets as well. Shot in an effortless and accessible style, *Man Bites Dog* is a deceptively complex study of violence and its insidious reach. The disarmingly humorous and charming Benoît has frightening outbursts of murder and abuse, and the audience's sympathies for his plight somehow remain intact through the majority of the film, until the members of the camera crew become active participants in his adventures.

The film was made by four student filmmakers, all of whom appear as major characters (and use their own names, to make it even more confusing to discern what is real and what isn't). Winner of two awards at the Cannes Film Festival, the low-budget Belgian film found a loyal following in America, where it was hugely influential to many fake documentary and found footage–style horror films, from *Behind the Mask: The Rise of Leslie Vernon* to *Long Pigs*.

Other Titles of Interest

The Silence of the Lambs (1991), *The Cell* (2000), *The Watcher* (2000), *The Crimson Rivers* (2000), *American Psycho* (2000), *Frailty* (2001), *The Poughkeepsie Tapes* (2007), *The Town That Dreaded Sundown* (1976 and 2014)

Shape-Shifter Horror

Why are we scared by the idea that something could look human while not being human? The instinct of humanity is to form everything into a shape that is pleasing to us, from our beliefs (more wars have been fought about the minor details of differing religions than almost anything else in the history of mankind) to our technologies (we want our computers to have voices and personalities) to our entertainment (cartoon animals always seem to stand on their hind legs, wear clothes, and speak). If we're so egocentric as to even see humanity in everyday objects (have you ever looked at the shape of the holes in a wall socket and instinctively seen a face staring back at you?), then why would we have such an issue with an alien, a machine, or a mutant creature of some kind that wanted to mimic that human shape?

It is possible that, where we attribute human appearance, we also attribute human thinking. We as a society know that the undesirables in our midst, the rapists and the murderers and the thieves, all have the same general appearance as the rest of us. That is, in fact, the reason that they try so hard to blend in; there is no foolproof way to look at a person and know that they are psychologically not like us. Though we try not to think about it consciously on a daily basis, we are always armed with the knowledge that evil walks among us without being seen.

Extrapolated in a horror context, the ability to look like us means that the enemy could be anyone, or everyone. It could even be us; if evil could look like someone else to you, why couldn't it look like you to someone else? The shape-changer in a horror film fools us by using our own expectations against us. We can't spend every second of every day watching all the people around us to figure out which ones are the murderers and rapists; we do the best we can, and we subconsciously hope that they will either be people we don't know, or that they simply won't target us. The same is true of the shape-changing villain in a horror film: the main characters can't spend every moment monitoring for slight personality changes, differing modes of speech, or telltale signs of altered identity. But unlike in real life, the characters in a horror film are always absolutely the target.

Elements of the Subgenre

Even the Audience Doesn't Know Sometimes: A good shape-shifter horror film keeps the characters in the film guessing who might be who, but a great one keeps the audience guessing as well. Sometimes up until the closing moments of the film, the audience may think they have the entire breakdown of humans versus shape-shifters figured out; but one surprising revelation can make the audience completely rethink the entire movie.

How Do the Clothes Fit?: When a person changes shape, the clothes don't change shape along with them. Sometimes, the clothes will be ripped to shreds by the transformation, leaving the new person standing naked in public, while at other times, the clothes will be ill-fitting but still cover all the important parts of the body. The amount of clothing remaining on the body often seems to be directly related to the level of fame of the person playing the shape-changer.

Recommendations from the Subgenre

Invasion of the Body Snatchers (1956)
Directed by Don Siegel
Written by Daniel Mainwaring (based on the story by Jack Finney)
Starring: Kevin McCarthy, Dana Wynter, Larry Gates

Dr. Miles Bennell, a doctor in the small town of Santa Mira, California, finds himself being consulted for numerous cases involving people who believe their loved ones have been

replaced by impostors. Upon further investigation, Bennell begins finding undeveloped, fea-
tureless human bodies hidden in cellars in the town. He learns that giant seed pods are appearing in people's homes and, when the people fall asleep, they are being replaced by exact
duplicates of themselves that grow out of the pods. The phenomenon is spreading, and Bennell
tries to flee in the hopes of warning others. One of the most famous science fiction conceits
of all time, *Invasion of the Body Snatchers* is a classic of American paranoid cinema that also
boasts one of the most memorable scenes of all time as Kevin McCarthy's Bennell runs wildly
through traffic trying to convince passing drivers of the conspiracy. Great lead performances
from McCarthy and Dana Wynter anchor a terrifying premise, and a solid script by *Out of
the Past* writer Daniel Mainwaring never lets up on the tension.

Though most people remember Don Siegel for his many collaborations with star Clint
Eastwood (*Dirty Harry* being the most famous), Siegel was a skilled crime and western director
before venturing into science fiction for this film. Much was made of its possible subtext
regarding communism and the McCarthy investigations, but director Siegel always maintained
that it was not intentional. The film has been remade three times, and each explored a different
possibility for the thematic representation of the "pod people." In 1978's *Invasion of the Body
Snatchers*, it dealt with conformity and individuality; in 1993's *Body Snatchers*, it discussed
military overreach; and in 2007's *The Invasion*, political power and corruption were its focus.

Terminator 2: Judgment Day (1991)

Directed by James Cameron
Written by James Cameron, William Wisher, Jr.
Starring: Arnold Schwarzenegger, Linda Hamilton, Edward Furlong

After the events of the original *The Terminator*, which had a hero from the future attempting to save Sarah Connor from the monstrous Terminator killing machine, Sarah is now housed
in a psychiatric facility. Her son John has been adopted by another family, and all seems fine,
until a new, shape-shifting robot comes back in time to kill John. Sarah escapes to save him,
only to find out that he's being protected by a different version of the same killing machine that
tried to murder her previously. They form an uncomfortable alliance to defeat the new robot
killer and stop the dystopian future which created them from ever coming about. The hugely
successful original film was already a classic when *Terminator 2: Judgment Day* came onto the
scene and became the highest-grossing film of 1991. The brilliant and unexpected decision
to make the villain of the first film the hero of the second one breathed new life into the concept, and a higher budget allowed for even more fantastic special effects and action sequences.

James Cameron had already created the hugely profitable sequel *Aliens* when production
company Carolco gave him the green light to create this sequel to his own creation. It was
the rare science fiction action film nominated for Academy Awards (it won four). The script
by Cameron and William Wisher Jr. is often called one of the perfect action movie script tem-
plates. Because shooting took so long on the film, young star Edward Furlong visibly aged
throughout, and most of his lines had to be re-dubbed after his voice changed partway through
the production.

The Thing (1982)

Directed by John Carpenter
Written by Bill Lancaster (based on the story by John W. Campbell, Jr.)
Starring: Kurt Russell, Keith David, Wilford Brimley

After a Norwegian helicopter attacks an American research station in Antarctica while trying to kill a dog, part of the research team heads to the Norwegian camp to investigate. They discover that everyone there is dead, probably killed by something that they found frozen for thousands of years in the ice. Some of the scientists begin to believe what was in the ice was a living creature which could take any shape. When communications are cut off, the group begins to suspect that the creature is among them in disguise. Combining claustrophobic paranoia with some of the most ambitious and mind-blowing practical effects ever committed to film, *The Thing* was a remake of a beloved classic that became a classic of its own. Employing a cast of recognizable veteran actors, from Wilford Brimley to Richard Masur, the film plays like *Ten Little Indians* with some alien shape-shifting thrown in for good measure.

Director John Carpenter had already worked with actor Kurt Russell twice when they re-teamed for this film (they would work together twice more after this). Though the entire on-screen cast is male, Carpenter's then-wife Adrienne Barbeau can be heard as the voice of the computer chess game. The special effects were created by Rob Bottin, hot off his fantastic werewolf work in *The Howling*. In a rarity for Carpenter, who often wrote and performed his own scores, he chose to have the score composed by his favorite musician, experimental icon and Sergio Leone collaborator Ennio Morricone.

Other Titles of Interest

Sleepwalkers (1992), *Cat People* (1942 and 1982), *Shapeshifter* (2005)

Siege Horror

There are certain human needs, beliefs, and instincts that transcend the need to be explained in great detail. Food, water, shelter, love. These are things which need no context, because we naturally and biologically seek them out. And the more necessary they are for existence, the less information an individual requires to understand them.

The human need for safety is one of these. We create our own places of safety in our homes or cars when we're adults, in our tree forts or blanket castles when we are children; we have an inherent desire to have a space of our own. With that desire to have our own space comes an equally strong need to protect it. Whatever that place may be, it is ours, and we do not want others intruding upon it (the exception of course being loved ones that we trust to enter our safe zones).

No child is ever instructed to feel territorial or to wish to have something of their own that belongs only to them, and no one needs to tell them they should protect it from others. It comes with the DNA, and we need never speak of it. Which is why, when that safety is threatened, there is just as little that needs to be said about the lengths we will go to in order to keep it.

The siege horror subgenre taps into that psychology in the most direct and uncomplicated way, by casting off the need for unnecessary context and placing the viewer in the same frightening situation as the characters on the screen. The greatest siege films will work with audiences in any country across the entire world, because we all have the same universal biological response to being attacked. And the very greatest of those films, films like *Assault on Precinct 13*, recognize that visceral experience works far better than complicated storytelling, and have entire passages of the movie that take place with nearly no dialogue.

It is of note that almost no siege horror film exists in which the people for whom we sympathize are on the outside, trying to get in. This is significant, because our very instincts tell us that whoever wants to force their way inside must be the villain. As viewers, our world shrinks to the size of a farmhouse or a school bus, and we're just as ready to defend it as the characters we're watching.

Elements of the Subgenre

Just a Simple, Little…: The places chosen for a siege are chosen because people want to (and expect to be able to) get inside. As such, none of the locations are particularly difficult to get into; you won't find a Fort Knox siege film out there. The quaint little country houses or old police precincts or abandoned toy factories are never built to withstand a battle, and that's what makes the attempted takeover so thrilling.

They Come Right Up to the Door: The people leading the siege are generally bold, or crazy, or they have nothing left to live for, and so they're not going to play it safe. They may come right up and ring the doorbell, or throw a jar of blood on the front porch, or fling a dead body through an un-boarded window. That is your first and last warning of what is to come.

Recommendations from the Subgenre

Straw Dogs (1971)
Directed by Sam Peckinpah
Written by David Zelag Goodman, Sam Peckinpah (based on the story by Gordon Williams)
Starring: Dustin Hoffman, Susan George, Peter Vaughn

American mathematician David and his English bride Amy move to the small town of Cornwall, the town where Amy grew up. Troubles in their relationship are compounded by a group of men from town, one of whom is Amy's old boyfriend. After Amy is sexually assaulted, and many of the townsfolk try to capture a mentally challenged man David is protecting, he decides he has to fortify his home and protect the three of them using whatever violent means necessary. A dark and brutal film known as much for its controversial scenes of sex as for its levels of violence, *Straw Dogs* is a true test of endurance. Dustin Hoffman was on an impressive run of performances with *Midnight Cowboy* and *Little Big Man* when he portrayed the repressed lead here, alongside newcomer Susan George. Though his role is small and uncredited, classic British actor David Warner is pivotal as the mentally challenged Henry.

After struggles in the U.S. on his last picture *The Ballad of Cable Hogue*, director Sam Peckinpah headed to England for this film. Co-writing the script with Oscar-nominated David Zelag Goodman (who would also go on to work on *Logan's Run* and *Eyes of Laura Mars*), Peckinpah returned to some of the themes of masculine violence he had explored in *The Wild*

Bunch. The notorious rape scenes take up an uncomfortable amount of time in the middle of the film, and he has been accused of misogyny and sadism. The complexities of its violent themes, however, are just as frequently noted as anti-retribution in their purpose as they are noted as glorifying vigilante action. The film was remade in 2011 by *The Contender* director Rod Lurie.

The Strangers (2008)
Written and Directed by Bryan Bertino
Starring: Scott Speedman, Liv Tyler, Gemma Ward

Kristen and James spend the night at a summer house in the secluded woods after attending a friend's wedding. When James runs to the store, Kristen is terrorized by a group of masked people ringing the doorbell, scaring her, and stealing her cell phone. James returns and the harassment worsens, with injuries sustained and a climbing body count. Kristen and James have no contact with the outside world, and have to find a way to get to safety. A film that begins with silence and discomfort and quickly escalates into life-threatening violence, *The Strangers* is a stripped-down, no-frills scarefest that makes a quick impact and doesn't overstay its welcome (unlike its main antagonists). With the action primarily on the shoulders of Scott Speedman and the lion's share of the emotional work done by Liv Tyler, the film balances the two threads of the story nicely, always allowing the lead characters and their concern for each other to shine through even the most disturbing of moments.

Director Bryan Bertino had never directed a film before this, and was not originally supposed to be the director; he stepped in to direct his own script after music video director Mark Romanek left the project. Combining a remembered childhood experience of a would-be invader with aspects of the Manson Family murders, Bertino delivered a tense script that was originally titled *The Faces.* Bertino's success with the film led to *Mockingbird,* a low-budget found footage thriller in a similar vein. A sequel for *The Strangers* was produced, based on Bertino's characters, but with no direct involvement from him.

Assault on Precinct 13 (1976)
Written and Directed by John Carpenter
Starring: Austin Stoker, Darwin Joston, Laurie Zimmer

Lieutenant Bishop is spending his first night on the job guarding a nearly empty police precinct which is soon to be closed. There is a skeleton crew there to answer phones, and a prison transfer bus has arrived with an ill prisoner. From out of nowhere, a traumatized man arrives on the doorstep of the precinct after having killed the gang member who killed his daughter. The gang surrounds and isolates the precinct, initiating a brutal attack intended to kill everyone inside. An existential conversation about what's worth dying to defend that is disguised as a low-budget crime thriller, *Assault on Precinct 13* represents much of what is great about the shift in filmmaking priorities in the 1960s and 1970s. Beautiful Panavision cinematography, a mysterious and seemingly endless group of street villains, and protagonists who are likable without being too heroic, combine to make for an intense and immersive experience that holds up better thirty years later than its 2005 remake does.

John Carpenter had only completed his student film *Dark Star* when he was given the opportunity to have complete creative control on this low-budget film. Working with the 1959 Western *Rio Bravo* as a template for his story (along with a healthy dose of *Night of the*

Living Dead), Carpenter shaped one of the most influential exploitation films of all time. References to the film would crop up in many of Quentin Tarantino's later work, as a direct influence on the script of *From Dusk Till Dawn*, and seen in the on-screen titles during *Jackie Brown*.

Other Titles of Interest

You're Next (2011), *The Mist* (2007), *Splinter* (2008), *The Purge* (2013), *Demon Knight* (1995)

Single Location Horror

Isolation is at the base of nearly every horror film ever made. Even when it is not explicit within the story or the source of the horror itself, isolation is one of the key elements that creates the suspense and dread necessary for a film to be considered horror.

No one is scared of the slasher that might be walking amongst them on the bustling streets of New York City; the slasher only becomes frightening when the victim is alone, in the dark or someplace where screams can't be heard, and the slasher can do his work in privacy without being interrupted. The idea that there is safety in numbers is a cliché for a reason. Though our ancient ancestors were often solitary beings who would fight each other for the scarce resources, it was when humanity started building communities and protecting themselves as a group that our species began to flourish.

This is why the single location horror film is so effective for fans who love true horror. A single character or small group of characters who find themselves trapped in a place (be it a broken elevator, a car, or a farmhouse in the midst of a zombie apocalypse) is a perfectly relatable circumstance to all of humanity. Though books, television, and movies can widen the scope of human knowledge, the human experience happens viscerally, in a single perspective. The world may be getting overrun by monsters, but the only experience an individual has with it is the one happening right at their door. To make a stronger real-world analogy, the horrifying events of September 11, 2001, may have a national impact that altered our collective consciousness, but everyone who lived through it has a very specific memory of where they were and what they were doing when they first heard.

Horror is personal. When the entire world is ready to explode and kill humanity forever, that is not a horror film, that is a disaster film. Horror is what happens to individuals.

The history of the single location horror film actually predates the medium of film itself. Many early films were based on popular stage plays of the time, translated to the screen for wider recognition (and because, in the heyday of filmmaking in the early 20th century, movie writers couldn't churn out scripts fast enough for the movie machine), and some of these stage plays contained in them the seeds for what would become the elements of horror: old dark houses, mysterious murders, characters with dubious motivations. A stage play, by its nature, works best when a single location can be constructed on the stage and used throughout the show, and many of those stories embraced the "chamber room" storytelling style.

It's a fun coincidence that a film made in a single location is always cheaper to produce and therefore more appealing to the financier, and that fact has kept the subgenre alive and doing well for the entire history of the filmic medium.

Elements of the Subgenre

I Can't Leave Because…: This conceit is as important as the story itself. A great single location horror film will have an extremely believable reason why none of the characters are able to open the door and walk away, because if they didn't, their audiences would spend the entire length of the film complaining about how the characters should just open the door and walk away. The most challenging part of the story isn't making a single room exciting and scary; it's making the characters stay in there for a logical reason.

Showy Camerawork: Any great filmmaker will tell you that the coolest single set in the world will get boring to look at if you have to stare at it uninterrupted for ninety minutes. One solution to that is to make the photography of that set adventurous and surprising. Split-screens, tilted angles, fast zooms, and varying shutter speeds are just some of the tricks that clever filmmakers will use to keep the visual excitement high in a static environment.

Don't Wear Out Your Welcome: Even though an audience may applaud a filmmaker for the audacity to make a film in a single location, the audience still doesn't want to get bored. An epic film can travel the world going to exotic locations, and the audience will often allow them the time to do so, but a smart filmmaker in a single location usually knows what his limits are, and makes sure to keep the pace brisk and the running time short.

Recommendations from the Subgenre

Rope (1948)

Directed by Alfred Hitchcock
Written by Hume Cronyn, Arthur Laurents (based on the play by Patrick Hamilton)
Starring: John Dall, Farley Granger, James Stewart

Moments before the beginning of a fancy society party they are throwing, two friends murder a former classmate and hide his body in a large wooden chest in the middle of the living room. During the party, they engage a former professor of theirs in an intellectual exercise on the efficacy of murder, something that he had spoken about in one of his classes. As the night continues on, the professor begins to sense that something strange is happening and decides to figure out what it is. An already audacious concept (a pair of murderers invite a group of friends over to have a party around the body of their victim) is made all the more ambitious in the film *Rope* by being filmed in a series of uninterrupted shots, giving the film the feel of a seamless eighty-minute take. Brilliant and twisty lead performances from John Dall, Farley Granger, and Jimmy Stewart give *Rope* a strong forward momentum, and the set design is immaculate; it even includes a slowly setting sun orchestrated by the lighting crew on the exterior backdrop.

Alfred Hitchcock had already taken on what seemed like an insurmountable challenge with the confines of *Lifeboat* when he signed on to make this film. The story, based on a Patrick Hamilton play, is inspired by the real-life Leopold and Loeb murder case. Much was made at the time of its homosexual subtext; though it somehow made it past the Hays Code to be released, modern audiences will recognize that lead actors Dall and Granger, as well as co-writer Laurents, were all actually gay as well, and the themes would have been largely intentional.

Bug (2006)

Directed by William Friedkin
Written by Tracy Letts (based on the play by Letts)
Starring: Ashley Judd, Michael Shannon, Harry Connick, Jr.

Still dealing with the psychological aftermath of her son's long-ago disappearance, Agnes drowns her sorrows in drugs and alcohol while trying to avoid contact with her abusive ex-spouse. When she meets fellow wounded soul Peter, a drifter with a military background, they immediately connect emotionally and physically. The troubles begin to compound, however, when Peter has some very strange theories about government activities and how they might relate to Agnes' child's mysterious disappearance. Though a few characters drift in and out of the room and their lives, *Bug* is primarily a doomed love story and a two-character *tour-de-force*. Ashley Judd, breaking from her crime and political thriller performances in *Double Jeopardy* and *High Crimes*, is matched well with Michael Shannon, a relatively unknown character actor at the time who would launch to stardom with award-nominated performances in *Revolutionary Road* and *Take Shelter*. The film's pace matches its characters' paranoia, starting slow and building to a devastating fever pitch.

After Agnes (Ashley Judd) sleeps with war veteran Peter (Michael Shannon), the mask of sanity slowly begins to slip in 2006's *Bug* (courtesy Lionsgate Publicity).

Director William Friedkin was already legendary in horror film circles for directing *The Exorcist*, and had revisited the genre only once in 1990 with *The Guardian*, before directing this film. The film is based on the play by Tracy Letts; Friedkin worked with Letts again translating his play *Killer Joe* to the screen. Letts' more recent *August: Osage County* garnered two Oscar nominations and won many other awards. With *Bug*'s themes of paranoia, sleepless nights, and destructive relationships, many have viewed it as a thinly veiled discussion of drug addiction and abuse.

Grave Encounters (2011)

Written and Directed by the Vicious Brothers (Colin Minihan, Stuart Ortiz)
Starring: Lance Preston, Ashleigh Gryzko, Merwin Mondesir

A popular television series called *Grave Encounters* ends when the crew (and the footage) disappears during the production of the sixth episode. When the footage is later discovered, the producer learns that the team visited Collingwood Psychiatric Hospital, a hotbed of paranormal activity. While shooting the episode, the crew members are killed one by one as the shape of the hospital changes and keeps them imprisoned inside, and they discover that one of the long-dead doctors dabbled in black magic along with horrifying medical experiments. Combining the often-used found footage concept with the claustrophobic confines of the real-life Riverview Hospital in British Columbia, *Grave Encounters* puts an interesting modern-day spin on a classic framework of supernatural investigations gone terribly wrong. Using the conceit of the "discovered final tapes" that has been popular in horror since *Cannibal Holocaust* and through to *The Blair Witch Project*, the gimmick builds in an effective ticking clock for the troubled characters.

The film was directed by the Vicious Brothers, the screen name for filmmakers Colin Minihan and Stuart Ortiz. It was their first feature-length project. They returned to script (but not direct) the sequel, *Grave Encounters 2*, before re-teaming for 2014's sci-fi–horror *Extraterrestrial*. *Grave Encounters'* characters and the concept are clearly influenced by several real ghost-hunting television series. Lead actor Sean Rogerson, as Lance Preston, seems to be channeling Zak Bagans from the Travel Channel series *Ghost Adventures*.

Other Titles of Interest

Exam (2009), *Right at Your Door* (2006), *The Killing Room* (2009), *Cube* (1997), *1408* (2007), *Fermat's Room* (2007)

Supernatural investigator Lance Preston (Sean Rogerson) finds proof of the paranormal in 2011's *Grave Encounters* (courtesy Shawn Angelski).

Single Person Horror

There are few ideas in the filmic world more audacious than the concept of creating a riveting feature-length film with limited locations and only a single actor carrying the entirety of the story. It can come across as more self-indulgent than simply daring, when in fact the truth is more often than not the opposite; the difficulty of securing budgets, locations, and high-quality actors on a low-budget film can lead to desperate methods on the storytelling front, which always breeds the most creative answers.

The results of that desperation, however, are fairly revealing about the nature of both film in general and horror films in particular. Single person films are not a common occurrence, certainly, but they happen more than one might initially think, especially if you factor in shorts and films in which most of the footage focuses on a single character (including Will Smith as Robert Neville in *I Am Legend* and Jeff Daniels as Ed Saxon in the underrated *Chasing Sleep*). Whatever we might theorize about the blockbuster epics of summer and their casts of thousands, we are for some reason drawn back time and again to single human beings and their very personal situations.

We all live as individuals, and if we're truly honest with ourselves, it is when we are with only ourselves that we often feel most comfortable. There is no judging, there is no measuring of oneself against another, no pretending to be polite or interested; we are our own favorite company. It certainly makes sense that, while watching a film about a single other human being, we would connect more directly than we could with a film that showed multiple stories and personalities and points of view. As Jean-Paul Sartre said in his play *No Exit*, "Hell is other people."

As many of the films in the single person horror subgenre will show us, though, hell can also be within. One of the strengths of the subgenre is that, by narrowing the focus of a film to a single human being, you have done away with the artifice of worldly problems that distract from the bigger, darker, more disturbing questions with which we all wrestle. In a single person film, if there is a conflict and no one else is there to struggle against us, then we must be our own enemy.

This kind of introspection, and the sophisticated way in which a seemingly physical story can take on epic psychological undertones, is rare in film of any kind, and particularly in your standard horror film, which is one of the reasons why the single person subgenre is such a vital and uniquely pleasurable part of the genre.

Elements of the Subgenre

The Voices of Others: Though the movie may contain only a single actor on-screen, it is nearly impossible to actually have a film with no other characters; if for no other reason, it makes it hard for the one character to have any kind of external conversation or action. That's where the disembodied voices come in handy: friends on the phone, delivery people outside the door, or perhaps the sounds of spirits long dead.

Breakdown in Real Time: Aside from having to carry the weight of the entire film on their shoulders, the single actors in these films are often asked to do even more heavy lifting in emotional scenes of a character breaking down from distress, fear, or isolation. This subgenre can be a *tour-de-force* for actors, but it can also be an exhausting challenge. With nothing else to cut to and no reactions from others to balance it, the actors crumbling emotionally in real time can be marvelous (or painful) to watch.

Recommendations from the Subgenre

The Last Will and Testament of Rosalind Leigh (2012)
Directed and Written by Rodrigo Gudiño
Starring: Aaron Poole

Leon returns to his recently deceased mother's house to take inventory of her many possessions. He remembers the struggle of their relationship, and how her fervent religious belief pushed them apart. Leon makes some surprising and dark discoveries about his mother and her involvement with a religious group, while also confronting his own isolation and fears about his level of success as an artist. Quiet and contemplative, *The Last Will and Testament of Rosalind Leigh* is a rare and touching horror film that is equally comfortable discussing loss and familial struggle as it is scaring the viewer. With a nuanced lead performance from Aaron Poole (the first of two great horror films from Poole in 2012, the other being *The Conspiracy*), it very effectively uses the beautiful and haunting voice of British actress Vanessa Redgrave to draw the viewer into the house and the psyche of the deceased mother along with Leon's character.

Rodrigo Gudiño had directed four similarly gothic-themed short films in the six years before writing and directing this film (and won multiple awards for his animated short film *The Facts in the Case of Mr. Hollow*). Though Gudiño has gone on to be recognized for this film and some of his other recent work (including directing an episode of the anthology horror series *Darknet*), he is also known as the founder of the Canadian horror magazine *Rue Morgue*, and has incorporated film festivals, podcasts, and even film production into its banner.

Leon Leigh (Aaron Poole) explores the creepy and cluttered estate of his recently deceased mother in *The Last Will and Testament of Rosalind Leigh* (courtesy Rodrigo Gudiño).

The Ceremony (2008)

Directed by James Palmer
Written by James Palmer, Ryan Cannon
Starring: Scott Seegmiller

Eric Peterson is at his house by himself when he finds an old text sitting inside a circle of burning candles. Extinguishing the candles and taking the book, he discovers that it is some sort of occult item. Some phone research and reading helps him figure out that he may have interrupted a complicated ritual. Trapped by the confines of the ritual he interrupted, Eric has only one hope to escape the inevitable fallout: find someone else to take his place. Influenced by films like 1963's *The Haunting* in its pacing and determination to let the audience fill in the gaps, *The Ceremony* takes a small budget and a single lead character and creates a remarkable piece of slow-burn horror. A great central performance by Scott Seegmiller is bolstered by clever camerawork that keeps arriving at the scene of the supernatural activity just after it happens, leaving the audience and the lead character to sift through the aftermath.

James Palmer had only worked in a limited capacity on a single short film when he and his producer Ryan Cannon made the bold leap to producing a feature film with *The Ceremony*. The Faustian tale was brought to the screen by a cast and crew of relative unknowns, with its premiere taking place at the South by Southwest Film Festival in 2009. Palmer has reteamed with Seegmiller, this time in front of the camera, to star in *Her Name Is Lily Grace*, based on the script by Palmer.

Eric Peterson (Scott Seegmiller) senses something isn't right inside his house in 2008's taut horror drama *The Ceremony* (courtesy James Palmer).

Buried (2010)

Directed by Rodrigo Cortés
Written by Chris Sparling
Starring: Ryan Reynolds

Paul Conroy, an American truck driver working as a civilian contractor in Iraq, is kidnapped by terrorists who bury him in a small wooden box with only a telephone and a cigarette lighter. He is given instructions to call and find ransom money to be delivered to the terrorists, or they will never find out where he is, and he will suffocate and die inside the box. Battling indifferent bureaucracy from the insurance companies, his own claustrophobia, and the sand slowly spilling in to fill the box, Paul races against time to find someone who can help him escape. Eschewing the supernatural in favor of the more visceral fears of claustrophobia and wartime terrorism, Buried is a thriller that is as tightly plotted and tense as it is self-contained. Carrying every frame of the film is the excellent Ryan Reynolds, proving he's more than a good-looking funnyman with this "raw nerve" performance.

Rodrigo Cortés had directed several short films and one comedy feature (The Contestant) when he embarked on the daring conceit for Buried. The film was nominated for numerous awards: for Cortés, actor Reynolds, and writer Chris Sparling, who scripted the similarly claustrophobic thriller ATM in 2012. Though Reynolds is the only actor appearing on-screen, viewers might recognize the voices of Stephen Tobolowsky (Groundhog Day) and Samantha Mathis (Pump Up the Volume) during his frantic phone calls.

Other Titles of Interest

Moon (2009), The Noah (1975), Silent Running (1972), Missing Link (1988), An Evening of Edgar Allan Poe (1970)

Slasher Horror

It is no coincidence that the heyday of the slasher films, the 1980s, was the same era that was synonymous with MTV and gloriously over-the-top rock stars. It would seem that the masked killers of the slasher film have more in common with the flamboyant personalities in hair metal bands of the '80s than they do with other villains from horror movies past.

Whether it be the flashy costumes (rock stars had their shoulder pads, spikes, makeup, and feather boas, while slashers preferred their masks and trenchcoats) or the hordes of fans who scream for their favorite classic performances (rock stars have their radio hits, and Jason Voorhees has his tried-and-true machete to the face), the 1980s had a way of creating larger-than-life characters that audiences turned into modern-day deities. Musicians and slashers both became such gigantic personalities that the material they were associated with wasn't even necessarily up to the level of quality that one would think necessary for such devoted followings; no one would accuse the later Friday the 13th or Nightmare on Elm Street entries of being excellent films, and much of the music of the '80s has been mercifully forgotten.

But the most striking similarity that slashers and rock stars share, and one that perfectly encapsulates the appeal of both, is the negative reaction that they both garnered in the estimation of parents and lawmakers. Disapproving looks, mass record burnings, heavy cuts and censorship from the MPAA—no one wanted these rebellious anti-heroes to succeed, and that was exactly what appealed to the fans. In a time of extreme social conservatism that included Republican president Ronald Reagan and Conservative Prime Minister Margaret Thatcher, the young people of the world were looking to rebel, and in the corporately driven media environment of the 1980s, a dollar was a vote.

In the same way that kids didn't listen to Twisted Sister because of the impressive musical talent or incisive lyrics, teens didn't flock to the theaters in droves to lie about their age and sneak into the newest slasher film because of the filmmaking skill. They wanted to be outrageous, to break rules and boundaries, and to partake in music and film that glorified the figures who didn't toe the line or obey their parents (in Jason Voorhees' case, quite literally). Parents fought it (with watchdog groups popping up constantly to boycott music or take "satanic" bands before Congress to defend themselves), lawmakers tried to stop it (the notorious Video Nasties list existed because the British government banned many horror films in the 1980s), and the attempts to destroy them only made them stronger. Like Freddy Krueger rising from the grave again and again due to the dreams of children, the slashers refused to be killed by the strict codes of the era, and their place in history has been secured (in many ways, to better effect than the careers of rock stars from the same time). Governments and ideologies change and die; masked killers live forever.

Elements of the Subgenre

Character Appropriate Deaths: One of the marks of a skilled slasher killer is the ability to make sure that people die in the way that they lived. If they were just horny kids, they'll probably die during sex; if they're gang punks, they might be murdered in front of their friends with a switchblade; and if they love to dress up and scare people by pulling mean pranks, you can be sure that they'll assume that the real killer is just someone pulling a prank on them, right up until the blade sinks into their forehead.

Gotta Have a Gimmick: In the musical *Gypsy*, the strippers said that in order to get noticed, you had to have something that makes you stand out (aside from the obvious). In the slasher film, the same holds true of the killer. It might be a specific kind of mask, a glove with blades on it, a catchphrase, or a style of killing people that no one else does (like locking them up and making them try to get out of traps).

Recommendations from the Subgenre

Halloween (1978)

Directed by John Carpenter
Written by John Carpenter, Debra Hill
Starring: Donald Pleasence, Jamie Lee Curtis, P.J. Soles

In the early 1960s, young Michael Myers stabs his older sister to death on Halloween night, dressed in a colorful clown's costume. He is sent to a sanitarium, where he spends the next fifteen years being studied by psychiatrist Dr. Samuel Loomis. On the fifteenth anniversary of the murders, a grown Michael escapes from the sanitarium and returns to his hometown, where he fixates on virginal Laurie Strode and her circle of babysitter friends, killing them one by one until only Laurie remains to defeat him. *Halloween*, a seminal film in the genre, was artistically impressive, hugely successful (making nearly $70 million in its initial release), and served as the template for nearly every slasher film of the next five years. The moody photography, brilliant score, and ambiguous conclusion add up to an intensely watchable film.

Lightning was captured when young director John Carpenter teamed for the first time with cinematographer Dean Cundey, producer Moustapha Akkad, and actress Jamie Lee Curtis (daughter of *Psycho* star Janet Leigh). Carpenter used cutting-edge film techniques (like the pioneering Steadicam opening shot) and surrounded himself with talented and likeminded individuals. Cinematographer Cundey was later nominated for an Academy Award for *Who Framed Roger Rabbit*, and producer Debra Hill helped bring *The Dead Zone* and *The Fisher King* to the screen. With seven sequels and a commercially successful remake by Rob Zombie, *Halloween* stands as one of the most profitable and artistically rewarding horror films of the modern era.

Reeker (2005)

Written and Directed by Dave Payne
Starring: Devon Gummersall, Eric Mabius, Michael Ironside

On their way to a rave in the middle of the desert, a group of friends are stranded at a hotel-diner after their vehicle stops working. While waiting it out, several of them begin to

Nelson (Derek Richardson) and Cookie (Arielle Kebbel) are among those stranded at an abandoned gas station in 2005's *Reeker* (courtesy Dave Payne).

see mysterious apparitions and violently injured people struggling to escape. Soon they are being picked off by a strange, dark entity whose presence can be predicted by the foul smell that fills the air moments before it strikes. A clever supernatural film that takes the conceit of the slasher framework and uses the set-up in a fresh and original way, *Reeker* is a modern take on the low-budget ingenuity of the original slashers of the 1970s and 1980s. With a cast that boasts genre mainstay Michael Ironside (*Scanners, Total Recall*) and television star Eric Mabius (*Ugly Betty*), the movie allows the cast to play against type and keeps the audience guessing until the final reveal.

After a series of low-budget crime thrillers and sci-fi action films (as well as a direct-to-DVD sequel to *The Addams Family*), Dave Payne directed this film, along with writing the script, producing, and even composing the score. This was the last film that actress Marcia Strassman, known from the *Honey, I Shrunk the Kids* film series, starred in before she died of breast cancer. Three years after the release of this film, Payne returned to the world of the story to create the prequel *No Man's Land: Rise of the Reeker*.

Scream (1996)

Directed by Wes Craven
Written by Kevin Williamson
Starring: Neve Campbell, Courteney Cox, David Arquette

On the eve of the one-year anniversary of her mother's death, teenager Sidney Prescott is still struggling to accept what happened even though the suspected killer is in jail. When there are new killings in their small town, everyone wonders if the murders might be connected; a local tabloid journalist who covered the previous murder shows up looking for a scoop. Sidney, her boyfriend, and several school friends throw a nighttime party to celebrate the town-wide curfew, which the journalist is monitoring. The mysterious ghost-masked killer is in attendance. From the opening moments of the film, reminiscent of the classic *When a Stranger Calls* but with a unique modern twist, *Scream* heralded itself as the leading contender to reshape the flagging and frequently uncreative slasher genre. A film that was cleverly aware of its clichéd tropes, while at the same time finding ways to both embrace and eschew them, *Scream* was at times both a parody and reinvention of the genre it emulated. A solid cast of popular young actors (Courteney Cox was at the height of her television popularity with *Friends*, and Neve Campbell was the star of *Party of Five*) brought in audiences and made *Scream* a surprising smash hit.

Kevin Williamson was an unproduced writer when his script for a meta-horror film (then called *Scary Movie*) was optioned to be made into a film directed by *A Nightmare on Elm Street* creator Wes Craven. A love letter to the heyday of the slasher film (the opening sequence alone name-checks all of the greats from *Halloween* to *Friday the 13th*), the film took advantage of the video-savvy audience by setting up what seemed like genre clichés, only to surprise viewers by turning the clichés on their heads. The film made almost $200 million and became a four-movie franchise. All of them involved Craven and Williamson in some capacity.

Other Titles of Interest

A Nightmare on Elm Street (1984 and 2010), *Slumber Party Massacre* (1982), *Maniac* (1980 and 2012), *I Know What You Did Last Summer* (1997), *The Prowler* (1981)

Split Personality Horror

In the world of the split personality tale, there is no story better known than *The Strange Case of Dr. Jekyll and Mr. Hyde*, written by author Robert Louis Stevenson in 1886. The story was as influential on the world of psychological horror as his earlier *Treasure Island* would be on future generations of stories about pirates and buried treasure. The circumstances of his writing the story, however, cast some interesting light on the psychology *behind* the story, and humanity's fascination with it and the thousands of stories like it.

In Graham Balfour's biography *The Life of Robert Louis Stevenson*, Stevenson's wife discusses how the first stirrings of the story came to Robert in a dream, and his son talks about how quickly and explosively the story came about: Robert wrote while confined to bed, and his story poured out of him in days. Some historians have claimed that he was on drugs at the time, and his family has said that he was sick and bedridden. Regardless of the explanation for the spectacular and difficult feat of creating a new subgenre of horror in mere days, it is a fascinating story.

One could even observe that the story had its roots in Stevenson's real-life behavior. The erratic hours writing the book, the evil coming to him in dreams, the illness that both held him in bed and drove him to complete the story—all the elements of a classic story about battling personas is present in Stevenson's story.

As they are in everyone's life. Decisions made in the spur of the moment that seem uncharacteristic in later reflection; angry outbursts that dissipate as quickly as they surface; reminders from loved ones of actions from our past of which we have no recollection. These are commonplace occurrences for the average human being, because we are constantly struggling within ourselves: who we are, what we believe, what we should do versus what we *will* do.

The true appeal of the split personality to most readers and viewers is less about the exotic surprise of the story than it is about the uncomfortable recognition of ourselves in the lead character. The human brain is a complex machine, one which we still don't fully understand, even with all our advanced technology. That mystery, that fear, that recognition of something inside us that is much more complicated and dangerous than we could ever understand or contain, is the connective psychological tissue that unites us with Robert Louis Stevenson and his creations, Dr. Henry Jekyll and Mr. Hyde.

Elements of the Subgenre

I Can't Remember What I Did: For some reason, when a brain has to deal with two personalities, it divides up the memory space as well. One identity can never remember what the other identity did, so neither of them is entirely aware of what is happening when they are unconscious. This creates much of the suspense in the story.

Wardrobe Change: When you have two characters who are exactly identical, there is usually some physical representation of one personality or the other. They might wear a watch as one and not the other; they might have different hairstyles; or perhaps one of them dresses a bit risqué. Whatever the difference, it is the signpost that filmmakers give the audience to remind viewers which of the characters they're following.

Recommendations from the Subgenre

Dr. Jekyll and Mr. Hyde (1920)

Directed by John S. Robertson
Written by Clara Beranger (based on the story by Robert Louis Stevenson)
Starring: John Barrymore, Martha Mansfield, Nita Naldi

Dr. Henry Jekyll is a great humanitarian. A discussion about the inherent dual nature of man inspires Jekyll to seek out a medical solution to dividing those conflicting aspects. He develops a potion that he uses on himself, and the effect creates dual personalities battling for the dominance of a single body: the kind Dr. Jekyll and the beastly Mr. Edward Hyde. Jekyll is overpowered by the growing strength of Hyde and is unable to control the frequency and intensity of the changes, and starts to feel he has completely lost control of himself. Released in 1920, thirty-four years after the release of the Stevenson novel, *Dr. Jekyll and Mr. Hyde* was a breakthrough for horror films at the time as it boasted a genuine star in lead actor John Barrymore. Though not the first screen version of the story, it closely follows the stage adaptation of the late 1880s, and is of note for Barrymore's largely makeup-free transformation sequences.

With over 125 versions of the story on film, *The Strange Case of Dr. Jekyll and Mr. Hyde* is one of the most interpreted stories in the history of modern storytelling. Versions of the story have been made by directors such as F.W. Murnau and Jerry Lewis, and played by such acting greats as Kirk Douglas, Christopher Lee, and John Malkovich. Because the 1920 film went into the public domain many years ago, clips will often be seen in documentaries, and whole scenes from it are often played in movies and music videos.

Sisters (1973)

Directed by Brian De Palma
Written by Brian De Palma, Louisa Rose
Starring: Margot Kidder, Charles Durning, Jennifer Salt

When deranged Dominique stabs her actress sister Danielle's lover to death in her apartment, Danielle's ex-husband Emil helps her cover up the murder. They don't know that the murder was witnessed by a reporter who lives nearby. As they attempt to clean up Dominique's mess, the reporter trails them with a detective, looking for clues to catch them. The mystery leads them to a mental hospital where they learn secrets about the sisters' past that reveal a deeper truth about the murders. A seedy psycho-thriller that breathed new life into the American mystery story, *Sisters* juggles multiple narrative threads to usher its audience to the fascinating climax. Beginning as a sweet romance, the film takes a huge left turn with the reveal of familial issues between the sisters played brilliantly by Margot Kidder (the year before her turn in *Black Christmas* and five years before her big break in *Superman*). The film does a great job of pointing the story in one direction, only to abruptly end that story and begin from a new angle.

Brian De Palma had already directed a couple of minor indie films such as *Greetings* and *Hi, Mom!* when he channeled his favorite filmmaker Alfred Hitchcock in the making of this movie. Using the mid-film twist and psychological identity disorders Hitchcock made famous in *Psycho*, and combining them with clever technical updates like extended P.O.V. shots and split-screen (something he would revisit in *Carrie*), De Palma continued the legacy of the artful thriller. He even had one of Hitchcock's most recognizable musical collaborators, Bernard Herrmann, do the score.

Identity (2003)
Directed by James Mangold
Written by Michael Cooney
Starring: John Cusack, Ray Liotta, Amanda Peet

During a terrible rainstorm, ten strangers take refuge in a remote Nevada motel. As they wait out the storm, people begin to die or disappear, and it is up to an ex–police officer to solve the mystery before they *all* die. Meanwhile, in a seemingly unrelated story, a convicted prisoner waits on death row for his coming execution....

Bringing the classic drawing room mystery together with the serial killer psychology of the modern era, *Identity* is a fun hybrid that makes the most of its trope-heavy influences. With a plot that is strikingly similar to Agatha Christie's *Ten Little Indians*, the film has fun with the genre expectations, presenting red herrings left and right ("Who is the body in the freezer?" "What is the officer's secret?") while simultaneously dropping little clues to the eventual (and somewhat expected) twist conclusion.

Director James Mangold has made a career out of hopping from genre to genre (*Walk the Line* was a musical biopic, *3:10 to Yuma* was a classic western action and *Kate & Leopold* played with the high-concept romantic comedy formula), and his foray into psycho-thrillers is equally successful. The style and cleverness of the film are sure signs of collaboration between Mangold and his wife Cathy Konrad, who produced the *Scream* franchise. A great cast of character actors (from stars Ray Liotta and John Cusack to the lesser known but brilliant John C. McGinley and Pruitt Taylor Vince) effectively avoid falling into the traps of genre cliché.

Other Titles of Interest

6 Souls (2010), *Secret Window* (2004), *Hide and Seek* (2005), *The Machinist* (2004), *Mr. Brooks* (2007), *A Tale of Two Sisters* (2003), *Mary Reilly* (1996)

Spooky Old House Horror

In the children's animated film series *Toy Story*, the audience learns about the secret life of all the games and toys that live in a little boy's upstairs bedroom. When he leaves the room, that's when the toys *really* start playing. There is something honest about that idea, that inanimate objects have their own existence, free from the use that we as humans have for them. Truth be told, though, not everything is as innocent and sweet as *Toy Story*.

When a family buys a house, unless it has been built specially for them, it is rare that they are the first people to live in it. Their name may now be on the mail, and their paint may be on the walls, and the cars in the driveway may be theirs, but it wasn't long ago that a completely different set of people inhabited those halls. And someday, perhaps because of financial issues or job relocation or a death in the family, the people who inhabit the home will leave, and the cycle will begin again. A new family, a new paint color.

Every family stands in the driveway and looks up at their new house. The more accurate reading of the situation would be that, every few years, the house looks down at its new guests. Being that humans are egocentric, we look at houses as objects that become part of our lives, when the reverse is far more accurate; in the lifetime of a single house, many families have come and gone, moved in and moved out. Chipped paint and shag carpeting and popcorn ceilings are the remnants of past stories that only the house knows entirely.

We are temporary objects that drift in and out of the life of the house; it is by definition a refuge for displaced souls, living and dead, a place for them to stay. When we move in, we don't know who lived there or died there, or who might have died there and is still living there.

It's all part of the story of the house, and we are merely players in the larger drama. And unlike *Toy Story*, the houses don't always wait until the humans aren't around to come to life.

Elements of the Subgenre

The Emotionally Troubled One: Someone in the house is always dealing with something pretty heavy emotionally. The death of a loved one, a series of psychological disorders, a disease or disability that has put them into a depression—whatever the issue they're dealing with, it puts them at a disadvantage. They're emotionally weaker than others, and therefore more susceptible to the disturbances in the house. And when something bad genuinely happens to them in the house, everyone else thinks it's all in their head.

The Disturbing Secret: Houses are private places where people keep everything they value. And when they die, some of those things are left behind. It might be jewelry or a will, or something much worse: a secret about the family history or evidence of a wrongdoing. Whatever the secret is, it will inevitably come out, either as a result of the construction the new owners are doing, or by the influence of the spirit which still haunts the premises.

Recommendations from the Subgenre

The Others (2001)

Written and Directed by Alejandro Amenabar
Starring: Nicole Kidman, Fionnula Flanagan, Christopher Eccleston

A stern mother hires new servants to help her care for her isolated country estate and her two ill children post–World War II. The rules for the house are strict, due to the rare disease that causes the children to be hurt by sunlight. As the servants adjust to their new jobs, they learn that the children have seen specters in the house. The mother, still reeling from news that her husband died in the war, is unwilling to believe the stories her children tell about the spirits in the house, until her own direct encounters with them reveal a horrible tragedy from the house's past. A brilliant twist on the standard clichés of the haunted house film, *The Others* bubbles with a quiet menace that peeks around the corner of every frame. The beautiful cinematography stands in juxtaposition to the muted, imprisoned lives of the lead characters, and the seemingly mundane activities of Nicole Kidman's Grace slowly build to an unexpected but inevitable climax.

Director Alejandro Amenabar already had two Spanish-language thrillers under his belt when he made his English-language debut with this film; his previous work, *Abre Los Ojos*, was eventually remade as *Vanilla Sky*. *The Others*, focused on a child's perspective of very adult subject matter, is similar to another Hispanic filmmaker's project the same year, Guillermo del Toro's *The Devil's Backbone*. Amenabar's script and Kidman's performance were nominated for awards. Kidman's then-husband Tom Cruise executive produced the film, but much of the publicity was overshadowed by their divorce the same year.

House (1986)

Directed by Steve Miner
Written by Ethan Wiley, Fred Dekker
Starring: William Katt, George Wendt, Richard Moll

Troubled horror novelist Roger Cobb has moved into his recently deceased aunt's house to work on a new book in the wake of a divorce brought on by the disappearance of his son. The new book, the story of his experiences in Vietnam, begins to have an effect on Roger, who begins seeing strange things in the house while remembering a tragic wartime event that cost a friend his life. With the help of a friendly neighbor, Roger discovers that the house is possessed by his friend's spirit, and that dealing with the demons from his past may lead him to find his missing son. Though the subject matter of *House* is certainly heavy (and one of the first times that mainstream film dealt with post–Vietnam veterans' issues), the film itself is surprisingly clever, spooky, and fun. Casting aside the clichéd ghost sightings in favor of mysterious portals that take Roger into the netherworld and his own past, the movie is as hilarious as it is frightening.

Originally intended as a serious psychological horror by concept creator Fred Dekker (of *The Monster Squad* fame), the film took on dark comedy elements in the final script by Ethan Wiley (who would return to script and direct its sequel, *House II: The Second Story*). Much of the creative team (including director Steve Miner, producer Sean S. Cunningham, and composer Harry Manfredini) re-teamed to make this film after creating the very successful *Friday the 13th* franchise. A brilliant turn from *Cheers* star George Wendt as neighbor Harold is one of the many comedic high points of a solid and exciting film.

House on Haunted Hill (1959)

Directed by William Castle
Written by Robb White
Starring: Vincent Price, Carol Ohmart, Richard Long

A millionaire invites five people to a spooky house for an all night party. They are all locked in, and each of them is promised ten thousand dollars if they are willing to stay the entire night, no matter what frightening events transpire. The millionaire's wife believes that he might be trying to kill her, and warns the guests of his possible motivations. The seemingly supernatural occurrences earlier in the evening turn deadly when someone is murdered and secret connections are revealed between the rich couple and their guests. The quintessential structure for a haunted house story, with strangers locked overnight in a purportedly haunted house, *House on Haunted Hill* is a fun and twisted little psychodrama that keeps the audience guessing on the origins (and even the reality) of the spooky events. A game cast makes the most of the premise (the humorously morose turn from Elisha Cook Jr. is a highlight). The always watchable Vincent Price steals the show as the eccentric millionaire.

Gimmick master William Castle had already found success in the low-budget horror arena with *Macabre* when he teamed with novelist Robb White to create this film; the two successfully worked together on five films. Forty years after the successful release of the original, makeup effects genius William Malone directed a big-budget remake which did well in theaters and spawned a direct-to-DVD sequel.

Other Titles of Interest

Darkness (2002), *Don't Be Afraid of the Dark* (1973 and 2010), *Dream House* (2011), *The Haunting in Connecticut* (2009), *House of Voices* (2004), *Rose Red* (2002)

Stalking Horror

Fear is one of the strongest emotions, and is a very effective emotion to elicit when making a film. Guilt is an emotion that is not as well noted as fear, but can be just as effective if properly used.

In a real-life situation that involves a stalker, there is the victim and there is the stalker himself (or herself). In a film that involves a stalker, however, there is a third party: the viewer. The simple addition of a third party into an already intimate relationship creates numerous emotions, among them fear and guilt.

As an audience member, we sympathize with the victim as they are being watched, followed, harassed, and in all likelihood ultimately attacked by their stalker. We root for them to find the hidden camera, get to the drawer with the big knife, and find a working phone in the abandoned building. We genuinely want them to be okay. This ignites our fear.

But we have watched these victims, too. Through windows, binoculars, and rear view mirrors. We have sat in cars with their stalkers in silence, observing the things they do when they think they are alone. We hope they are going to be okay, so we keep watching. Silently, secretly.

The first-person perspective of the film camera, putting the viewer in the same place as the stalker without their agreement or permission, creates guilt in audience members who have made a pact with the film to root for the hero while accompanying the villain. The push and pull of our instincts as decent people and our job as viewers of a film create a psychological circumstance called the Cassandra complex.

In Greek mythology, Cassandra was the daughter of the king of Troy, and she was gifted with prophecy. However, she was also cursed by Apollo that, no matter what she predicted, no one would believe her. She suffered from foreknowledge of bad events, coupled with the complete inability to do anything about them.

This is where the audience exists in a stalking horror film. Every viewer is a Cassandra who knows about the unstable person watching the hero's every move, but is helpless to do anything about it. The fear may come because the victims are in danger; but the guilt comes because the viewer watched it happen.

Elements of the Subgenre

Wordlessly Watching: One of the eerier aspects of the stalking horror subgenre is the largely wordless passages (with occasional creepy breathing) when the stalker is watching the stalked. Usually through a window or on a camera of some kind, the "stalkee" is entirely unaware of the viewing, and the silence on-screen makes the violation that much more unbearable to sit through.

It Could Have Been Love: The most frightening hate often blooms from the most ill-placed love, and this is true of the stalking horror film. It is rare that stalkers have no emotional investment in their quarry, and it usually began as some sort of twisted love gesture that, when rejected, turned dark and violent.

Recommendations from the Subgenre

Someone's Watching Me (1978)
Written and Directed by John Carpenter
Starring: Lauren Hutton, Adrienne Barbeau, Charles Cyphers

Leigh, a Los Angeles television director, has found a beautiful new apartment with a big balcony and large windows which draw the attention of a mysterious man who becomes obsessed with her. After Leigh receives a series of increasingly uncomfortable phone calls and gifts, she informs the police of the unwanted attention, but they dismiss it because of the lack of apparent threat. Leigh turns to her friends to take matters into their own hands. Taking standard subject matter of the era and heightening it with impressive filmmaking skill, *Someone's Watching Me* is a cut above the movie-of-the-week material in the same way that Steven Spielberg's *Duel* was. The film is heavily influenced by Hitchcock's *Rear Window*, with the interesting twist that the voyeur is a stalker and villain rather than the imprisoned hero of the piece. A solid lead performance from Lauren Hutton, who is in nearly every frame of the film, helps to ground the scares and connect the audience to the mounting tension.

After premiering as a writer-director with *Assault on Precinct 13*, John Carpenter did some for-hire work in film and television, usually writing spec scripts. One project that came about from that was his job writing and directing this project. Made and released in the same year that he set the horror world on its head with *Halloween*, *Someone's Watching Me* has many of the staples of what would become the Carpenter style: long tracking shots, strong female leads, and mysterious assailants. In one of her earlier television appearances, Adrienne Barbeau plays Hutton's work friend; she would collaborate with Carpenter again in film (*The Fog* and *Escape from New York*) and in real life (the two were married for five years).

Entrance (2011)
Directed by Dallas Richard Hallam, Patrick Horvath
Written by Karen Gorham
Starring: Suziey Block, Karen Gorham, Karen Baird

Suziey is a young woman working in a coffee shop in Los Angeles. Her life has become both stagnant and anxiety-filled. When her dog goes missing, she finally decides to leave Los Angeles and throws a party to say goodbye to her friends. During the party, Suziey heads into the garage to investigate a power outage and discovers that her anxious paranoia was well-founded, because a man who has been stalking her decides to kill everyone in the house so they can be alone together. A film whose visceral final act is all the more effective because of a slow, character-driven first hour, *Entrance* is a fascinating combination of low-budget horror and indie arthouse fare. The likable lead deals with harassing pedestrians and drivers on her daily walks, and those interactions add to the psychological weight of the sequences of perceived home invasion and stalking.

A strong script by Karen Gorham (who also acts in the film) anchors a solid thriller with equal footing in horror and mumblecore (an independent film movement focused on smaller, heavily improvised stories). The action culminates in a stunning continuous take that runs almost twenty minutes, showing Suziey's real-time attempt to escape her captor only to discover the trail of bodies left in his wake. The directors, Patrick Horvath and Dallas Richard Hallam, had previously worked together on a much more mainstream horror comedy called *Die-ner (Get It?)* before reteaming for this film and *The Pact II*.

The Loved Ones (2009)

Written and Directed by Sean Byrne
Starring: Xavier Samuel, Robin McLeavy, Victoria Thaine

High school student Brent is trying to enjoy his school year in the aftermath of his father's death. After rejecting Lola's invitation to the school dance, Brent is abducted and finds himself a prisoner in Lola's house. Her father has fashioned the house into a small version of the school dance, and Brent is Lola's date. As Brent tries to escape, he learns that he is not the first victim of the abductions, and most of them have been killed or lobotomized. Torture porn meets the John Hughes world with *The Loved Ones*, a horror film that is as absurdly funny as it is darkly disturbing. The father and daughter stalkers are perfectly cast; young Robin McLeavy's skills here won her a lead role on the AMC drama *Hell on Wheels*, and veteran John Brumpton is a staple of independent Australian thrillers like *Red Hill*, *Long Weekend*, and *Storm Warning*. The film's early deliberate pacing fools the audience into a sense of comfort that disappears in the relentless last hour, which deals with lobotomies, cannibalism, and incest.

The Loved Ones was the debut film of writer-director Sean Byrne, and one that brought an impressive amount of praise and attention; nominated for a dozen horror industry awards, it holds an impressive 98 percent approval rating on the critical aggregate site Rotten Tomatoes. The film courted controversy in 2013 when an Australian court found Gary George guilty of a brutal murder which the judge believed to be motivated by a keen interest in the movie and its depictions of torture.

Other Titles of Interest

One Hour Photo (2002), *Taxi Driver* (1976), *P2* (2007), *The Resident* (2011), *Play Misty for Me* (1971), *Single White Female* (1992)

Subway Horror

Humanity's love-hate relationship with the subterranean world has existed since the dawn of time. The caves where ancient man hid to escape predators were the same foreboding places that remained in darkness, even during daytime. The same fertile soil that grew crops to feed them eventually became their resting place in death. It seems appropriate that we would still find ourselves looking over our shoulders in fear as we head underground for the convenience of mass transit.

Some of our fear comes from the mundane, everyday instances of crime and violence that humanity visits upon itself. In films like Luc Besson's *Subway*, the Paris Metro system is a haven for eccentric weirdos and petty criminals like Christopher Lambert's safecracker. In a more sinister vein, the hellish underworld of Nimrod Antal's *Kontroll* shows the tedium of a job working as Kontroller, at constant peril from a serial killer operating in the tunnels. In the dark below the streets, the monsters feel free to come out and make themselves at home.

But our greater fears often come from the forgotten places underground, the caverns we created and abandoned in our effort to continue our progress technologically. In these old, unused tunnels underneath metropolitans like New York City and London, any number of civilizations, creatures, or secrets could be waiting for the unassuming commuter to make that single wrong turn. Guillermo Del Toro's *Mimic* used the forgotten subways of old New York as the setting for a battle against a quickly mutating strain of insect that has grown in size and found new prey: humans.

There is a deep biological warning signal in the human animal that begs us not to venture into the dark, into the cave, into the underground; that fear is one which we have decided in our enlightened age is an irrational and unnecessary one. We have used our technology and ingenuity to carve order into the chaos of the rock and dirt beneath us, and we like to think that there is nothing down there to surprise us.

The genre has been revisited many times in many iterations across the globe and over various mediums, from the Australian found footage thriller *The Tunnel* to the brilliant season eight *X-Files* episode "Medusa."

Elements of the Subgenre

Stupid Bureaucracy: Getting rid of monsters in the subway can never be easy, because there's always so much paperwork. The government closed down that tunnel decades ago, which trapped the parents of the mutated monster which is now attacking; or the head of transportation insists that the trains cannot be stopped, no matter how many homeless people have disappeared without a trace. In subway horror films, it's not just a battle with the monster: you also have to fight City Hall.

The Ladder to Safety: At some point during the frightening chase, the victim will see in the dark distance a single pool of natural light coming from above. Within that pool of light is a rusty old ladder that leads right up to the street, where pedestrians walk past without ever noticing the person screaming below and the monster that stalks them.

Society's Fringe: The subway is buried under the ground, a place that is unpleasant and not sought unless it is needed to reach a destination. The only people who spend lots of time there are the people who have no place else to be: the crazy, the homeless, the derelicts of society who are in no hurry to rush back up to the real world to be pushed aside and stepped over. The subway is a meeting place and safe haven for people who have no home above.

Recommendations from the Subgenre

Raw Meat (1973)

Directed by Gary Sherman
Written by Gary Sherman, Ceri Jones
Starring: Donald Pleasence, Norman Rossington, David Ladd

After finding and then losing a body in the London Underground station, young couple Alex and Patricia, along with a pair of Scotland Yard investigators, look further into the disappearance. They discover that, eighty years earlier, a tunnel collapse stranded several workers underground permanently, and the mutated ancestors of those workers are kidnapping subway patrons for food. When the last living mutant's mate dies, he goes looking for a new one, and Patricia looks to be the perfect candidate. *Raw Meat* (known as *Death Line* in the UK) is an archetypal British horror film in that it uses the subway monsters as a stand-in for the discussion of the class system in the United Kingdom. Produced and released at the summit of Hammer's horror film success (though not produced by Hammer), the film is more comfortable with unsavory subject matter and grimy locations than the gothic-minded Hammer, and the truly chilling mutant character (heard bellowing "Mind the doors!" as the only mode of spoken communication) also somehow elicits tragic sympathy.

Though a British production, the film boasts an American character in Alex and an American director, Gary Sherman (who went on to make the cult zombie film *Dead & Buried* and the third *Poltergeist*). Five years before he became known worldwide as Dr. Sam Loomis in *Halloween*, Donald Pleasence turned in a *tour-de-force* performance here, balancing the high-wire act of the cranky, hilarious, and sometimes drunken Inspector Calhoun. Hammer regular Christopher Lee pops up in a fun cameo as a meddling MI5 agent.

Creep (2004)

Directed and Written by Christopher Smith
Starring: Franka Potente, Vas Blackwood, Joe Anderson

At a party in London, young German girl Kate is convinced to leave in the late evening to attend a better party. While waiting for a train in the subway station, she falls asleep and finds herself waking to locked doors and no way to get to the surface. While trying to navigate the late-night trains and find a way out, she discovers that a mutated human is following and watching her and the homeless couple she meets. The mutant's intentions are disturbing and surgical in nature. A film that is somehow both a claustrophobic chamber piece inside the London subway and a clever observation on the interactions of different cultures, *Creep* makes great use of location and audience expectation to pull you in right from the opening moments of two sewage workers slogging through the underground. The film is carried largely on the shoulders of German actress Franka Potente (the breakthrough star of *Run Lola Run*), and her initially unlikable character grows on the audience as she is put through hell trying to survive the night.

Creep was director Christopher Smith's first foray into horror as well as film directing, and it shows the filmmaking promise that was later paid off in *Severance* and *Triangle*. The monstrous Craig is played by Sean Harris, a brilliant and versatile actor seen in Ridley Scott's *Prometheus* and the television series *Southcliffe*.

The Midnight Meat Train (2008)

Directed by Ryûhei Kitamura
Written by Jeff Buhler (based on the story by Clive Barker)
Starring: Bradley Cooper, Leslie Bibb, Vinnie Jones

Amateur photographer Leon has been searching New York City in the hopes of finding locations which will inspire him to take great pictures. He heads into the city's subway system in the late hours, hoping to break his habit of running away from danger in order to capture intense and vivid images. A woman he meets on the train goes missing, and as Leon looks into the mystery of her disappearance, he discovers that a butcher who frequents the subway has been murdering passengers and disposing of their bodies. When no one believes his story, Leon decides he has to stop the butcher himself. Combining the claustrophobia of the subway, the mystery of the serial killer, and some Hollywood-style romantic melodrama, *The Midnight Meat Train* is an unusual film that spends much of its time constructing an elaborate mystery that it resolves in a shocking and unexpected way. Though the CGI bloodletting gets a bit over the top, the story is intriguing, and the two central performers (*The Hangover's* Bradley Cooper and former footballer Vinnie Jones) play off each other well.

Silent killer Mahogany (Vinnie Jones) stalks New York City subway trains in 2008's *The Midnight Meat Train* (courtesy Lionsgate Publicity).

Director Ryûhei Kitamura was already well versed crafting horror films like *Alive* and *Versus* in his native Japan before making his American directing debut on this film, replacing production designer Patrick Tatopoulos in the position. Though generally very well-received, the film was buried upon release, making it to only a few theaters and primarily finding a cult audience once it reached the DVD market. Clive Barker, who penned the original short story, speaks highly of the film, which is one of his favorite adaptations of his work.

Other Titles of Interest

Mimic (1997), *End of the Line* (2007), *Quatermass and the Pit* (1967)

Surgical-Medical Horror

Though the study and practice of medicine has been around since the beginnings of human civilization, it is only within the past 150 years that the medical field has made its most groundbreaking and world-changing advancements. We've learned what germs are, what they do, and how to destroy them; we've discovered DNA sequencing and the secrets of genetic coding; and we've advanced the act of surgery, once a desperate battlefield choice likely to kill the patient, to an outpatient procedure that people can volunteer for when they don't like the contours of their faces. That magical future world we once read about in *Buck Rogers* and saw on *Disney's Tomorrowland* TV show, the world where lasers and pills cure terrible diseases, where robots and machine parts keep human bodies alive long past their probable life expectancy, is already upon us.

And yet ... we still hate going to the hospital. The astronomical costs, the secret language spoken between medical professionals, the impersonal treatment of the most intimate problems ... healing is hard work. Humanity's instinct to survive at all costs is nearly matched by its discomfort with pain and suffering, and our modern medicine is as good at prolonging the slow descent to death as it is at actually curing disease. Two hundred years ago, sickness happened quickly and life ended abruptly, but now we can drag out the length of time it takes to die in order to give ourselves time to panic, suffer, and waste away. The thought of that suffering is what nightmares are made of.

That is all before the discussion of the doctors themselves even begins. There is an inherent suspicion and mistrust in humanity towards doctors, and perhaps understandably so. Since the beginning of medicine, we have always questioned their methods and explanations; and they have often been wrong, in the cases of lobotomies, leeching, and even spiritual repentance. But even in the cases when their diagnoses are sound, the options are still not desirable: chemotherapy, surgery, a lifetime on prescription medication. The child in us still doubts that eating your vegetables, along with an apple a day, will keep you safely out of his reach. But we want to live, and so we follow his instructions, often blindly. We put our faith in a self-made god who can make mistakes as easily as we can.

The subgenre has been thriving for a long time, often in the guise of the "Mad Scientist" tale, dating all the way back to the original Universal classic *Frankenstein*. It eventually split from the science-gone-wrong thriller genre with classic films from the '70s through to the '90s, from early entries like Michael Crichton's medical thriller *Coma* and the more gory '80s entry *Blue Monkey* to the tongue-in-cheek sadism of *Dr. Giggles*.

Elements of the Subgenre

Unnecessary Operations: One might argue that the subgenre wouldn't exist without this particular element. There is nothing scary about a necessary operation that goes well and helps a patient, but everyone is terrified of being told that they have to get an organ removed or lose a limb and finding out after the procedure that it had less to do with their health and more to do with the perverse desires of a sadistic medical professional.

Unnerving Calmness from the Doctor: A crazed medical professional doesn't get into a position of power by running around covered in blood, laughing maniacally as he dismembers his victims. In order to operate (no pun intended) within the medical community, there must be an air of reasonableness about him, something that convinces us he is rational and trustworthy. He may consume human flesh and watch plastic surgery videos for fun, but in public, he is even-keeled and focused.

Recommendations from the Subgenre

Eyes Without a Face (1960)

Directed by Georges Franju
Written by Pierre Boileau, Thomas Narcejac, Claude Sautet (based on the story by Jean Redon)
Starring: Pierre Brasseur, Alida Valli, Juliette Mayniel

A series of mysterious killings are plaguing a small town in France; the bodies of women are found with their faces mutilated beyond recognition. A surgeon has been kidnapping them and surgically removing their faces in an attempt to graft them to his daughter, who has been disfigured due to a car accident. Trapped by her frightening appearance and her reluctance to participate in the killings, the daughter decides to take matters into her own hands. A truly disturbing horror film, *Eyes Without a Face* is a triumph of mood and atmosphere. In the central role of Christiane, a woman with a disfigured face who spends most of the film under a protective mask, Edith Scob works wonders, connecting with the audience using little more than her eyes and mannerisms.

Director Georges Franju was well-known for his co-founding (with Henri Langlois) of the Cinémathèque Français, the French film archive, before making this film. Carefully balancing the needs of multiple censors (each country would have issues with subject matter in the film), Franju assembled an impressive writing team to steer the story. Working from the source material of original novelist Jean Redon, Franju's assistant director Claude Sautet collaborated with famed writing team Pierre Boileau and Thomas Narcejac (whose novels had already been made into the successful films *Diabolique* and *Vertigo*) to create a story that was intense and frightening without being exploitative.

Dead Ringers (1988)

Directed by David Cronenberg
Written by David Cronenberg, Norman Snider (based on the story by Bari Wood and Jack Geasland)
Starring: Jeremy Irons, Geneviève Bujold, Stephen Lack

Identical twin brothers Beverly and Elliot Mantle are highly successful gynecologists who jointly run a fertility clinic, though their familial dynamic is unusual, and they often share sexual conquests without making their bedmates aware of it. When an actress visits the office, Elliot seduces her and convinces Beverly to sleep with her. Beverly's delicate emotional state, coupled with his territorial feelings towards the actress and his drug addiction, send him into a spiral of paranoia and delusion which begins to destroy the brothers' business and relationship, and possibly their lives. A disturbing medical horror film that is made all the more frightening by its quiet unease and coldly beautiful cinematography, *Dead Ringers* combines surgical discomfort with the eeriness of the doppelganger subgenre. The film surpasses the normal level of body horror by inventing new kinds of gynecological creepiness, and the creation of instruments for working on mutant women is a particularly horrifying image.

Director David Cronenberg was already versed in the body horror arena with *Rabid* and *Videodrome* when he came upon the book *Twins* by Bari Wood and Jack Geasland. The twins are portrayed in the film by Jeremy Irons in a career-defining set of performances, creating two distinct characters with simple changes in his subtle physicality. The Genie- and Saturn Award–winning score was composed by Howard Shore, who has worked with Cronenberg fifteen times since they met on *The Brood*.

No Telling (1991)

Directed by Larry Fessenden
Written by Larry Fessenden, Beck Underwood
Starring: Miriam Healy-Louie, Stephen Ramsey, David Van Tieghem

Lillian's husband is a research scientist, and his career has afforded them a nice lifestyle which includes a pleasant summer retreat. While vacationing, she meets an animal activist who opens her eyes about the frightening realities of animal experimentation and torture in the field of research science which makes her question her husband's career and motivations. Little does she know how much darker her husband's current experimental activities are. A horrifying exploration of the lengths to which a scientist will go to make a breakthrough, *No Telling* is all the more frightening because the premise itself is not outlandish at all. Inspired by the original *Frankenstein* as well as true stories of animal laboratory testing and chemical farming at the time, the film juxtaposes the lives of people on opposite ends of the controversial subject to great effect. Well-researched sequences of laboratory experimentation and footage of animal abuse make for uncomfortable but eye-opening viewing in this unique sci-fi–horror hybrid.

Director Larry Fessenden had worked for several years in short form and video work; *No Telling* was his first feature-length release. The themes of environmental concern would continue throughout his career, cropping up again in *Wendigo* and *The Last Winter*. The film was co-written by Fessenden and his wife Beck Underwood; the couple has worked together on numerous projects at their company Glass Eye Pix.

Other Titles of Interest

American Mary (2012), *The Skin I Live In* (2011), *Altered States* (1980), *Pathology* (2008)

Scientist Geoffrey Gaines (Stephen Ramsey) allows his medical curiosity to take him to strange, dark places in 1991's *No Telling* (courtesy Larry Fessenden).

Swamp Horror

If the Earth were a creature with the ability to think and communicate, we might recognize the various biospheres of the planet as personality traits that express aspects of who Earth really is. Sometimes cold and remote, sometimes dry and withering, sometimes lush and vibrant, Earth is a well-rounded individual and seems to have a variety of facets to her psyche.

One of the most baffling is the swamp. A confusing mash-up of aspects of other biomes that seems to contradict itself, it is the schizophrenic part of our friend the Earth that we'll never fully understand. The vegetation is lush and green, supporting the life of trees, bushes, and other plants, which can give it the appearance of connection to grasslands and forests; yet half of the life of the swamp exists under the murky surface of the water, putting it seemingly more in the camp of the aquatic biome. Though the heat in the swamp may be moist, it is still a strong heat, reminding us of the climate of a desert (with the unpleasant addition of massive humidity). And the difficulty of survival for humanity, whether because of the multiple dangerous species or the landscape which is nearly impossible to navigate on foot, is reminiscent of the tundra.

So what are we to make of this bizarre amalgamation of land and sea, welcoming vibrancy and life-threatening creatures? Perhaps the swamp is nature's way of saying that it would like some private time. Humanity has spread all across the planet, adapting to varying climates and geography, and the Earth has silently let us go about our business. However, the Earth might also have some piece of its personality that just wants to be alone every once in a while.

The creatures (and occasional humans) that call the swamp home do so with the understanding and agreement that they live there as solitary beings. While they are all connected in the ecological sense, they also all have an understanding of their oneness in life, their isolation from other places and their reliance only on themselves. The swamps are the places where the Earth stops looking out for everyone else and gives herself some much-deserved alone time.

But be warned: When the Earth isn't watching you, who knows what else might be.

Elements of the Subgenre

Exotic Company: From the toothless wildmen who live on airboats to the stunning variety of poisonous and dangerous bugs and reptiles, the swamp is one of the most alarmingly diverse places on the planet. The culture and borders blend and disappear without roads and signs, and you never know if the next human you meet might be a climate scientist or a Creole-speaking turtle hunter.

We Don't Get Many Visitors Round Here: The unique purpose and location of the swamp makes it a rather unlikely locale for vacations and tourism. If you end up there, you either have some business to attend to (or bodies to dispose of), or you stumbled upon it by accident. And any time someone new shows up with no warning, there's bound to be some problems with the locals.

Recommendations from the Subgenre

Creature from the Black Lagoon (1954)
Directed by Jack Arnold
Written by Harry Essex, Arthur A. Ross, Maurice Zimm
Starring: Richard Carlson, Julie Adams, Whit Bissell

When an expedition to the Amazon unearths a skeletal webbed hand that might have belonged to a Missing Link, an expanded expedition on a steamer ship is arranged to find the rest of the skeleton. Arriving at the expedition camp, they find that the two natives left behind were killed under mysterious circumstances. Investigations into a nearby lagoon reveal that the creature they are seeking does exist and is not as long-dead as they had expected. Originally released in 3-D, *Creature from the Black Lagoon* ended up benefitting from the depth of frame that was created by the technique, and it accentuated the beautiful underwater photography. Restructuring a classic myth that has populated horror from *Beauty and the Beast* to *King Kong*, the story finds an interesting ecological angle with the undisturbed lagoon as a hiding place for a missing link creature.

Directed by sci-fi mainstay Jack Arnold, who also brought audiences *The Incredible Shrinking Man* and *It Came from Outer Space*, the film was a hit for Universal; though the Gill Man was created over two decades after the original Universal horror monsters, the film's popularity and the unique character design won him a place in the iconic pantheon. The film was followed by two sequels in 1955 and 1956, and the legend of the creature has maintained a presence in film and television through loving references in places as disparate as *Buffy the Vampire Slayer* and *The Nightmare Before Christmas*.

Eaten Alive (1977)

Directed by Tobe Hooper
Written by Alvin L. Fast, Mohammed Rustam, Kim Henkel
Starring: Mel Ferrer, Carolyn Jones, Marilyn Burns

In a decrepit hotel on the edge of a swamp, its owner Judd lives a relatively isolated and private life with his pet crocodile Nile; on occasion, he murders a person or two and feeds them to Nile. When the parents of one of his victims come looking for their daughter at the same time that a family is falling victim to his habits, Judd goes on a rampage and provides a feast for his pet. While it doesn't reach the fevered pitch or artistic heights of director Tobe Hooper's previous film *The Texas Chain Saw Massacre*, *Eaten Alive* is an interesting and always watchable exploitation film with recognizable faces both old (Mel Ferrer and Carolyn Jones) and new (Kyle Richards a year before her performance in *Halloween* and a pre–Freddy Krueger Robert Englund). With an over-the-top script co-written by his *Chain Saw* script collaborator Kim Henkel, the film trades in the dry open spaces of Texas for the dank atmosphere of the swamp, complete with sleazy brothels and crazed locals with pet maneaters.

With several of his previous co-workers present for his second film, director Hooper found himself attempting to recapture the anarchic intensity of his first film with mixed success through several low-budget entries until he was chosen to direct *Poltergeist* in 1982. Hooper's collaboration on the *Eaten Alive* score with Wayne Bell (still a well respected dialogue and sound editor) produced the high point of the film, a music-light soundscape comprised largely of noises and eerie vocal effects.

The Legend of Boggy Creek (1972)

Directed by Charles B. Pierce
Written by Earl E. Smith
Starring: William Stumpp, Willie W. Smith, Vern Stierman

The town of Fouke, Arkansas, has long been plagued with appearances and attacks from a Bigfoot-like creature called the Fouke Monster. A young boy terrified of a monster he saw in the woods narrates a series of encounters that Fouke residents had with the monster, running from strangely humorous to downright terrifying. Voice-over narration and dramatic re-enactments of the events track the attacks and the eight-year disappearance of the creature, culminating in its inevitable return. A homegrown indie film made near the Texas-Arkansas border, *The Legend of Boggy Creek* is a triumph of ingenuity over budget. The film, though shot on 35mm film stock, has the grain of an old newsreel, and its lack of technical gloss helps to sell the conceit all the more effectively. The style of this film, which is similar to television documentary series like *In Search of...*, has been borrowed and paid homage to in films like *The Blair Witch Project*.

Charles B. Pierce was a salesman before embarking on the journey to make this unlikely drive-in hit which earned over $20 million in its theatrical run; Pierce later made other Southern-focused horror-thrillers like *The Evictors* and *The Town That Dreaded Sundown*, though no other film he directed would ever be nearly as successful. The script by constant Pierce collaborator Earl E. Smith gave the film its pseudo-documentary sensibility; it was so well-received that two sequels were produced (only one of which involved director Pierce). It has also been the inspiration for other similar but unconnected *Boggy Creek* films.

Other Titles of Interest

Swamp Thing (1982), *Hatchet* (2006), *Venom* (2005), *Man-Thing* (2005), *Swamp Devil* (2008), *Rugaru* (2012)

Terror in Suburbia Horror

In many ways, suburban living is both representative of the greatest achievements of modern humanity, and also a symbol of the tenuous grasp we have on those achievements.

Suburban life is generally defined not as much by its location (though it takes its name from a specific kind of lifestyle), but more about what that location represents. The suburbs were designed as a place well away from the bustling city where the jobs and traffic and pollution and corruption choke away the ability for families to live in happiness and tranquility. Beautifully constructed and brightly painted homes, row upon row of them, were lined up neatly in small towns where the grass is the same height, teenagers are discouraged from "hanging out" in public, and the scourge of drugs and alcohol simply don't exist.

This construct is the pleasant face suburbanites have put onto their true desires: to remove themselves from the horrible reality of what society actually creates. The cities, as dirty and crowded and uncomfortable as they may be, have an inherent geographic honesty. In New York City, a rich person traveling the streets is forced to be at least somewhat aware of the fact that the drug addicts, prostitutes, and homeless people are present around them, the unwanted end result of the process called capitalism. They may choose to ignore them, but they are there.

In suburbia, however, even the reminders are gone. No graffiti on the walls, no blanketed bums on benches, no protests in the town park. It creates a brilliant false utopia for those wealthy or lucky enough to pay or marry their way into it.

Of course, the utopia is impossible, because the people in suburbia are just as susceptible to the problems of modern society as the derelicts in the cities, and those problems can seep their way into the suburbs quietly. An unfaithful husband can bring home a disease from an illicit affair, a housewife weighed down under the burden of expectation can seek out more and more extreme medical solutions to her mounting anxieties. Scratching at the surface of those bright colors reveals a dark truth underneath.

Horror films often go beyond the literal truth to get to the underlying spiritual truth of a situation. While not all suburban neighborhoods may secretly hide criminal enterprises, cult activity, rape and serial killings, the terror in suburbia subgenre always reminds us of the constant fear that, underneath the veneer of civilized humanity, there is a savage nature waiting to be let out.

Elements of the Subgenre

Turning a Blind Eye: Suburbia isn't just about finding your own perfect little home; it's also about knowing that everyone else around you is doing the same. Sure, the lady next door might have a black eye, but it must have been some sort of accident. People don't investigate the dark possibilities of the lives around them in suburbia, because it's all too possible that they will find something. And if they find something, then they have to do something. It's much easier to simply look the other way.

But They Looked So Wholesome and Innocent: None of the suburban monsters who torture and murder their families look like monsters, or someone would have caught on to them years earlier. No, the most dangerous man on the block will likely wear a suit and a practiced smile, and his answers to leading questions will always be just a little too slick. You might, for just a second as the door is closing, see the smile slide away and catch a momentary glance at the evil underneath.

Recommendations from the Subgenre

The Stepfather (1987)
Directed by Joseph Ruben
Written by Carolyn Lefcourt, Brian Garfield, Donald E. Westlake
Starring: Terry O'Quinn, Jill Schoelen, Shelley Hack

Real estate agent Jerry Blake has just married single mother Susan, and is having trouble connecting with her teenage daughter Stephanie. Noticing his strange behavior and tendency to lose his temper easily, Stephanie begins to suspect that her new stepfather is not who he says he is. Mysterious deaths lead Stephanie to the discovery that Jerry is a madman who has previously killed whole families and then disappeared, and they might be next. A slasher-influenced thriller film that came at the peak of the slasher craze, *The Stepfather* raises the bar on the domestic suspense film with great performances and a scathing commentary on 1980s America. Rather than simply rehashing the Hitchcockian premise that someone you know may be a killer, the film takes the clichés of the American dream, with its happy families and perfect suburban houses, and gives it a nasty twist. The possible mystery element of "Is he a killer?" is done away with in the opening moments, leaving the film to play cat and mouse with Jerry and Stephanie very effectively.

With a screenplay from crime novelist Donald E. Westlake (whose previous book *The Grifters* was turned into an Oscar-nominated film) and a career-making performance from lead actor Terry O'Quinn, director Joseph Ruben crafted a promising follow-up to his previous thriller *Dreamscape*. Clips from *Mr. Ed* accentuate Jerry's old-fashioned fantasies while creating dual feelings of fear and sympathy from the audience, and even the B-story of the amateur detective on his trail is handled with intelligence and mounting suspense. The film was followed by two sequels (only one of which brought back the stellar O'Quinn) and a remake in 2009.

The Girl Next Door (2007)
Directed by Gregory Wilson
Written by Daniel Farrands, Philip Nutman (based on the story by Jack Ketchum)
Starring: William Atherton, Blythe Auffarth, Blanche Baker

Grown-up David, after witnessing a violent encounter that left behind an abandoned victim, remembers his childhood in the late 1950s. Young David lived next door to two young girls who had come to stay with their aunt after the death of their parents in a car accident. As he becomes closer to one sister, Meg, he discovers that the abusive aunt and cousins have been systematically beating and raping her. Wanting to help but unsure of what a ten-year-old boy can do, he becomes trapped in his inability to convince adults of the secret truth next door. Not to be confused with the raunchy 2004 comedy, *The Girl Next Door* is an unrelenting look into the dark heart of suburban America. With a lead cast made up almost entirely of excellent young actors, the film doesn't pull its punches in portraying the sordid events at hand (even when you want it to).

Based on the novel by horror writer Jack Ketchum, who wrote the book after learning of the real-life torture and murder of a young girl in 1965, it is a powerful piece of filmmaking that is always effective but never particularly enjoyable. Co-writer Daniel Farrands is something of an expert in the horror arena, having written one of the *Halloween* films and produced retrospective documentaries about several others including *Friday the 13th* and *A Nightmare on Elm Street*. Producer Andrew van den Houten, after successfully translating Ketchum's work to screen in this film, worked with his source material twice more to produce *Offspring* and the award-winning *The Woman*.

Benjamin Ross Kaplan as Donny Chandler in the chilling period piece *The Girl Next Door* (2007) (courtesy Andrew van den Houten).

The 'Burbs (1989)

Directed by Joe Dante
Written by Dana Olsen
Starring: Tom Hanks, Bruce Dern, Carrie Fisher

During a week-long vacation, suburbanite Ray Peterson substitutes relaxation with suspicion when he begins to get the impression that the new neighbors might be hiding some strange secrets. Along with two other nosy friends, Ray starts digging into the activities of the weird Klopeks, from midnight yard-digging to beating up their trash to running their monstrous noisy basement incinerator. *The 'Burbs* is a hilarious and knowing comedy that brilliantly turns the clichés of the terror in suburbia horror film on their heads without ever allowing the characters to wink at the viewer. All the beats from the subgenre are there: the missing neighbor, the strange behavior, and the stories of horrifying small-town secrets. But it is the over-the-top score and twists on the tropes (the dramatic zoom on the face of the neighbor's dog) that make the film fun and original.

Director Joe Dante, already known for the satirical genre hybrids *Piranha* and *Gremlins*, teamed with writer Dana Olsen (who was also versed in writing comedy hybrids with *Wacko* and *Memoirs of an Invisible Man*) to create this cult classic. Die-hard Dante fans will recognize familiar faces Robert Picardo and Dick Miller (a character actor who appears in every film Dante directs), and dramatic star Bruce Dern does a brilliant comic turn as retired military man Mark Rumsfield. Hints of Hitchcock's *Rear Window* lace the film, and Tom Hanks makes a convincingly befuddled everyman lead.

Other Titles of Interest

The Stepford Wives (1975 and 2004), *Happiness* (1998), *Bully* (2001), *Arlington Road* (1999), *Disturbia* (2007), *House at the End of the Street* (2012)

Theatrical Performance Horror

In a theatrical performance, there is an obvious deception that is accepted by both the audience and the performers. Viewing a stage seventy-five feet wide with a fake sunset painted on a backdrop and plywood castle walls dressed in colored construction paper, the audience must be willing to buy into the blatant fantasy that is *Hamlet's* Denmark. The performers accept it as well, altering their natural voice and body to the over-enunciation, volume, and broad gestures necessary for the performance to reach audience members in the back of the theater.

Everything about it is fake, and yet we have all agreed to believe it. And we do it precisely because it is safe. We can watch the actor portraying Count Dracula, or we can watch the magician sawing his assistant in half, and allow ourselves to be taken in by the story because we know we are in no danger. The classic Grand Guignol stage shows of Paris, where horrible violence was visited on victims while a crowd watched, became so popular because audiences could witness the immediacy of the violence while still protected by the unspoken agreement between audience and performer. We don't believe the magician has truly sawed a woman in half, but we like to be fooled.

But an agreement only works when both parties abide by the rules. A deranged performer, who already has the trust of his audience, can betray that trust: He can actually injure, murder, or dismember someone in front of them, psychologically implicating them in the violence and murder. A brief but brilliant example of this is seen in the Vampire Theater in director Neil Jordan's *Interview with the Vampire*: An audience witnesses a coven of vampires feeding on an innocent woman, but they suspect it to be nothing more than a strange, gothic performance.

That is where theatrical performance and horror film meet. We all know horror movies aren't real, but we like to be fooled anyway. And every once in a while, with a truly amazing special effect or a disturbing performance from an unknown actor in a found footage film, we might wonder to ourselves … it's not possible that this is real, right?

Elements of the Subgenre

The Charismatic Weirdo: In almost any theatrical performance horror film worth noting, there is a mysterious figure with possibly shady intentions and surprisingly compelling motives. Whether his face is disfigured and he hides behind a mask, or he performs graphically violent stage shows that almost dare the audience to investigate further, there is something about him that draws the audience in. And that is right where he wants you.

Effects Too Good to Be Fake: We can't help but look away, and yet we perhaps peek through our fingers to continue watching the carnage unfold. After all, those aren't real deaths being committed, right? The blood is too bright, the screaming too stiff and staged. But then again…

Recommendations from the Subgenre

The Phantom of the Opera (1925)

Directed by Rupert Julian
Written by Raymond Schrock and Elliot J. Clawson (based on the novel by Gaston Leroux)
Starring: Lon Chaney, Mary Philbin, Norman Kerry

When the management of the Paris Opera House quits during the new season due to the mysterious Opera Ghost, the new owners laugh off the legends and continue the performances. Christine, the new understudy for the lead role, finds herself the focus of the Opera Ghost's interest, and he threatens the safety of the production if she is not featured in the lead role. The threats continue, and Christine's career begins to flourish, but she finds herself as the prize in a struggle between her love interest, Raoul, and the mysterious Ghost, whose presence becomes all the more real. The most well-known screen adaptation of Gaston Leroux's 1910 novel, *The Phantom of the Opera* is a classic gothic romance whose influence would reach through generations to become a successful musical stage production. The mysterious machinations and physical deformities of the masked Phantom created the template of the tragic hero which has influenced films like *Twilight* and *Frankenstein*.

Produced by Carl Laemmle for Universal Studios, the film was a precursor to the Universal horror monster boom that began in 1931 with *Dracula*. Lon Chaney, the actor known for

The Phantom (Lon Chaney) makes a terrifying entrance at the annual masked ball in 1925's *The Phantom of the Opera*.

his stunning performances in complicated makeup, created the skeletal face design for the Phantom. *Phantom* was pioneering in its use of color film during the Bal Masque sequence. The Paris Opera House set built for the film was so elaborate and sturdy that it remained standing until it was demolished in 2014.

Wizard of Gore (2007)

Directed by Jeremy Kasten
Written by Zach Chassler, Herschell Gordon Lewis (based on his original story)
Starring: Kip Pardue, Bijou Phillips, Crispin Glover

A magician named Montag the Magnificent has a stage show in which he seemingly murders women from the audience in graphic ways, only to reveal that they are still alive and well. However, the women are later found dead, and the cause of death seems to be wounds that exactly match the faked injuries from Montag's stage show. A young journalist looking to make a name for himself decides to investigate. As he becomes enmeshed in Montag's following and watches more of his shows, he begins to lose his hold on reality. A loving advertisement for the parts of downtown Los Angeles not usually seen on film, *Wizard of Gore* is a modern film with a decidedly nostalgic bent. A film built on set-piece magic shows and the brilliantly demented performance of Crispin Glover, it also works off the stage due to the performance of Kip Pardue as the seemingly time-displaced journalist Ed Bigelow.

Director Jeremy Kasten and his writing collaborator Zack Chassler bring some of the energy and flair of Kasten's previous film *The Attic Expeditions* to this remake of the not-quite-classic 1970 film by Herschell Gordon Lewis. Many of the victims of Montag the Magnificent are famous pin-up models from the Suicide Girls website, and there are brief appearances by horror industry veterans Jeffrey Combs (*Re-Animator*) and Brad Dourif (*Child's Play*).

Montag the Magnificent (Crispin Glover) mesmerizes audiences with his stage magic in the 2007 remake of *Wizard of Gore* (courtesy Jeremy Kasten).

The Theatre Bizarre (2011)

Directed by Douglas Buck, Buddy Giovinazzo, David Gregory, Karim Hussain, Jeremy Kasten, Tom Savini, Richard Stanley
Written by Zack Chassler, Richard Stanley, Scarlett Amaris, Emiliano Ranzani, Buddy Giovinazzo, John Esposito, Douglas Buck, Karim Hussain, David Gregory
Starring: Udo Kier, Virginia Newcomb

Young Enola Penny is curious about the abandoned theater down the street. The door mysteriously opens one evening and Enola goes in to find a strangely lifelike puppet named Peg Poett onstage. Peg introduces a series of bizarre and haunting stories inspired by the Grand Guignol, and as the evening of storytelling progresses, Enola finds Peg becoming more and more lifelike as she slowly turns into a giant human puppet herself. An anthology film which makes the most of its wild framework to bring several stylistically varied short films together, *The Theatre Bizarre* is a horror film tinged with nostalgia about the stage and decidedly international in its influences. The six stories veer from supernatural (encounters with a creepy witch) to perversely clinical (a woman steals memories by feeding on people's eyes), all anchored by the effectively eerie performance of Udo Kier as the puppet narrator.

Seven filmmakers from different artistic disciplines (Gregory is a documentarian and producer, Giovinazzo works primarily as a novelist, Hussain is an award-winning film–TV cinematographer, etc.) were brought together by Severin Films with the intent of creating a dark homage to Grand Guignol, the French theatrical movement focused on physical brutality and live staged gore effects. The most well-known filmmaker of the bunch, Richard Stanley, is known for his African horror film *Dust Devil* and for being fired from directing *Island of*

Disturbingly lifelike puppet Peg Poett (Udo Kier) inches closer to becoming human with every story he tells in the 2011 anthology film *The Theatre Bizarre* (courtesy Jeremy Kasten).

Dr. Moreau. Many of this anthology's filmmakers worked together again on a documentary about Stanley's *Moreau* experience, called *Lost Soul: The Doomed Journey of Richard Stanley's Island of Dr. Moreau.*

Other Titles of Interest

The Brighton Strangler (1945), *A Double Life* (1947), *The Hypnotic Eye* (1960), *Stage Fright* (2014), *Theatre of Death* (1967), *The Flesh and Blood Show* (1972), *Theater of Blood* (1973), *Stage Fright: Aquarius* (1987)

Tool Horror

Though the First World War has been eclipsed historically by other more prominent wars (as well as the simple march of time), it will always be remembered as the first major war to enlist the use of mechanized warfare. The creation of tanks and machine guns during that war changed the face of warfare forever.

Before mechanized warfare, two armies would meet on a field of battle, under generally understood laws of war, and they would battle until one side was defeated or surrendered. Every man in an army was fighting other men, and they looked into the eyes of the men whom they fought. It was a miserable and violent task, but it was a direct one.

The advent of killing machines changed not only the way we went to war, but how we looked at the enemy we were fighting. Mowing downs tens of people with a single gun in the blink of an eye, or crushing a body underneath the tracks of a moving tank, were new tactics employed by an army, and in order to remain sane and believe they were not monsters, soldiers who used these weapons had to adjust their thinking regarding those they were killing. No longer were they human beings with opinions that *they* must have believed were worth fighting for; now, they were dead-eyed villains whose desire was simply to murder before they could be murdered.

What little humanity had existed in the idea of warfare was gone, and what replaced it was the ingenuity of death. Faster and deadlier weapons meted out quicker results, and soldiers became more removed from the idea that the victims of the war were really even victims at all.

This skewed view of certain parts of humanity, seen as a problem to solve or an impediment to remove, has also extended to our other mechanized technology. Murders committed with power tools and advanced weaponry dehumanize the victims, turning them into nothing more than the target for the weapon or the material for the tool. Humanity is seen now as little more than a plank of wood to be shaped or a nail to be driven down. This turn in psychology is vividly rendered in the subgenre of tool horror.

Killers eschew the simple kills of the knife or bare hands, instead opting to distance themselves from the real act itself by executing it with the impersonal machinery of death. Humanity is in need of repair, and the killer knows exactly how to handle it.

Elements of the Subgenre

If You Treat Them Like Objects, They Will Kill with Objects: The closest that the tool horror films tend to come (in terms of commentary) is when they point out that the people who use tools to kill do so after they themselves have been dismissed as useless or trivial. They're using common household objects to lash out at lovers that have spurned them, bosses who ridiculed them, and a society that pushed them to the side.

Creative. Gross, But Creative!: One of the strongest elements of the subgenre of tool horror is the inventiveness that comes with the kills. While that may not be something that seems noteworthy, the films focus on it, often to the detriment of characterization or story. We may not know or care about any of the main characters, but these films guarantee the most unusual methods of extermination, the more elaborate the better.

Recommendations from the Subgenre

The Toolbox Murders (1978)

Directed by Dennis Donnelly
Written by Neva Friedenn, Robert Easter, Ann Kindberg
Starring: Cameron Mitchell, Pamelyn Ferdin, Wesley Eure

At an apartment complex in Los Angeles, women are being murdered in horrible ways that all involve the use of some kind of tool: a drill, a hammer, a screwdriver, a nail gun. When the MO of the killer changes to the kidnapping of a young girl, her brother Joey begins to investigate. The police and Joey soon learn that someone from inside the apartment complex is the kidnapper-killer, and that not only is he out of his mind, he may not be acting alone. A dark and unrelentingly violent film for the first half, *The Toolbox Murders* becomes a strangely compelling psycho-thriller in the last half, which focuses on the motives of the killer and owes a debt of inspiration to films like *Psycho* and *The Texas Chain Saw Massacre*. Combining the newly created slasher genre with the police investigative procedural, the film's pacing is slow but the story's payoff is worth the time invested.

Dennis Donnelly was an assistant director working in action films and B-movies of the 1960s and 1970s before stepping into the role of director for the only time in his career. Co-writer Ann Kindberg moved into producing and directing for such prominent television series as *Grey's Anatomy* and *The Shield*. Star Wesley Eure is known to cult TV fans as Will Marshall on *Land of the Lost*. The false "based on a true story" framework from director Tobe Hooper's original *The Texas Chain Saw Massacre* was used for this film; it is ironic that Hooper would direct the supernaturally tinged 2004 remake.

The *Saw* series (2004–2010)

Directed by James Wan, Darren Lynn Bousman, Kevin Greutert, David Hackl
Written by Leigh Whannell, James Wan, Darren Lynn Bousman, Thomas Fenton, Patrick Melton, Marcus Dunstan
Starring: Tobin Bell, Costas Mandylor, Shawnee Smith

In an unnamed industrial American city, the authorities are on the trail of a serial killer named Jigsaw who kidnaps people he has deemed unworthy and puts them through deadly

Jigsaw disciple Detective Hoffman (Costas Mandylor) readies a deadly new trap in 2010's *Saw: The Final Chapter* (courtesy Lionsgate Publicity).

tests that they must survive. This has resulted in many deaths and several physically damaged survivors. As the police net tightens and Jigsaw's fatal illness is revealed, others start to pick up where he left off and continue the testing as his disciples. Cleverly combining the "locked room" mysteries from British authors like Agatha Christie and Dorothy L. Sayers with the graphic violence of modern horror, *Saw* is a perfect modern take on the tool horror film. Reducing people to parts of a mechanical process in which they must use ingenuity and inner strength to survive, the series comments on the increasing alienation of people due to technology.

The creation of director James Wan and writer Leigh Whannell (who went on to co-create the *Insidious* film series), *Saw* was a surprise breakout hit that became a yearly horror phenomenon with a new release every October for seven years straight. The compressed release schedule and the return of many creative and production team members on subsequent entries make this one of the most serialized and intricate storylines in a horror film franchise, and it rewarded loyal viewers with constant twists and surprises.

The Driller Killer (1979)

Directed by Abel Ferrara
Written by Nicholas St. John
Starring: Abel Ferrara, Carolyn Marz, Baybi Day

Angry young artist Reno lives in a rundown apartment in New York City. His career is going poorly, he can't pay his rent, he sees his father's face in every bum on the street, and his girlfriend is cheating on him. He buys a portable battery pack for his electric drill, and after he is driven over the edge by the constant loud music from the band next door, he starts murdering homeless people by drilling them to death. Teeming with grimy life from its practical locations in Union Square of the late 1970s, *The Driller Killer* is a primal scream of exploitation horror that put director Abel Ferrara on the map. Combining religious iconography with the punk music scene of the time, the film feels like a juxtaposition of old and new world values clashing in the life of lead character Reno. Many consider this film to be the prototype for Ferrara's later New York City nightmare film *Bad Lieutenant*.

Directing as well as playing the lead role, Ferrara worked with longtime collaborator Nicholas St. John on the script. (They made nine films together, including *Body Snatchers* and *The Addiction*.) The film was low budget and shot on 16mm film, its gritty imagery accurately reflecting the feel of New York City of the era. Though the film was released to relatively little fanfare in the U.S., it was the target of British censorship, being one of the major motivations for the creation of the notorious "Video Nasties" list of films banned in the U.K.

Other Titles of Interest

Nail Gun Massacre (1985), *The Texas Chain Saw Massacre* (1974 and 2003), *Machete* (2010)

Underwater Horror

The more advanced and civilized humanity becomes, the less equipped we are to protect and defend ourselves without the civilization and the technological advances. The world itself seems to be aware of our inherent weakness and actively tries to confine us in the narrow window where we can survive; gravity keeps us out of the cold vacuum of space, and buoyancy keeps us out of the crushing depths of the ocean. Constantly being pushed down from the sky and up from the water, and we still have the audacity to consider ourselves the superior species.

As if it weren't humbling enough that our planet is the only speck of inhabitable dirt for billions of miles, we also look around this planet to see that two-thirds of it is covered in water. Water is the lifeblood and poison of humanity; too little and we die of dehydration, too much and we drown. The relationship between humanity and water, much like any tenuous relationship, is a matter of degrees.

But humanity refuses to be told what we can and cannot do. Our ego tells us that there is nothing that ingenuity and hard work cannot achieve, and so we venture into the murky deep with a level of confidence matching our lack of preparedness. In a sealed suit made of metal, thick fabric, and tanks of air to keep our fragile bodies from suffocating, freezing, or being crushed, we bob in the water, barely able to move and appearing not much different from the fish pulled from the ocean and left to flail about on the deck of a boat. We may not die because of the water, but we certainly do not look at home in it.

And it is that battle, the fight between the inherent danger of the depths of the ocean and the hubris of man, which creates situations rife with the real-life and not-so-real-life terrors from beneath the surface.

Elements of the Subgenre

Scuba Breathing as Scoring: Taking a cue from the granddaddy of all underwater horror movies, *Jaws* (which is just as much part of this subgenre as it is the animals attack subgenre), filmmakers love to have tense moments with characters underwater, their action punctuated only by the rhythmic and eerie breathing and bubbling from scuba gear. While music and sound effects can be effective, there's just something about the muted silence of the ocean and a single human being breathing...

A Stronghold Filling with Water: When you're underwater, your submarine-base-boat-diving gear is all that is between you and certain death, and that is why there is always a slow and unpreventable leak that is filling up the place where the characters felt safe. As if to remind the characters and the audience that they don't belong there, water is constantly and persistently working its way into man's temporarily safe environment.

Sitting Ducks: The lack of navigational skill that humans have when underwater inevitably leads to a confrontation between a character and something else, something much better in water than them, swirling around them and ready to strike. Maybe it's a monster, or a shark, or just a spy in a mini-sub, but it's faster and more agile than them, and it's coming.

Recommendations from the Subgenre

The Deep (1977)

Directed by Peter Yates
Written by Peter Benchley, Tracy Keenan Wynn (based on the novel by Benchley)
Starring: Jacqueline Bisset, Nick Nolte, Robert Shaw

While on vacation in Bermuda, a couple goes scuba diving and finds artifacts from a sunken ship. At first they believe them to be pieces from a downed ship from World War II. The couple becomes embroiled in a plot that involves sunken Spanish treasure, drug dealers, Haitian black magic, and shifting loyalties. While much of the action and intrigue does take place on land, it is during the diving sequences where the film really comes to life. Though the film is not strictly horror in the sense of graphic violence or supernatural occurrences, the tense and fearful underwater segments are fantastically engrossing and help to keep the viewer engaged during the rather pedestrian landlocked love story.

Based on the novel by Peter Benchley (who had already proven his underwater thriller skills by writing *Jaws*), the film was directed by Peter Yates, who made the fun fantasy of *Krull* and the cool action of *Bullitt*. Another *Jaws* alumnus, actor Robert Shaw, nearly steals the film in the role of lighthouse watchman-treasure seeker Romer Treece. The rest of the supporting cast does an excellent job of covering for the strange chemistry between leads Bisset and Nolte. Yates boldly decided to do much of the underwater filming in open water, and the risky effort pays off with spectacular underwater imagery.

Sphere (1998)

Directed by Barry Levinson
Written by Kurt Wimmer, Stephen Hauser, Paul Attanasio (based on the story by Michael Crichton)
Starring: Dustin Hoffman, Samuel L. Jackson, Sharon Stone

A group made up of a biologist, a mathematician, a psychologist, and an astrophysicist, gathered to be the first contact team in the event of an alien encounter, are taken to a Navy ship in the middle of the ocean. It seems that a spaceship has been found on the floor of the ocean, and it looks to have been there for several hundred years. While exploring the ship and the strange hovering sphere contained within it, the scientists and the military crew find themselves facing off against a mysterious intelligence that seems to be able to tap into their deepest fears and make them real.

Sphere is moody, surprising, and well-orchestrated. There are sequences (including the appearance of thousands of tiny submerged eggs surrounding the station) that are undeniably unnerving. A sci-fi thriller written by the king of the sci-fi thriller, Michael Crichton, *Sphere* was a critical and commercial flop upon release. Director Barry Levinson and actor Dustin Hoffman were doing double duty during the shooting of the film, also making the political comedy *Wag the Dog* on sets nearby. Excellent visuals, a smart and talented cast (including Queen Latifah and a not-yet-famous Liev Schreiber), and a cerebral take on a science fiction mystery were lost on audiences looking for something more action-oriented. The film is in many ways a love letter to *Twenty Thousand Leagues Under the Sea*, specifically folding the novel itself into the plot of the film.

DeepStar Six (1989)

Directed by Sean S. Cunningham
Written by Lewis Abernathy, Geof Miller
Starring: Miguel Ferrer, Nia Peeples, Matt McCoy

The crew of an underwater military outpost called DeepStar Six find themselves in charge of both underwater colonization experiments and the placement of a nuclear weapons storage platform. A depth charge causes a cave-in of underwater caverns, and the crew of the station race against time to escape the station and the mysterious creature that is attacking them due to the cavern explosions. *DeepStar Six* came out in 1989, and is clearly a product of the decade. Classic elements of the underwater subgenre, including claustrophobia, hallucinations, and unbelievably fast decompression (i.e., people exploding), make this a perfect template for the era and the subgenre.

The *other* "monsters under the water" film that came out in 1989 (the more prominent one being the James Cameron film *The Abyss*), *DeepStar Six* was directed by *Friday the 13th* creator Sean S. Cunningham. Getting lost in the sea of lower-budget underwater films the same year (including *Leviathan*, *Lords of the Deep*, *The Evil Below*, and *The Rift*), the film had little chance to distinguish itself. Cameron was coming off the one-two punch of *The Terminator* and *Aliens*, and *The Abyss* was the box office winner, while *DeepStar Six* was relegated to VHS bins and relative obscurity.

Below (2002)

Directed by David Twohy
Written by Lucas Sussman, Darren Aranofsky, David Twohy
Starring: Matthew Davis, Bruce Greenwood, Olivia Williams

When a British nurse is saved from a sinking medical ship by an American World War II submarine, her welcome is not warm (given the superstition regarding bad luck that accompanies women on submarines). She discovers it extends much deeper than that: The captain of the ship died days earlier in a suspicious accident, and strange supernatural occurrences on the ship may be connected somehow. Combining hints of the supernatural, the real-life fears of claustrophobia, and the intensity of a maritime military suspense film, *Below* is a brilliant and effective horror-thriller. The script carefully balances all the moments of possible supernatural occurrence, providing reasonable scientific explanations for the activity (are there really ghosts, or is the crew breathing too much carbon dioxide?) and making the extended denial all the more plausible.

Another great film from a filmmaker whose career has skirted breakout success for years without ever fully landing, *Below* came from director David Twohy after the clever *The Arrival* and the franchise-starting Vin Diesel film *Pitch Black*, making it (along with *A Perfect Getaway*) another frustrating almost-success that never gained wide recognition. It is filled with brilliant character actors who are terribly underrated (including *Star Trek*'s Bruce Greenwood and *Scandal* star Scott Foley) and an early appearance from *The Hangover* superstar Zack Galifianakis. The biggest mystery about the film is its lack of connection with an audience.

Other Titles of Interest

Deep Blue Sea (1999), *Shark Night* (2011), *The Reef* (2010), *Black Water* (2007)

Urban Legend Horror

Humans love to believe in something. Rumors, ghost stories, myths, and conspiracies all feed into that deep psychological need to believe. Even atheists are adamant about their belief in the absence of something. To a degree, it is our beliefs that define who we are.

As a race, we have advanced, and science has replaced superstition in large part throughout the world. Religion still exists, but few people seek religion for the answers to pragmatic questions, because science has given us definitive answers. The idea of believing something has been replaced by the ability to know it.

That is precisely why we are drawn to things like Bigfoot and the Loch Ness Monster, stories of secret societies and massive government conspiracies. In all likelihood, they are not true, and we're glad to know that; but the possibility exists that they could be true, and it is in the narrow margin between belief and knowledge that those things exist.

Urban legends are the modern-day mythology for a jaded scientific age. The stories people share in oral tradition (like our ancestors did before the advent of the printing press) have taken on that same mystical quality, that mystery of possibility that has yet to be entirely proven or disproven. And the outrageous coincidences that most of the stories contain, the timing and circumstances necessary to make the final revelation hit home ("It wasn't a bear she shot in the dark, but her husband!" "The sheriff opened the tent to see that it was his own daughter inside!") are so unrealistically impossible that to believe them is to mirror the faith necessary to believe in the deities that much of modern science has dismissed.

In many ways, urban legends are the weapon that mankind has used to push back against the enveloping finality of knowledge. Learning will always be an important foundation, and truth should always be the measure against which all decisions are ultimately made; but the ability for mankind to look into a seemingly cruel and arbitrary world and find in it some kind of clarifying pattern, a story that makes sense of a troubling and indifferent circumstance, will always lie somewhere deep inside our hearts. For now, though, it lies quietly in the back seat of your car as you pull away from the gas station, and the attendant tries to warn you but it's just too late...

Elements of the Subgenre

The Dramatic Surprise!: The entire premise of the urban legend story is that, by the end of the story, the listener will be shocked and surprised by what the eventual revelation is. In a form similar to Rod Serling's *Twilight Zone* series, the goal of a great urban legend is to lead you in one direction, and then have an amazing final act twist that leaves everyone with their jaws hanging open in disbelief.

Someone Tells the Story: This is a classic element of any kind of mythical storytelling, and it continues into the modern myth of the urban legend: Someone tells another listener the secret background that no one else knows. The history of the killer whose hand was replaced by a hook, the truth behind the pirate's shipwreck off the coast of a small town, the secret connection between the town sheriff and the bones found in the desert. All of it happened in the murky past, and in order for you to know the truth, this storyteller has to provide it.

Recommendations from the Subgenre

When a Stranger Calls (1979)

Directed by Fred Walton
Written by Steve Feke, Fred Walton
Starring: Carol Kane, Charles Durning, Ron O'Neal

Babysitter Jill finds herself plagued with annoying phone calls one night as the children are asleep upstairs. The calls go from innocuous to threatening, and Jill contacts the police about tracing them. They discover that the calls are coming from inside the house, and Jill barely escapes being murdered by the madman within, who had already killed the sleeping children. Years later, when the madman escapes from an asylum, he is drawn to find Jill and finish what he started. With a first act that is claustrophobic and filled with tension, *When a Stranger Calls* perfectly captures quiet suburban paranoia. Great performances from Carol Kane (playing her character as both a teenager and a married adult) and Charles Durning help to smooth a rough second half when the action expands outside of the single house. The classic set-up of the call from inside the house was the inspiration for numerous horror films, including *Black Christmas* from five years earlier, but it has never been more effectively rendered.

In his feature directorial debut, Fred Walton adapted his successful short film into a feature to cash in on the sudden popularity of films like *Halloween*. Walton's filmic output was a mixed bag; he even directed *April Fool's Day*, often considered to be the film that marked the end of the golden age of slasher films. Fourteen years after the release of the original, Walton returned along with star Kane for a made-for-TV sequel, *When a Stranger Calls Back*.

Candyman (1992)

Directed by Bernard Rose
Written by Bernard Rose, (based on the story by Clive Barker)
Starring: Virginia Madsen, Tony Todd, Xander Berkeley

Graduate student Helen is working on a thesis project that revolves around urban legends. She learns about a local legend in the Cabrini-Green area named Candyman: The story revolves around the son of a slave disfigured and murdered when people discovered that he had impregnated a white woman; saying his name in front of a mirror can summon his vengeful spirit back into the world. Helen finds out that the legend is all too real, as Candyman becomes obsessed with her and orchestrates a series of murders to frame her. Combining themes of racism with growing interest in the modern urban legend movement, *Candyman* is a surprisingly considerate horror film that allows for understanding on the part of the killer, played brilliantly by Tony Todd in one of the unfortunately rare iconic horror performances for a black actor. Leaning heavily on the original novella *The Forbidden* by Clive Barker, the story is switched from the U.K. to a housing project in America to great effect.

British director Bernard Rose was a great choice for the film, having previously married horror with character drama in 1988's *Paperhouse*. Actress Kasi Lemmons, who played Helen's colleague in the film, later went on to become a well-known director, creating the excellent black-centric horror-thrillers *Eve's Bayou* and *The Caveman's Valentine*. The Candyman proved to be a popular horror icon and the series continued on for two more entries, with Tony Todd reprising the role in both.

Urban Legend (1998)

Directed by Jamie Blanks
Written by Silvio Horta
Starring: Jared Leto, Alicia Witt, Rebecca Gayheart

On a college campus, a series of murders have been taking place, all of which conform to well-known urban legends. Natalie, a friend of one of the victims, teams with a campus journalist to investigate the killings. As the bodies continue to pile up, Natalie discovers that her previous participation in an urban legend–inspired car pursuit that ended in tragedy might be the reason that people are being targeted for death. A self-referential horror film populated with young television stars, *Urban Legend* was the direct result of the popularity of *Scream* two years earlier. Like the previous year's *I Know What You Did Last Summer*, the film takes a well-known premise (a series of American urban legends) and puts a cast of young actors in the midst of murders based upon them, allowing the kids to use meta-knowledge of the stories to play a cat-and-mouse game with a masked killer.

This was director Jamie Blanks' first major film, which he followed with 2001's *Valentine* before heading back to his native Australia to make the outback horror film *Storm Warning*. The film is even more self-referential than *Scream*, and has several cameos from famous horror industry faces: Danielle Harris, Robert Englund, and Brad Dourif (who represent characters from three of the biggest horror franchises: *Halloween*, *A Nightmare on Elm Street*, and *Child's Play*). The film was followed by the sequels *Urban Legends: Final Cut* and *Urban Legends: Bloody Mary*.

Other Titles of Interest

Boogeyman (2005), *The Mothman Prophecies* (2002), *The Curve* (1998), *Alligator* (1980), *Carved* (2007), *La Llorona* (1960)

Vampire Horror

We recognize vampires. They used to be us, and we once knew them. Often, the vampire doesn't even have to use his or her powers of flight, metamorphosis, or superhuman strength; they simply need to come near enough to us that we can get a look at the faces that were once familiar to us and now gone from our lives, and then we open our doors and our lives. And our veins.

This analogy is an apt one when it comes to the psychology of the vampire as well. We like vampires as a story element because we recognize them. They were human (meaning that they resemble us inside and out), but they have a distance that makes us comfortable enough to assume commentary about vampires isn't actually commentary about humanity. Deep down, we know it is, though.

Humanity sees within itself all the egocentric, violent, base sensibilities of the vampire, but the supernatural veneer allows us to continue looking without fear of the true recognition that comes from glancing in a mirror. We see the ability that vampires have, to take advantage of (and power over) other people, to abuse others for their own gain, and we know the same potential exists within us as well. The logical extension of biological predation, of hunter and prey, taken to its most extreme and clear-cut conclusion, is apparent not only in the bloodlust of vampires, but in the everyday activities of one human interacting with another. The methods are different, but the desire is the same.

So why, then, are we drawn to stories which depict these creatures in their vicious glory, and then have them destroyed by noble heroes?

Because we hope to embody those heroes as well. Those stalwart, shining examples of humanity, people willing to give up their lives to save others, they are the characters of the story to whom we secretly hope to measure up. If the vampire, cloaked in darkness and dripping human blood from its fangs, represents the demon aspect of our nature, then the heroic hunter, with his icons of a holy God and a selfless desire to rid the world of evil, represents the light within us.

To watch these two battle is to fully recognize the war of humanity on both its grandest and most intimate scale: light versus darkness, good versus evil, played out simultaneously across the entire world and inside every human heart.

Elements of the Subgenre

Eternal Life: Though much of the other mythology changes according to the whims of the creators involved in the individual story, there are a couple of elements that always seem to be a part of the vampire mythos. The first is the ability to live forever, to retain a youthful appearance over generations, even as your mind and spirit continue to mature and learn. And with that gift of forever comes the curse of…

The Need to Feed: The second element that exists in nearly every vampire myth is the need to take blood (or life force of some kind) from others by force. This is the punishment that comes with the gift, the dark flip side of the coin of eternity. Some vampires have no issues with it, and some struggle endlessly with their humanity every time they feel the need; but it is always a biological force that they have to embrace if they wish to continue living.

A Human Relationship: There is a need in vampire movies for the vampires to be constantly reminded of what they once were, and what they sometimes still strive to be. This is usually done by having a vampire connecting in some way with a regular human. Their relationship (whether it be romantic or platonic) is the reflection of the vampire's lost humanity, and always reminds the audience that even though vampires may be immortal and strong, they are the ones who need humans rather than the other way around.

Recommendations from the Subgenre

Nosferatu (1922)

Directed by F.W. Murnau
Written by Henrik Galen
Starring: Max Schreck, Gustav von Wangenheim, Greta Schröder

On a journey for his employer, Thomas Hutter goes to Transylvania to visit Count Orlok, a new client. He is captured by Orlok (who Hutter discovers is a vampire) and held in the

The rays of the morning sun destroy the vampiric Count Orlok (Max Schreck) in the 1922 F.W. Murnau classic *Nosferatu*.

castle, but narrowly escapes and ends up in a hospital. Meanwhile, Orlok travels to Hutter's home city and finds himself enamored with Ellen, Hutter's wife. Knowing that she must destroy the creature that is haunting the city, Ellen sacrifices herself to keep Orlok in her room until daybreak, when he is destroyed by the first rays of the rising sun. *Nosferatu* is undoubtedly one of the most influential horror films in existence, and the truly impressive part is that the ninety-plus year-old silent film still holds many subtle shocks and beautiful images for modern-day viewers. The shadowplay in Orlok's castle and his rise from the coffin during the schooner voyage have been influential on nearly every serious vampire film since.

Directed by German Expressionist filmmaker F.W. Murnau, *Nosferatu* is bursting with stunning camera angles and set design. The story is based directly on Bram Stoker's novel *Dracula*, though permission was never obtained for the making of the film; a court ordered that every print of *Nosferatu* be destroyed, but luckily for film history someone didn't obey that order. It was remade in 1979 by another famed German auteur, Werner Herzog, and the supernatural "true story" of the film's making was explored in the horror comedy *Shadow of the Vampire*.

Let the Right One In (2008)

Directed by Tomas Alfredson
Written by John Ajvide Lindqvist (based on his story)
Starring: Kåre Hedebrant, Lina Leandersson

Passive young Oskar spends his days being tortured and beaten up by school bullies, and his nights fantasizing about how he would take revenge on them. When a young girl named Eli moves into the apartment nearby with her older companion, Oskar begins a tentative friendship with her. Discovering her true nature as a vampire, Oskar grows closer to her while her older companion is captured trying to harvest blood from victims in town. *Let the Right One In* effectively marries the eternal torture of immortality with the youthful angst of not fitting in, allowing the two leads to fantasize about the better life the other lives. The moody winter locale and scenes of silent interaction create a subtle and beautiful rhythm which is occasionally punctuated by shocking but brief violence. Young stars Hedebrant and Leandersson are mesmerizing, and their performances are leagues away from the precocious Hollywood children that films are comfortable showing audiences.

Based on a Swedish horror novel, the story struck at just the right time when the world was starting to recognize the seriousness of bullying. The film sidesteps some of the more difficult themes from the book such as pedophilia and gender-swapping, choosing instead to hint at these elements through clever film techniques; Eli is played by a girl, but her voice is dubbed by a much older person, lending a sense of androgyny and ambiguity to her character. Though there are several moments of overt violence, from the acid-burning to the swimming pool attack, director Alfredson chooses to shoot them at a distance, effectively muting the graphic imagery without diminishing the emotional impact. The film was remade for American audiences as *Let Me In*.

Habit (1995)
Directed and Written by Larry Fessenden
Starring: Larry Fessenden, Meredith Snaider

With the death of his father as just the latest in a series of depressing setbacks that include being robbed and breaking up with his girlfriend, Sam finds solace in alcohol. After

a chance meeting with the mysterious and aggressive Anna, Sam finds himself drawn into her world. Several dark sexual encounters and some coincidental quirks of Anna's get Sam thinking that Anna might be a vampire, and that he is the person she is using to feed on in order to stay alive. The striking city cinematography and claustrophobic emptiness of

Troubled Sam (Larry Fessenden) is haunted by the mysterious presence of the captivating Anna (Meredith Snaider) in 1995's *Habit* (courtesy Larry Fessenden).

Habit make for a tough but powerful exploration of the dissolution of a man on the edge. The skillful ambiguity the film employs to toy with the audience's expectations of a vampire film pay off in fascinating ways, and when the story is over, viewers might be left wondering if there ever was a vampire to begin with.

The film was a labor of love for Larry Fessenden who, aside from starring in the lead role, also wrote and directed it. Only his second feature-length theatrical release, the film is based on an even lower-budget video version of the story that Fessenden shot thirteen years earlier. The vampirism in *Habit* is clearly allegorical in nature, and Fessenden wisely allows the audience to decide what the allegory might be about: alcoholism, destructive relationships, inability to deal with loss, or unmotivated existence.

Other Titles of Interest

Interview with the Vampire (1994), *The Lost Boys* (1987), *Dracula* (1931 and 1992), *30 Days of Night* (2007), *Underworld* (2003), *Blade* (1998), *Vampires* (1998), *Near Dark* (1987), *Thirst* (2009), *Daybreakers* (2009)

Voodoo Zombie Horror

Today it's hard to argue that there is an iconic horror figure more popular than the zombie. From film to television to comics, the living dead have done to popular culture what they do to human flesh: They have devoured en masse and made converts of us all. The ultimate irony is that the creatures that populate these movies and shows that we love so much aren't actually zombies at all.

The beginning of what we call the modern zombie began with George Romero's seminal 1968 horror film *Night of the Living Dead*; however, anyone who remembers the film well will know that they were never called zombies. They were called ghouls in the script, referred to as many things by the characters themselves, and the film was originally named *Night of the Flesh Eaters*.

The reason they became known as zombies (from *Dawn of the Dead* forward) was because of the superficial similarities they bore to the actual historical legend of the Zombie, known from West African and Haitian folklore. The slow movement and seeming lack of cognitive thought in Romero's flesh-eating monsters got them dubbed zombies, when in fact the truth of zombies, and the voodoo that supposedly creates them, is far more fascinating in its origins as a horror trope.

Since Bela Lugosi starred in the 1932 *White Zombie*, the first feature film to discuss zombies, there has been a clear message about what there is to fear about the voodoo zombie: the master. Voodoo zombies, legend has it, are controlled by a master who uses witchcraft and drugs to either bring a person back from the dead to command them, or to gain control over the will of a living person. Often, as in the case of *I Walked with a Zombie*, or the character of Lugosi's Murder Legendre in *White Zombie*, it is the affluent white settlers who have come to the new and mysterious land and learned the ancient voodoo arts for themselves. Now that they have control over the native population, they can exert their will over the others of their own race that dare to confront them.

Much of the fear and panic these films induced came from an unfortunate and xenophobic place within the largely white American film-going audience: the "barbaric" and "devilish" practices of non–Christian and non–Anglo people across the world. The films tapped into a fear that nice, regular white people (who had violently taken over countries that belonged to native populations, like Haiti and Africa) could suddenly have revenge visited upon them by the arcane practices of people they felt they were trying to civilize.

The subgenre of the voodoo zombie film went out of style in mainstream horror film for the simple reason that it represents an antiquated practice (colonialism) and an unenlightened perspective (the mysterious evil magic of foreigners).

It makes perfect sense that in 1968, a hippie and progressive like George Romero would not only do away with the ridiculous portrayal of zombies as an evil created by minorities, but would in the same film create one of the great lead roles for a black character in the history of horror film. The audience, a hip and forward-thinking group of young people ready to cast off what came before, ate it up, and there was no looking back. There may someday be a resurgence of the voodoo zombie subgenre, some way that it can connect thematically to something that the world is dealing with in our time; but for now, they remain a relic of an unenlightened age.

Elements of the Subgenre

Rich White People: The lifeblood of this subgenre is the subjugation of one person or group by another, more powerful one. Who better to subjugate than the ones who have been doing it throughout the entirety of history, white people? Whether the rich white people are the ones who have abused and enslaved people and are deserving of voodoo retribution, or they've co-opted the secrets of voodoo rituals in order to make themselves more powerful, they're always there causing trouble in some way.

The Ritual: The basis of any voodoo magic is the ritual that is performed to enact it, and from here the set piece scene of the movie is often derived. Painted priests and priestesses, pounding drums, strange powders and flames, chanting, and all under a pitch black sky—this is the moment of mysterious imagery and driving sound on which the film is built.

Not Really Dead: The lowered heart rate, lack of response, and clammy skin that certain drugs create in living human beings is what created the original myth of people dying and coming back as voodoo zombies. So in any voodoo zombie film, the audience must always be aware that anyone who dies in the story may not truly be dead. In fact, it may all be part of some elaborate plan.

Recommendations from the Subgenre

I Walked with a Zombie (1943)
Directed by Jacques Tourneur
Written by Curt Siodmak, Ardel Wray
Starring: Frances Dee, Tom Conway, James Ellison

A nurse is hired to come to the West Indies to care for the ill wife of a sugar plantation owner. She begins to fall in love with the owner, while discovering that his wife's illness is not a physical one, and may have something to do with the incessant jungle drumming and the strange rituals of the local islanders. The film is classic slow burn horror, and was based in part on Charlotte Bronte's novel *Jane Eyre*. Capturing one of the more mesmerizing sequences of a voodoo ritual in film, which begins with a walk through a sugar cane field at night to meet the haunting zombie guard Carrefour, *I Walked with a Zombie* uses stunning cinematography and an image-driven story with sparse dialogue to slowly enmesh the viewer in the exotic locales and rituals.

The film was produced by Val Lewton, in his second of three filmic collaborations with director Jacques Tourneur; Tourneur went on to a successful mainstream career, revisiting the horror arena fifteen years later with *Curse of the Demon*. Writer Curt Siodmak was also well versed in horror, having previously written entries in Universal's Invisible Man, Franken-stein, Wolf Man, and Dracula franchises. Lead actor Tom Conway, who worked with Lewton on several projects, later did voice work for Disney animated films.

Sugar Hill (1974)

Directed by Paul Maslansky
Written by Tim Kelly
Starring: Marki Bey, Don Pedro Colley, Zara Cully

An urban horror tale, *Sugar Hill* sees the titular hero's boyfriend murdered by gangsters in their neighborhood for not paying protection money. Rather than back down, Sugar decides to partner with an elderly voodoo queen to help her call upon Baron Samedi and raise a zom-bie army that wreaks revenge on the people who killed her love. The music and the clothes are painfully dated, but some of the horror moments (in particular, the scene of Sugar feeding a gangster to pigs) are well-executed and suspenseful. Surprisingly sincere performances from lead actress Marki Bey and *The Jeffersons* actress Zara Cully (as Mama Maitresse) make this a fun and effective entry in the voodoo zombie subgenre.

In the aftermath of the release of Melvin Van Peebles' pimp-on-the-run film *Sweet Sweet-back's Baadasss Song*, Hollywood found a thriving market for blaxploitation films, and many were churned out. Within that subgenre was yet another one, the horror blaxploitation, with titles like *Blacula*, *Blackenstein*, and *Dr. Black and Mr. Hyde*. Black casts populated the films, which were mostly directed and written by white filmmakers. In the case of *Sugar Hill*, zombies were the horror icons adapted to an urban setting. Paul Maslansky, who never directed another film, became known as a producer and the creator of *Police Academy*.

The Serpent and the Rainbow (1988)

Directed by Wes Craven
Written by Richard Maxwell, Adam Rodman (based on the story by Wade Davis)
Starring: Bill Pullman, Zakes Mokae, Paul Winfield

The Serpent and the Rainbow is the story of anthropologist Dennis Alan, who is sent to Haiti by a pharmaceutical company to find a drug used in Haitian voodoo rituals which will be studied and used as an anesthetic. Facing distrust from the locals and hostility from the military, Alan finally gets ahold of the drug, only to learn that some secrets come at too high a cost. Though the film has a contemporary setting, the same themes of European infringement on island life are prevalent through medical companies rather than sugar plantations or slave traders. The cast is comprised of excellent black character actors (Paul Winfield and Zakes Mokae are standouts), and their skill on-screen has the unfortunate side effect of pointing out the lack of charisma on the part of lead actor Bill Pullman.

A film worth seeing because of its intention rather than its execution, Wes Craven's voodoo zombie story was that rare thing: a serious and high-minded horror film based (loosely) on a non-fiction book. What resulted was a fascinating attempt and a confusing mess, with moments of bizarre humor and a disturbing scene of a nail driven through a man's scrotum. Craven made the film during a run of unusual and lackluster entries (along with *Deadly Friend*, *Shocker*, and *Vampire in Brooklyn*) that came after his *Nightmare on Elm Street* success but before his career resurgence with the *Scream* franchise. Though it still packs a punch in some ways, the film feels more like the product of several cooks making different meals.

White Zombie (1932)

Directed by Victor Halperin
Written by Garnett Weston (based on the story by William Seabrook)
Starring: Bela Lugosi, Madge Bellamy, Joseph Cawthorn

When a young woman and her fiancé arrive in Haiti, a plantation owner interested in winning her affections plots to steal her away by making a deal with voodoo master Murder Legendre to turn her into a zombie who must obey his every command. Once the plan is set in motion, the plantation owner regrets his actions and wishes to change her back, but Legendre makes him one of his zombie horde. The young woman's husband must battle Legendre and his zombie guardians to save her. Though not historically as well remembered as *Dracula* (released a year earlier), Lugosi's turn in *White Zombie* is a stunning performance from the Hungarian actor in a groundbreaking film. Generally considered to be the first feature-length zombie film ever made, it was the template for the classic voodoo zombie film with its Haitian locales and rich white aristocrats.

The film was based on the book *The Magic Island* by Wil-

Bela Lugosi is the murderous Legendre in 1932's *White Zombie*.

liam Seabrook, an author and journalist known to dabble in the occult and, in one instance, even cannibalism. Due partly to the film's public domain status, it is a mainstay in classic horror film collections. It has been influential on generations of filmmakers, among them Rob Zombie, the *House of 1,000 Corpses* director who named his band after the film.

Other Titles of Interest

Ritual (2002), *The Plague of the Zombies* (1966), *Voodoo Dawn* (1991), *King of the Zombies* (1941)

War Horror

Films about war contain such an impressive spectrum of human experience that it's not hard to understand why the war film seems to stand on its own as a genre unto itself. The war film can be so many other things (drama, comedy, action, horror) while still retaining the accurate description of war film. Therefore it is difficult to discuss as simply something which can be married to horror.

Nearly any war film, if portrayed in an accurate light to the circumstances at hand, can be considered a horror film. As the expression goes, "War is hell." Violent sudden death, something that would immediately turn a drama or comedy into something entirely other, is not only right at home in the war film, it is a fully expected plot point. So if all war is horror, then what differentiates a war film from a war horror film?

The introduction of a supernatural circumstance can obviously change a straightforward tale of battle into something darker and more foreboding, as can a simple shift in the visual representation of the visceral and graphic results of war. More disturbing than that, though, is the idea of what heights and depths that average humans can go to as a result of the war itself.

The goal of war, to defeat another group of people with violence and, if necessary, murder, has its roots in a lot of uncomfortable and unsavory human instincts: jingoism, perceived moral superiority, scapegoating, and subjugation. It should be worrisome that our initial reaction to resistance regarding ideals, laws, and beliefs is to raise up arms against our fellow man. Of equal concern is the fact that humanity is never more creative or ingenious than when it comes to hurting each other for a cause.

Through the marvelous inventions of war that find increasingly impersonal and depersonalizing ways of destroying other human beings, we have learned to hurt others with clinical distance and emotional reserve. Bombing someone from an automated machine piloted from thousands of miles away removes most of our sense of responsibility regarding taking lives. Wartime tactics like torture, along with the terrorist acts that bring about that torture, reduce human beings to pawns on a board, so many disposable figures to be moved around.

The lives at stake are no longer real to us, and so we treat them accordingly. People live and die; it is part of a process, and nothing more. Humanity is stripped away, and one day the idea of what is worth fighting for is so clouded that it can no longer be seen. War may be hell, but it's someone else's hell, and we don't care to see it.

Elements of the Subgenre

A War on Two Fronts: A horror movie with one struggle is good; a horror movie with many struggles is great. One of the most effective aspects of the war horror film is that there is always another enemy, and that is the *actual* enemy. Sure, there might be ghosts or zombies, but even if you defeat them, there are still all the other men on the other side of the battlefield who want you dead.

The Unquiet Dead: It is no coincidence that a large percentage of the plots in war horror films revolve around dead people (soldiers or civilians) who refuse to go quietly into the afterlife. War itself is a rumination on the constant presence of death in the lives of the living, and war horror films take that abstract concept and make it an immediate and disturbing reality.

Sarge Has Lost His Mind: Another classic war trope right at home in the war horror film is the slow dissolution of the human mind. It happens all the time in war films (and in real war), when a normal man can't take the unrelenting violence and permeating fear of wartime, and his mind shatters. In horror, those tragically realistic elements take on a frightening grandeur.

Recommendations from the Subgenre

Isle of the Dead (1945)
Directed by Mark Robson
Written by Ardel Wray
Starring: Boris Karloff, Marc Cramer, Jason Robards

During the Balkan Wars, a general and an American journalist travel to the Isle of the Dead to visit the resting place of the general's wife. While there, they hear whispers of the presence of a Vorvolaka, a malicious supernatural creature disguised as a human, somewhere in their midst. Overnight, one of the island residents dies, and when a doctor says it was due to a plague, he quarantines the entire island. When the island residents continue to die one by one, the survivors begin to wonder if there is indeed a Vorvolaka in their midst, and who it might be. A somber and funereal film, *Isle of the Dead* plays with atmosphere and dread like all of producer Val Lewton's best films. The title is an apt one, as the film opens with a general's demand for a soldier's suicide due to his failure, and it ends with another death due to a different but equal failure.

Lewton often worked with the same team on multiple pictures, and Robson and Wray were frequent collaborators of his. Due to a troubled production and the need for Boris Karloff to take a break for surgery, the movie was shot in two sessions; in the interim, Lewton made an entire other film, *The Body Snatcher*, also starring Karloff. Director Martin Scorsese is a huge fan of Lewton's work and in particular *Isle of the Dead*, and several references to *Isle* can be found throughout Scorsese's *Shutter Island*.

Deathwatch (2002)
Written and Directed by Michael J. Bassett
Starring: Jamie Bell, Matthew Rhys, Andy Serkis

A World War I British squad fights their way through a mysterious mist into the labyrinthine trenches of the German enemy. Finding a few survivors who quickly surrender, they fortify their position and consider the battle a success. Something is lurking in the trenches, though, as the men discover when they find dead bodies of German soldiers who look to have been killed by their own men. The claustrophobia and fear begin to coalesce in the British soldiers, who slowly begin to lose their grip on reality and turn against one another. Taut and thoughtful, *Deathwatch* sheds light (along with some blood) on World War I. Young lead actor Jamie Bell is supported by a cast of great British character actors, in particular Matthew Rhys and Laurence Fox.

Director Michael J. Bassett began his feature career with *Deathwatch* before graduating to big-budget horror with *Solomon Kane* and *Silent Hill: Revelation*. The film's influences, from *Predator* to *The Fog* to *All Quiet on the Western Front*, are sometimes too apparent, but the set design and period detail are immaculate. Though he goes a bit over the top late in the film, Andy Serkis' performance as the unhinged Private Quinn is anarchic fun. It was one of his first live-action performances after his motion-capture work as Gollum in *Lord of the Rings*.

The Objective (2008)
Directed by Daniel Myrick
Written by Daniel Myrick, Mark A. Patton, Wesley Clark Jr.
Starring: Jonas Ball, Michael C. Williams, Jon Huertas

During America's occupation of Afghanistan, a military Special Forces team is tasked with helping a CIA agent find a strategically important Afghan cleric. The mission seems dangerous enough to begin with, and the added mysteries of disappearing soldiers, loss of communication, and strange symbols marked on the mountainsides make a bad situation worse. The quickly dwindling group of soldiers discovers that the CIA agent was trying to find something far more dangerous than a cleric. Combining the technical accuracy and unglamorous action of a war film like *The Hurt Locker* with the science fiction–fantasy of *Predator*, *The Objective* succeeds in making the audience think while they're feeling. The creatures in the film, based on tales from ancient Sanskrit epics, are barely seen but their presence is palpable and frightening.

Directed by Daniel Myrick, co-director of *The Blair Witch Project*, the film toys with visual perception and the battle of reality versus the recorded image. A science fiction extrapolation of an ancient myth allows the audience to draw thoughtful comparisons to the religious aspects of the film, marking one of the few post–9/11 films in which the discussion of differing belief systems is complex and respectful. The script was co-written by Wesley Clark, Jr., son of presidential candidate and retired Army general Wesley Clark.

Other Titles of Interest

Revolt of the Zombies (1936), *Red Sands* (2009), *War of the Dead* (2011), *R-Point* (2004), *The Squad* (2011), *The Bunker* (2011), *The Devil's Tomb* (2009), *Death Ship* (1980), *Osombie* (2012)

Werewolf Horror

The mythology of the werewolf runs well back into the literature of ancient Greece, and came to particular notoriety in Europe in the 1400s and 1500s. At one time as common in trials as witches themselves, the defendants were accused of murder and cannibalism (many of those accusations were true) brought on by the transformation from man to wolf. There are those who believe that superstitions like werewolves are what prevented the world from recognizing the very real existence of serial killers until well into the 1800s.

Interestingly, there are many reports throughout history of other kinds of animalistic shape-changers as well. In Chinese myth, the Huli jing are fox spirits that possess the ability to take on human form. In some African cultures, there is the ancient belief in the Bultungin, a creature which could transform back and forth between human and hyena.

Human literature and mythology is replete with mentions of such creatures, and yet the popular lexicon seems able to contain only one shape-shifting human-animal: the lycanthrope, the man who becomes a wolf. Of all the creatures through history, what is it about the wolf that has driven such fear and fascination into us as a species?

Whatever high-minded theories we might put forth about ancient man's instinctive fear of a creature who would be a competitor for food and who had a bloodthirsty nature, the truth is likely much more simple and honest: Werewolves look really cool and scary.

The swell of interest surrounding werewolves to the exclusion of other shape-shifting creatures can possibly be traced to the coverage of werewolves in books of the nineteenth century such as the classic Sabine Baring-Gould work *The Book of Were-Wolves*. Many of them had crude drawings and woodcuts of the monsters attacking and killing families, stealing livestock, and making off with children. The images of the werewolves are impactful, and part of the reason is because wolves lend themselves to human form in a more interesting way than other creatures.

Most other animals, even the other vicious man-eaters, don't make the transition to humanoid without some issues. The stripes and spots of cheetahs and tigers, the giant mane of the lion, the weird skin and nose of the snake or the crocodile; the bear already resembles a human form when standing, which makes an effective transformation difficult. Whether by luck of the genetic draw, or the inability of ancient artists to effectively capture the raw monstrosity of other species and couple them with people, the werewolf has his position as top shape-changer secured in history. Because apparently, looks *can* kill.

Elements of the Subgenre

The Transformation: For as far back as the werewolf movie subgenre goes, filmmakers have been determined to bring the viewer into the transformation. With varying levels of success and quality, each film brings its own unique flavor to the most iconic part of the werewolf mythos, when man loses his control and changes his shape.

That Time of the Month: Every month, like clockwork, the full moon brings about the transformation of man to wolf. Why does the full moon affect him? We don't know, but it doesn't stop the townsfolk (and the recently bitten) from living twenty-eight days a month in fear of the inevitable.

Where Do They Come From?: One of the tropes of the werewolf film is that the main character is always bitten by a werewolf and starts becoming one himself; however, there usually aren't any explanations for the *first* werewolf, how it became a werewolf, or if there is any actual origin or Patient Zero to the werewolf lineage. Perhaps filmmakers understand that the mystique wears off when too much is explained, or perhaps there's just no explanation more effective than the mystery.

Recommendations from the Subgenre

The Wolf Man (1941)

Directed by George Waggner
Written by Curt Siodmak
Starring: Lon Chaney, Claude Rains, Bela Lugosi

Returning home to Wales after the death of his brother, Larry Talbot attempts to reconnect with his titled father while courting a young lady named Gwen. While protecting Gwen's friend from a wolf attack, Larry is bitten himself. He learns from an old gypsy woman that the creature which attacked him was her son, a werewolf, and that because Larry was bitten and survived, he will also transform into a werewolf at night. *The Wolf Man* was the last of the original iconic Universal monsters to be introduced to the American public, a full decade after Lugosi's *Dracula*. Steeped in the same European moodiness as *Frankenstein*, the film focused less on the science and more on the gypsy culture clash and wolf mythology, and made actor Lon Chaney a horror star. Bela Lugosi added the afflicted werewolf gypsy to his impressive list of Universal characters, which already included Dracula, mad scientist Dr. Mirakle, and hunchback Ygor.

The film was scripted by Curt Siodmak, one of the few writers to tackle the characters of Dracula (*Son of Dracula*), the Wolf Man (*The Wolf Man*), and Frankenstein's Monster (*Frankenstein Meets the Wolf Man*). Though the original film spawned a successful series of sequels in which the Wolf Man interacted with the other monsters, the character has had a troubled return journey to the big screen, appearing in two would-be franchises that never rated sequels: 2004's action-horror *Van Helsing* and the 2010 remake *The Wolfman*, starring Benecio Del Toro.

Bad Moon (1996)

Written and Directed by Eric Red (based on the story by Wayne Smith)
Starring: Mariel Hemingway, Michael Paré, Mason Gamble

After Ted and his girlfriend are attacked by a werewolf in Nepal, survivor Ted heads back to America and lives in isolation in a trailer in the woods, fearful of the changes that periodically overcome him. After fleeing the woods due to the mauling deaths of nearby hikers, Ted decides to visit his sister and nephew, hoping that familial bonds will quell the frightening changes. The family dog, Thor, senses something is amiss with him, and the struggle for dominance begins. *Bad Moon* is a clever conceit for a film, a combination of the children's adventure films of the Spielberg-soaked 1980s and a much darker werewolf tale. The most successful element is the perspective of the film, which begins through Ted's experience but then largely becomes a story through the eyes of the dog.

Director-writer Eric Red had already shown his skill in combining fantastical supernatural characters with a gritty real-world aesthetic in *Body Parts* and his scripts for *Near Dark* and *The Hitcher*. The story, based on the novel *Thor*, plays like a domestic drama with a sprinkling of classic horror. While it was not successful in its initial theatrical run, the film has become a cult hit, and was clearly influential on a new generation of gritty werewolf films like *Dog Soldiers*.

Ginger Snaps (2000)

Directed by John Fawcett
Written by Karen Walton, John Fawcett
Starring: Emily Perkins, Katharine Isabelle, Mimi Rogers

The Fitzgerald sisters are high-schoolers who don't fit in because of their morbid fascination with creating photos of deaths and fake crimes scenes. When they're out one night seeking revenge on a bully, the older sister is bitten by a mysterious furry creature. She recovers quickly, but the attack changes her behavior, popularity, appearance ... and desires. One of the few films to take the werewolf mythos and translate it through the lens of female sexual maturity, *Ginger*

Uncle Ted (Michael Paré) becomes this fully transformed werewolf in 1996's *Bad Moon* (courtesy Eric Red).

Snaps is a surprisingly thoughtful and clever entry in the subgenre. Touching on the connection between lunar cycles and menstrual cycles, the inborn social fear of aggressive women, and a witty use of silver in an unexpected way, it finds ways to breathe life into the myth of lycanthropy by making it modern and switching the gender.

Though the film was a low-budget Canadian production, the filmmakers made the most of their concept, and it's no surprise that both director John Fawcett and writer Karen Walton later had big success creating and writing the sci-fi television series *Orphan Black*. The lead actresses returned for two back-to-back sequels in 2004, and Katharine Isabelle used the series as a springboard into more work in the horror arena like *Freddy vs. Jason*, *American Mary*, and the *Hannibal* television series.

Other Titles of Interest

WereWolf of London (1935), *Dog Soldiers* (2002), *The Howling* (1981), *An American Werewolf in London* (1981), *The Company of Wolves* (1984), *Silver Bullet* (1985), *Cursed* (2005), *Teen Wolf* (1985)

Western Horror

Isolation and loneliness are often at the heart of any situation that instills irrational fear in humanity, and nothing is more isolated and lonely than the untamed American West. With hundreds of lawless miles between outposts of civilization, a single human being is at constant threat from rough terrain, weather, and both animal and human predators. When he finds himself dehydrated, starving, lost, or injured, he becomes imprisoned by that distance.

It is also a great place to explore supernatural themes, because of the built-in "myth of the West." Westerns take place in the adolescence of America, a time of pioneer spirit when manifest destiny beckoned brave travelers to venture into the vast and unexplored landscape barely touched by human influence. This was a place of mystery to European settlers, who would probably have found that an imagined Wendigo sighting wouldn't have been any more frightening than a real-life encounter with a lunatic prospector, a Native American in war paint, or even an unusual new animal species like a hyena, rattlesnake, or horned toad. The myth of the West is America's Arthurian legend, with cowboys as the Knights of the Round Table and gold rush boom towns as myriad Camelots. It only seems appropriate that Merlin would show up in the form of an Indian medicine man, or that a hero would battle a ghost rider as his own personal black knight.

Some of the greatest horror stories thrive because of the clearly drawn lines between good and evil, and the ensuing battle between them. What better place to draw those lines than in a Western, where intent can be divined by whether a cowboy's hat is black or white, and where the line between civilization and chaos is often nothing more than a single man with a tin star?

The hybrid genre of the western-horror has had a checkered and unusual past, lurching from terrible to inspired and back again. In 1966 a double bill brought about the unusual pairings of famous monsters with historical cowboy figures: *Billy the Kid versus Dracula* and *Jesse James Meets Frankenstein's Daughter*. Obviously confused about how to successfully integrate them, the genre floundered along until the 1980s, when writer Eric Red created two modern horror-westerns, the Rutger Hauer chase film *The Hitcher* and the vampire crime drama *Near Dark*. Subsequent entries in the genre have more effectively balanced the two genres.

Elements of the Subgenre

Wide Open Spaces… A Little Too Wide Open: Forget no cell phone signal or a car that has run out of gas; when you're stranded in a western, you're on your own. Entire books and films have been devoted to the tragedies to be found simply traveling from one side of the country to the other by covered wagon: being killed by animals, freezing to death, resorting to cannibalism. All of these were realities of the West, and every one of them makes for an effective horror trope.

Around a Roaring Fire: It just wouldn't be a western without a scene around the campfire, and it doesn't hurt that a scene lit by campfire is fairly spooky-looking. The idea of a small group of people in the middle of an unimaginably vast wilderness becomes even more terrifying when their world is narrowed down to the ten feet of visible dirt illuminated by the flickering flames of a fire.

That Poor Lady!: The West is no place for a woman, or at least that's the misogynist cliché. In a horror western, however, that tends to be true. Whether they end up dead, sexually assaulted, or paralyzed and buried under the ground to be eaten later, the womenfolk of the West don't tend to get a very fair deal.

Recommendations from the Subgenre

High Plains Drifter (1973)
Directed by Clint Eastwood
Written by Ernest Tidyman
Starring: Clint Eastwood, Verna Bloom, Geoffrey Lewis

A stranger rides into the western town of Lago, immediately killing some men who taunt him in the local bar. The townspeople, already fearful of the criminals being released from prison that might be returning to the town later that day, ask the stranger to act as their protector. The town is turned into a nightmare vision for the arriving criminals, who also have an unknown past connection to the mysterious stranger and sins to answer for. A classic revenge western with a slight tinge of supernatural horror and the darker sensibilities of the early 1970s, *High Plains Drifter* is a reinvention of the western right at the time that the genre was becoming a cliché. Its imagery, particularly the transforming of the entire town into Hell on Earth (complete with all the buildings painted blood red), effectively takes the already symbolic good versus evil elements and gives them a dark spiritual component, a theme which Clint Eastwood later revisited in a more positive light with *Pale Rider*.

The seemingly simple revenge story holds hidden complexity from the very beginning, when the ostensible hero of the piece rapes a local woman for little more than ruining his cigar. With a script from Ernest Tidyman (the author of the novel *Shaft* and writer of the Oscar-winning screenplay for *The French Connection*), taciturn star Clint Eastwood follows up his directorial debut on *Play Misty for Me* with this competent and stylish hybrid with early appearances from classic character actors Geoffrey Lewis and John Hillerman.

Dead Birds (2004)
Directed by Alex Turner
Written by Simon Barrett
Starring: Henry Thomas, Patrick Fugit, Isaiah Washington

During the Civil War, a group of Confederate soldiers flees the Army, joined by an escaped slave and a nurse, and robs a bank in order to survive. Hiding out on an abandoned plantation, they discover that black magic rituals were used on the grounds to bring back the dead, and those spirits still haunt the premises. A film which touches equally on horror, westerns, and some thoughtful social commentary about forced servitude, *Dead Birds* follows many of the conventions of the horror genre to good effect, including eerie spectral faces which should haunt your dreams.

A troubled production for first-time director Alex Turner (on his DVD commentary he speaks in detail about the struggle) still manages to shine a good light on the script by writer and future *V/H/S* franchise regular Simon Barrett. Cast members, varying from former child stars (*ET*'s Henry Thomas) to stars soon-to-be-discovered (Isaiah Washington was only a year away from *Grey's Anatomy* and Michael Shannon would make an Oscar-nominated impact four years later in *Revolutionary Road*), acquit themselves admirably in this low-budget but inventive entry in the western horror genre.

The Burrowers (2008)

Directed and Written by J.T. Petty
Starring: Clancy Brown, William Mapother, Karl Geary

When a young Irish immigrant discovers that the woman he loves has mysteriously been taken from her prairie home along with the rest of her family, he joins a search party. They discover that the creatures responsible for the abduction are a deadly race which the settlers have never seen or dealt with. Only a captured Native American seems to have any idea what to do to stop them. Combining the beautiful location photography and languid pacing of a western with the inventive graphic violence of a horror film, J.T. Petty's *The Burrowers* effectively exists as a film in two genres simultaneously. Period details about the Native American tribes and languages bring authenticity to a story that is primarily about the desire for dominance and the inability to properly communicate.

Excellent performances from character actors Clancy Brown (remembered best as the villain in *Highlander*) and Doug Hutchison (brilliantly evil in *The Green Mile*) anchor a strong

John Clay (Clancy Brown) and immigrant Fergus Coffey (Karl Geary) are shocked to find still-living Audrey (Seri DeYoung) buried in the ground in 2008's western-horror *The Burrowers* (courtesy Lionsgate Publicity).

cast, and cinematographer Phil Parmet finds a way to make wide open spaces claustrophobic. The theme of the film explains the monster as a naturally occurring creature forced to feed on humans after the population of its normal prey, buffalo, dwindles due to over-hunting. The environmental message is appropriate without being too heavy-handed.

Other Titles of Interest

Jesse James Meets Frankenstein's Daughter (1966), *Grim Prairie Tales* (1990), *Curse of the Undead* (1959), *Sundown: The Vampire in Retreat* (1989), *Billy the Kid versus Dracula* (1966), *Gallowwalkers* (2012), *Undead or Alive* (2007), *The Quick and the Undead* (2006)

Witchcraft Horror

Women are mysterious; even in our enlightened and educated times, the modern male is aware of the imbalance between the sexes. Women are the ones who give birth to the next generation of life, putting them in the driver's seat when it comes to biology. Women have instincts and emotions that exist beyond the obvious and pragmatic awareness that most males tend to exist with on a day-to-day basis, which some call women's intuition, and some mistakenly confuse as "being too emotional." Any man who truly weighs the pros and cons of gender knows that the men get superior physical strength, and that's about it.

And that is why society and culture (which have been male-dominated since their inception) have spent so much time attempting to keep women in their place. In an existence where the male is the more disposable of the two genders, the only choice the disposable gender has is to subjugate the gender that holds more power and sway. In a way, it kind of evens the odds.

So the women get the blame for most things. Bad children? Terrible mother. Man cheated on his wife? It was probably the fault of the trollop who seduced him, or perhaps the wife who wasn't loving enough for his needs. Somehow, it always ends up *her* problem.

Add to that the irrational fears that cropped up when ancient man believed women to be tapping into "dark powers" because their menstrual cycle was seen to be connected to the phases of the moon, and then you have witchcraft. Though there are men (warlocks) involved in witchcraft, you'd barely know it from the portrayals of witches throughout history, which always portray covens as groups of women with some mysterious connection to evil through their very femininity. The New Age ideas of female spirituality, Mother Earth and the traditional worship of goddesses like Diana tap into that same separation of male and female, with the female holding a special connection unattainable by men.

Though a brilliant indictment of McCarthyism in its day, the play *The Crucible* is actually about the Salem Witch Trials, and the play reveals a society wherein witchcraft is so woven into the female psyche that women of the time even used it against each other. And that struggle, not only to divide men and women along gender lines, but also to divide women amongst themselves, is the interesting keystone to many of the best horror films revolving around witchcraft. (Note: No discussion of witchcraft would be complete without a mention of the film *Haxan: Witchcraft Through the Ages*, but it has been left off this list only because it is a documentary rather than a horror film.)

Elements of the Subgenre

The New Girl: Every portrayal of witches has their own specific rules and boundaries (much like vampires), and no two films treat them exactly the same. So, in order for audiences to have a character with whom they can relate and who needs to learn all about it themselves, witchcraft films often have a "new girl" arriving to the town-school-neighborhood who must learn the truth and be inducted into the group.

Ineffective Men: As many of the films in the subgenre have a theme of women's empowerment to them, no witchcraft film would be complete without at least one useless man. He might be a sad excuse for a husband or an uncaring father, but they never have the skills necessary to solve the problem at hand. Luckily, these women learn to solve it without him.

Unwanted Gifts: It's rare that a woman in these films is actively seeking witchcraft as a way of life; more often than not, it is an inborn ability, foisted on them by nature and genetics. Whether they want the abilities or not, they have them, and often they interact with the coven just to understand what is happening to them.

Recommendations from the Subgenre

Suspiria (1977)

Directed by Dario Argento
Written by Dario Argento, Daria Nicolodi
Starring: Jessica Harper, Stefania Casini, Falvio Bucci

When American student Suzy Bannion arrives in Germany to attend a prestigious dance academy, a series of strange events (a fainting spell, a dog attack, and maggots falling from the ceiling) leads her to believe that all is not right within the school walls. Research brings her to the discovery of the school's founding by a cruel Greek witch who it turns out is still alive and living in secret passages within the school. A feast of stunning visual stylization and color saturation, *Suspiria* is *the* uber-witch horror film. With a bold and shocking score by the band Goblin that was written in collaboration with the director (the soundtrack incorporates echoing voices whispering the word "witches"), the film is driven so much by mood rather than dialogue that it would make an effective silent film or opera adaptation.

The first film in the Mothers trilogy (followed in 1980 by *Inferno* and in 2007 by *Mother of Tears*), this is undoubtedly one of Italian director Dario Argento's most successful and well-respected films and is frequently cited as one of the greatest horror films of all time. The entire dialogue track was dubbed in after the film was finished rather than being recorded on the set (a common practice in Italy at the time), and the effect gives the entire movie an air of distance and eeriness.

Season of the Witch (1972) (aka Hungry Wives)

Directed and Written by George Romero
Starring: Jan White, Bill Thunhurst, Joedda McClain

Though she is intelligent and sophisticated, Joan Mitchell's personal life is in turmoil. Her businessman husband has buried violent tendencies, her teenage daughter is rebellious, and she is unhappy with her life as a housewife. A neighborhood party leads her to a local coven, and suddenly Joan begins to realize that the rituals in which she is participating are having lasting and possibly positive changes on her personal life. While only tangentially a film about witchcraft (Romero is really discussing the growing feminist movement), this film touches on many of the subgenre staples, from nightmarish imagery to female empowerment, and allows the "witches" of the film to be fully developed figures rather than crones and villains.

Romero's first foray back into horror after *Night of the Living Dead* had trouble finding an audience as he was interested in making a social drama; the abstract horror elements serve only to frustrate fans seeking a scary experience. Part of a trilogy of smaller films (including *The Crazies* and *Martin*) Romero made before returning to the zombie world with *Dawn of the Dead*, *Season of the Witch* is a fascinating experiment that captures its time and place effectively while also heralding the "angry woman" films to come later that decade.

The Woods (2006)

Directed by Lucky McKee
Written by David Ross
Starring: Agnes Bruckner, Patricia Clarkson, Bruce Campbell

In rural New England in the mid–1960s, a young woman sent to a girls' boarding school by her parents discovers that the troubles at home are the least of her worries. While struggling against mysterious instructors and investigating the disappearances of fellow students, she discovers that the impenetrable woods surrounding the school hold frightening ancient secrets. With a script that reinterprets the best of *Suspiria* through a distinctly American lens, *The Woods* excels in its focus on effective creation of mood and a reliance on the talents of its largely female cast. The slow burn pays off in the final act, as the coven is revealed and seemingly simplistic images such as piles of leaves and glasses of milk take on sinister significance.

The focus on female characterization should come as no surprise to fans of director Lucky McKee, whose more well-known recent films are other horror-based gender commentaries like *The Woman* and *All Cheerleaders Die*. *Evil Dead*'s Bruce Campbell, in a small but pivotal role, seems perfectly at home in a film about living vines that kidnap and kill. Sharp-eared viewers will notice that a voice in the woods sounds familiar: It is the voice of Angela Bettis, actress and collaborator of Lucky McKee, with whom she has worked six times.

Other Titles of Interest

Burn Witch Burn (1962), *The Craft* (1996), *Witchfinder General* (1968) (aka *Conqueror Worm*), *Black Sunday* (1960), *The Witches* (1990), *The Lords of Salem* (2012), *The Witches of Eastwick* (1987), *Little Witches* (1996), *Witchboard* (1986)

Zombie *see* Modern Zombie; Voodoo Zombie

Further Resources

Gambin, Lee. *Massacred by Mother Nature: Exploring the Natural Horror Film.* Baltimore: Midnight Marquee Press, 2012.

Harper, Jim. *Legacy of Blood: A Comprehensive Guide to Slasher Movies.* Manchester, UK: Critical Vision, 2004.

Heller-Nicholas, Alexandra. *Found Footage Horror Films: Fear and the Appearance of Reality.* Jefferson, NC: McFarland, 2014. http://public.eblib.com/choice/publicfullrecord.aspx?p=1674887.

Kay, Glenn. *Zombie Movies: The Ultimate Guide.* Chicago: Chicago Review Press, 2008. http://public.eblib.com/choice/publicfullrecord.aspx?p=445248.

Koven, Mikel J. *La Dolce Morte: Vernacular Cinema and the Italian Giallo Film.* Lanham, MD: Scarecrow Press, 2006.

Marrero, Robert. *Vampire Movies.* Key West, FL: Fantasma Books, 1994.

McCarty, John. *Splatter Movies: Breaking the Last Taboo of the Screen.* New York: St. Martin's Press, 1984.

Newman, Kim. *Apocalypse Movies: End of the World Cinema.* New York: St. Martin's Griffin, 2000.

Index

The A-Team (TV series) 22

Abbott, Bud 57

Abbott, Jack Henry 134

Abbott and Costello Meet Frankenstein 57

Abbott and Costello Meet the Killer, Boris Karloff 57

Abernathy, Lewis 199

Abrams, J.J. 146

Abre los Ojos 173

The Abyss 199

Academy Awards (Oscars) 10, 28, 52, 63, 110, 112, 125, 131, 132, 136, 151, 154, 161, 167, 187, 217, 218

Ackles, Jensen 100

Adams, Brooke 122

Adams, Julie 184

Adam's Rib 131

The Addams Family 61, 168

The Addiction 196

Adrien, Gilles 46, 52

The Adventures of Baron Munchausen 48

Afghanistan 212

Agnew, Jim 97

AIDS 114

Akkad, Moustapha 167

Alba, Jessica 94

Albarn, Damon 46

Aldrich, Robert 125

Alfredson, Tomas 204

Alias 146

Alice in Wonderland 52

Alice Sweet Alice 64

Alien 6, 139

Alien: Resurrection 46

Aliens 154, 199

Alive 135, 179

All Cheerleaders Die 221

All Quiet on the Western Front 119, 212

Allen, Nancy 136

Alligator 202

Alone in the Dark 21

Altered 93

Altered States 182

Altieri, Mitchell 69

Alucarda 56

Amaris, Scarlett 192

The Amazing Transparent Man 111

Amelie 46

Amenabar, Alejandro 172

American Film Institute 91

American Gothic 61

American International Pictures (AIP) 14

American Mary 182, 215

An American Werewolf in London 35, 59, 132, 215

Amicus 37

Amity Island 12

The Amityville Horror 74, 128

Anamorph 67

Anders, David 26

Anderson, Brad 22

Anderson, Joe 178

Anderson, Maxwell 63

Anderson, Melissa Sue 101

Anderson, Michael J. 88

The Andromeda Strain 11

Ang, Michelle 125

Angel (TV series) 149

Angel Heart 32

Angelica 144

Angelski, Shawn 161

Anguish 72

Animal House 39

Annabelle 76, 77

Antal, Nimrod 177

Antarctica 155

Anthopophagus 46

Apollo 18 40

April Fool's Day 70, 101, 201

Apt Pupil 121

Arachnophobia 12

Aranofsky, Darren 199

Arbogast, Thierry 119

Arctic National Wildlife Refuge 84

Argento, Dario 71, 95–97, 137, 220

Arkansas 185

Arkush, Allan 104

Arlington Road 189

Armstrong, R.G. 128

Army of Darkness 73

Arnold, Jack 184

Arnold, Tracy 151

Arquette, David 168

The Arrival 199

Arterton, Gemma 4

Arthur and the Invisibles 119

Artigue, Kevin 69

As Above, So Below 92

Ashfield, Kate 58

Ashmore, Shawn 85

Ashworth, Piers 35

Assault on Precinct 13 156–157, 175

Astor, Mary 125

Asylum 37

The Asylum (film studio) 104

Asylum Blackout 21

Atherton, William 38, 187

Atkins, Tom 100

ATM 165

Atrocious 92

Attanasio, Paul 198

The Attic Expeditions 192

Audrey Rose 64

Auffarth, Blythe 187

August: Osage County 161

Australia 17, 138

Automatons 33

Autumn, Emilie 49

Avatar 129

The Baby 60

Babylon 13

Backus, Richard 25

Backwoods 141

Bacon, Kevin 41, 109

Bad Dreams 83

Bad Lieutenant 196

Bad Moon 214

The Bad Seed 63, 130

Bad Taste 8

Badalamenti, Angelo 52, 88

Baesel, Nathan 88

Bagans, Zak 161

Bailey, Colley 139

Baird, Karen 175

Baker, Betsy 28

Baker, Blanche 187

Baker, Dylan 15, 114

Baker, Rick 132

Balagueró, Jaume 107

Balderston, John L. 118

Baldwin, William 129

Balfour, Graham 169

Balkan Wars 211

Ball, Jonas 212

The Ballad of Cable Hogue 156

Band, Charles 76

Band, Richard 134

Bangkok Dangerous 94

Banks, Elizabeth 8

Banks, Leslie 102

Bannister, Reggie 81, 120

Baquero, Ivana 51

Barbeau, Adrienne 155, 175

Barberini, Urbano 71

Barcelona 107

Baring-Gould, Sabine 213

Barker, Clive 179, 201

Barker, David 5–6

Barrett, Simon 14, 217

Barrymore, John 170

Bart, Roger 143

Barton, Charles 57

Basement 30

The Basement 30

Basket Case 79

Bass, Saul 10

Bassett, Michael J. 211

Bates, Kathy 112

Bates, Norman (character) 96, 151

Bates, Richard, Jr. 143

Batman Begins 21

The Battery 18

Battle Royale 104

Bava, Lamberto 71

Bava, Mario 13, 72, 95

The Bay 86

Beaird, John 100

Bear 11

Beauty and the Beast 184

Bedlam 24

Behets, Briony 84

Behind the Mask: the Rise of Leslie Vernon 88

Bell, Ashley 72
Bell, Jamie 211
Bell, Tobin 195
Bell, Wayne 185
Bellamy, Madge 209
Below 199
Belvaux, Rémy 152
Benchley, Peter 12, 198
Beneath 85
Beneath the Planet of the Apes 61
Bening, Annette 81
Beranger, Clara 170
Berberian Sound Studio 97
Berger, Sidney 48
Bergman, Ingmar 4
Berkeley, Xander 201
Bermuda 198
Berryman, Michael 33
Bertino, Bryan 157
Bertolucci, Bernardo 97
Bervoets, Gene 38
Besson, Luc 119, 177
Bettinelli-Olpin, Matt 14
Bettis, Angela 221
Bevilacqua, Alberto 13
Bey, Marki 208
The Beyond 117
Beyond Re-Animator 135
Bibb, Leslie 179
Big Trouble in Little China 54
Bigfoot 199
Billy the Kid versus Dracula 216, 219
Bird, Antonia 45
Bird with the Crystal Plumage 96
The Birds 10
Birthistle, Eva 63
Bishop, Wes 69
Bisley, Steve 17
Bissell, Whit 184
Bisset, Jacqueline 198
Black Belly of the Tarantula 98
Black Book 110
Black Christmas 26, 96, 99, 170, 201
Black Narcissus 87
Black Sabbath 13
Black Sheep 12
Black Sunday 221
Black Swan 79
Black Water 199
Blackenstein 208
Blackwood, Vas 178
Blacula 208
Blade 206
A Blade in the Dark 72
Blade Runner 139
Blade II 52
The Blair Witch Project 18, 91, 161, 185, 212
Blakeson, J. 4
Blanks, Jamie 84, 138, 202
Blatty, William Peter 126

Blazing Saddles 36
Blindness 20
The Blob 39, 49
Bloch, Robert 151
Block, Suziey 175
Blood and Black Lace 98
Blood Creek 27
Blood Dolls 77
Blood from the Mummy's Tomb 120
Blood Simple 40
Blood Ties 116
Bloodlust 105
Bloody Disgusting (website) 15
Bloom, Verna 217
Blue Monkey 181
Blue, the grizzly bear 11
Blue Velvet 144
Blunt, Emily 146
Boardwalk Empire 94
Bodega Bay 10
Body Parts 214
The Body Snatcher 35, 211
Body Snatchers 154, 196
Boehm, Carl 87
Boileau, Pierre 181
Bond, Timothy 101
Bonet, Lisa 32
Bonner, Beverly 79
Bonzel, André 152
Boogeyman 202
The Book of Eli 20
Book of Shadows: Blair Witch 2 92
The Book of Were-Wolves 213
Boorman, John 138
Boothe, Powers 139
Borey, Chris 39
Borey, Eddie 39
Borgnine, Ernest 18
Born American 134
Borrelli, Christopher 66
Botched 67
Botko, Huck 72
Bottin, Rob 155
Bourgoin, Louise 119
The Bourne Identity 32
Bousman, Darren Lynn 49, 196
Bowden, Katrina 140
Bowen, A.J. 15
Bowie, David 137
The Box 82
A Boy and His Dog 20
The Boys from Brazil 121
Boys Life 85
Brach, Gerard 142
Bradbury, Ray 48
Brake, Richard 21
Bram Stoker's Legend of the Mummy 120
Brasseur, Pierre 181
The Brave Little Toaster 127
Brazil 46

Breakdown 141, 145
The Breakfast Club 149
Bride of Frankenstein 109
The Brighton Strangler 193
Brimley, Wilford 154
British Independent Film Awards 98
Britton, Connie 84
Brody, Adrien 95, 97, 145
The Broken 79
Brolin, James 128
Brolin, Josh 109
Bronte, Charlotte 208
The Brood 64, 182
Brooks, Mel 36
Brooks, Stephen David 128
Brown, A. Michael 81
Brown, Clancy 218
Bruckner, Agnes 221
Bruckner, David 14–15
Brumpton, John 176
Bruno, John 129
Bubba Ho-Tep 119
Bubba Nosferatu: Curse of the She-Vampires 120
Bucci, Flavio 220
Buck, Douglas 192
Buddhism 37
Buffy the Vampire Slayer (film) 149
Buffy the Vampire Slayer (TV series) 148, 185
Bug 160
Buhler, Jeff 179
Bujold, Geneviéve 78, 182
Bullitt 198
Bully 189
The Bunker 212
The 'Burbs 64, 189
Burgess, Tony 116
Buried 165
Buried Alive 38
Buried Alive II 39
Buring, MyAnna 66
Burke and Hare 35
Burke, Charlotte 82
Burke, William 35
Burn Witch Burn 221
The Burning 41, 43
Burning Bright 12
The Burning Hell 33
Burns, George 31
Burns, Marilyn 60, 185
Burnt Offerings 74
Burroughs, William S. 112
The Burrowers 218
Bush, Dan 15
Bustillo, Alexandre 131
The Butcher Brothers 70
Butler, Michael 128
Byrne, Gabriel 31
Byrne, Sean 176

Caan, James 112
Cabin Fever 43, 72

The Cabin in the Woods 140
The Cabinet of Dr. Caligari 23
Cage, Nicolas 69, 97
California 76, 145, 154
Callies, Sarah Wayne 66
Camelot 216
Cameron, James 8, 129, 154, 199
Camp Blood 42
Camp Crystal Lake 41
Camp Kill Yourself 43
Campbell, Bruce 28, 119, 221
Campbell, John W., Jr. 154
Campbell, Neve 168
Campfire Tales 43
Campillo, Robin 25
Campion, Paul 122
Canada 116
Candyman 82, 201
Cannavale, Bobby 94
Cannes Film Festival 152
Cannibal Ferox 46
Cannibal Holocaust 90, 161
Cannon, Ryan 164
Cape Fear 36, 101
Captivity 6
The Car 128
Carducci, Mark Patrick 38
Carlin, Lynn 25
Carl's Jr. 141
Carlson, Richard 184
Carlyle, Robert 45
Carmen, Julie 113
Carnival of Souls 48
Caro, Marc 46, 52
Carolco 154
Carpenter, John 8, 18, 54, 110, 113, 154, 157, 166, 175
Carradine, David 104
Carradine, John 122
Carradine, Keith 139
Carrie 78, 136, 170
Carriers 107
Carroll, Lane 106
Caruso, David 22
Carved 202
Casablanca 23, 121
Cashtown Corners 116
Casini, Stefania 220
Cassandra Complex 174
Cassavettes, John 131
Castle 110
Castle, Nick 18
Castle, William 131, 173
Cat Ballou 128
A Cat in the Brain 88
Cat People 26, 155
Catholicism 52, 54
Cat's Eye 16
Cave, Nick 134
The Caveman's Valentine 201

Caviezel, Jim 84
Cawthorn, Joseph 209
The Cell 152
The Cellar 28
Cemetery Man 27
The Ceremony 164
Chain Gang Women 69
Chan, Dennis 93
Chaney, Lon 55, 190, 214
Chaney, Lon, Jr. 57
Channel Islands 122
Chaplin, Charlie 34, 46
Charlot, Alexandre 133
Chase, Chevy 110
Chasing Sleep 162
Chassler, Zach 191, 192
Cheers 173
Chicago 75
Childers, Ambyr 44
The Children 63
Children of Men 130
Children of the Corn 64
Children Shouldn't Play
   with Dead Things 26
Child's Play 75, 124, 192,
   202
Child's Play III 76
Chillerama 126
China 93
Chiodo, Charles 49
Chiodo, Stephen 49
Chiomak, Robert 114
Chiou, Tim 93
Chou, Lawrence 94
Christ 13
Christie, Agatha 171, 196
Christine 129
A Christmas Story 26, 99
Chromeskull (character)
   139
Chucky (character) 75,
   124
The Church 56
Ciardi, Francesca 90
Cinecitta Studios 88
Cinémathèque Français
   181
Circus of Horrors 49
Citizen Kane 82, 125
City of Lost Children 52
Civil War 217
Clark, Bob 25, 99
Clark, Wesley 212
Clark, Wesley, Jr. 212
Clarkson, Patricia 221
Clash of the Titans 124
The Class 25
Clawson, Elliot J. 190
Clayton, Jack 48
Cleopatra 10
Clerici, Gianfranco 90
Clifford, John 48
Clooney, George 65
Cloverfield 92
Cobb, Lee J. 126
Code Name: Trixie 107
Coen Brothers 112
Cognard, François 133

Cohen, Larry 132
Cohen, Laurence D. 136
Coldplay 58
Collector, Robert 110
Collet, Christopher 43
Colley, Don Pedro 208
Colossus: The Forbin Proj-
   ect 129
Columbo 145
Coma 181
Combs, Jeffrey 192
Comer, Anjanette 60
The Company of Wolves
   215
Compston, Martin 4
The Conjuring 76
Conkie, Gene 134
Connell, Richard 102
Connelly, Jennifer 137
Connick, Harry, Jr. 160
Connolly, Billy 114
Conqueror Worm 221
The Conspiracy 163
Constantine 33
The Contender 157
The Contestant 165
Contracted 140
The Convent 56
Conway, Tom 207
Cook, Elisha, Jr. 174
Cooney, Michael 171
Cooper, Alice 55
Cooper, Bradley 179
Copley, Sharlto 39
Coppola, Francis Ford
   97
Corman, Roger 14, 104
Cornillac, Clovis 133
Cornwall 156
Corridors of Blood 37
Cortés, Rodrigo 165
Cosby, Bill 32
The Cosby Show 32
Coscarelli, Don 27, 81,
   119
Costello, Lou 57
Cotton, Joseph 125
Coughlin, Brendan
   Michael 11
Courtés, Alexandre 21
Cox, Brian 15
Cox, Courtney 168
Coyote, Peter 139
The Craft 221
Craig, Eli 140
Cramer, Grant 49
Cramer, Marc 211
Craven, Wes 4, 42, 69, 80,
   100, 168, 208
Crawlspace 77
The Crazies 106, 221
Creature from the Black La-
   goon 184
Creelman, James Ashmore
   102
Creep 178
Creepers 137
Creepshow 16

Crichton, Michael 11, 181,
   198
Criminal 146
The Crimson Rivers 152
Critters 49
Cronenberg, David 78,
   112, 182
Cronheim, Adam 18
Cronyn, Hume 159
The Crucible 219
Cruise, Tom 173
Cuaron, Alfonso 130
Cube 161
Cul-de-Sac 142
Cully, Zara 208
Cundey, Dean 66, 167
Cunningham, Sean S. 4,
   41, 173, 199
Currie, Andrew 114
Curry, Tim 31, 35
Curse of the Demon 208
Curse of the Undead 219
Cursed 215
Curtis, Jamie Lee 129,
   148, 166
The Curve 202
Cusack, John 171
Cushing, Peter 25, 121,
   122
Cyphers, Charles 175
Cyrus, Billy Ray 88
Czerny, Henry 116

Dagover, Lil 23
Dahl, John 146
Dall, John 159
Dalle, Béatrice 131
Dalton, Timothy 36
Damici, Nick 44
Damon, Mark 13
Dance of the Dead 149
Dane, Lawrence 101
Daniell, Henry 35
Daniels, Jeff 162
Dante, Joe 82, 189
Danvers State Hospital
   22
Darabont, Frank 38
The Dark Half 113, 134
Dark Horse Comics 129
Dark Ride 49
Dark Skies 9
Dark Star 157
Dark Water 94
The Darkest Hour 9
Darkness 174
Darknet 163
Davenport, Nigel 10
David, Keith 154
Davies, David A. 38
Davies, Jeremy 46
Davis, Bette 125
Davis, Judy 112
Davis, Matthew 199
Davis, Ossie 119
Davis, Wade 208
Dawn of the Dead 26, 58,
   97, 114, 116, 206, 221

Dawn of the Mummy 120
Dawson's Creek 100
Day, Baybi 196
Day of the Animals 84
Day of the Dead 117
The Day the Earth Stood
   Still 35
Daybreakers 206
Daylight 5–6
Dead & Buried 178
Dead Alive 9, 117
Dead Birds 217
Dead End 145, 147
Dead End Drive-In 20
Dead of Night 13, 77
Dead Ringers 78, 112,
   182
Dead Silence 75
Dead Snow 121
Dead Snow 2: Red vs. Dead
   122
The Dead Zone 137, 167
Deadly Friend 129, 209
Deadwood 105
Death Line 178
Death Proof 147
Death Race 2000 104
Death Ship 212
Deathdream 25
Deathsport 104
Deathwatch 211
De Brulier, Nigel 55
Dee, Frances 207
The Deep 198
Deep Blue Sea 199
Deep Red 72, 98, 137
DeepStar Six 199
Dekker, Fred 173
de Haviland, Olivia 125
Delicatessen 46
Deliver Us from Evil 71
Deliverance 138, 139
Del Toro, Benecio 214
del Toro, Guillermo 51,
   173, 177
De Luca, Michael 113
Demon Seed 132
Demons 71–72
Demons 2 72
Deneuve, Catherine 142
DeNiro, Robert 31–32
Deodato, Ruggero 90
De Palma, Brian 78, 96,
   136, 170
The Department of
   Health 20
Depeche Mode 135
Dern, Bruce 125, 189
Dern, Laura 78
De Roche, Everett 84
Dersu Uzala 84
The Descent: Part Two 5
Desperado 149
Devil 33
The Devil and Daniel Web-
   ster 31
Devil Doll 77
The Devil Inside 71

The Devil Wears Prada 146
The Devils 56
The Devil's Advocate 31
The Devil's Backbone 52, 173
The Devil's Carnival 49
The Devil's Rejects 8, 141
The Devil's Rock 122
The Devil's Tomb 212
DeYoung, Seri 218
Diabolique 181
Die Hard 39
Die-ner (Get It?) 176
Diesel, Vin 199
Dirty Harry 154
The Disappearance of Alice Creed 4
Disney, Walt 10
Disney's Tomorrowland 180
District 9 40
Disturbia 189
The Divide 20
Divine 61
Dixon, James 132
The Doctor and the Devils 36
Dr. Black and Mr. Hyde 208
Dr. Giggles 181
Dr. Jekyll and Mr. Hyde (characters) 58
Dr. Jekyll and Mr. Hyde (film) 170
Dr. Mabuse (film series) 51
Dr. Strangelove 142
Doctor Who 67
Doctor X 46
Dog Soldiers 215
Dolls 77
Dolores Claiborne 32, 112
Donahue, Heather 91
Donkey Punch 64
Donnadieu, Bernard-Pierre 38
Donnelly, Dennis 194
Donnie Darko 82, 85
Donovan, Martin 146
Don't Be Afraid of the Dark 174
Don't Look in the Basement 30
Don't Torture a Duckling 98
Doomsday 20
Dorm 149
Double Jeopardy 160
A Double Life 193
Dougherty, Michael 15
Douglas, Kirk 170
Dougnac, Marie-Laure 46
Dourif, Brad 75, 126, 136, 192
Down Terrace 67
Downey, Robert, Jr. 81

Dracula 119, 122, 190, 206, 209, 214
Dracula (character) 208
Dracula (novel) 204
Dracula 2000 100
Draper, Don (character) 107
Dream House 174
Dreamcatcher 112
Dreamscape 83, 187
Dreamworks Animation 28
Dressed to Kill 144
Dreyfus, Jean-Claude 46
Dreyfuss, Richard 12
The Driller Killer 196
Drinkwater, Karlos 122
Drive Angry 100, 147
The Driver 8, 139
The Drowning Pool 8
Drye, Jenny 152
Duangtoy, Jinda 94
Duel 128, 145, 175
The Duellists 8
The Duke of Burgundy 98
Dullea, Keir 99
DuMaurier, Daphne 10
Dun, Dennis 54
Dunaway, Faye 136
Dune 36
Dunning, John 101
Dunstan, Marcus 195
Dupieux, Quentin 58
Durning, Charles 170, 201
Dust Devil 134, 192
Du Vall, Clea 148

Ealing Studios 58
Easter, Robert 194
Easter Bunny Kill Kill 101
Eastman, Marilyn 29
Eastwood, Clint 154, 217
Easy Rider 69
Eaten Alive 185
Eating Raoul 46
Eccleston, Christopher 172
Echternkamp, G.J. 91
Eden Lake 141
Edgar Allan Poe Award 97
Egender, Joe 69
Eggleston, Colin 84
Egypt 118
8½ 88
Eight-Legged Freaks 12
Ekland, Britt 68
El Topo 61
The Elephant Man 36
Ellison, James 207
Elvis (TV movie) 18
Emge, David 116
Emilfork, Daniel 52
The Empire Strikes Back 137
End of Days 31, 33
End of the Line 180

England, Eric 139
English, Evan 134
Englund, Robert 88, 128, 185, 202
Entrance 175
ER 66
Ershov, Konstantin 54
Escape from L.A. 18, 110
Escape from New York 18, 175
Esposito, John 192
Essex, Harry 184
ET: The Extra-Terrestrial 218
Eure, Wesley 194
Evans, Rupert 21
Eve's Bayou 201
An Evening with Edgar Allan Poe 165
The Evictors 185
Evigan, Briana 49
The Evil Below 199
The Evil Dead 28, 43, 73, 119, 123, 221
Evil Dead 2: Dead by Dawn 59
Exam 161
Excision 143
Exists 93
The Exorcist 71, 74, 161
The Exorcist II: The Heretic 126
The Exorcist III: Legion 126
The Expelled 149
The Extraordinary Adventures of Adéle Blanc-Sec 119
Extraterrestrial 161
The Eye 94
Eyes of Laura Mars 136
Eyes Without a Face 37, 181

Fabian, Patrick 72
The Faces 157
The Facts in the Case of Mr. Hollow 163
The Faculty 148
The Fades 64
Fallen 74
Falling Angel 32
Fame 32
Family Plot 95
Fangoria 141
Fansten, Jérôme 21
Fantasia Film Festival 134
Fantasm Comes Again 84
Farmer, Todd 100
Farnsworth, Richard 112
Farrands, Daniel 187
Farrell, Henry 125
Farrell, Sharon 132
Farrow, Mia 131
Fast, Alvin L. 185
The Fast and the Furious (film series) 97
Fast Five 97

Fawcett, John 215
The Fearless Vampire Killers 59, 142
Fear(s) of the Dark 16
Feist, Frances 48
Feke, Steve 201
Feldman, Dennis 129
Felicity 146
Fellini, Federico 88
Femme Fatale 78
Fenton, Thomas 195
Ferdin, Pamelyn 194
Fermat's Room 161
Ferrara, Abel 196
Ferrer, Mel 185
Ferrer, Miguel 199
Ferrini, Franco 71, 134
Fessenden, Jack 85
Fessenden, Larry 36, 84, 182, 205
Fido 114
Field, Chelsea 134
Field, David 134
A Field in England 67
Fiennes, Ralph 121
Fierman, Hannah 14
Fillion, Nathan 8
The Final 149
Final Destination 110
Finch, Paul 122
Fincher, David 8, 103
Finney, Jack 154
Fire, Richard 151
Fire in the Sky 9
The Fisher King 167
Fisher, Carrie 189
Flanagan, Fionnula 172
Flanery, Sean Patrick 49
Flatliners 83
The Flesh and Blood Show 193
Flores, Phil 69
The Fly 113, 132
The Fog 18, 94, 100, 175, 212
Foley, Scott 199
Fonda, Peter 31, 69
Fondato, Marcello 13
Foot, Sean 124
The Forbidden 201
Ford, Glenn 101
Foree, Ken 58, 116
Forster, Robert 66
Fougerol, Martin 21
Fouke Monster 185
The Fountain 116
1408 161
Fox, Laurence 212
Fox, Michael J. 86
Fragile 52
France 38, 138, 181
Francis, Freddie 36
Franju, Georges 181
Frankenstein (character) 208
Frankenstein (film) 37, 56, 109, 118, 129, 181–182, 190, 214

Frankenstein Meets the Wolf Man 214
Frankenstein's Army 124
Fraser, John 142
Freaked 49
Freaks 49
Freddy vs. Jason 215
Frederick, Lynne 10
Freeman, Martin 58
The French Connection 217
Frenzy 95
Freund, Karl 118
Friday Night Lights 85
Friday the 13th 26, 41, 96, 138, 148, 165, 168, 173, 188, 199
Friedenn, Neva 194
Friedkin, William 160
Friends 168
Fright Night 59, 75
The Frighteners 59
Frogner, Charlotte 121
From Dusk Till Dawn 45, 64, 158
From Hell 67
Frontier(s) 46
Frost, Lee 69
Frost, Nick 58
The Frozen Dead 121, 124
Fugit, Patrick 217
Fujiwara, Tatsuya 104
Fukasaku, Kenta 104
Fukasaku, Kinji 104
Fulci, Lucio 88, 122
Full Moon Pictures 77, 134
The Funhouse 49
Funny Games 6
Furlong, Edward 154
The Fury 137
Fusco, Cosimo 97

Gains, Courtney 64
Galen, Henrik 203
Galifianakis, Zach 199
Gallowwalkers 219
Gamble, Mason 214
A Game of Death 103
A Game of Thrones 105
Gangemi, Joseph 146
Gardner, Jeremy 18
Garfield, Brian 187
Garner, Julie 44
Gates, Larry 154
Gayheart, Rebecca 202
Geasland, Jack 182
Gein, Ed 151
Genie Awards 182
Gentry, Jacob 15
George, Gary 176
George, Susan 156
German expressionism 23, 204
Germany 220
Get Shorty 112
Gevedon, Steven 22
Ghost Adventures 161

The Ghost and the Darkness 12
The Ghost Writer 113
Ghosthouse Distribution 93
Ghosts … of the Civil Dead 134
The Ghoul 27
Giallo 95, 97
Giamatti, Paul 120
Gibson, Mel 17
Giger, H.R. 8
Gil, Vincent 135
Giler, David 139
Gillet, Tyler 14
Gilliam, Terry 46
Gilroy, Tony 31
Ginger Snaps 215
Ginsberg, Allen 113
Giovinazzo, Buddy 192
The Girl Next Door 187
Glass Eye Pix 182
Glazyrin, Aleksey 54
Glee 66
Glosserman, Scott 88
Glover, Crispin 191
Gobert, Fabrice 25
Goblin 137, 220
God Told Me To 132
Godere, Michael 5
Gogol, Nikolai 54
The Golden Egg 38
Goldman, William 110, 112
Goldsmith, George 64
The Good Son 64
The Good Wife 144
Goodfellas 11
Goodman, David Zelag 136, 156
Gordon, Ruth 131
Gorham, Karen 175
Gothika 24
Gottlieb, Carl 12
Grabbers 9
Grace 132
Grand Guignol 189, 192
Grandmother's House 126
Granger, Farley 159
Grant, John 57
Grau, Jorge Michel 44
Grave Encounters 161
Grave Encounters 2 161
Gray, William 148
The Great Depression 9
Greay, Karl 218
Greek mythology 174
The Green Mile 218
Greenwell, Emma 69
Greenwood, Bruce 199
Greetings 170
Gregory, David 192
Gremlins 59
Greutert, Kevin 195
Grey's Anatomy 195, 218
Grier, Pam 66
Griffin, Ted 45
Griffith, D.W. 13

Griffiths, Louise 26
The Grifters 187
Grim Prairie Tales 219
Grindhouse 45, 66
Grisham, John 31
Grizzly 43
Grodin, Charles 131
Groundhog Day 165
Gryzko, Ashleigh 161
The Guardian 161
Guardians of the Galaxy 8
Gubler, Matthew Gray 143
Gudiño, Rodrigo 163
Guilfoyle, Paul 82
Guinness, Alec 35
Guinness Book of World Records 18
Gummersall, Devon 167
Gunn, James 8
Gurland, Andrew 72
Guza, Robert, Jr. 148
Gyllenhaal, Jake 82
Gyllenhaal, Maggie 82
Gypsy 166

Habit 205
Hack, Shelley 187
Hackford, Taylor 31
Hackl, David 195
Hairspray 61
Haiti 208
Hall, Craig 122
Hall, Kenneth J. 76
Hallam, Dallas Richard 175
Halloween (original film) 18, 22, 41, 54, 66, 89, 96, 99, 134, 137, 148, 166, 168, 175, 178, 185, 188, 201, 202
Halloween (remake) 117
Halloween: Resurrection 89
Halloween III: Season of the Witch 55
Halo 4: Forward Until Dawn 66
Halperin, Victor 209
Hamilton, Linda 64, 154
Hamilton, Patrick 159
The Hamiltons 70
Hamlet 189
Hammer horror 35, 69, 119, 122, 178
Hammon, Ken 8
Hang 'Em High 61
The Hangover 179, 199
Hanks, Tom 189
Hannah, Daryl 110
Hannibal (TV series) 215
Hansel & Gretel: Witch Hunters 5, 122
Hansen, Gunnar 60
The Happening 83, 86
Happiness 189
Happy Birthday to Me 101
Happy Tears 144

Hard Core Logo 116
Hard Target 105
Hardman, Karl 29
Hardy, Robin 68
Hare, William 35
Hargreaves, John 84
Harlin, Renny 134
Harper, Jessica 220
Harpster, Michael 21
Harrigan, William 109
Harring, Laura 87
Harris, Danielle 202
Harris, Sean 179
Harrison, John Kent 122
Harry Potter films 21, 98
Hartley, Hal 146
Hartnett, Josh 148
Harvey, Herk 48
Harwood, Ronald 36
Hatchet 186
Hauer, Rutger 149, 216
Haunted Prison 135
The Haunting 35, 164
The Haunting in Connecticut 174
Hauser, Stephen 198
Hauser, Wings 58
Haxan: Witchcraft Throughout the Ages 220
Hayes, Isaac 18
Hays Code 103
Headley, Glenne 82
Healy-Louie, Miriam 182
The Heartbreak Kid 131
Hearts in Atlantis 112
Heathers 149
Heaton, Dennis 114
Heavenly Creatures 9
Hedebrant, Kåre 204
Hedren, Tippi 10
Heffernan, Gavin 125
Hell 20
Hell Night 149
Hell on Wheels 176
Hellbound: Hellraiser 2 113
Hellboy 21, 52
Heller, Lukas 125
Hellraiser 89
Helter Skelter 70
Hemingway, Mariel 214
Hendler, Stewart 66
Hendry, Ian 142
Henenlotter, Frank 79
Henkel, Kim 60, 185
Henriksen, Stig Frode 121
Henry, Gregg 8
Henry: Portrait of a Serial Killer 151
Henry: Portrait of a Serial Killer 2: Mask of Sanity 152
Hensley, John 144
Hepburn, Katherine 131
Her Name Is Lily Grace 164

Herrmann, Bernard 78, 132, 171
Herthum, Louis 73
Herzog, Werner 204
Hess, David 4
Hi, Mom! 170
Hickey, William 76
Hicks, Catherine 75
Hide and Seek 171
High Crimes 160
High Plains Drifter 217
High Tension 119, 131
Highlander 218
Hiles, Tony 8
Hill, Debra 166
Hill, Dulé 66
Hill, Marianna 60
Hill, Walter 8, 139
Hillcoat, John 134
Hillerman, John 217
Hilligoss, Candace 48
The Hills Have Eyes 33, 61, 69, 144
The Hills Run Red 141
Hiltzik, Robert 43
Hinzman, Bill 107
History of the World, Part 1 36
A History of Violence 116
Hit and Run 147
Hitchcock, Alfred 10, 28, 38, 78, 95, 103, 136, 151, 159, 170, 175, 187
The Hitcher 144, 214, 216
Hjortsberg, William 32
Hoel, Vegar 121
Hoffman, Dustin 156, 198
The Hole 82
Holland, Tom 75
Hollow Man 109
Holloway, Josh 66
Holm, Ian 112
Holmes, Ashton 146
Holstenwall 23
Holy Ghost People (documentary) 70
Holy Ghost People (horror film) 69
Home Movie 92
Homebodies 126
Honey, I Shrunk the Kids 168
The Hoodlum Priest 137
Hooper, Tobe 60, 128, 185
Horta, Silvio 202
Horton, Peter 64
Horvath, Patrick 175
Hostel 72
Houle, Lisa 116
The Hour 64
House 12, 173
House at the End of the Street 189
House of Dracula 122
House of Frankenstein 122
House of 1, 000 Corpses 61, 209

House of the Devil 15, 33
House of Usher 40
House of Voices 174
House on Haunted Hill 173
House II: The Second Story 173
Hovey, Natasha 71
Howard, Shemp 43
The Howling 155, 215
Huertas, Jon 212
Hughes, John 176
Hugo, Victor 55
Hui, Yuet-Jan 94
The Hunchback of Notre Dame 55
The Hunger Games 98, 104
Hungry Wives 220
Hunter, Evan 10
Hurd, Gale Ann 129
Hurley, Elizabeth 31
Hurt 52
The Hurt Locker 212
Hush 147
Hush ... Hush, Sweet Charlotte 125
Hussain, Karim 192
Hussey, Olivia 99
Huston, Walter 31
Hutchison, Doug 218
Hutton, Lauren 175
The Hypnotic Eye 193
Hypothermia 33

I Am Legend 162
I Come in Peace 105
I Know What You Did Last Summer 168, 202
I Saw the Devil 67
I Sell the Dead 36
I Spit on Your Grave 83
I Stand Alone 119
I Walked with a Zombie 206
Identity 171
Ihaka, Brett 122
Ilsa: She-Wolf of the SS 121, 124
In a Lonely Place 113
In Dreams 81
In Fear 145
In Search of ... 185
In the Belly of the Beast 134
In the Mouth of Madness 113
In the Realm of the Senses 144
The Incredible Shrinking Man 184
Indiana Jones (character) 122
Infection 108
Inferno 220
Inland Empire 78
The Innocents 36, 48
Insane Clown Posse 49

Insanitarium 24
Inside 131
Insidious 52, 76
Institute Benjamina 98
Interview with the Vampire 81, 206
Intolerance: Love's Struggle Throughout the Ages 13
Invaders from Mars 9
The Invasion 154
Invasion of the Body Snatchers 149, 154
Invisible Agent 124
Invisible Avenger 111
Invisible Invaders 111
The Invisible Man (character) 208
The Invisible Man (film) 109
INXS 134
Iron Man 82
Iron Sky 121
Irons, Jeremy 78, 182
Ironside, Michael 167
Irreversible 119
Isabelle, Katharine 215
Islam 37
Island of Dr. Moreau 192
Isle of the Dead 211
It Came from Outer Space 184
It Lives Again 128
Italy 97
It's Alive 132
Ivy, Bob 120
Iwerks, Ub 10

The Jacket 24
Jackie Brown 66, 158
Jackson, Michael 35
Jackson, Peter 8
Jackson, Samuel L. 198
Jacobs, Gregory 146
Jacobs, Matthew 82
Jacob's Ladder 83
James, Brion 139
Jane Eyre 208
Janowitz, Hans 23
Janssen, Famke 94
Jason X 100
Jaws 12, 128, 197–198
Jeepers Creepers 147
The Jeffersons 208
Jennifer's Body 74, 144
Jennings, Claudia 104
Jesse James Meets Frankenstein's Daughter 216, 219
Jeunet, Jean-Pierre 46, 52
Jobin, Peter 101
Johann, Zita 118
Johnny Mnemonic 104
Jones, Caleb Landry 72
Jones, Carolyn 185
Jones, Ceri 178
Jones, Doug 51
Jones, Duane 29, 117
Jones, Gemma 82

Jones, Harold Wayne 106
Jones, Henry 63
Jones, Jeffrey 45
Jones, Toby 97
Jones, Tommy Lee 136
Jones, Vinnie 179
Jordan, Neil 36, 81
Joston, Darwin 157
Joy Ride 146
Joy Ride 2: Dead Ahead 146
Joy Ride 3: Road Kill 146
Joyce, Ella 119
Joyner, C. Courtney 134
Ju-On: The Grudge 94
Judaism 37
Judd, Ashley 160
Julian, Rupert 190
Jump, Amy 66
June 9 92
Jungle Holocaust 91
Jurassic Park 66
Jurgenson, Morgan 140
Just Before Dawn 138

Kane, Carol 201
Kane, Michael 139
Kanin, Garson 131
Kaplan, Benjamin Ross 188
Karloff, Boris 13, 35, 118, 211
Karvan, Claudia 84
Kasten, Jeremy 191, 192
Kate & Leopold 171
Katt, William 173
Katz, Steven 146
Kaufman, Lloyd 8
Kaycheck, Michael 104
Kebbel, Arielle 167
The Keep 124
Keitel, Harvey 31, 65
Keller, David Henry 28
Keller, Sean 97
Kelly, Nancy 63
Kelly, Richard 82
Kelly, Tim 208
Kendall, Suzy 96
Kennedy, John F. 119
Kentucky 139
Kerman, Robert 90
Kerouac, Jack 113
Kerry, Norman 55, 190
Kershner, Irving 136
Ketchum, Jack 187
Kidder, Margot 99, 170
Kidman, Nicole 172
Kidnapped 6
Kier, Udo 192
Kiersch, Fritz 64
Kill Bill 40, 66, 104
Kill Buljo 122
Kill Buljo 2 122
Kill List 66
Killer Joe 161
Killer Klowns from Outer Space 49
The Killing Gene 63

The Killing Room 161
Kilpatrick, Patrick 28
Kimmel, Bruce 148
Kind Hearts and Coronets 58
Kindberg, Ann 194
King, Adrienne 41
King, Jaime 100
King, Jonathan 123
King, Stephen 64, 78, 107, 112, 113, 128, 136
King Kong 103, 184
King of the Mountain 40
King of the Zombies 210
Kiss the Girls 6
Kitamura, Ryûhei 179
Kitano, Takeshi 104
Kneale, Nigel 55
The Knick 146
Knife in the Water 142
Knights of the Round Table 216
Knowland, Nicholas 98
Konrad, Cathy 171
Kontroll 177
Kove, Martin 4
Krabbé, Tim 38
Krampus 15
Krauss, Werner 23
Kretschmann, Thomas 39
Kropachyov, Georgi 54
Krueger, Freddy 4, 80, 88, 128, 166, 185
Krull 198
Kuravlyov, Leonid 54
Kuriyama, Chiaki 104
Kurosawa, Akira 84
Kurtzman, Robert 65
Kuzui, Fran Rubel 149
Kwaidan 16
Kwanten, Ryan 75

Labine, Tyler 140
Labute, Neil 69
Labyrinth 137
Lack, Stephen 182
Ladd, David 178
Ladd, Diane 48
The Ladykillers 58
Laemmle, Carl 190
Lafia, John 75
Laid to Rest 140
Laing, R.D. 22
Lambert, Christopher 177
Lambert, Mary 113
Lamont, Davina 124
Lancaster, Bill 154
Land of the Lost (TV series) 195
Landau, Martin 21
Landham, Sonny 139
Landis, John 35
Lang, Fritz 23, 51
Langlois, Henri 181
Lansdale, Joe R. 119
Laroche, Gérald 133
Larson, Jill 125

Lassie 116
The Last Circus 49
The Last Days 107
The Last Exorcism 72, 91
The Last House on the Left 4, 42
The Last Seduction 146
The Last Will and Testament of Rosalind Leigh 163
The Last Winter 84, 182
Laudenbach, Philippe 133
Laurant, Guillaume 52
Laurents, Arthur 159
Laurie, Piper 136
Lawless 135
The League of Extraordinary Gentlemen 111
Leandersson, Lina 204
Leatherface: Texas Chainsaw Massacre 3 117
Leaver, Robert 84
Lee, Ang 144
Lee, Angelica 93
Lee, Christopher 35, 68, 170, 178
Lees, Robert 57
Lefcourt, Carolyn 187
The Leftovers 25
The Legend of Boggy Creek 185
Legeno, Dave 21
Legion 126
Le Gros, James 84
Leguizamo, John 102
Leigh, Janet 151, 167
Leigh, Jennifer Jason 38
Lellouche, Gilles 119
Le Mat, Paul 76
Lemkin, Jonathan 31
Lemmons, Kasi 201
Leon the Professional 119
Leonard, Joshua 91
Leone, Sergio 97, 155
Leonetti, John R. 76
Leopold and Loeb murder case 159
Leroux, Gaston 190
LeRoy, Mervyn 63
Let Me In 205
Let the Right One In 204
Leto, Jared 202
Letts, Tracy 160
Leviathan 199
Levin, Ira 131
Levine, Ted 128, 146
Levinson, Barry 198
Lewis, Dylan 39, 143
Lewis, Geoffrey 217
Lewis, Herschell Gordon 191
Lewis, Jerry 170
Lewis, Juliette 65
Lewis, Patrick Scott 11
Lewton, Val 35, 208, 211
Lichtenstein, Mitchell 144

The Life of Robert Louis Stevenson 169
Lifeboat 159
Lifeforce 9
The Lift 129
Lindqvist, John Ajvide 204
Link, Andre 101
Lionsgate Entertainment 73, 160, 179, 196, 218
Liotta, Ray 102, 171
Lister, Tom "Tiny" 134
Lithgow, John 78
Little Big Man 156
Little Britain 58
Little House on the Prairie 101
Little Witches 221
Livid 131
A Lizard in a Woman's Skin 98
La Llorona 202
Lloyd, Kathleen 128
The Locals 141
Loch Ness Monster 199
Logan's Run 156
Lohman, Alison 73
London 114, 177
Long, Justin 73
Long, Richard 173
A Long Night at Camp Blood 42
Long Pigs 152
Long Weekend 84, 176
López-Gallego, Gonzalo 39
López, Sergi 51
The Lord of the Rings (film series) 9, 124, 134, 212
Lords, Tracy 143
The Lords of Salem 221
Lords of the Deep 199
Lorre, Peter 51
Los Angeles 176, 192, 194
Losey, Joseph 51
Lost 66
The Lost Boys 206
Lost Highway 79
Lost Soul: The Doomed Journey of Richard Stanley's Island of Dr. Moreau 192
Louisiana 139
Lovecraft, H.P. 29, 113, 123
The Loved Ones 176
Lovely Molly 93
Lowe, Alice 67
Lowe, Edward T., Jr. 55
Lowes, Katie 11
Lowndes, Jessica 49
Lucas, Henry Lee 152
Lucas, Josh 22
Lucas, Matt 58
Lugosi, Bela 35, 209, 214
Luppi, Federico 52
Lurie, Rod 157
Lussier, Patrick 100

Lynch, David 52, 78, 87
Lynch, Paul 148
Lynch, Richard 104

M 51
M*A*S*H (TV series) 69
Mabius, Eric 167
Macabre 72, 174
Machete 196
The Machinist 22, 171
MacMillan, Will 106
Mad Dog and Glory 151
Mad Max 17
Mad Men 107
Madison County 139
Madsen, Virginia 201
Maeda, Aki 104
Magic 77
The Magic Island 209
Magnier, Franck 133
Mahin, John Lee 63
Maléfique 133
Malkovich, John 170
Malone, Jena 82, 85
The Maltese Falcon 125
Mama 52
Man Bites Dog 152
A Man Called Horse 128
The Man from Elysian Fields 113
Man-Thing 186
The Man Who Haunted Himself 79
Mancini, Don 75
Mancino, Antonio 97
Mandylor, Costas 195
Manfredini, Harry 42, 173
The Mangler 128
The Mangler 2 129
The Mangler Reborn 129
Mangold, James 171
Manhattan 11
Manhattan Melody 122
Maniac 168
Maniac Cop 27
Manic Street Preachers 135
Manners, David 118
Mansfield, Martha 170
Manson, Marilyn 59
The Manson Family 157
Mantione, Ry 76
Manwaring, Daniel 154
Mapother, William 218
March, William 63
Marcus Welby, M.D. 128
Marianne Dreams 82
Marjoe 72
Marks, Leo 87
Marley, John 25, 128
Marlowe, Andrew W. 109
Marnhout, Heidi 120
Marrero, Ace 139
Marsan, Eddie 4
Martha Marcy May Marlene 70
Martha's Vineyard 12

Martin 221
Martin, Ivan 5
Martinez, Justin 14
Martyrs 131
Mary Reilly 171
Maryland 61, 91
Marz, Carolyn 196
MASH (film) 11
Maskell, Neil 66
Maslansky, Paul 208
Massachusetts 12
Massey, Anna 87
Massey, Edith 61
Masur, Richard 155
Matheson, Richard 145
Matheson, Tim 38
Mathis, Samantha 165
Matlin, Marlee 143
Matmor, Daniel 128
The Matrix 32
Maury, Julien 131
Maximum Overdrive 129
Maxwell, Richard 208
May 77, 143
Mayer, Carl 23
Mayniel, Juliette 181
Mayo, Simon 10
McBain, Ed 10
McBride, Jim 87
McCarthy, Brendan 69
McCarthy, Kevin 154
McCausland, James 17
McClain, Joedda 220
McCollough, Paul 106
McCord, AnnaLynne 143
McCormack, Patty 63
McCoy, Matt 199
McCrea, Joel 102
McDonald, Bruce 116
McDonald, Philip 35
McDonnell, Mary 83
McDonough, Neal 46
McGillis, Kelly 45
McGinley, John C. 171
McHattie, Stephen 116
McKean, Michael 110
McKee, Lucky 143, 221
McKellen, Ian 121
McKenney, James Felix 32
McLeavy, Robin 176
McNaughton, John 151
McQuaid, Glenn 14, 36
Meatballs 2 122
Meet the Feebles 9
Megan Is Missing 6
Meierhans, Alexandra 5–6
Meloni, Christopher 107
Melton, Patrick 195
Memoirs of an Invisible Man 110, 113, 189
Memorial Day 101
Men in Black 112
The Mephisto Waltz 33
Mercer, Matt 139
Mercier, Michéle 13
The Mercury Theatre 125
Mercy 126

Meredith, Burgess 31
Merlin 216
The Messenger: The Story of Joan of Arc 119
Metropolis 51
Mexican-American War 45
Mexico 66, 85
MI-5 178
Mickle, Jim 44
Micmacs 52
Middle East 3
Midnight Cowboy 156
Midnight Express 32
The Midnight Meat Train 179
Mikey 64
Mile Zero 116
Miles, Vera 151
Milius, John 86
Miller, Chris 28
Miller, Deron 43
Miller, Dick 189
Miller, Geof 199
Miller, George 17
Miller, Jason 126
Miller, Patsy Ruth 55
Miller, Stephen 100
Miller, Victor 41
Milton, John 32
Mimic 177, 179
Minahan, Daniel 104
Miner, Steve 173
Minihan, Colin 161
Minority Report 137
Mir space station 129
Miracle, Irene 76
Miramax 149
Misery 112
Miska, Brad 15
The Missing 64
Missing Link 165
The Mist 158
Mr. Brooks 171
Mr. Ed 187
Mr. Oizo 59
Mister Roberts 63
Mitchell, Cameron 194
Mockingbird 157
Mokae, Zakes 208
Moll, Richard 173
Mom 126
Monaghan, Dominic 36
Mondesir, Merwin 161
"The Monkey's Paw" 26
Monroeville Mall 117
The Monster Squad 120, 173
Monteith, Cory 66
Moon 165
Moorcroft, Nick 35
Moore, Gene 48
Moore, Roy 99
Moore, Stephen Campbell 63
Moorehead, Agnes 125
Morricone, Ennio 97, 155
Mortensen, Viggo 31, 134

Moseley, Bill 49
Moss, Carrie-Anne 114
The Most Dangerous Game 102
Mother of Tears 97, 220
Mother's Day 101, 138
The Mothman Prophecies 202
MPAA (Motion Picture Association of America) 166
MTV 165
Mulberry Street 45
Mulholland Drive 79, 87
Mullan, Peter 22
mumblecore 176
The Mummy (character) 58
The Mummy 118
Murders in the Rue Morgue 119
Murnau, F.W. 23, 170, 203
Murphy, Michael 10
Murphy's Law 3
Musante, Tony 96
My Bloody Valentine 100, 148
My Super Psycho Sweet 16 16
Myers, Michael (character) 96
Myrick, Daniel 91, 212

Nahon, Philippe 119
Nail Gun Massacre 196
Naked Lunch 112
Naldi, Nita 170
The Nameless 108
Narcejac, Thomas 181
Nash, Jamie 93
Nazis 76
Neal, Edwin 60
Near Dark 94, 206, 214, 216
Nebraska 64
A Necessary Death 72, 91
Necronomicon 8
Neiderman, Andrew 31
Neill, Sam 110, 113
Nelson, Tim Blake 116
Nercessian, Jacky 119
New England 18, 41, 113
New Line Cinema 22, 113, 134
New Orleans 32
New Year's Evil 101
New York City 18, 32, 79, 131, 158, 177, 179, 186, 196
New Zealand 8
Newcomb, Virginia 192
Nicholson, Jack 31
Niciphor, Nicholas 104
Nicolodi, Daria 137, 220
Nielsen, Leslie 148
Night Gallery 145
Night of the Creeps 59

Night of the Demons 28
Night of the Flesh Eaters 206
Night of the Lepus 12
Night of the Living Dead 29, 61, 107, 113, 157, 206, 221
Night of the Living Dead (remake) 151
"Night Surf" 107
The Nightmare Before Christmas 185
Nightmare Concert 88
Nightmare Honeymoon 128
A Nightmare on Elm Street 80, 168, 209
A Nightmare on Elm Street (film series) 27, 165, 188, 202
A Nightmare on Elm Street 2: Freddy's Revenge 22
A Nightmare on Elm Street 3: Dream Warriors 39
A Nightmare on Elm Street 4: The Dream Master 134
9/11 212
90210 143
The Ninth Configuration 24
No Escape 102
No Exit 162
No Man's Land: Rise of the Reeker 168
No Telling 85, 182
The Noah 165
Nolte, Nick 198
Nosferatu 23, 203
Nuremberg War Crimes Trial 121
Nutman, Philip 187
Nyman, Michael 46

Oasis of the Zombies 124
Oates, Warren 69
O'Bannon, Dan 7
The Objective 212
O'Brien, Alana 18
O Brother, Where Art Thou? 116
Obsession 78
Ocean's 11 46
O'Dea, Judith 29
The Office 58
An Officer and a Gentlemen 32
Offspring 188
Oh God, You Devil! 31
O'Herne, Peter 8
Ohmart, Carol 173
The Old Dark House 61, 109
Old State Prison 134
Olsen, Dana 110, 189
The Omen 33, 142
Once Upon a Time in the West 97

One Flew Over the Cuckoo's Nest 137
One Hour Photo 176
100 Feet 94
One Missed Call 134
O'Neal, Ron 201
Open Grave 39
Opera 72
O'Quinn, Terry 187
Oram, Steve 67
The Ordeal 138
Ormsby, Alan 25
Orphan Black 215
Ortiz, Stuart 161
Osombie 212
OT: la Película 108
The Other 79
The Others 173
Out of the Past 154
Outpost 124
OZ the Great and Powerful 73

P2 176
Pacino, Al 31
The Pact II 176
Páez, Daniel 5
Pailhas, Géraldine 25
Pais, Josh 144
Palance, Jack 21
Pale Rider 128, 217
Palmer, Betsy 41
Palmer, James 164
Pang Chun, Oxide 94
Pang, Danny 94
Pan's Labyrinth 51
Paperhouse 82, 201
Paquin, Anna 15
Paradis, Allyson 131
Paradise Lost 32
Paranormal Activity 74
Paranormal Entity 104
Pardue, Kip 191
Paré, Michael 214
Parents 46
Paris Opera House 190
Parker, Alan 32
Parker, Jameson 54
Parks, Michael 45, 66
Parmet, Phil 219
Party of Five 168
Pastor, Alex 107
Pastor, David 107
Pat and Mike 131
Pataky, Elsa 97
Pathology 182
Patrick 84, 137
Patton, Mark A. 212
Payne, Dave 167
Pearce, Guy 45
Pearl, Daniel 60
Peckinpah, Sam 21, 156
Pee-Wee's Big Adventure 49
Peeping Tom 87
Peeples, Nia 199
Peet, Amanda 171
Pegg, Simon 35, 58

Pennsylvania 106, 117
Penny Dreadful 64
The People Under the Stairs 52
Perabo, Piper 107
Pereira, Hugo 5
A Perfect Getaway 199
Perkins, Anthony 151
Perkins, Emily 215
Perlman, Ron 36, 52, 84–85
The Pest 102
Pet Sematary 64, 113
Petty, J.T. 218
Peyton Place 61
Pfarrer, Chuck 129
Phantasm 33, 37, 81, 120
The Phantom of the Opera 190
Phase IV 10
Phenomena 137
Philbin, Mary 190
Phillips, Bijou 191
The Pianist 97
The Piano Teacher 144
The Piano Tuner of Earthquakes 98
Picardo, Robert 189
Pichel, Irving 102
Pierce, Charles B. 185
Pierrot, Frédéric 25
Pine, Chris 107
Pinhead (character) 89
Pink Flamingos 61
Pinner, David 68
Pinocchio's Revenge 77
Pinon, Dominique 46, 52
Piranha 12
Pirates of the Caribbean (film series) 48
Pitch Black 199
Plague of the Zombies 210
Planet of the Apes (film series) 101
Play Misty for Me 176, 217
Plaza, Paco 107
Pleasence, Donald 18, 21, 31, 54, 137, 166, 178
Pleshette, Suzanne 10
Poe, Edgar Allan 39
Poelvoorde, Benoît 152
Polanski, Roman 97, 130, 142
Police Academy 208
Poliziotteschi 96
Polsky, Abe 60
Poltergeist 52, 89, 185
Poltergeist III 178
Pontypool 116
Poole, Aaron 163
Popcorn 89
Porky's 26
Posse 134
Post, Ted 60
Potente, Franka 178
Potter, Terry 8
The Poughkeepsie Tapes 152

Powell, Michael 87
Predator 9, 212
Premature Burial (film) 40
"The Premature Burial" (story) 39
Presley, Elvis 119
Pressburger, Emeric 87
Preston, Lance 161
Price, Vincent 57, 76, 173
Prince of Darkness 54, 110, 113
The Princess Bride 112
Principe, Nick 139
Prior, Kerry 26
Prison 134
Prison Break 66
Prochnow, Jurgen 113
Prom Night 148
Prometheus 179
Proof of Life 32
Prophecy 86
The Proposition 135
The Prowler 168
Pryce, Jonathan 36, 48
Psych 66
The Psychic 137
Psycho 10, 151, 170, 195
Ptushko, Aleksandr 54
Pucci, Lou Taylor 107
Pullman, Bill 208
Pulp Fiction 15, 66
Pulse 94
Pump Up the Volume 165
Puppet Master vs. Demonic Toys 77
Puppetmaster 76
The Purge 158
Puss in Boots 28
Putnam, Nina Wilcox 118
PVC-1 5

Quarantine 108
Quartermain, Allan (character) 122
Quatermass (film series) 55
Quatermass and the Pit 180
The Quay Brothers 98
Queen Latifah 198
The Quick and the Undead 219
The Quiet Earth 20
Quinn, Aidan 81

R–Point 212
Rabid 108, 182
Rabid Grannies 126
Race with the Devil 69, 139
Race, Hugo 134
Rackham, Arthur 52
Radio Silence 14
Rage 97
Raimi, Ivan 73
Raimi, Sam 28, 43, 73, 93
Rains, Claude 109, 214
Raising Cain 78

Rampo 104
Ramsey, Anessa 15
Ramsey, Anne 125
Ramsey, Laura 85
Ramsey, Stephen 182
Randel, Tony 113
Ranzani, Emiliano 192
Rao, Dileep 73
Rataud, Dimitri 133
Ravenous 45
Raver, Lorna 73
Raw Meat 178
Ray 32
Razorback 84
Rea, Stephen 36, 82, 145
Reagan, Ronald 166
Real Housewives of Beverly Hills 128
The Real World 105
Reality 59
Re-Animator 37, 192
Rear Window 175, 189
Rebel, John 11
REC 107
Red, Eric 94, 214, 216
Red Eye 6
Red Hill 176
Red Sands 212
The Red Shoes 87
Red State 45
Redgrave, Vanessa 163
Redon, Jean 181
Reeder, Calvin 14
The Reef 199
Reeker 167
Reeves, Keanu 31
Reilly, Georgina 116
Reiné, Roel 11
Reiner, Rob 112
Reitman, Ivan 110
Repo! The Genetic Opera 49
Repulsion 142
The Resident 176
Resident Evil 117
Return of the Living Dead 114
Return of the Living Dead 2 122
Return to Oz 48
Return to Sleepaway Camp 43
The Returned 25
Reubens, Paul 149
The Revenant 26
Revolt of the Zombies 212
Revolutionary Road 160, 218
Reynolds, Ryan 165
Rhys, Matthew 211
Richards, Erin 39
Richards, Kim 128
Richards, Kyle 128, 185
Richardson, Derek 167
The Rift 199
Right at Your Door 161
Rin-Tin-Tin 116
Rinaldo, Frederic 57

Rio Bravo 157
Ripper Street 64
Ritchkoff, Jennifer 42
The Rite 74
Riverview Hospital 161
The Road 20, 135
Road Games 84, 145, 147
Road Kill 147
The Roaring Twenties 9
Robards, Jason 48, 211
Robertson, Cliff 78
Robertson, John S. 170
Robinson, Bruce 81
Robitel, Adam 125
RoboCop 110
Robot Chicken 43
Robson, Mark 211
Rodman, Adam 208
Rodriguez, Robert 65, 148
Rogers, Buck (character) 180
Rogers, Mimi 215
Rollerball 104
Roman, Ruth 60
Romanek, Mark 157
Romasanta: The Werewolf Hunt 108
Rome 88
Romeo & Juliet 99
Romero, George A. 29, 97, 106, 113, 116, 206, 220
Rooker, Michael 8, 66, 151
Roosevelt, Franklin D. 111
Rope 159
Rose, Bernard 82, 201
Rose, Felissa 43
Rose, Louisa 170
Rose Red 100, 174
Roseanne 149
Rosemary's Baby 61, 130
Ross, Arthur A. 184
Ross, David 221
Ross, Gaylen 116
Rossington, Norman 178
Roth, Eli 72
Rotten Tomatoes 176
Rounders 146
Rourke, Mickey 32
Roussel, Nathalie 131
Rubber 58
Ruben, Joseph 187
Rubinstein, Zelda 89
Rue Morgue (magazine) 163
Rugaru 186
The Ruins 85
Run Lola Run 178
Runaway 129
The Running Man 105
Russell, Kurt 18, 154
Russo, John A. 29
Rustam, Mohammed 185
Ryan, John 132

S. Darko 82
Sacchetti, Dardano 71
The Sacrament 16, 70
Sage, Bill 44
Saint, H.F. 110
St. John, Nicholas 196
Salem Witch Trials 219
Salerno, Enrico Maria 96
Salt, Jennifer 170
Salvage 108
Samuel, Xavier 176
Samuels, Joanna 17
Sánchez, Eduardo 91, 93
Sandweiss, Ellen 28
Sanskrit 212
Santa Sangre 49
Sarandon, Chris 75
Sartre, Jean-Paul 162
Satan Hates You 32
Saturn Awards 182
Sautet, Claude 181
Savage Messiah 70
Savini, Tom 117, 192
Savoy, Suzanne 28
Saw (film series) 49, 76, 195
Saxon, John 66
Saxton, John C.W. 101
Sayers, Dorothy L. 196
Scandal 199
Scanners 137, 168
Scary Movie 168
Schayer, Richard 118
Scheider, Roy 12
Schmoeller, David 76
Schoelen, Jill 187
Schon, Kyra 29
Schrader, Paul 78
Schreck, Max 203
Schreiber, Liev 198
Schrock, Raymond 190
Schröder, Greta 203
Schultz, Dwight 22
Schwarzenegger, Arnold 154
Scorsese, Martin 87, 211
Scotland Yard 178
Scott, George C. 126
Scott, Ridley 7, 179
Scream 149, 168, 171, 202, 209
Scrimm, Angus 32, 37, 81
Seabrook, William 209
Season of the Witch 61, 107, 220
Secret Window 171
Seegmiller, Scott 164
Segal, Nanu 64
Seigner, Emmanuelle 97
Series 7: The Contenders 104
Serkis, Andy 35, 211
Serling, Rod 200
The Serpent and the Rainbow 208
Serrano, Jorge-Yaman 107
Session 9 22
Seven 67

Seventh Moon 93
Severance 179
Severin Films 192
Sexton, Brendan, III 22
Shadow of the Vampire 204
Shaffer, Anthony 68
Shaft 217
Shankland, Tom 63
Shannon, Michael 160, 218
Shapeshifter 155
Shark Night 199
Shaun of the Dead 58
Shaw, Robert 12, 198
The Shawshank Redemption 39
Shaye, Robert 21, 134
Shearer, Moira 87
Sheehan, Perley Poore 55
Sheffield, Jeremy 63
Sherman, Gary 178
Sherriff, R.C. 109
The Shield 195
The Shining 113
Shipka, Kiernan 107
Shivers 108
Shock Waves 122
Shocker 209
Shoesdack, Ernest B. 102
Sholder, Jack 21
Shore, Howard 182
Shrek 28
Shrooms 64
Shryack, Dennis 128
Shue, Elisabeth 109
Shusett, Ronald 7
Shutter Island 24, 211
Shuttle 6
The Sick Fucks 22
Siegel, Don 154
Sightseers 67
The Signal 15
Signs 9
The Silence of the Lambs 30, 125, 128, 146, 151–152
Silent Hill: Revelation 212
Silent Night, Deadly Night 101
Silent Running 165
Silver Bullet 215
Silverstein, Elliot 128
Simonelli, Giovanni 88
A Simple Plan 85
Singer, Bryan 126
Single White Female 176
Sinister 113
Siodmak, Curt 207, 214
Sirk, Douglas 116
Sisters 170
6 Souls 171
The Skeleton Key 126
Skellern, Anna 21
Skerritt, Tom 7
The Skin I Live In 182
Sky Captain and the World of Tomorrow 119
Slate, Lane 128

Sleepaway Camp 41, 43
Sleepwalkers 155
Slither 8
Sluizer, George 38
Slumber Party Massacre 168
Smart, Amy 93
Smiley, Michael 66
Smith, Brooke 104
Smith, Carter 85
Smith, Christopher 178
Smith, Earl E. 185
Smith, Kerr 100
Smith, Scott B. 85
Smith, Shawnee 195
Smith, Terri Susan 79
Smith, Wayne 214
Smith, Will 162
Smith, Willie W. 185
Smith, Zane 100
Snaider, Meredith 205
Snakes on a Plane 12
Snider, Norman 182
Snyder, Suzanne 49
Sobieski, Leelee 146
Soderbergh, Steven 146
Soles, P.J. 136, 166
Solomon Kane 212
Someone's Watching Me 175
Something Wicked This Way Comes 28, 48
Somos Lo Que Hay 45
Son of Dracula 214
Sonatine 104
Sonnenfeld, Barry 112
Sons of Anarchy 52
Sorority Row 66
Sorvino, Paul 49
Sotomura, Joanna 140
Sound of My Voice 70
South America 3
South by Southwest Film Festival 164
South Carolina 8
Southcliffe 179
Southern Comfort 139
Southland Tales 82
Soylent Green 20
Spaced 58
Spacek, Sissy 136
Spain 52
Sparling, Chris 165
Species 9
Speed 32
Speedman, Scott 157
Spencer, Christine 32
Sphere 198
Spider Baby 61
Spider-Man 3 73
Spielberg, Steven 12, 145, 175, 214
Spiers, Elliot 82
Spinella, Stephen 58
Spliced 89
Splinter 158
Spoorloos (The Vanishing) 38

The Squad 212
Stage Fright 193
Stage Fright: Aquarius 193
Stakeland 45
Stamm, Daniel 72, 91
The Stand 107
Stand by Me 112
Stanley, Richard 192
Stanton, Harry Dean 7, 18, 79
Star Trek (film series) 107, 199
Star Trek (TV series) 36
Star Wars 7, 81, 127, 142
Starks, David 140
Starrett, Jack 69
Starship Troopers 110
Stathoulopoulos, Spiros 5
Staunton Hill 141
steadicam 167
steampunk 52
Stefano, Joseph 151
Stella, Christian 19
The Stepfather 187
The Stepford Wives 149, 189
Stephen King's It 136
Stevens, Casey 148
Stevenson, Robert Louis 35, 169
Stewart, Donald E. 104
Stewart, James 159
Stierman, Vern 185
Stieve, David J. 88
Stiller, Ben 85
Stir of Echoes 94
Stoker, Austin 157
Stoker, Bram 204
Stole, Mink 61
Stone, David 142
Stone, Sharon 198
Stonehearst Asylum 24
Storaro, Vittorio 97
Storm Warning 138, 176, 202
Storr, Catherine 82
Strange, Glenn 57
The Strange Case of Dr. Jekyll and Mr. Hyde 169
Strange Invaders 9
The Strangers 157
Strassman, Marcia 168
Straw Dogs 156
Streamers 144
Stresisand, Barbara 137
Strickland, Peter 97
Stuart, Gloria 109
Stuck 145
The Stuff 108, 132
Stumpp, William 185
The Substitute 26, 149
Suburban Gothic 143
Subway 177
Sugar Hill 208
The Sugarland Express 12
Suicide Girls 192
Suicide Kings 66
Sullivan's Travels 103

Summerisle 68
Summer's Moon 6
Sunderland, Matthew 122
Sundown: The Vampire in Retreat 219
Superman 99, 170
Superman Returns 126
Supernatural 100
Survivor 105
Suschitzky, Peter 113
Suspiria 97, 137, 220, 221
Sussex 109
Sussman, Lucas 199
Sutherland, Donald 129, 149
Swamp Devil 186
Swamp Thing 186
Swanberg, Joe 14
Swanson, Kristy 149
Swayze, Patrick 83
Sweeney Todd: The Demon Barber of Fleet Street 46
Sweet Sweetback's Baadasss Song 208
Swit, Loretta 69
Syfy Channel 77
Sykes, Brad 42

Takami, Koushun 104
Take Shelter 160
The Taking of Deborah Logan 125
Tale of the Mummy 120
A Tale of Two Sisters 171
Tales from the Crypt (film) 13, 25, 37
Tales from the Crypt (TV series) 128
Tales from the Crypt Presents Demon Knight 158
Tales from the Crypt Presents Ritual 210
Tales from the Hood 16
Tangy, Laurent 21
Tarantino, Quentin 65, 104, 158
Tardi, Jacques 119
Tarver, Clay 146
Tatpoulos, Patrick 180
Tavier, Vincent 152
Taxi Driver 78, 176
Taylor, Michael 42
Taylor, Richard 124
Taylor, Rod 10
Teaching Mrs. Tingle 149
Technicolor 14
Teen Wolf 215
Teeth 144
Ten Little Indians 155, 171
Tenney, Kevin 28
Tentori, Antonio 88
The Terminator 129, 154, 199
Terminator 2: Judgment Day 154
Terraza, Ferran 107
Terror Train 148
ter Steege, Johanna 38

Texas 41, 60, 65, 145, 185
The Texas Chain Saw Massacre 60, 140, 151, 185, 195, 196
Texas Chainsaw Massacre 2 129
Thaine, Victoria 176
Thanksgiving 59
Thatcher, Margaret 166
The Thaw 86
Theater of Blood 193
The Theatre Bizarre 192
Theatre of Death 193
Theron, Charlize 31
Theroux, Justin 78, 87
They Came Back 25
They Live 110, 113
A Thief in the Night 33
The Thing 8, 84, 149, 154
The Thing with Two Heads 69
Thirst 206
13 Ghosts 94
30 Days of Night 206
Thomas, Dylan 36
Thomas, Henry 217
Thompson, David L. 88
Thompson, Gary Scott 109
Thompson, J. Lee 101
The Thompsons 70
Thor (novel) 214
388 Arletta Avenue 92
Three Extremes 16
Three Mothers trilogy 97
Three O'Clock High 86
The Three Stooges (characters) 43, 121
3:10 to Yuma 171
Thriller (music video) 35
Thriller (TV series) 14
Thunhurst, Bill 220
Tidyman, Ernest 217
Tiersten, Jonathan 43
Tighe, Kevin 100
Tijou, Brigitte 25
Tilly, Matthew 91
Timber Falls 43
The Tingler 76
Titanic 129
To the Devil a Daughter 33
Tobolowsky, Stephen 110, 165
Todd, Tony 201
Tointon, Hannah 63
Toledo, Fabiola 71
The Tomb of Ligeia 27
The Tommyknockers 136
The Toolbox Murders 194
Toole, Ottis 152
Top Gun 45
El Topo 61
Total Recall 168
Tourist Trap 77
Tourneur, Jacques 207
Towers, Harry Alan 128
Towers, Richard 4
Towles, Tom 151

The Town That Dreaded Sundown 152, 185
The Toxic Avenger 83
Toy Story 171
Tracy, Spencer 131
Trane, Reuben 122
Transmorphers 104
Transsiberian 22
Transylvania 203
The Travel Channel 161
Travolta, John 66, 136
Treasure Island 169
Tremors 59
Triangle 179
Trick 'r Treat 15
Trilogy of Terror 16
Troll Hunter 92
True Blood 70, 105
Tucker & Dale vs. Evil 140
Tudyk, Alan 140
The Tunnel 177
Turner, Alex 217
Tutankhamun 119
28 Days Later 114, 117
24 Exposures 15
Twenty Thousand Leagues Under the Sea 198
Twiggy 36
Twilight 190
The Twilight Zone (TV series) 8, 200
Twilight Zone: The Movie 16, 35
Twin Peaks 59, 79, 88
Twins (novel) 182
Twisted Sister 166
Twitch of the Death Nerve 98
Two Evil Eyes 16
2001: A Space Odyssey 99
2001 Maniacs 126
2001 Maniacs: Field of Screams 126
Twohy, David 199
Tyler, Liv 157

Ugly Betty 168
Umbrellas of Cherbourg 142
Undead or Alive 219
Underwood, Beck 182
Underworld 206
The Uninvited 94
Union Square 196
Universal Soldier 134
Universal Studios 56, 57, 118, 190, 208
Urban Legend 84, 202
Urban Legend: Bloody Mary 202
Urban Legend: Final Cut 89
Urch, Walter Montague 27
Urquia, Merida 5
The Usual Suspects 15
Utah 128

V/H/S 14, 218
V/H/S 2 15, 93
V/H/S: Viral 15
Valentine 84, 202
Valette, Eric 133
Valletta, Amber 75
Valli, Alida 181
Vampire Circus 49
Vampire in Brooklyn 209
Vampires 206
Vampyr 83
van den Houten, Andrew 188
Van Helsing 214
van Hentenryck, Kevin 79
Vanilla Sky 173
Van Lidth, Erland 22
van Peebles, Melvin 208
Van Sloan, Edward 119
Van Tieghem, David 182
Varga, Kalatin 98
Varley, Natalya 54
Vaughn, Peter 156
The Vault of Horror 37
Veidt, Conrad 23
Velasco, Manuela 107
Venom 186
Verhoeven, Paul 109
Vernon, John 49
Versus 180
Vertigo 11, 78, 181
A Very Long Engagement 46
The Vicious Brothers 161
Video Nasties 166, 196
Videodrome 182
Vietnam War 26, 173
Village of the Damned 64
Villela, Chad 14
Vince, Pruitt Taylor 171
The Violent Kind 70
The Virgin Spring 4
Virus 129
The Visit 126
Viy 54
von Harbou, Thea 51
von Wangenheim, Gustav 203
Voodoo Dawn 210
Voorhees, Jason (character) 4, 88, 138

Wacko 189
Wag the Dog 198
Waggner, George 214
Wahlberg, Donnie 75
Wait Until Dark 94
Wales 214

Walk the Line 171
Walker, Paul 146
Walker, Shirley 110
The Walking Dead 39, 66, 129
Walton, Fred 201
Walton, Karen 215
Wan, James 75, 195
War of the Dead 212
The Ward 24
Ward, Fred 139
Ward, Gemma 157
Warhol, Andy 61
Warm Bodies 117
Warner, David 156
Warner Brothers 63
Warning Sign 108
The Warriors 139
Washington, Isaiah 217
The Watcher 152
The Watcher in the Woods 28, 48
Watergate 18, 106
Waters, John 61, 143
Watts, Naomi 87
We Are What We Are 44
Weaver, Dennis 145
Weaver, Sigourney 7
Wechter, David 148
The Wedding Banquet 144
Weixler, Jess 144
Welborn, Justin 15
Welcome to the Jungle 46
Weller, Peter 112
Welles, Orson 125
Wells, H.G. 109
Wendigo 182
Wendigo (myth) 46
Wendt, George 173
WereWolf of London 215
Wernicke, Otto 51
Wes Craven's New Nightmare 89
West, Ti 14
West Side Story 11
Westlake, Donald E. 187
Weston, Garnett 209
Westwick, Ed 94
Wet Hot American Summer 43
Weta Workshop 124
Whale, James 109
Whannell, Leigh 75, 195
What Ever Happened to Baby Jane? 125
Wheatley, Ben 66
Whedon, Joss 149
When a Stranger Calls 99, 168, 201

When a Stranger Calls Back 201
When Harry Met Sally 112
Whisper 66
White, Jan 220
White, Robb 173
White Noise 2 100
White Zombie 206, 209
Who Can Kill a Child? 64
Who Framed Roger Rabbit? 167
Wicked Little Things 64
The Wicker Man 67–68
The Wicker Tree 69
Widman, Ellen 51
Wiederhorn, Ken 122
Wiene, Robert 23
The Wild Bunch 156
Wild Things 151
Wiley, Ethan 11, 173
Wilkinson, Tom 35
Willard 12
Williams, Gordon 156
Williams, John 12
Williams, Michael C. 91, 212
Williams, Olivia 199
Williams, Paul Andrew 63
Williamson, Fred 66
Williamson, Kevin 148, 168
Williamson, Nicol 126
Wilson, Gregory 187
Wilson, Scott 88
Wimberley, Darryl 28
Wimmer, Kurt 198
Wind Chill 146
Winfield, Paul 208
Wingard, Adam 14
Winter, Ariel 143
Wirkola, Tommy 121
Wise, Robert 35
Wisher, William, Jr. 154
Witchboard 221
The Witches 221
The Witches of Eastwick 221
Witchfinder General 221
Within the Woods 43
Witt, Alicia 202
Wizard of Gore 191
Wolf Creek 43
The Wolf Man (character) 208
The Wolf Man (film) 214
The Wolfman (remake) 214
The Woman 188, 221
The Woman Hunt 105

Wong, Victor 54
Woo, John 21
Wood, Bari 81, 182
Wood, Don 32
Wood, Elijah 148
Woodbury, Mark 104
The Woods 221
Woodward, Edward 68
Woodward, John 28
World War I 193, 211
World War II 76, 121, 122, 198, 199
World War Z 117
Worsley, Wallace 55
Wrath of the Gods 69
Wray, Ardel 207, 211
Wray, Fay 102
Wrecked 145
Wright, Edgar 58
Wrights Hill Fortress 124
Wrong 59
Wrong Cops 59
Wrong Turn 46
Wylde, Chris 26
Wynn, Tracy Keenan 198
Wynter, Dana 154
Wyoming 134

The X-Files 177
The X-Files: I Want to Believe 137
X-Men 85, 94, 126
X-Men: The Last Stand 124
X-Men 2 15
Xtro 132

Yablans, Irwin 134
Yagher, Kevin 75
Yates, Peter 198
Yorke, Carl Gabriel 90
Young, Tim 42
You're Next 15, 158

Zabriskie, Grace 59, 79
Zaccaï, Jonathan 25
Zahler, S. Craig 21
Zahn, Steve 146
Zdunich, Terrance 49
Zimm, Maurice 184
Zimmer, Laurie 157
Zodiac 103
The Zodiac Killer 103
Zombi 122
Zombie, Rob 8, 167, 209
Zombie Death House 135
Zombie Lake 124
Zombieland 117
Zsigmond, Vilmos 78